Thinking with the Harrisons:
Re-imagining Art in the Global Environment Crisis

Thinking with the Harrisons

Re-imagining Art in the
Global Environment Crisis

Anne Douglas
Chris Fremantle

Leuven University Press

This book will be made open access within three years of publication thanks to Path to Open, a program developed in partnership between JSTOR, the American Council of Learned Societies (ACLS), University of Michigan Press, and The University of North Carolina Press to bring about equitable access and impact for the entire scholarly community, including authors, researchers, libraries, and university presses around the world. Learn more at https://about.jstor.org/path-to-open/

ISBN 978 94 6270 426 8
eISBN 978 94 6166 574 4 (ePDF)
eISBN 978 94 6166 616 1 (ePUB)
https://doi.org/10.11116/9789461665744
D/2024/1869/55
NUR: 642
Cover design: Daniel Benneworth-Gray
Cover illustration: Helen Mayer Harrison and Newton Harrison 'Book of the Lagoons' (1985). Courtesy of the Newton and Helen Harrison Family Trust.
Typesetting: Crius Group

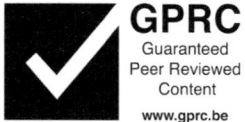

GPRC
Guaranteed
Peer Reviewed
Content
www.gprc.be

In memory of Helen Mayer Harrison (1927-2018)
and Newton Harrison (1932-2022),
pioneers of art and ecology

Contents

Acknowledgements

This book emerged out of many conversations with Helen Mayer Harrison and Newton Harrison, since we met them at the Dawin Symposium, Shrewsbury in 2005, co-ordinated by our friend and colleague David Haley. The friendship that that event seeded, along with the many questions of the place of art in the environmental debates, will outlast us all. This book is a step along that remarkable and challenging enquiry, and we hope it inspires many more.

We want to acknowledge the invaluable role of our publisher Mirjam Truwant who has been a great support and guide in bringing this book to fruition in a timely way. We have been gently nudged and provoked by the reviewers to look more closely and think more deeply through their insightful comments and questions. These have helped us clarify important sections of the argument. Tim Ingold inspired an adventure with the writing of Alfred North Whitehead that left none of our early assumptions unexamined. We draw extensively on Isabelle Stengers' remarkable understanding of Whitehead and his relevance to present day challenges. We would like to thank Roger Berkowitz and the Hannah Arendt Center's Virtual Reading Group at Bard College, New York for helping us rethink the political through the work of Hannah Arendt.

We would also like to thank Brandon Ballengée, Lauren Bon, Tim Collins and Reiko Goto-Collins, Annie Sprinkle and Beth Stephens, and Ruth Wallen for various conversations and interviews which have enabled us to better articulate the ways in which they were in conversation with Helen and Newton.

We are very grateful to the Harrison family for their support and engagement, and to the team at the Harrison Studio including Justin LaneLutter. Mark Hope co-produced *On the Deep Wealth of this Nation Scotland* (2018). We owe a debt to others who have provided opportunities to present aspects of the argument, including Tatiana Sizonenko and Heath Fox, curators of the 'Helen and Newton Harrison: California Work' exhibition. They organised the *Listening to the Web of Life* (2022) where we first explored Isabelle Stengers and Alfred North Whitehead's philosophy as a way to open up the importance of the Harrisons' work. Grant Kester enabled us and other contributors to publish from that event in *Field* 2023. Others including Jim Fairley and Jake Fremantle have offered expert commentary on specific sections. Jo Macdonald has guided and enriched new ways of exploring the meaning of 'nature' in the 21ˢᵗ century. Our families, all three generations, and friends have supported the many hours of grappling with the complexities of the Harrisons' work in a rapidly changing world.

We thank the various rights owners of images including principally the Newton and Helen Harrison Family Trust as well as galleries and museums for allowing us to use the images. These include Ronald Feldman Gallery, New York; Various Small Fires, Los Angeles; Flat Time House and the Lisson Gallery, London; Paula Cooper Gallery, New York and the Department of Special Collections, Stanford University who hold the Harrisons' archives.

The process of collaborating to create something is challenging. Co-authoring this book makes clear what a remarkable collaboration Helen and Newton developed, one which produced deep, clear and sophisticated works of art, whilst allowing for disagreement, evident in their performance lectures. Their collaboration gave us the courage to keep going, to uphold our different specific interests and perspectives as authors, to come together in agreement from time to time, and at others to agree to disagree in friendship.

CHAPTER 1

Introduction: Seeking a Different Place for the Arts in Survival

The global environment crisis already constitutes 'an unbearable intrusion on someone's beliefs, values and interests' (Latour 2020, 13).[1] How might arts practices be reimagined in the face of the escalating number of manifestations of the crisis? How might they help us re-imagine ourselves in the world outside of human exceptionalism and progress, cultural narratives that have dominated the Western world for more than 500 years since the Renaissance? Can the arts offer alternative ways of knowing that counter the authority of 'technoscience' to shape Earth as an object for our human convenience? Technoscience is a term that philosopher of science Isabelle Stengers (b. 1949) uses to describe the ways science has been 'enslaved' by the state and industry, capitalism and growth, in the development of what is called the economy of knowledge (Stengers 2011, 11; 2023, 53, 56). Multiple articulations of this challenge come from within the arts, and from practices and disciplines collaborating with the arts. These pose a question as to what sorts of arts practices face the challenges of this time. Helen Mayer Harrison (1927–2018) and Newton Harrison (1932–2022), 'the Harrisons', have for more than 50 years pioneered a practice that is focused by ecologies and have sought to engage in precisely such a re-thinking. Their response to the intrusion has been to only make work that in some sense addresses the well-being of the environment. They made this decision in 1969-70. It is not made in a moment but rather sets the artists on an adventure, as is clear from their own description of their chronology in *The Lagoon Cycle* catalogue (referring to themselves in the third person):

> 1970
> The Harrisons begin collaboration as artists. Through 1973 they develop *The Survival Series*, from which they develop a discourse or theory they call the ecological argument. (H. M. Harrison and Harrison 1985b, 99)

The 'ecological argument' has been explored by the Harrisons in different ways and at different scales, first in quasi-scientific experiments, then in watersheds and bioregions, and eventually at continental scale. Entropy has been a key organising concept in this work, particularly since 2007 in the *Force Majeure* projects.[2]

We believe that present day capitalism, unless it finds the way to give back to the life web more than it takes, by internalizing biological exchange, will continue to generate [a] sixth extinction and the overarching simplification and further degeneration of the web of life. The partial collapse of the life web is highly probable, as demonstrated by the physical laws of the conservation of energy. We know that when energy is changed from one form to another there is always a net loss, thermodynamically expressed as entropy. (N. Harrison 2021a, 63)

A healthy low entropy system is one where the transformations of energy (the processes of living, reproducing, and dying) mean that energy in the system can continue to work, in other words that energy is not dispersed, becoming unusable and inert.[3] The Harrisons express this as part of the framing of the *Force Majeure* in a short text[4]:

Matter/energy can be transformed from one form to another.
Matter/energy can be neither created nor destroyed.
When matter/energy is transformed from one form to another,
there is a net loss of available energy to perform work.
This loss is called entropy.
A system that has been so transformed and has lost energy
moves towards higher local entropy.
A system that maintains its ability to take useful energy into itself
and dissipate unuseful energy
tends to be a healthy, low-entropy system.
(H. M. Harrison and Harrison 2016, 374)

Nature constantly reuses waste (biological exchange) whereas Western cultures have not prioritised this, resulting in the simplification and degeneration of the web of life. We face a 'force majeure', that is, we have created the circumstances, in terms of exponential population growth, sudden increases in energy consumption, and runaway economic development, which can only be characterised as a high entropy system resulting in the climate crisis and sixth extinction. In a playful reversal of the meaning of force majeure as an 'escape' clause, the Harrisons propose that there is no escape as long as we continue along the current trajectory of creating high entropy systems (2016, 426ff.). The escalating environmental crisis is the context that makes the Harrisons' work over the past 50 years particularly prescient. The speed and scale of change is now a matter of scientific fact that in turn generates matters of shared concern for how to imagine and organise a common future. High entropy, as the Harrisons recognise, is a useful way to understand the underlying problem as it characterises the consequences of not thinking ecologically.

It is noticeable that many ecological scientists are increasingly turning to the arts to help society to think through how best to move forward. In a recent collaboration between the philosopher of science Bruno Latour (1947–2022) and the curator of arts and media Peter Weibel (1944–2023) in 2020, Latour suggests we are no longer equipped to deal with the terrifying news of environmental devastation. He appeals to scientific colleagues to rethink what they might expect from the arts as something more than popularisation and ornamentation, indicating that the arts can be an important contributor to understanding and acting in the world differently (Latour 2020). He is joined by contemporaries such as Isabelle Stengers, as well as Donna Haraway (b. 1944), and Anna Tsing (b. 1952), in turning towards artists as public intellectuals in a far-reaching reappraisal of what it means to be human. Haraway, a feminist in the biological sciences, increasingly uses science fiction as an opening to a more than human world (Haraway 2011). Tsing, an anthropologist, investigates life 'in the ruins' through the experiences of mushroom pickers improvising their existence in the margins of mainstream society. The mushroom economy forms a powerful image of a dystopian future (Tsing 2016). Stengers, like Latour, is a philosopher of science in search of a different science, one that is freed from the dictates of capitalist interests, free to ask questions that matter to the future of humanity.

These important thinkers from their diverse discipline perspectives share with the Harrisons the enormity of the challenge of what it means to be human from an ecological perspective. All acknowledge that aesthetics has an important role to play in encouraging this different imaginary. Less well developed is an understanding of what and how the arts contribute. It is a truism to say the arts affect our subjectivity, affect how we imagine ourselves to be, but what does it mean to do so when the arts enter the public realm, as in this case seeking to actively contribute to issues outside of art? Frequently the art is ignored or reduced to good social work or ecological work or damned as inadequate science. It is initially to Stengers and her major undertaking to 'think with' the mathematician and philosopher, Alfred North Whitehead (1861–1947), that we turn to think through this question of art and the radical shift the Harrisons make in repositioning the arts within an ecological argument. Stengers in her practice of 'thinking with Whitehead' has opened the opportunity for us to engage with Whitehead's writings on process philosophy. We share with her a sense that his thinking has been critical to the development of ecological thinking beyond the narrow confines of the biological sciences just as the Harrisons have sought to shape a form of art and poetics beyond the narrow confines of the art institution.[5]

Before embarking on this venture, it is important as a first step to reflect on what the arts to date have specifically offered to social environmental challenges. Diego Galafassi et al. in their sociological analysis of this issue draw on a range of case studies and reveal a wide range of possibilities (2018, 71–79). Artists can communicate science in ways that extend its reach, a function not far perhaps from Latour's notion of 'popularization'.

> In a quieter period, it might make sense for scientists to reject the collaboration of artists, or to limit their help to decoration and popularization. Not in a time of crisis such as that of the newly moving Earth. (Latour 2020, 18)

Artists can open the imagination to serendipity and develop forms of experimentation that are different from positivist science and that explore futures imaginatively. They can embrace the complexity of emotions and values that confront human beings and construct spaces of interaction engaging the human and non-human in processes of knowledge exchange and civic participation. These largely positive qualities of the arts are tempered by writers such as Amitav Ghosh (b. 1956), who, as a writer of fiction and non-fiction, raises questions about what form of art serves the challenges we face appropriately. Ghosh questions whether the modern Western novel and its particularly narrow focus on the subjective experiences of individual characters can sufficiently address the scale of the issues involved in environmental change (2016). As a form the novel may in fact depend upon an assumption of ecological stability and therefore exacerbate the problem. Such examples across the arts and humanities reveal a restless search for a different future, one that is wide-eyed to the challenges we face but also refuses to be crushed by the overwhelming evidence of the speed and criticality of the change, and the need for rapid forms of adaptation against time.

Why are the Harrisons important to this discussion? For some contemporary artists like Ghosh the environmental crisis emerges as something of an intrusion in thinking and being that challenges their ways of working and the institutions that support them and their audiences. The Harrisons also experienced the intrusion from the mid-1960s, Newton as an established gallery artist and Helen as a Geoffrey Chaucer (c. 1340s–1400) scholar and educationalist. They committed to addressing the environment in response to profound, personal, and disruptive experiences, including reading Rachel Carson's *Silent Spring*, which explored the effects of dichlorodiphenyltrichloroethane (DDT) on biodiversity (1962). Over 50 years they painstakingly evolved a form of practice in which environmental well-being is front and centre, simultaneously subject, content, and to an extent process. While the Harrisons' projects resulted in exhibitions in a wide range of conventional and unconventional spaces, they have also been included in most major group exhibitions that define the development of art and ecology,[6] and been included in both the Venice Biennale and Documenta.[7] They were represented from the late 1970s by a major New York commercial gallery where many of their key projects were re-exhibited.[8] They have had to reinvent themselves as individuals and create a way of working appropriate to their commitment to only make work that would help them understand the web of life and *its* needs, not the narrow interests of humans alone. Their work is open to the world and its mutability. It is in their terms 'post-categorical' (H. M. Harrison and Harrison 2007b, n.p.) or 'post-disciplinary' (Ingram Allen 2008, 30), led by circumstances on the ground. It is situated in the sense that they begin in particular places and raise questions in response to what they find through conversation. They create opportunities for discourse and the sharing of knowledge and experience in which the voice of the farmer or birdwatcher is as relevant as that of the expert scientist. They become saturated in knowing a place and connect place with ecological systems, creating feedback loops that allow for new learning. They describe their process as a form of 'conversational drift', a key concept underpinning the work's 50-year evolution. It is through conversational drift as a process that is informed and open-ended, participatory and generative, that they tackle the challenge of high entropy systems. Importantly, this approach stimulates and provokes emotional intelligence and the energy to rebuild a world in common through the coming together of plural, potentially contradictory perspectives. These characteristics, carefully developed as a practice that is profoundly aesthetic, poetic and artistic, find interesting parallels in the ways the scientists mentioned above are currently rethinking science and its relevance to the future of the planet.

As authors we have written on the Harrisons' practice from a diversity of perspectives: on metaphor, on improvisation, on inconsistency and contradiction, as a poetic form, in relation to policy and governance, and in relation to irony and the absurd.[9] We also have experience of working closely with the Harrisons to produce the work. Anne Douglas, as a Board member at the time of an arts organisation located in a town in the Northeast of Scotland impacted by flooding, was instrumental in inviting the Harrisons to help the community to come to terms with the flooding as an experience of climate change. This resulted in Newton Harrison's work *On the Deep Wealth of this Nation, Scotland* (2018) (fig. 1-2)[10]. Chris Fremantle was producer for the Harrisons' *Greenhouse Britain: Losing Ground, Gaining Wisdom* (2006–09) (fig. 3-6) that investigated the patterns and implications of sea level rise on the island of Britain.[11] Both were involved in supporting the other project as well. Our research to date has largely addressed artists and their audiences interested in exploring new forms of artistic practice. We have researched how the Harrisons work with scientists and the relationship between their work and environmental policy and governance. In this book, we read more deeply into the philosophy of science and have uncovered shared concerns that point to an underlying commonality between the domains of science, art, and politics. By connecting these diverse bodies of work, including Stengers and Whitehead in the philosophy of science with the Harrisons and related thinkers in art, noting synergies and contradictions, it becomes possible to encounter and cross-fertilise a plurality of perspectives that have hitherto been siloed. This book explores this commonality and its implications for making a 'world in common' as a political process that is grounded in individual judgement. It explores the implications for a different aesthetic, an ecological aesthetic (Steiner 2019), one that is more than a sensory exchange between people and their environments. An ecological aesthetic, eminent designer, and regional planner, Frederick Steiner argues, is capable of taking into account socio-cultural and political interrelationships countering entropy by working with the organisation, structure, and function of ecosystems, understood through aesthetic as well as analytic means.

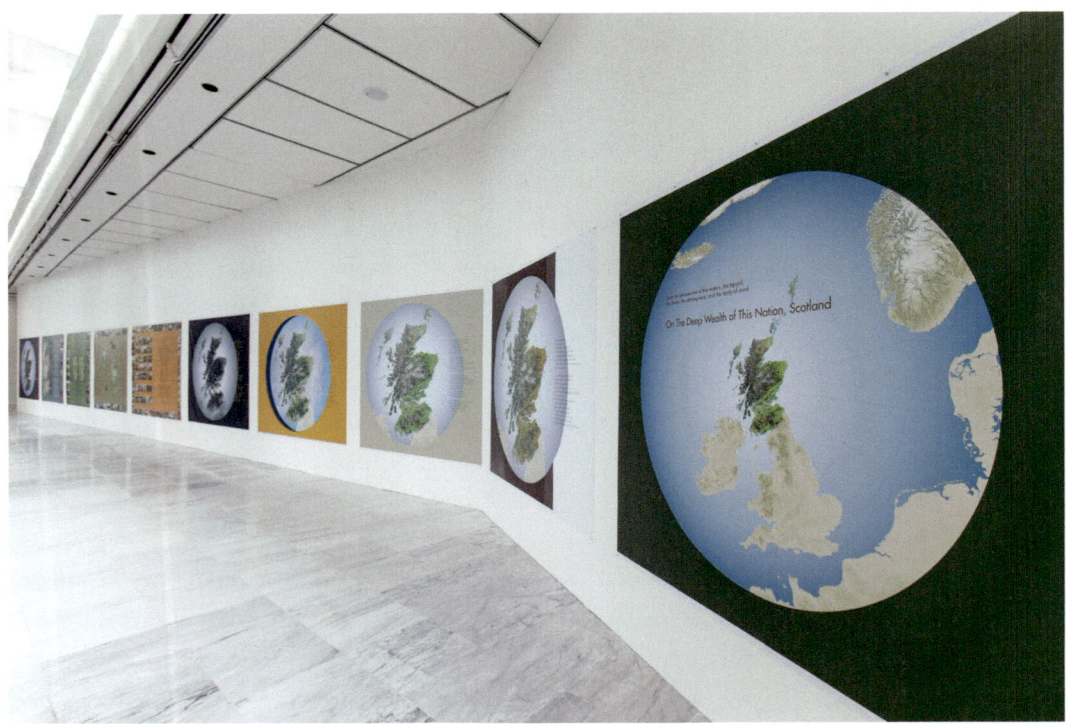

Figure 1: 'On the Deep Wealth of this Nation, Scotland' (2018) Installation view at Taipei Biennial, Taiwan (courtesy of the Newton and Helen Harrison Family Trust)[12]

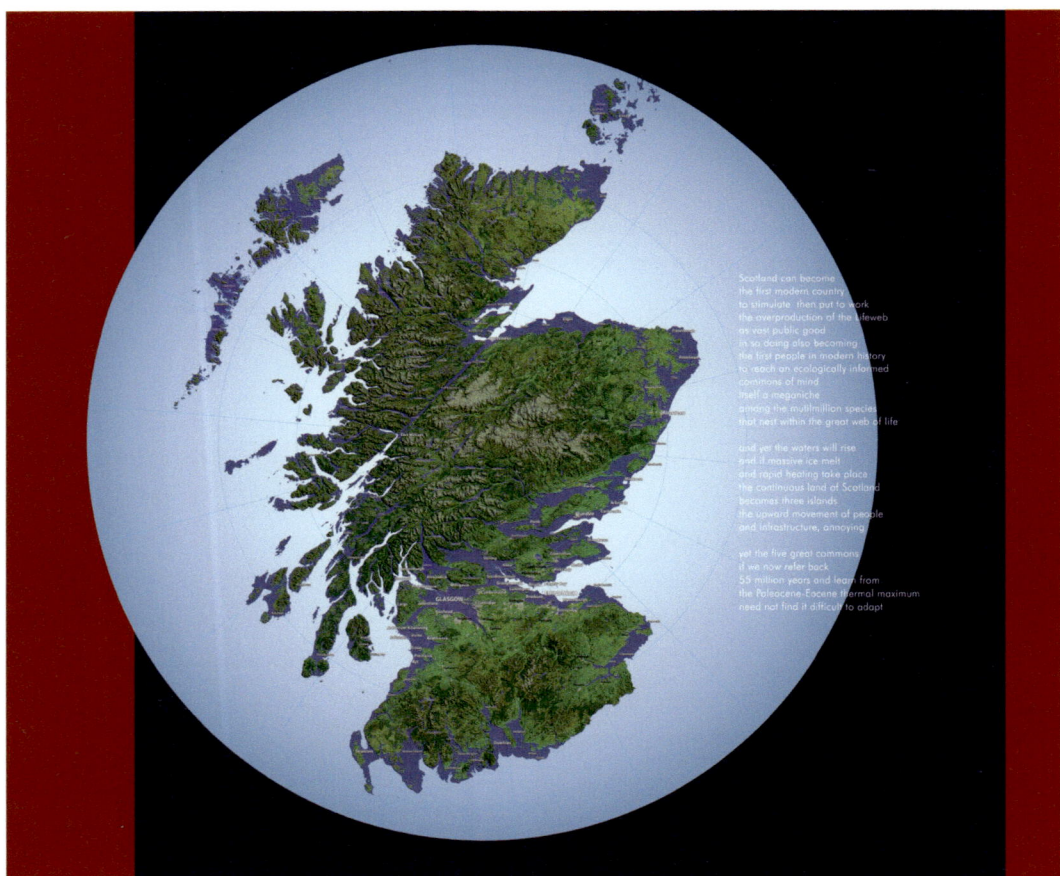

Figure 2: 'On the Deep Wealth of this Nation, Scotland' (2018) detail (courtesy of the Newton and Helen Harrison Family Trust)

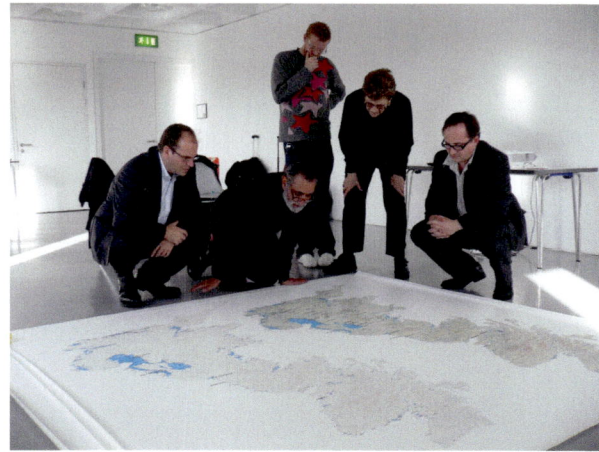

Figure 3: 'Greenhouse Britain: Losing Ground, Gaining Wisdom' Reviewing initial sea level rise maps at the Arnolfini Gallery, Bristol, England. From left: Tom Trevor (Director), Newton Harrison, Martin Clarke (Curator), Helen Mayer Harrison, Chris Fremantle (2006) (courtesy of David Haley)

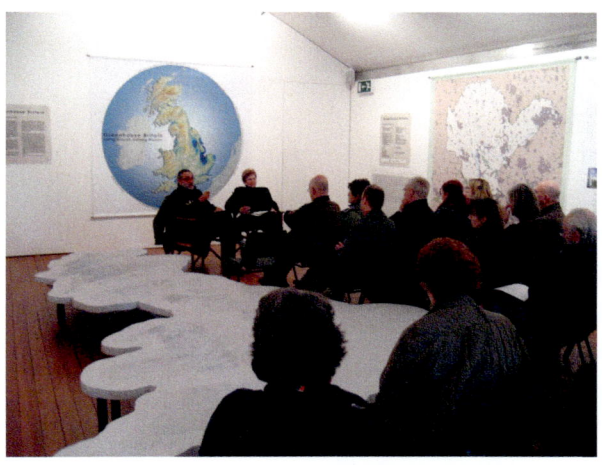

Figure 4: 'Greenhouse Britain' – Lecture at exhibition opening, Centre for Contemporary Art and the Natural World (CCANW), Haldon Forest, Exeter, England (2007) (courtesy of CCANW)

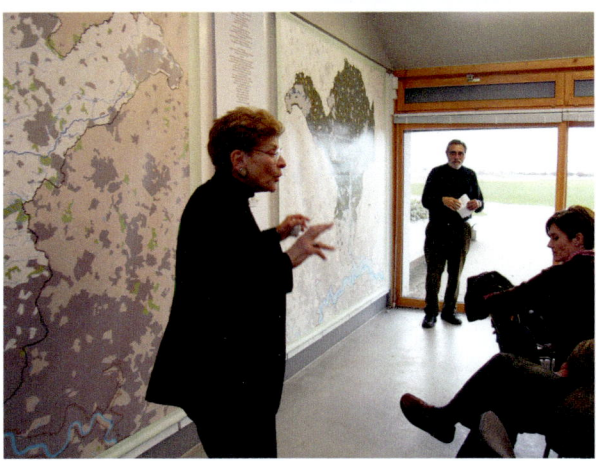

Figure 5: 'Greenhouse Britain' 'Bright Sparks' workshop with associated installation, Gunpowder Park, Essex, England (2008) (courtesy of David Haley)

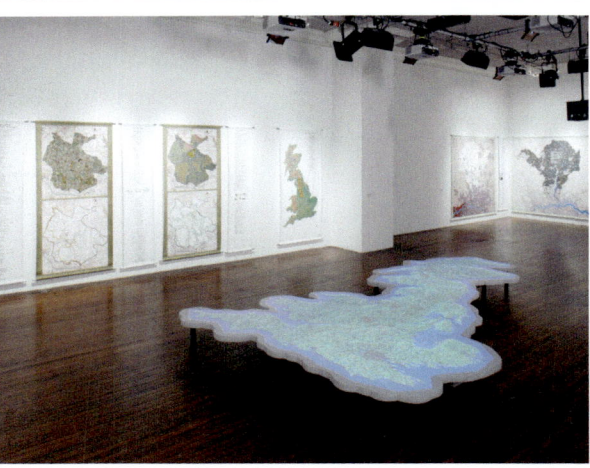

Figure 6: 'Global Warming: Greenhouse Britain, 2006-2009, and Related Works 1974-2009' (January 10 – February 7, 2009) Installation view Ronald Feldman Gallery, New York. (Private collection courtesy Ronald Feldman Gallery, New York)

Why have we, as authors and artist researchers, made the unlikely choice to work with on the one hand Whitehead's process philosophy and writings on science (2022, 2015, 1985, 1978, 1967, 1948), and on the other Stengers, who works with Whitehead's philosophy.

> ...I am part of a motley crew of 'Whiteheadians', of those ecologists, feminists and educators, theologians, and so on, who have discovered that Whitehead helped them to imagine and to fight against "ready-made" models. and above all not to despair. (Stengers 2011, 11)

As authors and artists researchers, we are also part of that motley crew resisting the despair of runaway environmental change. One of the precepts of artistic research is to consider practice in relation to the different histories of ideas that inform and shape the work. This is our motive for turning predominantly to Whitehead and Stengers as critical friends and to others as relevant to the issues under discussion. Whitehead and Stengers are deeply concerned with a similar challenge, in their case constructed as a rethinking of science's understanding of nature through philosophy. At a moment of societal change, artistic research supports a process of examining the assumptions, values, and ways of working through which the Harrisons' practice has evolved. That being said we are not experts on Whitehead's work, and we focus, with the assistance of Stengers, on key concepts that offer a side light on the work of the Harrisons and on how we might re-think the arts.[13] Stengers not only offers an up-to-date reading of Whitehead and his relevance to our time of technoscience, but also acts as a bridge to our understanding.

The crisis is one in which no-one, let alone a single discipline or discipline group, has the solutions. It invites us, even compels us, to reach out of knowledge domains and comfort zones, to undertake an 'adventure'. Stengers' approach to Whitehead gives us permission to undertake the adventure of ideas, of hope, and of experiment that Whitehead proposes. 'Adventure' in Whitehead, she argues, characterises that we are dealing with reality and situates us in speculative thinking (Stengers 2011, 18). She further inflects this as 'accepting an adventure from which none of the words that serve as our reference points should emerge unscathed but from which none will be disqualified or denounced as a vector of illusion' (Stengers 2011, 15). In doing this Stengers offers an approach to a discourse that is different from conventional forms of account such as art history or critical theory. She does not seek to create a 'history', just as we are not seeking to create a history of the Harrisons' work (Stengers 2011, 23–24). In her approach to Whitehead, she takes up the central problem of the 'bifurcation of nature' and develops key concepts such as 'leap of the imagination' and 'adventure'. She develops further concepts out of her reading of Whitehead such as 'inventing a field' and 'storytelling'. She provides an approach to the process of 'thinking with' offering a series of questions that she understands to be necessary correlates.

Every adventure thus calls forth the generic question 'what does it make matter?' which can also mean 'how is the contrast between success and defeat defined for it?' (Stengers 2011, 19)

And:

[T]he point is to experiment with the effects of that leap: what it does to thought, what it obliges one to do, what it renders important, and what it makes remain silent. (Stengers 2011, 22)

These questions, which so clearly draw on Whitehead's writings, will underpin our approach as we seek to rethink the role of the arts.

Whitehead's process philosophy, which we explore in relation to the Harrisons' work in Chapter 2, is called a philosophy of the organism. Whitehead starts with the 'bifurcation of nature'. For Whitehead this highlights the way the sciences split nature between abstracted, measurable aspects organised around a particular notion of 'causality' stripping away all sensory qualities of an experience, *and* the way nature is 'apprehended' by separating subject from object, reducing perception to visual perception (Whitehead 2015, 18-32). The bifurcation, and each of its resulting forms – the reduction to measurement and the separation of viewer and viewed – are both equally problematic. The subject/object split structures our relationship to knowledge as a duality between the knower (subject) and what is known (object) and this duality in turn frames our relations with the environment, severing in our minds the profound entanglement and co-dependence of humans with the life around them. This in turn has encouraged the licence to use and exploit. Whitehead proposes a different idea of nature within an expanded notion of perception, one based in process and 'event' where organic and inorganic entities interact and co-create their environments. It is through process and event that all life emerges. Life is an 'adventure', thinking is an adventure of ideas, and language an adventure in interpretation. Inertia at all levels of existence and within all forms of life results in mere repetition. While repetition is necessary to sustaining life through objects and processes that endure, creativity and experimentation, taking 'a leap of the imagination' beyond the assumptions and 'safe limits of learned rules of taste' (Whitehead 1985, 279), create the circumstances for novelty and change. Where excessive repetition and inertia leads to death, creativity and the imagination enable us to renew life always within some degree of constraint.

We might imagine the central concept of 'event' through some examples, including the practice of drawing; the work of anthropologist and theorist of entanglement Tim Ingold, who has studied Whitehead; and works by the British conceptual artist John Latham (1921–2006). In drawing from life, for example, it would be easy to describe the experience in terms of the separation of subject and object: the model or still life presents an array of objects to me, the drawer. These transmit information to the brain that in turn 're-pictures' the image, presenting this back in a new form through materials such as paper, lead pencil, and charcoal. However, our experience of drawing suggests something different. Drawing is more like suspending any sense of intention, giving oneself over to tracing an experience of a small part of the world, creating 'a moment' in which I am present, active, and alive. This experience gives way to a 'perishing' in Whitehead's terms. It undergoes a transition, becoming a resolved drawing that can be experienced in a new way. It becomes potential for new experience. This new experience could be one of simply viewing the new drawing (by myself or by another) as aesthetic pleasure or it could offer the potential, the energy, to embark on a different drawing. The way anyone draws is also connected to and influenced by their own physiology, life history, and cultural histories of representation, acting as 'eternal objects' perhaps, along with qualities of material, tone, colour, and so on. 'Perishing' is interesting in this respect. A drawing can appear 'unfinished' and yet be no longer open to the creative potential of the moment. Its perishing and transition into new potential is palpable to the drawer and often determined by the drawing, out of the control of the drawer.

Turning to Ingold, he discusses the relationship between trees and wind asking us where the tree that has grown bent by the prevailing wind on the coast 'ends' and the wind 'begins'. He asks of quivering leaves of the Aspen trees, the rustling reeds, the ripples on water, do these cause the wind, to which he answers, 'Of course not!' but goes on to say, 'if, by wind, we mean its music to our ears, or its sun-dance to our eyes, then yes – leaves, ripples and reeds do make the wind. For when I say I hear the wind, or see it on the surface of the lake, the sounds I hear are made by leaves just as much as is the light I see made by ripples' (Ingold 2021, 24). Ingold is interested in the affective relation that means that every entity participates in generating nature's capacity to endure. He is drawing attention to this complex corporeal entangled understanding of the world, rather than one understood in terms of discrete objects. He explores this through 'lines', trajectories more than graphics, as a conceptual device with which, like Paul Klee, he can focus on the world as we experience it.

> One could perhaps compare wandering to drawing: as the draughtsman traces a line with his pencil, so the wanderer – walking along – paces a line with his feet. Paul Klee had explicit resort to this comparison in his celebrated definition of drawing as 'taking a line for a walk'. (Ingold 2015, 60)

For Ingold the example of the bent over tree is a 'knot' (entangled lines) where tree and wind and ground and topography are inseparable. It is also a very clear way to focus on event, the inseparability of the spatial and the temporal in the process of becoming. Ingold says, 'So entangled are these lines that it is scarcely possible to say with any certainty where any particular tree ends and the rest of the world begins. Is the bark a part of the tree? If so, then what of the insects which burrow in it, or the lichens that hang from it? And if the insects are part of the tree, then why should we not also include the bird that nests there? Or even the wind…?' (Ingold 2013, 87). This approach, where the phenomenal is intrinsic to being rather than something to do with human perception attributed to objects, might help us to understand Whitehead's construction of event as not subject to the bifurcation.

The third way to imagine event might be through two works by John Latham. Latham grappled with quantum physics and made two groups of artworks in response to his understandings, works that might speak to Whitehead's notion of 'event'. Whether Latham was aware of Whitehead or not, he shared the insight that scientific systems should take account of human actions, that art could be considered a kind of intuitive science that makes clear "what is for and what is against mankind" (Marlis Grüterich quoted in Conzen-Meairs 1991, 10).

> [L]atham regards the artist as an individual who is capable of universal insight; the purpose of art is, for him, the recreation of the lost relationship between the individual and the whole. As a result, he is engaged in a critique of the Natural Sciences, since he feels they have failed by not taking human existence into account within their system. The result of this has been an alternative formulation of a theory of time which includes the person and his motivation. By regarding the fundamental unit of the universe not as a particle but as an event, the traditional dualistic separation of material and consciousness becomes invalid. (Conzen-Meairs 1991, 9)

Latham conceives of the artist, himself included, as an 'incidental person' integral to the society in which they find themselves, rather than a maker of objects. The latter would involve conformity to the marketplace, which Latham, like the Harrisons, refuses to do.[14] In his *One-Second Drawings* (1970–77), Latham used spray paint on unprimed canvas to enact and create a visual manifestation of what he termed a 'least moment' or event. In the *Time-Base Roller* works (1972–87) (fig. 7) Latham presents his theory of time in relation to a length and width of flat canvas, wound on a roller, which is operated by an electric switch. Along the top of the canvas, time is divided into intervals that mirror the way the human mind imagines time. A in the top left-hand corner marks a 'least event', the shortest duration; M at a halfway point marks the present of an individual; P marks an event of human time, approximately 30 years; Q marks 'the boundary of Reason or society and its rules, the rational/structural'. RST marks intuition and consciousness and STU the domain of truth where U is the time base of the whole universe (Douglas 2013a, 211). The roller unfurls in response to the switch. Most of the canvas is obscured from view. The narrow visible strip that can be seen represents 'now' and the face against the wall is 'then', the past. It is interesting to note that Whitehead also creates a paradoxical image of the world disclosed within that which remains undisclosed. In discussing the experience of an event, he suggests that whatever is made apparent through an event, another part that anchors the event in the world is 'out of sight'. Far from being Plato's hidden, more ideal, determined world, the other side of Latham and Whitehead's reality is the indeterminate potential from which an occasion of experience selects.

These three examples suggest ways of imagining 'event' in the Whiteheadean sense. The experience of drawing characterised by what one brings to it, what is going on during the process of drawing, as well as how one knows when it is 'done', is 'captured' in Whitehead's articulation of event. Ingold's experiential articulation of wind and trees provides an account beyond mere causality. Latham foregrounds the temporality of event.

In Chapter 2 '*Thinking with*' we explore how Whitehead's process philosophy and Stengers' particular questions can help us understand the Harrisons' *Survival Pieces* (1970–74) and the ways in which they are key to the development of the Harrisons' 'ecological argument'. The *Survival Pieces* are a series of quasi-scientific experiments modelling and recreating ecosystems exhibited as artworks.

Whitehead's conceptualisation of event and the way Stengers draws their relevance to new forms of human–environmental relations, invite us to ask questions about what is made to matter and how differing criteria of judgement are revealed in the *Survival Pieces*. These works produce collisions between values associated with ecology and high cultures. While the works look novel and to some un-art-like, they are informed by specific previous experiences of the Harrisons, as well as fundamentals such as colour and pattern. The Harrisons treat each work as an opportunity from which to learn and grow the practice through ecological insight.

In Chapter 3, *The Lagoon Cycle,* unresolved issues identified in the *Survival Pieces* give form to the Harrisons' seminal work of that name (1974–85). This work marks a step change from modelling partial ecosystems in galleries to exploring actual damaged ecosystems and developing reflective and critical thinking. The story told in the *The Lagoon Cycle* starts from an exploration of the potential of the *Scylla Serrata* crab, native to Sri Lanka, for aquaculture farming in California. The implications of bifurcating nature become very clear within this work. The Harrisons start out along a very conventional pathway of technoscience where the goal of the research is to build a system, in this case of industrial fish farming. The further the Harrisons as artists travel along that path, the clearer becomes the potential damage to the environment. The work is constructed as a dialogue between two positions, the active Lagoon Maker, the embodiment of creativity, and the reflective Witness who tracks the implications of actual and proposed experiments undertaken by the artists. Whitehead's key concepts of life as a process of emergence and perishing bring into a sharp focus the transition that the Harrisons undergo as they shift from imagining crab farming at scale to speculating on the disastrous environmental consequences of their proposal. The differences between technoscience founded in the bifurcation of nature and those of art and its 'indirect power...to express the truth about the nature of things' (Whitehead 1985, 249) become apparent as the artists increasingly rely on their sense of judgement and deepening feeling for the dependence between the crab and its environment to guide their choices.

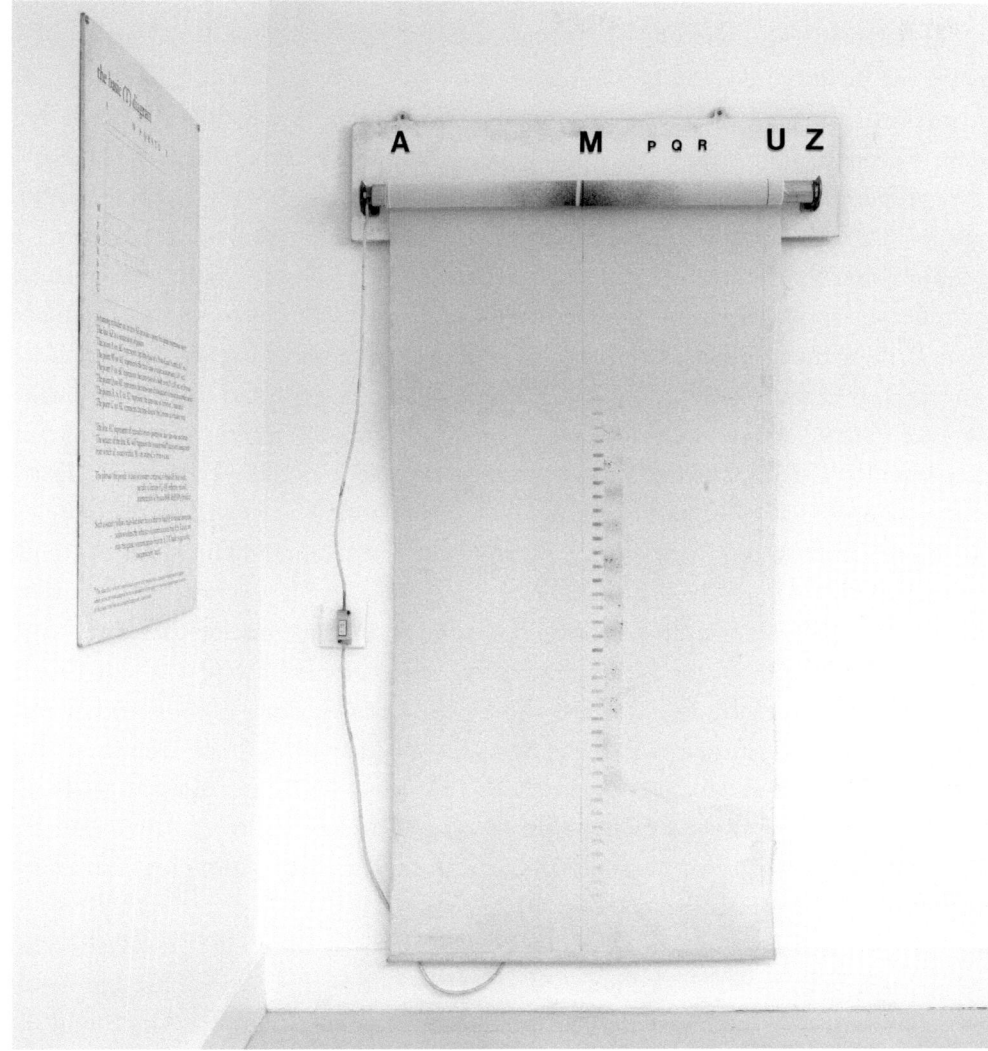

Figure 7: John Latham, 'Time-Base Roller with Graphic Score' (1987) (with Basic T Diagram on left). Canvas, electric motor operating metal bar, wood, graphite. Photo Ken Adlard (courtesy of John Latham Foundation and Lisson Gallery, 2005)

They notice that the natural world and human cultures share a dynamic in common: both are forms of improvisation. They also notice patterns of continuity across time and space that endure, offering potential for new life. The next two chapters, 4 and 5, pick up on both improvisation and systems in relation to the Harrisons' work and reveal that they are connected, the one acting as a foil to the other.

Chapter 4, *On Improvisation*, explores the Harrisons' work through one of Whitehead's key pairings, constraint and freedom. The pairings, like truth and beauty or appearance and reality, are a way of ordering and characterising ideas and how they relate among alternatives. We often interpret human history in terms of constraint and freedom, Whitehead observes, conferring value on what otherwise might become a meaningless succession of events (Whitehead 1967, 8). Whitehead's construction of event can be imagined as improvisatory in the sense that organisms are free to inherit from the past selectively in new occasions of experience in the environment. Such freedom is dependent upon constraints to channel and intensify experience. The body of a living organism functions in this way (Whitehead 1978, 107). The process frequently results in novelty, such as organisms evolving from simple to more complex states. For the Harrisons constraint and freedom characterise their understanding of improvisation as underpinning both natural systems and cultural processes. Improvisation is their way of describing the meeting of fresh and salt water in an estuarial lagoon along with the fluctuations of abundance and scarcity in cultures, always at risk and changeable. An array of different perspectives enriches and expands this understanding of improvisation. Massumi (b. 1956), philosopher and social theorist, in search for a different politics, situates improvisation in nature, using Whitehead's notion of process to explore play in animals as an aesthetic experience. Play allows for variation and breaks with simple repetition. Chaudhuri (b. 1962) and Peters (b. 1952), key writers and musicians on improvisation, explore improvisatory skill, discipline, and imagination that is necessary to holding a crucial tension between adventure and communicability. Where Ghosh looks for a suitable form in the arts to address the environmental crisis, improvisation offers a practice oriented towards the livingness of the world. It can take shape as a predicament, such as the environmental crisis. To avoid becoming trapped, we create ways to escape, generating a 'more to life' or what Whitehead calls 'a creative advance'. As a practice in the world improvisation can be imagined as a counterpoint to the 'mere repetition' of industrial productivity.

Chapter 5, *On the Poetics and Aesthetics of Systems*, starts from the observation that the Harrisons frequently use the language of systems in their work, through words in their poetic texts such as 'database', 'boundary', 'stability', 'changes of state' and the forms such as maps and diagrams as visual elements. However, these are used playfully and plastically, in ways that are interpreted through understandings from art practice. We might understand that the Harrisons are improvising with systems. Fritjof Capra (b. 1939) and Donella Meadows (1941–2001) offer an alternative to the mathematical and modelling focused articulation, understanding systems as both human constructs and also literal, manifest in flows of energy and materials that are affected by metaphors and paradigms. This links with the Harrisons' concern with entropy. The language of systems and ecosystems co-evolved during the 20th century. Burnham (1931–2019), whose critical writing in the late 1960s and early 1970s references the Harrisons' practice and who was in correspondence with them, argues that we need to pay attention to the aesthetic dimension of systems 'revealed in the principles underlying the progressive reorganisation of the natural environment' for better or worse (Burnham 1974, 18). His argument was that artists' poetics were shifting from 'object' to 'process' and that this needed to be understood in terms of a capacity to shape or influence systems, including ecosystems. One focus was on metaphor. The work of Mierle Laderman Ukeles

(b. 1939) engaged with the waste management system in New York City is a complementary example. The Harrisons' work *Spoils Pile Reclamation* (1977–78) provides a
useful example of a work that improvises a very successful system and yet fails, perhaps
through a lack of attention to metaphor. This work shares much with the *Survival Pieces*
while also harking forward to important works such as *The Endangered Meadows of
Europe* (1996).

Whitehead's process philosophy has some resonances with systems theory, in particular the role of repetition. Process philosophy is most resonant with those approaches to systems that are concerned with openness and emergence.

Chapter 6, *On the Political*, shows in what sense the Harrisons' life-long aim to put
the well-being of the life web first has political implications. They recognise that their
ecological concerns fundamentally challenge narrow Western notions of progress and
economics that build on scientific materialism. They also recognise that their position
on the environment invokes a form of authoritarianism or even ecofascism. This is al-
luded to in their 1977 work *Meditation on the Great Lakes of North America* in which
they explore the proposition of a 'dictatorship of the ecology'. They acknowledge this
danger within the ecological turn, in part through irony. Their work as artists focuses
on the question of what can be done in the shared space of public life by bringing
aesthetics and judgement to bear in real situations. Positioning the aesthetic within the
political is also a quality in the work of Hannah Arendt (1906–1975). Writing in the
late 1960s as a political theorist she draws on Immanuel Kant's (1724–1804) late work
in an unusual articulation of his political philosophy. She sees that the formation of
aesthetic judgement in the individual is critical to creating a world in common through
a plurality of experiences and perspectives. The Harrisons and Arendt follow a similar
trajectory and it is different from a construction of the political driven by interests,
strategy, and efficiency, a matter for experts or of populism. There are resonances with
Whitehead in the way he develops his idea of the importance of freedom for creativity in society, also informed like Arendt by the fear of its suppression in 'totalitarian'
regimes (Whitehead 1948, 52–53). Whitehead suggests that plurality is immanent
in the way life emerges in an actual occasion of experience, in the way that vectors of
feeling from the past are complex, multi-perspectival, and conflicted. This is mirrored
in some of the Harrisons' works with the incorporation of multiple voices articulating
contradictory positions. Force Majeure works tend to give voice to the life web directly
also drawing out contradictions. Discourse as an occasion of experience or event affords
the making of meaning in common as an active working with contradiction. Arendt
and Whitehead offer concepts and tools that are important to the political implications
of ecological mindedness, but there are also blind spots. The danger implicit in adopting
ecosystemic well-being as a principle tends towards universalising. Mandating ecosystemic well-being as a goal, driven by intention, derives action from principles and can
in its actualisation become an ideology rather than a question of attention, at worst a
form of eco-fascism. The Harrisons' use of 'dictates' and 'dictatorship' is provocative

and requires us to attend to this challenge. Their dialogue frames the issue as a debate with which they struggle. The question arises about the relevance of their political perspective for today. Their emphasis on dialogue does not directly address the complexity of issues that the ecopolitical needs to address today, such as the increased domination of elite interests over aspects of the social/political (Táíwò 2022), as just one example.

Chapter 7, *Artists 'thinking with' One Another*, returns to the question of understanding how the arts address global environmental challenges, and how the arts need to be rethought in the process. We imagine this through Whitehead's idea of immanence: the environment that an 'actual occasion' inherits is immanent within each occasion and each occasion is immanent within the environment that it helps to transmit (Whitehead, 1985, 63). Chapters 1 to 6 explore how the Harrisons' practice has been formed and is formative of a step change in positioning the artist in society. They acknowledge a debt to, for example, the Renaissance, particularly Giotto's *St Francis* cycle of frescos at Assisi (1297–1300). This both offers a form for *The Lagoon Cycle* – a 360 ft 'mural' in seven parts – and prompts them to reflect critically on the apparent absence of shared guiding narratives in the present. This chapter also explores how other artists close to the Harrisons have entered into long-term conversations, 'thinking with' the Harrisons and the Harrisons thinking with them. They include Brandon Ballengée (b. 1974), artist and environmental activist, and his work including *Atelier de la Nature* (2017–) in Louisiana; Lauren Bon (b.1962), founder director of Metabolic Studio in Los Angeles, in particular *Bending the River* (2006–ongoing); Tim Collins (b. 1956), a Scottish American artist and Reiko Goto Collins (b. 1955), a Japanese artist, both now practising in Scotland and their work with the Black Wood of Rannoch (2011–ongoing); Annie Sprinkle (b. 1954) and Beth Stephens (b. 1960), the queer activist ecosexual artists and their various ways of relating to Earth as lover such as through a series of *Weddings* (2008–2016); and Ruth Wallen (b. 1953), who as a trained scientist and artist develops ecological art in relation to environmental justice, in particular *Learning to Think Like a Forest* (2023). In the past, discourse in the arts might have described this as 'influence'. Whitehead enables us to see the individual presence of one artistic practice in terms of his conception of 'event'. Each practice is a unique moment drawing on the potential at hand within an artist's experience of life as it presents to that practice. A creative process emerges by drawing together the different forms of potential in an occasion of experience, a unique growing together of different feelings from the past. Event, in this sense, could refer to a moment, the work of a lifetime, or a trajectory over generations. Sometimes the processes of transmission between one artist and another, between the artist and their environment, are very close and apparent; at others they are more distant and diffused. Whatever the degree, each is immanent within the other – Giotto within the Harrisons, the Harrisons within Bon or Goto-Collins, Wallen within the Harrisons and within the landscapes in which she walks and meditates.

In *Science and the Modern World* (2022, 80–103) Whitehead devotes a chapter to tracing the relationship of poets to the developments of science in their day, starting with John Milton (1608–1674). He discusses the poets of the Romantic period, particularly William Wordsworth (1770–1850) and Percy Bysshe Shelley (1792–1822) and their relationship with science and industrialisation. Whitehead suggests that their survival as great poets is evidence that they express deep intuitions of humankind, penetrating into what is universal in concrete fact. He says:

> Remembering the poetic rendering of our concrete experience, we see at once the element of value, of being an end in itself, of being something which is for its own sake, must not be omitted in any account of an event as the most concrete actual something. 'Value' is the word I use for the intrinsic reality of an event. Value is an element which permeates through and through the poetic view of the world. (Whitehead 2022, 101–2)

Value is one of the aspects that the bifurcation of nature has stripped out and Whitehead's philosophy of the organism seeks to re-introduce it into science. It is reality and, in not addressing it, science limits itself to a distorted truth. If philosophy in surveying the sciences confronts science with concrete facts of experience, the English poetic tradition of 18th and 19th centuries, Whitehead argues, drew attention to the discord between aesthetic intuitions and the mechanics of science. The Harrisons and others continue to grapple with this discord, not through a juxtaposition with a different, romantic nature but by entering into and revealing moments of that discord in their experience.

In the conclusions we return to the questions with which we opened: How might arts practices be re-imagined in the environmental crisis? How do they help us to re-imagine ourselves as humankind in relation to the natural world? What might be drawn from the Harrisons' approach? What might be understood from the dialogue and relationships between artists addressing common questions and issues?

Stengers' 'thinking with' Whitehead throws the Harrisons' approach to the primacy of environmental well-being into sharp relief. She leads us to Whitehead and as we become more familiar with his writings, their relevance to the Harrisons' work becomes more apparent, in content and approach, and in spirit. Whitehead, Stengers, and the Harrisons are all unprepared to slip into accepted modalities of thought at their respective times. Stengers and the Harrisons increasingly question the way technoscience of the mid- to late 20th into 21st century creates environmental devastation through its success as an economic force. They all disrupt the uncritical faith in this modality, demonstrating a respect for life and a deep curiosity about how to reimagine humans within life. They all undertake this as a philosophical question that leads into rethinking their respective fields of the philosophy of science and art.

What does Whitehead offer us? His unpacking of 'event' provides a set of concepts that reveal in what ways life is emergent, creative, and indeterminate. While there are recognisable patterns and repetitions, these are never exact, opening the potential for novelty through degrees of freedom within constraint. Whitehead's construction of 'event' resonates with the creative process in art, centred on judgements that in turn support the development of a world 'in common'. Just as the individual organism at all levels of life evolves through a dynamic relation with everything around them, so artists judge and negotiate the character of their practices in relation to the worlds they find themselves within. Whitehead's event works 'all the way down' through the different levels of organic and inorganic life – the ecological question as not restricted to interhuman relations. The Harrisons' radical poetics ask what it means for the human to be an element of Earth's system – to understand how we are 'niched' and to organise ourselves around exchange rather than production. No aspect of this dynamic can be assumed – it is always evolving, critical, and relational. The Harrisons characterise this saying:

> THEN
> A NEW REVERSAL OF GROUND COMES INTO BEING
> WHERE HUMAN ACTIVITY BECOMES A FIGURE
> WITHIN AN ECOLOGICAL FIELD
> AS SIMULTANEOUSLY THE ECOLOGY CEASES TO BE
> AN EVER SHRINKING FIGURE
> WITHIN THE FIELD OF HUMAN ACTIVITY
> (H. M. Harrison and Harrison 1993, 3)

The next chapter will develop the articulation of Whitehead's philosophy, drawing on Stengers' elucidation of key concepts, and discuss two of the Harrisons' *Survival Pieces* in particular, focusing on the multiple collisions of values that these works generated. The Harrisons' adventure is driven by the question of how we feed ourselves, and this is a question that also concerns Whitehead, who describes the interplay between living beings and the environment as a form of robbery with higher lifeforms frequently 'disintegrating' less evolved ones. Whitehead also conceives of food as 'repair' (1978, 106). The Harrisons' adventure into this tension develops the form of their 'ecological argument' and leads to the critical questioning that is central to the story of *The Lagoon Cycle*, the subject of Chapter 3.

CHAPTER 2

'Thinking With' Whitehead, Stengers and the Harrisons

The approach of 'thinking with' is not unique to Stengers. A few writers, including Hannah Arendt, have worked with this concept to forge a different pathway with past and current experience that is neither writing a history nor producing models that can be applied uncritically. Stengers stresses the rigorous listening she has undertaken in relation to Whitehead. We draw on her writing as an example of an approach to 'thinking with' as becoming deeply and critically immersed in a specific body of work, for her Whitehead and for us the Harrisons. We draw on Whitehead's original writings for key concepts of process philosophy, including his critique of the 'bifurcation of nature', his construction of 'event' as a process through which all life emerges, his speculative stress in thinking as 'adventure' and 'taking a leap of the imagination' that may bring about new forms through which life keeps going. Together they provide a point of entry into learning what our responsibility towards the work of the Harrisons might be, and how to take it forward. The chapter focuses on the Harrisons' early exploration of what it means to attend to the well-being of the environment, through their early work, the *Survival Pieces*. It then explores four experiences, precursors to the *Survival Pieces*, that deeply informed their poetics at this stage of development. While it is not known if they had read Whitehead, there are resonances with his thinking and the Harrisons' emergent approach that are significant to the project of thinking ecologically. The chapter begins by introducing Whitehead's concepts and then explores their relevance to this early work.

Whitehead, writing in the early 20th century, was radical in understanding life as a process of co-creation throughout its organic and inorganic forms. He prefigured ecological thinking in the sense of understanding nature as emergent through a process of deep entanglement at all levels at a time when the damage to the environment of industrialisation was less apparent than in the present. Stengers and the Harrisons in the latter half of the 20th century share the recognition that the time is now over to imagine Earth as a totality of resources available for our use. All three share the sense that positivistic materialism not just in science, but in the practice of everyday life, is exhausted. Whitehead is particularly critical of 'the science of materialism' (16th to 19th centuries and we would argue beyond into 20th and 21st centuries) because it fails to address life and nature as a unified concept that takes into account sensory experience, feelings, and emotions. As a scientist and mathematician, he is in search of a unified idea of nature and to achieve this he needs to draw on philosophy to examine some of the fundamental assumptions on which science is founded. The science of materialism is unsuited to the circumstances of the early 20th century through new discoveries particularly in physics. It confines itself to certain types of facts, abstracted from the circumstances in which these occur. Whitehead characterises the problem in terms of the 'bifurcation of nature' (Whitehead 2022, 1985).

The Bifurcation of Nature

Whitehead explains the bifurcation as follows: the one branch focuses on the measurable aspects of nature organised around a particular notion of 'causality' that strips away, through quantification, all sensory qualities of an experience including aesthetics, interest, and values. The second branch of the bifurcation does address perception and experience, but again in a reductive way by focusing predominantly on vision. Nature is 'apprehended' between a subject and an object: I, as subject, receive information about the world as an array of objects before me. The eye transmits this information to the brain that in turn 'remakes' the world in my mind. The bifurcation of nature impacts on the way we imagine knowledge and come to know the world. By dividing experience between subject and object, we also divide knowledge into a relationship of knower to known in ways in which knowledge becomes highly abstracted. This fails to account for how the world evolves through experience, through processes of affective judgement. The basis of experience for Whitehead is emotional. Knowledge through experience is triggered by what is felt to be important in the situation. Whitehead draws on the Quaker term 'concern' to describe this, as it places the object of knowledge as a component of the experience of a subject. It is through this quality of affective relation that every entity participates in generating nature's capacity to endure. For Whitehead causation or 'causal efficacy' is quite different from causality in terms of cause-and-effect relations, 'mere causality', though he acknowledges that there are occasions when mere causation is appropriate and useful. Causal efficacy refers to a mode of perception by which feelings are inherited from the past into the present and interpreted in association with experiences in that past life newly encountered in the present. Feeling the weight or coldness of a stone is dependent upon some prior knowledge or experience by the subject that feels, that is prior experiences of weight and cold. In seeking coherence, and not causality, Whitehead is looking to a scheme in which 'no entity can be conceived in complete abstraction from the system of the universe, and that it is the business of speculative philosophy to exhibit this truth' (Whitehead 1978, 3). He saw one of the functions of philosophy to be that of scrutinising and making explicit the ideas that shape our views of the nature of the world (Whitehead 2022, vii).

What Stengers sees in Whitehead is a serious attempt to rethink the bifurcation of nature by acknowledging that more than one way of knowing is important for the furthering of life. The separation of explanation and understanding in the production of 'facts' (the world constructed by science) from meaning and values (the world of aesthetics, the senses and perception) is problematic, she argues, because it has given rise to highly successful forms of technoscience that remain unchecked. That in turn has brought about human alienation from the conditions on which our lives depend. As a result, we find ourselves valuing high entropy systems and the associated characteristics (the great acceleration in population, energy consumption, and economic development) without taking the responsibility to address the consequences. Whitehead suggests that part of the problem of bifurcation is that science has confined itself to 'How?' questions since the Renaissance (Whitehead 2022, 9, 41–59). Stengers highlights this separation in the ways in which 'why' questions, such as 'What has happened to us?' are never allowed to be addressed. This was the sense in which Galileo proposed to distinguish between what he had succeeded in demonstrating, 'how' bodies fall, and the question of 'why' they fall in that way, a question that, as he remarked, there was 'no great use' in asking: this is the domain of the imagination and of undecidable fiction (Stengers 2011, 13–14).

Helen and Newton, in discussion with Michael Auping, curator of the exhibition 'Five Artists in the Florida Landscape' (1982), directly address this same issue in terms of fragmentation, reiterating Whitehead's bifurcation.

> NH: We see modernism as beginning with the Renaissance. We see modernism as the successive division into smaller and smaller categories, of all human knowledge. The operant being that the establishment of micro categorization permits a clear perception of individual phenomenon and therefore, deeper understanding.
> HH: We feel that we know more about something out of the context in which that something occurs leads to less and less understanding of the something since everything exists in context. I consider this one of the great problems of our culture…we have so much information and yet so little understanding. Indeed, modernism reflects the conditions that separate people from the ground they stand on. It is a power and control centred belief-system in immediate need of revision, particularly of its guiding metaphors. (Auping 1982, 102–3)

The parallels between the Harrisons' articulation and that of Whitehead are striking if we read the effects of modernism and its dependence upon quantification and classification that Newton Harrison points out in terms of a misleading idea of what is believed to be knowledge. The Harrisons committed to developing alternative understandings through experiencing things in everyday life in their contexts, along with identifying new guiding metaphors through which experience gains meaning and value in terms of understanding. Whitehead's process philosophy, particularly his construct of event, places experience and context at the core of understanding.

Nature as emergent

For Whitehead any scientific understanding of nature needs to treat nature as a whole, in its livingness and in the ways that we come to know through experience. Perception is crucial to this understanding, and it is not limited to sight and its implicit separation of subject from object. A philosophy of the organism engages the whole organism or entity at all levels of existence and from moment to moment. The whole body in its environment intensifies and augments experience. Life emerges from such processes of intensification and amplification, that is, it is created from moment to moment. In so called higher organisms the sensory is active through all the organs including internal organs. We experience the world through 'eyes, palates, noses, ears, and the diffused bodily organization furnishing touches, aches, and other bodily sensations' (Whitehead 1985, 177–78). Consciousness comes into play in higher organisms, though consciousness does not need to be present for life to be present.

Whitehead meticulously constructs this idea of nature through the notion of 'event', the immediate, actual occasion of experience, the moment in which experience is augmented and intensified, 'lured' by a desire to create harmony with the environment. While a term such as 'harmony' may sound odd to us now, Whitehead carefully aligns this as the underpinning of all science, that is, the assumption that nature is not arbitrary but functions in relation to some sort of order. Harmony in this context could mean survival or the furthering of life, but not in a narrow instrumental sense as it involves aesthetics, a sense of beauty, desire, and judgement. It is through thought that we can access this order. For Whitehead this belief or faith in the order of nature as opposed to arbitrariness and mystery has made science possible.

> It springs from direct inspection of the nature of things as disclosed in our own immediate experience. [...] To experience this faith is to know that in being ourselves we are more than ourselves: to know that our experience, dim and fragmentary as it is, yet sounds the utmost depths of reality: to know that detached details merely in order to be themselves demand that we should find themselves in a system of things: to know that this system includes the harmony of logical rationality, and the harmony of aesthetic achievement. (Whitehead 2022, 20)

The search for harmony is the basis on which science is built, but we need to take care of what abstractions we create and how we work with them. In Whitehead's thinking actual occasions occur, exist momentarily, and then perish to become new potential for life. The process draws on vectors of feelings, which Whitehead terms 'prehensions', a rich potential of what has gone before that is full of contradiction, competing with other mutual interests and perspectives. Feelings inform and shape events but do not determine experience. In any single event or actual occasion, a process of 'concrescence' takes place, a growing together of a selection of prehensions from the past, lured into the present to achieve the satisfaction or definiteness that creates a better chance of survival, though it may not necessarily guarantee success.

In Whitehead's construction 'actual occasions' inherit from the past not only through the feelings or prehensions of an individual atom, entity, or organism but also through a shared and deep history of the character of planetary life, through 'eternal objects' such as colours, shapes, patterns of growth, patterns of sound, or musical composition. These more stable aspects of inheritance ingress into an actual occasion, participating in the forming of new, emergent life. In non-material entities such as stones or less evolved organisms, actual occasions of experience mainly simply repeat the past. In more developed organisms the potential of the past uniquely occurring in the present may offer an opportunity for transformation through the creation of novelty, though repetition and inertia also occur. Eternal objects (colours, shapes, patterns) do not determine what emerges in an actual occurrence. Like 'prehensions' or feelings from the past, they offer potential. While Whitehead's eternal objects appear to be like Plato's eternal forms, there is an important difference. For Plato the world of experience is a shadowy version of a truer reality that is out of sight. Whitehead's philosophy of organism inverts this: reality emerges out of and is created through events that draw on these forms or objects as potential in creating new life.

Adventure and/as a 'leap of the imagination'

Adventure is the core meaning of 'process' in 'process philosophy'. There is no sense in which life maintains or perfects itself by remaining static, standing still. Process means becoming and perishing.

> Thus each actual thing is to be understood in terms of becoming and perishing. There is no halt in which the actuality is just its static self, accidently played upon by qualifications derived from the shift of circumstances. The converse is the truth. (Whitehead 1985, 274–75)

Whitehead takes the example of culture. Although civilisations strive for perfection, this can only be maintained if they are open to experimentation.

> But when these minor variations are exhausted, one of two things might happen, Perhaps the society in question lacks imaginative force. Staleness then sets in. Repetition produces a gradual lowering of vivid appreciation. Convention dominates. A learned orthodoxy suppresses adventure. (Whitehead 1985, 277)

Feelings or prehensions are gifted, given in a moment of experience, and in turn the experience that emerges is gifted back into reality. For Whitehead the steps within an event or actual occasion, that is, concrescence, actualisation and perishing to become new potential, are profoundly aesthetic, artistic and ecological, and destabilising.

> [G]iven the vigour of adventure, sooner or later the leap of imagination reaches beyond the safe limits of the epoch, and beyond the safe limits of learned rules of taste. It then produces the dislocations and confusion marking the advent of new ideals of civilised effort. (Whitehead 1985, 279)

This philosophical perspective casts a useful side light on the Harrisons' articulation of nature when discussing the composition of images.

> Nature, the life web in its entirety, appeared interactive, interdependent, mutually evolving and, therefore, in various degrees indeterminate and frameable only in a narrow way. As a result, any central images that appeared seemed to exist for only a moment and thereafter to fade back into a pattern of moments grouped within moments. (H. M. Harrison and Harrison 2001a, n.p.)

Further their repeated description of their process as 'joining a conversation' captures a sense of always foregrounding experience, but an experience that inherits both deep experience and also the feelings and prehensions of the ongoing circumstances.

We see the Harrisons' leap of the imagination, 'the flying dart, of which Lucretius speaks, hurled beyond the bounds of the world' (Whitehead 1985, 177), in their decision to do no work that did not in some way address ecosystemic well-being, in later formulations, giving back more to the web of life that we take. The Harrisons initially talked about their commitment to the well-being of the web of life in terms of conceptual art strategies. The Harrisons are not easily definable as conceptual artists, not least in their insistence of working with the specificity of place. That said, they drew on some of its principles.

> One of the tenets of conceptual art, which strongly influenced our conceptual art-making, was to make a single decision and follow it relentlessly to its unknown, unknowable outcomes. The outcomes were simply the result of continuous creativity, investigation and enactment, referenced always to that initial single decision. (H. M. Harrison and Harrison 2001a, n.p.)

In 1971–72 they realise a series of experimental works resulting from the leap, the single decision, to always attend to the well-being of the environment. These works form the foundations of the Harrisons' approach and emerge through a process of trial and error. The cluster included the piece *Part One of an Ecological Nerve Center* in the exhibition 'Furs and Feathers' in New York as well as seven *Survival Pieces* (*Survival Piece #1: Air, Earth, Water, Interface: Annual Hog Pasture Mix* (hereafter *Hog Pasture*);

Survival Piece #II: Notation on the Ecosystem of the Western Saltworks with the inclusion of Brine Shrimp (hereafter *'Brine Shrimp Farm'*) (figs. 8-10); *Survival Piece #III: Portable Fish Farm* (hereafter *'Portable Fish Farm'*) (figs. 11-14); *Survival Piece #IV: La Jolla Promenade; Survival Piece #V: Portable Orchard* (figs. 47-48); *Survival Piece #VI: Full Farm: Photographs and Drawings: Part I, Eight Horizontal Pastures; Part II: Ten Upright Pastures; Part III: Potato Patch and Portable Orchard* (hereafter *'Full Farm'*); and *Survival Piece #VII: The Crab Farm* (hereafter *'The Crab Farm'*)).[1]

By 1974 this phase of work stops. The Chronology in *The Lagoon Cycle* catalogue says:

HMH [Helen Mayer Harrison] examines their survival pieces and their initial work. Concludes that it was an inherently alienated metaphor and was not energy-efficient. Using photographs and proposal making as a medium, the Harrisons change the direction of their work. (H. M. Harrison and Harrison 1985b, 101)

The aim of the following discussion is to understand the collisions and contradictions that shaped the judgements made by the artists and informed their conclusion that the forms of these works was fundamentally flawed.

Brine Shrimp Farm, for example, involves four large ponds, in its first iteration using existing ponds outside the Los Angeles County Museum of Art (LACMA). Each pond has a slightly different combination of an ecosystem of brine shrimp and algae. This was one of two works that Newton Harrison contributed to the famous 'Art & Technology' exhibition in 1971.[2] It starts from the observation of the amount of algaecide being used to keep the water in the existing ponds clean. This leads to an investigation of the potential of algae, in their ability to change colour, to create a colour field. A species of algae called *Duniella* found in sea water is capable of surviving in high salinity and normally appears as blue-green. As water evaporates in more confined conditions such as ponds the algae produce carotene as a survival tactic to resist the increased salinity. The algae change from blue-green through a spectrum to brick red. They discover that *Duniella* co-exist with brine shrimp forming the simplest known ecosystem. They introduce algae inoculated with brine shrimp eggs so that the work is both a colour field and an ecosystem. The shrimp grow, the water evaporates, the algae change colour, but in due course fade. At this point they harvest. They sell the salt at a price below that of supermarkets. Helen Mayer Harrison creates a feast from the shrimp but it is inedible even with the addition of capers (H. M. Harrison and Harrison 2016, 26). *Brine Shrimp Farm* draws attention to dependencies: human > nutrient > algae > shrimp > human. In Stengers' terms the fields we need to invent in order to be able to tackle the problems are generative and central to any conception of situated knowledge. The way that Stengers and Whitehead construct situated knowledge is closely aligned with what we perceive in experience, that is, a world that is given to us through the senses more complex than one that is read through models or paradigms, or a sense of perception restricted to the visual. Situated knowledge always brings together time and space in an event, the event here being the whole experiment.

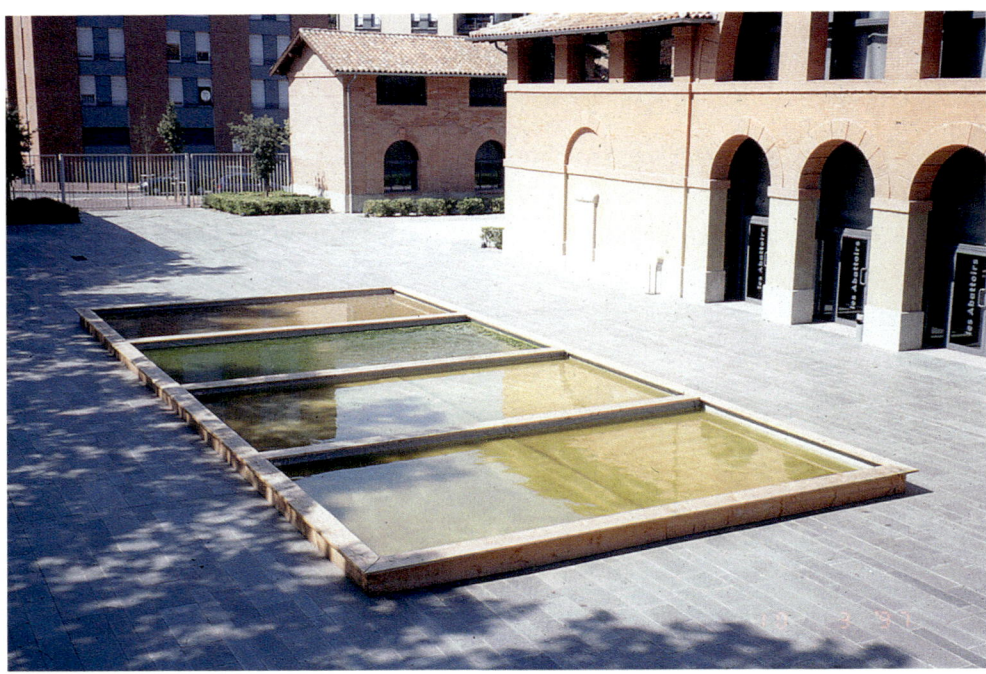

Figure 8: 'Survival Piece #II: Notation on the Ecosystem of the Western Saltworks with the inclusion of Brine Shrimp' (2002) Reconstruction at Les Abbatoirs, Toulouse, France (courtesy of the Newton and Helen Harrison Family Trust)

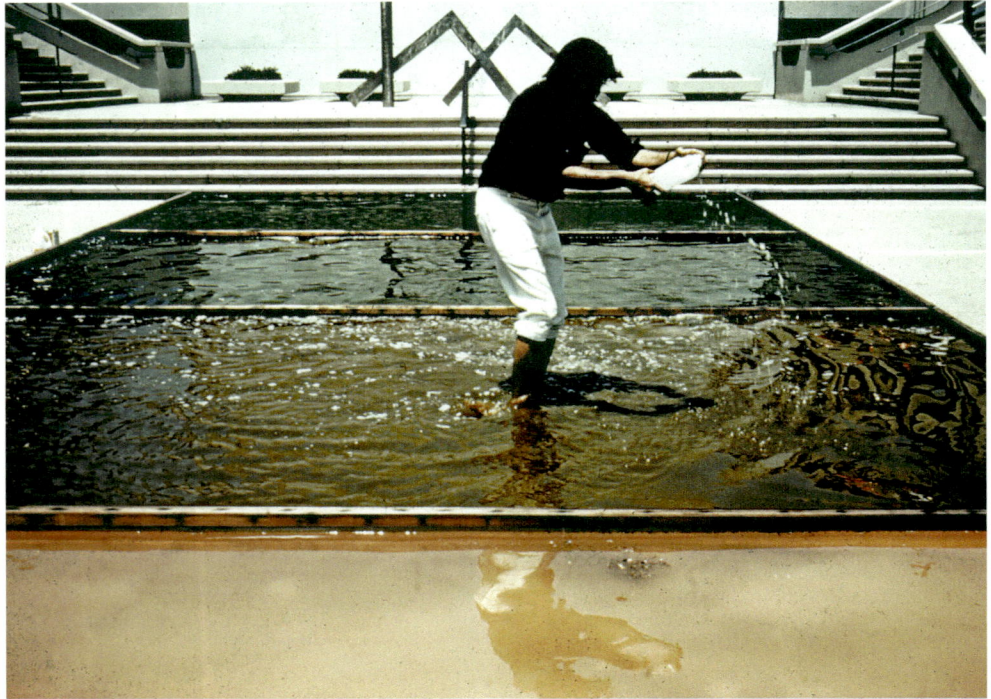

Figure 9: 'Brine Shrimp Farm' (1971) Feeding in process with entrance to the Los Angeles County Museum of Art behind (courtesy of the Newton and Helen Harrison Family Trust)

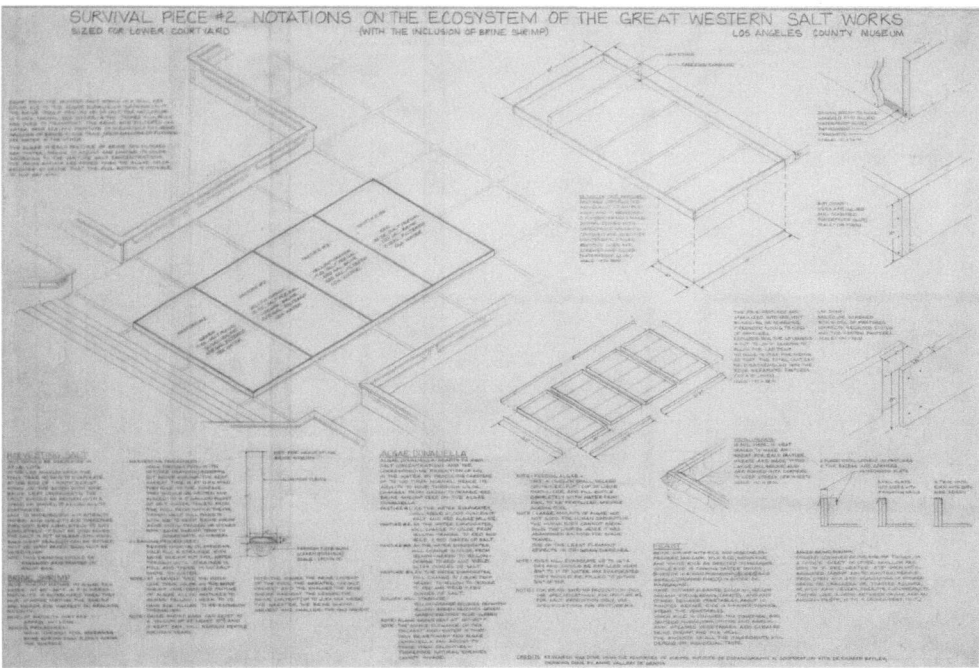

Figure 10: 'Brine Shrimp Farm' (1971) Diagram (courtesy of the Newton and Helen Family Trust and Various Small Fires, Los Angeles / Dallas / Seoul)

In terms of Whitehead's notion of event, *Brine Shrimp Farm* draws into an actual occasion multiple kinds of experience: 'vectors of feeling' or 'prehensions'. These offer potential to the new work and include the Harrisons' knowledge of art and the knowledge they had acquired from scientists of the ecosystem of shrimp and algae, the smallest eco-system that they could work with in the outdoor space assigned to them by the curators. The expectations of the curators and their audiences, along with the Harrisons' urge to grow their understanding of ecology through each new work, also offer potential, acting as vectors of feeling. The work can be experienced on the one hand as a colour field, and on the other as a quasi-scientific experiment. A collision occurs between these perspectives that are 'inherited'. The algae/shrimp become entangled with the lives of the artists, curators, and audiences, and the specific environment and its conditions, all of which interact in ways that augment and intensify the moment of experience, lured by the need to create some kind of harmony. Newton Harrison characterises the new emergent form as a 'Dadaist gesture' (2016, 25). The growing together of widely separate realities, that of modernist art, of science, and of living systems, creates a spark that initially disorientates and deprives us of a familiar frame of reference. In this sense, *Brine Shrimp Farm* exposes the absurdity of high art being celebrated at the cost of the ecosystem. By attempting to make sense of the experience, we create new meaning. At this point the event becomes something else, potential for a new work, a 'perishing' in Whitehead's terminology. *Brine Shrimp Farm* enriches the work that follows, *Survival Piece #III Portable Fish Farm*.

Collectively, the *Survival Pieces* are open-ended experiments that are speculative, generated by a question: How do we feed ourselves? (Burnham 1974, 163–66). This is a question that comes out of everyday life. Each work constitutes an experiment and an experience, for the artists, for the curators, and for the audience. It is interesting to note two synergies here, one with Stengers on experiment and the other with Whitehead on the centrality of food for imagining co-dependence and the potential for exploitation. Stengers uses experiment in the French sense, which includes the idea of experience overtly. She says, 'Unlike French, English does not allow the word "experiment" to be used for an experience that implies an active, open, and demanding attention' (Stengers 2011, 22). We could equally say that the Harrisons' *Survival Pieces* and subsequent work constitute an experiment in these terms, that is, one that requires an active, open, and demanding attention in which we are never not involved. For Stengers the problem with the English construction of 'experiment' is that it denies interdependence. Our thinking with the Harrisons is, like Stengers' relation with Whitehead, an experiment or experience in and with that question, 'What has happened to us?'.

Brine Shrimp Farm was the first work that included a 'feast', initiating a significant dimension of the Harrisons' work thereafter, in which the Harrisons connect humans to their environments and other organisms through food and convivial forms of sharing food. The Harrisons share with Whitehead the importance of food as the means of sustaining life, and as core to the relationship with the environment. The kinds of exchanges that occur across the whole of organic life undergo change. They are processes of transmission.

> Salt dissolves in water, and can be recovered from it. Gases interfuse in liquids. Molecules arise from a patterned interfusion of atoms. Food interfuses with the body and produces an immediate sense of diffused vigour. (Whitehead 1985, 207)

Such life-giving processes also involve destruction.

> The societies which [a living society] destroys are its food. This food is destroyed by dissolving it into somewhat simpler social elements. It has been robbed of something. Thus all societies require interplay with their environment; and in the case of living societies this interplay takes the form of robbery. The living society may, or may not, be a higher type of organism than the food it disintegrates. But whether or no it be for the general good, food is robbery. It is at this point that with life morals become acute. The robber requires justification. (Whitehead 1978, 105)

For Whitehead the preservation of life is not a matter of concern. The ongoing-ness of life is a core concern, and it is concentrated in each actual occasion of exchange, in the intensities that such an occasion affords, and its depth of satisfaction. He describes this as a process in which 'The many become one and are increased by one' (Whitehead 1978, 21).

The change that is undergone in each actual occasion is the creation of a new 'object', that is, something that becomes potential to be actualised in new events. In *Brine Shrimp Farm* the foundational question of survival and what it takes to feed us led to a pivotal point in their work, the harvesting of salt to create a feast, folding humans into the chain of dependencies around foods. It creates a transformation in their way of working where one set of concerns, those of the dominant art world at the time – in this case technology – are superseded by questions of survival and the process of understanding how living systems work.

What is 'adventure' in the Harrisons' works?

Each of the Harrisons' *Survival Pieces*, one could argue, constitutes an adventure, increasingly finding ways to draw us in and feel the interdependencies within living systems. Where *Brine Shrimp Farm* intentionally uses absurdity to highlight such interdependencies, subsequent works develop more and more ecologically complex systems and become generative of contradictions. Contradictions are in turn generative for the Harrisons, constitutive of a different form of practice.[3] They reveal the points of tension between conflicting values and beliefs in culture and society. This is well exemplified with *Survival Piece #III: Portable Fish Farm*, described below, which unintentionally became read as a work of 'shock' art (Walker 1999, 52–57). Whitehead's notion of adventure allows us to enter into the dynamicity of being, to become part of the world in its making. Stengers builds on this, imagining thinking as entering into the mobile reality of this unfolding world, following its curves and adopting the movements of its inner life (Stengers 2011, 57).

Inhabiting the bifurcation of nature

Portable Fish Farm was an experiment that to a lot of people looked like science or fish farming. It was part of a group exhibition '11 Los Angeles Artists' curated for the Hayward Gallery in London by Maurice Tuchman, the curator of LACMA and the 'Art & Technology' exhibition. The Harrisons' work involved a series of tanks installed in the Hayward Gallery, London (and later other venues). The tanks provided habitats for catfish and bottom feeders at different stages of development. The intention was to have an aquaculture system in which the catfish reproduced. As with *Brine Shrimp Farm*, human dependence was built in, both in terms of care of the system – it needed to be looked after; and in terms of sustenance – it did produce fish for feasts.

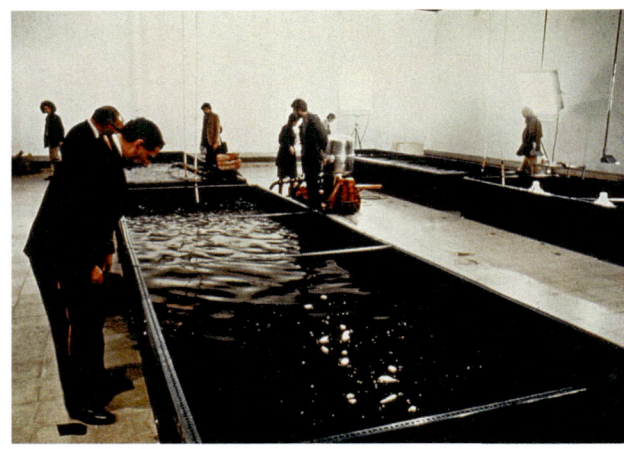

Figure 11: 'Portable Fish Farm:
Survival Piece #III' (1971)
Installation view (courtesy
of the Newton and Helen
Harrison Family Trust

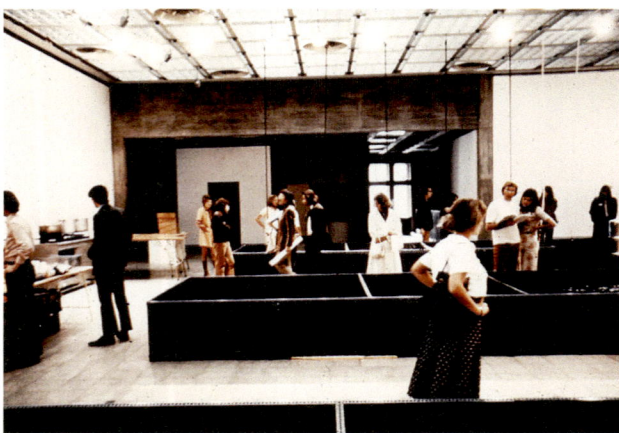

Figure 12: 'Portable Fish Farm:
Survival Piece #III' (1971)
Installation view (courtesy
of the Newton and Helen
Harrison Family Trust)

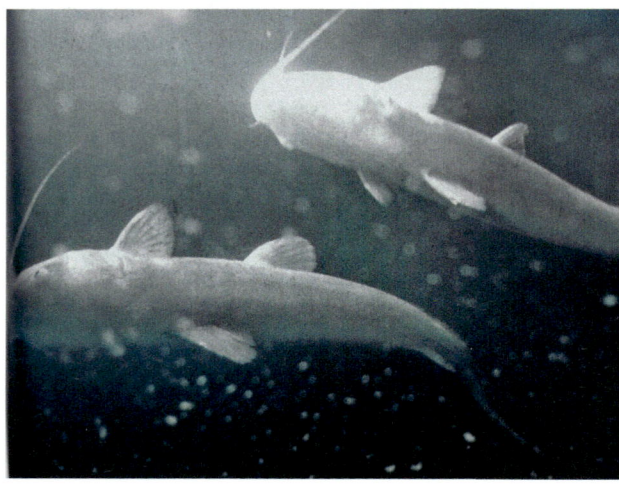

Figure 13: 'Portable Fish Farm:
Survival Piece #III' (1971)
Detail of catfish (courtesy
of the Newton and Helen
Harrison Family Trust

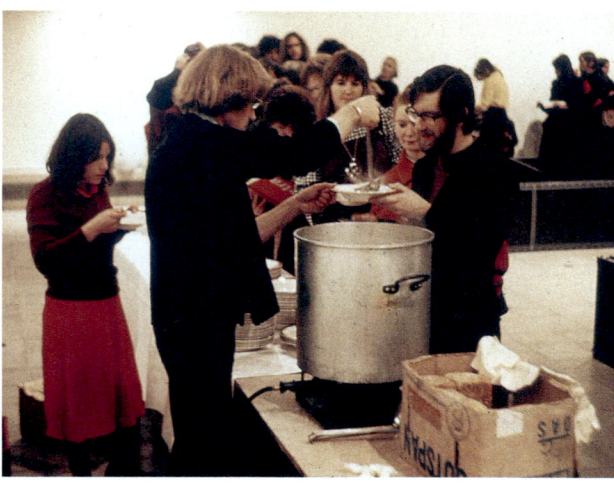

Figure 14: 'Portable Fish Farm:
Survival Piece #III' (1971)
Detail of soup feast (courtesy
of the Newton and Helen
Harrison Family Trust)

The first of the contradictions that emerged was between American and British values around catfish. In the United States catfish farming was a growth industry – the Harrisons had researched catfish farming at Brawley in California – however in the United Kingdom some species of catfish were pets. The plan to electrocute the fish in public in preparation for creating a feast for the audience was met with outrage. In fact, Newton tells us that the scandal led Sonnabend Gallery in New York to be interested in representing them, but they turned this down.[4] The Harrisons' concern was with learning more about the implications of their commitment, and not becoming more successful as producers of shock art.

The reading as 'shock art' amplified in the press in turn meant that the ritual and reflective intentions of the work were overwritten, the second collision between conflicting values. The contradiction is clear in a letter to the Harrisons where Norbert Lynton, art critic and historian, grasped the artists' intention, commenting on the feasts,

> It seemed to me to be exactly the rounding out with life, event, ritual, service, receiving, the exhibit requires. The atmosphere was not party-ish but happily peaceful [...] (Cassidy Rogers 2016, 232)

The third contradiction has to do with success and failure. The last of Stengers' key questions cited in the Introduction asks us to pay attention to what changes the criteria in defining success and defeat in an open-ended experimental adventure. The catfish did not mate and reproduce as hoped, 'so in the strict ecological sense *Portable Fish Farm* did not succeed' (H. M. Harrison and Harrison 2016, 32). In the end this failure was more important to the Harrisons than its apparent success as an artwork. It led them to create *Survival Piece #VII The Crab Farm*, which is a key part of *The Lagoon Cycle*. The contradictions that *The Crab Farm* in turn generated are at the heart of the debate between the two main protagonists in this work, the Lagoon Maker and the Witness.

In these various ways the Harrisons enable the energy of their processes of encounter and learning to continue to work generatively, rather than dissipate. Failure works for them and towards the next adventure. It also speaks to Whitehead's notion of event that inherits from the past, drawn by the lure to create harmony or satisfaction, in this example encountering and addressing the contradictions that arise in the experience of making the work in public. The actual experience or occasion perishes becoming new potential for a different experience/event. It is possible to imagine the cluster of seven *Survival Pieces* as a nexus of events, each of which inhabit the problem of the bifurcation of nature in different ways. They are set up as quasi-scientific experiments on the one hand, placed within the aesthetic space of the museum and art gallery, spaces that conventionally focus the eye and privilege the visual. According to the Harrisons' own telling each fail as scientific experiments, generating unintended consequences, for different reasons: the fish do not mate and reproduce in *Portable Fish Farm*. In *Survival Piece #IV: La Jolla Promenade* the ducks consume their food source and litter

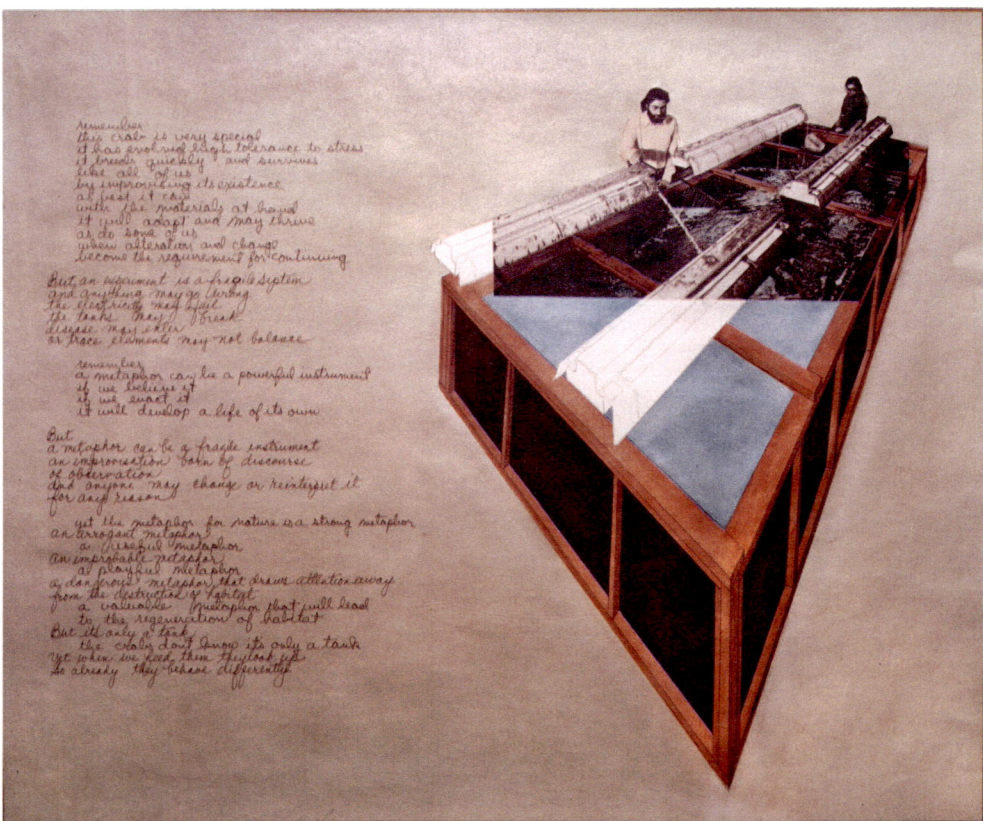

Figure 15: 'Book of the Lagoons' (1985) Detail of 'Second Lagoon' showing the crab farm tanks (courtesy of the Newton and Helen Harrison Family Trust)

the pristine gallery yard in poop (H. M. Harrison and Harrison 2016, 36). The feast for *Survival Piece #V: Portable Orchard* gives everyone acid stomachs, and some trees do better than others (2016, 41). Insects infest the potato patch and someone introduces marijuana with the bean sprouts in *Full Farm* (2016, 44). As noted earlier the Harrisons abandon this way of working, but not for the same reasons as Whitehead's grounds for criticising the bifurcation and his proposed alternative in a philosophy of organism. As quoted, the Harrisons' reasons for changing direction was Helen's analysis that the works were 'not energy-efficient', and Jonathan Benthall's review of *Portable Fish Farm* noted that although it claimed to model an ecosystem it was totally dependent on external energy inputs (Benthall 1971). Helen's analysis also highlights the alienated metaphor. They are clearly caught in the bifurcation by 'doing an experiment' that separates organisms from ongoing life. In line with Whitehead's criticism, they find this approach 'alienating' and this becomes the focus of a key debate in the Second Lagoon (H.M. Harrison and Harrison 1985b, 44–45) (fig. 15), which we will return to in our discussion of *The Lagoon Cycle*.

The *Survival Pieces* emerged out of four earlier experiences in the Harrisons' growing awareness and activism and their understanding of what survival might mean.

We might imagine these precursors as acting as potential for the nexus of events in Whitehead's terms that became the *Survival Pieces*. They include Helen's reading of Rachel Carson's *Silent Spring* (Carson 1962); their first collaborative essay 'Dropouts and a "Design for Living"', published in a collection of essays that focused on possible remedies to poverty and education in the US (H. M. Harrison and Harrison 1965); an early art science experiment *The Slow Birth and Death of a Lily Cell* (1968) and a collaborative artwork, *An Ecological Nerve Centre* (1970–71), exhibited in 'Furs and Feathers'.[5] The context for these experiences was the social and political turmoil of the Cold War and the Vietnam War and the impact of such events not least in connecting emergent environmental concerns with education and societal values. These wider societal occurrences prompted a number of artists at the time to rethink the place and form of their practices in public life (David and Eleanor Antin, Agnes Denes, Hans Haacke, Allan Kaprow, Mierle Laderman , and Robert Smithson among others (Matilsky 1992, Spaid 2002, Kester 2004)).

Carson's *Silent Spring* (1962) opens up the sensual, human dimension of survival, and in so doing creates the possibility of dealing with scientific material in ways that were not restricted to ecological scientists. Everyone can relate to the issues and participate in a dialogue that positions survival as a matter of shared concern. The Harrisons have always acknowledged the pivotal role of this text in their decision to focus on the environment, helping them to conceptualise 'survival' in this early work as a thread that reorders values in ways that make concrete their commitment to attend to the well-being of the web of life. Carson exposed the devastating effects of the pesticide DDT. It was not only carcinogenic, but also depleted the earth's biodiversity at a terrifying rate despite being presented as a miraculous solution for disease control and food protection. More importantly for our concerns,

> Carson's 'subversive and transformative' prose instructs readers to regard themselves less as DDT-armed pest-combatants than as affected and affecting cohabitants of overlapping human and nonhuman milieus. (Chisholm 2011, 570)

Helen had read Carson's book in the year of its publication while also acting as the first New York co-ordinator for the *Women's Strike for Peace* (C. A. Jones 2018). She had also given birth to their fourth child, Joy Eden Harrison. Their involvement in the strike was particularly driven by the discovery of Strontium 90 in breast milk.

The second key moment in the evolution of their approach was the Harrisons' first collaborative essay entitled 'Dropouts and a "Design for Living"'.[6] It reflects Helen's particular expertise and interest in public education and also built on Newton's experiences of teaching experimental painting to children at housing settlement projects and neighbourhood centres (N. Harrison 1996).[7] The essay addresses the circumstances of young people whom the system of conventional education has failed and asks us to consider 'survival' in a much richer way, beyond mere physical survival. It opens the question of 'what matters' in such a way that the young people are invited to become participants and to recognise their own agency. In this way the Harrisons shift the challenge from 'learning trade skills and the mechanics of getting a job', survival as a minimum achievement, to survival as engaging with the key questions that start with the self and our fears, and from there move out to the wider world. This idea that survival, value, and meaning are deeply connected underpins the *Survival Pieces* and changes our understanding of success and defeat.[8]

To this end the Harrisons propose an educational programme structured around a series of questions that range from the personal and practical to the existential. They begin with 'What are you most afraid of?' and move to 'Why is everything as it is? [...] How would you like the world to be? What do you have to do with the world? What does the world have to do with you? [...] What is the meaning and function of a good environment? Health? Food? Effective childcare? What is the role of the parent? Why use decoration or plan for visual effect? Why plan? How can we handle money? Time? Energy? Leisure? What is the value of continuous inquiry? Why keep an open mind?' (H. M. Harrison and Harrison 1965, 176).

The Harrisons talk about disadvantage through the metaphor of nutrition. The individual is undernourished culturally and socially. '[A]rt, literature, drama, and the play of ideas have neither part nor function, have been neither seen nor heard, [...] discussed nor questioned' (H. M. Harrison and Harrison 1965, 174). Even at this stage the Harrisons saw everyday matters and planetary issues as part of a continuous enquiry. They set out to stimulate aesthetic sensations alongside thought processes by means of lectures, trips, and discussion groups. The point was to explore how values control human actions, where limits are self-imposed and where they are culturally imposed, where assumptions could be challenged, and new opportunities developed. This prefigures the approach to survival that becomes central in the *Survival Pieces* in being led by questions, critical and value-driven, and recurs in their proposal for a 'New Curriculum' discussed in Chapter 7.

While their chapter is a contribution to research in education, it reveals characteristics and priorities that become increasingly evident in the Harrisons' approach to making work, in particular the importance of discourse in exploring beliefs and values as a social experience. This short essay addressing 'dropouts' could be read as an allegory for human relations with the environment, a push back against inertia in culture and society and a refusal to be consumed by existing institutions and inert ideas. There is a common thread of a question-led approach that is shared with Whitehead and Stengers and has its roots in experience-based education and philosophy (Dewey 2011, Whitehead 2022).

Whitehead took his process philosophy into all aspects of culture and society, not just the sciences, writing from the perspectives that the Harrisons also undertake in thinking ecologically, including politics, education, and aesthetics. Education in his view needed to be useful, relevant to making sense in the present by building connections with the past in the present for the future.

> [I]deas which are not utilised are positively harmful. By utilising an idea, I mean relating it to that stream compounded by sense perceptions, feelings, hopes, desires and of mental activities adjusting thought to thought, which forms our life. (Whitehead 1967, 3)

We might now describe this as thinking relationally and it is clear that in evoking utility, Whitehead is not meaning instrumentality. Education is learning how to use knowledge as a living process, not just accumulate it as material. The best education is 'gaining the utmost information from the simplest apparatus' (1967, 11). The Harrisons evoke this simplicity by positioning their questions firmly in life, in ways that are open to everyone, and encourage thinking as being receptive to beauty and feeling for humanity. Education is about values that individuals judge for themselves in relation to the society in which they live. 'What do you have to do with the world? What does the world have to do with you?' (H. M. Harrison and Harrison 1965, 176). For Whitehead education constitutes an adventure, 'an art of life' that guides the adventure. It is corporeal and rhythmic, from the very first stages of infancy of learning to walk, speak, and then write to later stages of becoming a valuable social being through self-development.

> It is a moot point whether the human hand created the human brain, or the brain created the hand. Certainly the connection is intimate and reciprocal. (Whitehead 1967, 50)

A third precursor was a series of experiments that Newton undertook in 1968 with growing lily and tobacco cells. The lily cell succeeded. Newton never took this work, entitled *The Slow, Birth and Death of a Lily Cell*, forward to exhibition, nor are there any material remains for this work (Cassidy Rogers 2016, 75, 117–19). However Newton frequently acknowledged the importance of its underpinning research in making possible the later *Survival Pieces*, particularly '*Hog Pasture, Brine Shrimp Farm, Portable Orchard* and *La Jolla Promenade*' (H. M. Harrison and Harrison 1985b, 99).

A fourth influential moment in the Harrisons' development is their joint work *An Ecological Nerve Centre* in 'Furs and Feathers' (1971). Historically this work significantly prefigures an approach in which existing research is gathered and presented in such a way that also invites participation. The context was an exhibition that largely presented playfully intriguing artefacts. The curator wanted the exhibition to acknowledge and go beyond the luxury and sensuous beauty of the materials and to highlight the ecological and conservational crisis of the world (Smith 1971). The Harrisons were invited to address this aspect and their work comprised a large-scale world map (14ft x

14ft), a Rolodex, and an audio track, all documenting endangered and extinct species. The World Wildlife Fund (WWF) acting as a partner provided some information, extensively supplemented by Helen and students under her supervision from the Visual Arts Department at the University of California, San Diego (UCSD) (Cassidy Rogers 2016, 147–49). This is the first appearance of large-scale mapping as a representational device in their work, one that they have since exploited in a range of ways. It engaged partnerships that mattered to the political status of the work and its public significance.

The work is concerned with survival, though not named a *Survival Piece*. It also does not address how we feed ourselves. It provokes existential questions – if the trajectory of threat and disappearance in animal species is allowed to continue, human beings themselves become a threatened species. It also has an educational dimension. What is left out in this case is the entangled relations on which each of these species is dependent. In some respects, this work is a manifestation of the bifurcation problem previously discussed. Species are isolated from other organisms and environments on which their life is dependent (and also at risk from). *Brine Shrimp Farm* and *Portable Fish Farm*, which are exhibited later in the same year, both go some way towards addressing this complexity (although as noted the Harrisons change direction from these too). From this point on an artistic practice started to emerge, one that was enquiry-led, driven by carefully framed questions, shared with a public in ways that invited feedback and engagement. The *Survival Pieces* are all at 1:1 scale focused on actual interactions within the web of life (fish, shrimp, algae, lobsters, crabs, ducks, snails) and it is not until 1974 and really not until 1976 that they revisit works using 'mapping' scales.[9]

To conclude this chapter, the global environmental crisis demands a radical reimagining of how to keep life going in all its aspects and manifestations and from a diversity of perspectives, including scientists, philosophers, and political thinkers as well as artists. The key concepts through which Whitehead builds his process philosophy into a 'philosophy of the organism', allow us to interconnect the sciences with the arts, a set of relations the Harrisons always sought to address as fundamental to ecological thinking. What has their work helped us to discover thus far? The construction of 'nature' that is split between experience and data, where 'how?' questions are separated from 'why?' questions, is deeply problematic in not allowing us, humankind, to risk forms of enquiry that embrace a full understanding of how perception, experience, emotions, and values shape knowledge. In the separation our imaginations do not stray towards responsibility to what we understand.

Events are characterised by diversity and complex interdependencies. We have shown how Whitehead helps us understand the Harrisons' early works differently. Stengers paraphrases Whitehead's process philosophy/philosophy of organism in terms of lifeforms composing the world together, at the mercy of one another, and sharing fate in life and death. In this she is drawing closely on the evolutionary biologist Lynn Margulis (1938–2011). The question underpinning the Harrisons' early works, particularly the *Survival Pieces*, 'How do we feed ourselves?', acts as a powerful anchor, refocusing our attention on the conditions for life itself. David Antin, the Harrisons' colleague at the University of California, San Diego, said in 1970, 'The idea of an ecological art is the idea of an art that articulates dependencies: its own condition for existence or those of the world' (1970, 90). Antin uses the term 'dependence', and we might think that this has evolved into what is now more frequently interdependence as used by Stengers, Haraway, Latour, and others. In fact, Stengers illuminates this difference.

> Nor should the intertwining interdependencies be confused with a network of interlinking dependences. It is easy to understand why, without water or light, a plant dies. This fits the definition of 'dependence'. But interdependence implies a way of being sensitive that is a form of venture. (Stengers 2020, 231)

Dependency is directly related to survival. The fragmentary methods of technoscience are problematic in isolating living things from the complexity of their conditions of survival and assuming that this provides complete knowledge. As we have seen the Harrisons seek to reveal both dependency and the conditions of survival as well as the interdependence of living things even in the early works. Stengers also offers us a different and useful reading of interdependence in saying 'letting [our]selves be touched by the reasons of others'. The Harrisons' multi-vocal poetics is an example of the thing that does the touching. Stengers' understanding of 'letting ourselves be touched' highlights the importance of the 'middle voice' neither the active nor the passive, nor the subject nor object. She continues that it is 'a transversal path connecting the most diverse earthly interdependencies ... where touch is not an impact that a being endures but a prerequisite for this being to be affected'. This suggests an openness to the potential and risk involved in experience. She demonstrates 'the letting ourselves be touched' as a particular construction of interdependence through our sense of taste. 'Knowing how to taste is an integral part of the adventure of life in a world that requires of us an ability to discern between what feeds us, what poisons us, and what heals us'. For Stengers the daring involved in allowing ourselves to touch and be touched is a manifestation of interdependence. It is generative and therefore a particularly suitable way to imagine some forms of art. (Stengers 2020, 235)

The Lagoon Cycle follows the *Survival Pieces*, and the learning from the latter becomes potential in the new work, a different event that draws their concrete experience into a new form, in this case of storytelling. Within the story that forms the next chapter, the Harrisons conduct a new experiment, this time inhabiting the role of scientists and receiving a research grant. Their experience of earlier work enables them to clearly evaluate their experimentation speculatively before it results in an ecological disaster.

CHAPTER 3

The Lagoon Cycle

The Lagoon Cycle marks a step change in the Harrisons' approach. They acknowledge it as a seminal work, an adventure reconstructed as story, that gives form to subsequent works. Over 10 years the Harrisons undertook experiments, conceived of landscape scale interventions, researched the history of the Salton Sea in Southern California, and travelled to Sri Lanka. Individual parts of the work were exhibited at different stages of development and in different combinations from 1974. The whole story as a 360 ft installation comprising larger and smaller panels using maps, photographs, drawings, and text, was only finally exhibited in 1985.[1]

The Lagoon Cycle starts from an unresolved aspect of *Portable Fish Farm*. The catfish at the Hayward Gallery had not mated as hoped, posing a new question, that of how to create the conditions that would ensure life continuing through successful reproduction. Instead of catfish, the artists work with a different species, the *Scylla Serrata* crab native to Sri Lanka. The crab was considered both locally and internationally to be an excellent and increasingly sought-after food source. The Harrisons' adventure initially follows a very conventional pathway in technoscience. They set up an experimental space at Pepper Canyon on the University of California, San Diego campus and, having successfully prototyped the process, secure a National Sea Grant, a Federal-University science-based partnership programme that brings science together with communities 'for solutions that work'. Their task was to research, innovate, and exploit the potential of the crab for industrial level fish farming in the United States. *The Lagoon Cycle* is the story of this research and their growing realisation of the implications of their scientific approach for the environment. As the story unfolds, they increasingly become aware of the conflicts that this conventional research approach generates and work with intuition and judgement to steer a different course, rediscovering their understanding that human survival is integral to that of the natural environment. We might understand *The Lagoon Cycle* as wrestling with the dominant and problematic paradigm of Western culture and certainly the one that is at the core of Whitehead's thinking on the bifurcation of nature.

The Harrisons do not reject science as some of the romantic Poets had done, notably Wordsworth, but rather wrestle with the complexities, in particular how science is shaped by experience, and needs to be underpinned by philosophy, or in their case an 'ecological argument'. They continue to work with environmental scientists throughout their career. Newton Harrison says in 2021:

> The best of us have good relationships with the way science works because we [artists and scientists] both work with discovery, but then we [artists] work with a level of risk taking and improvisation that works against the theoretical basis [of science, that is] the preponderance of evidence proving something. [...] We early on figured out we didn't have to do that. We had to make work that was *prima facie – prima facie* means true to the face of it. (N. Harrison 2021b, loc. 14.50)

The Harrisons use *prima facie* to talk about 'envisioned actions that most people would accept as *prima facie* good to do, whether or not they believed they *could* be done' (H. M. Harrison and Harrison 2001a, n.p. italics in original). This construction also includes a suspension of judgement as to where the enquiry will lead.

Whitehead's process philosophy – his focus on 'event' as a way to approach organisms as integral with their environments, keeping experience in time and space as the root of understanding – is curiously resonant in *The Lagoon Cycle*, despite some clear differences, not least in that we experience the work as a story that gives it a particular sort of coherence. The Harrisons are artists, and their work is sensory, performative, and place specific. *The Lagoon Cycle* takes form as an exhibition where its discourse invites participation by the audience, not least in engaging with the adventure. It seeks to address a wide range of audiences, drawing them into experiencing the issues. Neither Stengers, Whitehead, nor the Harrisons are 'against' science, but they are critical of its current economic and political objectives that amount to an absence of shared responsibility and the space to think freely, to confront reality in a world that has become dominated by private interests. Their shared concern is to open practices to questions, to reclaim public space as a space of responsibility.

Turning first to the form of the work and the language, we have drawn on the text as reproduced in the exhibition catalogue (1985b) in this discussion. For the visual aspects, we have used the *Book of the Lagoons* as reproduced in *The Time of the Force Majeure* (2016). The images in the latter function more powerfully in terms of telling a visual story, whereas the text in the former is clearer for the purposes of reading and analysis.[2] The story unfolds in seven episodes, named 'Lagoons'. It takes the form of a dialogue predominantly between two characters, the active Lagoon Maker, who embodies creativity and bold speculation, and the reflective Witness who tracks and questions the implications of the proposed courses of action. The whole work is structured around a dynamic back and forth exchange between these two characters and, from time to time, with others who can inform understanding of what is at stake. The text rarely

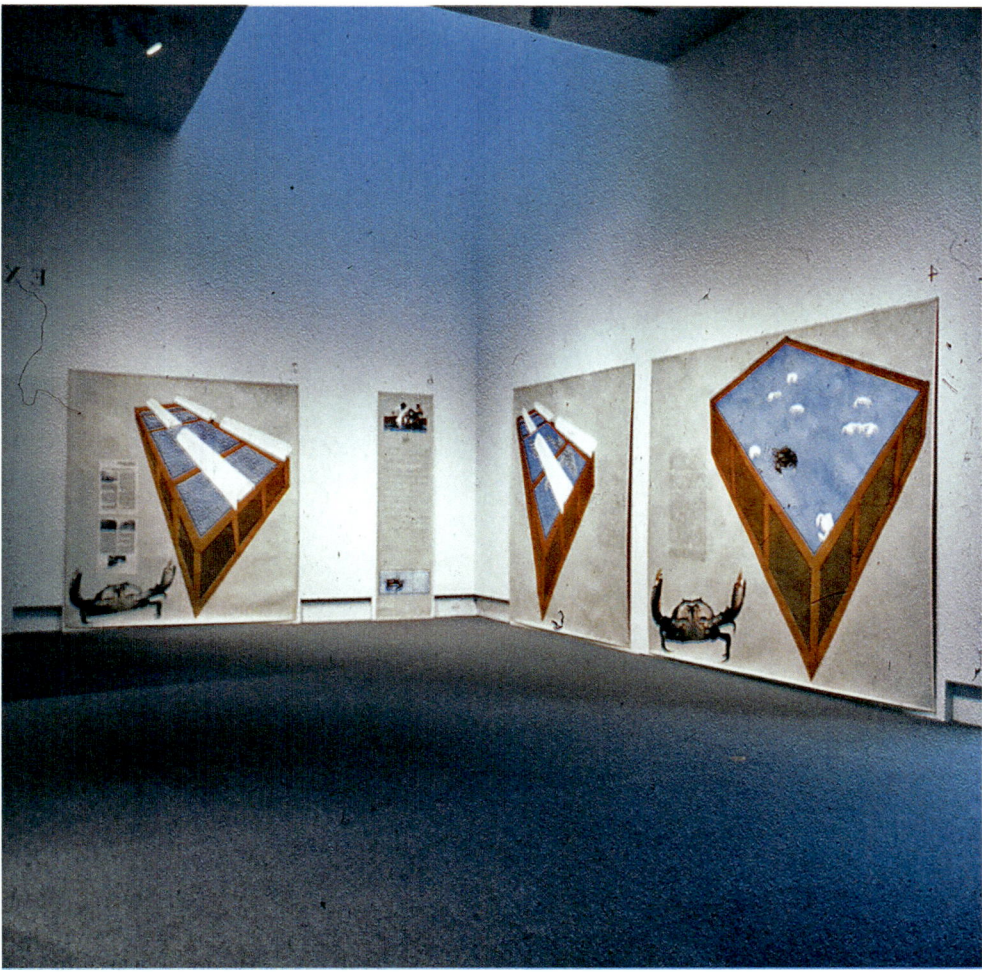

Figure 16: 'The Lagoon Cycle' (1985) Installation at the Herbert F. Johnson Museum at Cornell University (courtesy of Newton and Helen Harrison Family Trust)

names any of the characters other than through their roles as fisherman, friend, guide, or water department official, in the manner of *dramatis personae*. It never specifies that Helen is the Witness, or that Newton is the Lagoon Maker, though the perspectives that each embody in terms of unchecked creativity and more cautious critical reflection are unequivocal. In visual terms in the *Book of the Lagoons* the words of the Witness and the Lagoon Maker are in two different hands.

The Lagoon Cycle, while having significant elements characteristic of epic poetry (the vast setting; beginning in the middle, *medias res*; use of epithets rather than names; use of lists; the transformative trajectory), can also be understood, as noted by French Philosopher Michel de Certeau (1925–1986) in his introductory essay, as having some elements of the picaresque. Many of the characters, particularly in the Third Lagoon, are roguish. The Lagoon Maker starts out pursuing his own desires. The use of epithets is also reminiscent of medieval 'Everyman' plays, in which characters personify moral qualities or abstractions such as death or youth, or here hubris checked by reality. As noted elsewhere, Helen had studied literature, in particular Chaucer, and *The Lagoon Cycle* draws on and works with different aspects of poetic tradition, as well as the development of ethnopoetics. This movement emerged in the 1960s through the work of Jerome Rothenberg (b. 1931), their colleague at University of California, San Diego during the 1970s and 1980s (Manolescu 2021, 102; Douglas and Fremantle 2016b, 456). Ethnopoetics starts from the recognition that poetry is a necessity in life, is found everywhere, is rooted in orality, and like all art is, in Whitehead's terms, an activity of intensifying and amplifying experience. Reflecting in *The Time of the Force Majeure* (H. M. Harrison and Harrison 2016, 49) on the central characters, the Witness and the Lagoon Maker, the Harrisons describe them as 'exaggerations of ourselves'. They also describe, in developing the performative practice, choosing to 'represent ourselves as a simple "Mom and Pop" operation' (H. M. Harrison and Harrison 2016, 49). These two principal characters, though not heroic, are drawn into an extraordinary adventure. Their dialogues, even disputations, lead to deeper insights and 'an ecological ethos emerges' (Matilsky 1992, 70).

The Poem as Visual Essay

The 'Introduction' to *The Lagoon Cycle* comprises a short text surrounding a single image – a world map centred on San Diego (fig. 17). This map is drawn from an earlier work *San Diego as the Center of a World* (1974). Carter Ratcliff (b. 1941), American art critic who writes the other critical essay in the catalogue, focuses the role of this.

> From the start the Lagoonmaker and the Witness treat large questions of creation and self-creation, will, and belief and action with a confidence that usually only occurs at the end of a cycle of experience, not at the start. (H. M. Harrison and Harrison 1985b, 11)

The text establishes the dialogue between the two, at this point unnamed, characters. It positions them at the core of the work and articulates their process of negotiating meaning. It starts:

> *For us it was a moment*
> *We didn't know it had begun until we*
> *were already in the middle*
> *Then we looked forward and knew how it*
> *should end*
> *but we didn't know how to get there*
> *You could as well say that knowing the ending*
> *we worked backward to what we must have been*

to begin it
as forward to what we must become to end it
Introduction/26

The characters as archetypes cannot be conflated, but they are in relation to each other. The text is juxtaposed with a world map, evoking the iconic blue dot of Planet Earth in the photograph taken in the 1960s, but intentionally centred on the place in which the Harrisons were living at the time, the place inhabited by the two characters. The dialogue that follows introduces several key ideas. Time, influenced by ideas of quantum theory ('Every time we recreate the past it is different', Introduction/26), is framed in terms of a series of articulations of what 'moments' are, including 'a radioactive moment with/a ten-year half-life' (Introduction/26). This is a way of noting the duration over which the work was created, the duration across which this epic is played out. They reverse the meaning of half-life, making it a generative period rather than one of decay. The idea of half-life also directs us to the other half: the work continues to live in our experience, through exhibition, readings, interpretations, and responses.

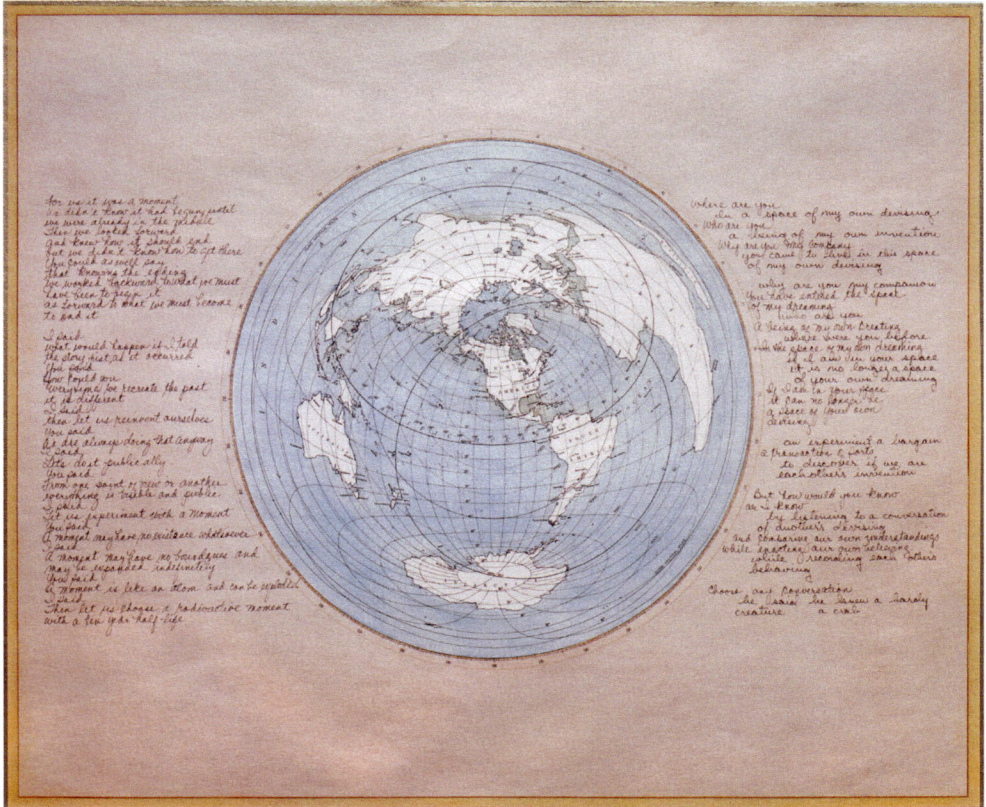

Figure 17: 'Book of the Lagoons' (1985) Introduction (courtesy of the Newton and Helen Harrison Family Trust)

At the end of this Introduction the crab enters as simply another conversation among many possibly conversations, a context in which to figure out what it means to work together.

> *Choose any conversation*
>   He said he knew a hardy creature
>   a crab

This comes at the end of an exchange that starts with:

> *Where are you*
>   In a space of my own devising
> *Who are you*
>   A being of my own invention
> *Why are you my company*
>   You came to live in the space
>   of my own devising
> Introduction/26

This interaction is at the heart of the whole narrative of *The Lagoon Cycle*, moving from two individual or even individualistic characters through an intuitive transformation into an understanding in common. Discussion takes form through a series of encounters and experiences during which their working practice and relationship develop. *The Lagoon Cycle* is one of very few of the Harrisons' works that has this particular self-reflective dimension. Although other works continue to be constructed around dialogue, none apart from *Atempause für den Save-Fluss* (*Breathing Space for the Sava River*) (1989) (figs. 37-40) revisits this negotiation.[3] Helen reflects on the changes they undergo to develop the quality of relationship that characterises their partnership from this point onwards.

> One of us – who had been an artist from early adolescence on – had to change completely to do this. The other of us – who had been a lifelong teacher, researcher, educational philosopher, and student of psychology and literature – had to change completely to do this. We were convinced that neither of us had the capability to become eco-systemically empowered without the help, encouragement, and dramatically different talents, experience, and tolerance of ambiguity of the other. We began to imagine that there was a third party, a unique co-creator, and that we were assistants to this entity – the real artist only visible to us.
> We were teaching each other to be each other, but not completely each other. (2016, 53)

Where epic poetry conventionally starts with an invocation to a muse, *The Lagoon Cycle* starts with this dialogue on time, co-creation, and what it might mean to tell a story of an adventure. It then turns immediately to Sri Lanka.

The First Lagoon
The Lagoon at Uppouveli
In the First Lagoon the narrative starts with the natural habitat of the crab in the lagoons particular to Sri Lanka. This sequence is visually akin to an ethnographic study comprising notes and images (fig. 19-21). The opening image is of an individual working in a mangrove in a lagoon (fig. 18). Various Sri Lankan 'icons' are used alongside documentary photography. The issues of modernisation are articulated in relation to the longer history of Sri Lankan civilisation. The brutality of British colonial authority is present through a reproduction of a poster mandating killing men over 18, pulling down and burning houses, felling fruit trees, breaching irrigation tanks and canals, and destroying cattle. The sequence ends with a large image of a fisherman holding a basket of crabs.

The Second Lagoon
Sea Grant
The Second Lagoon focuses on a period of experimentation in which this natural habitat of the crab is reproduced as polycultural aquaculture tanks in California. Problems are encountered and gradually solved to the point that the question of mating in artificial conditions is successfully addressed.[4] Visually this sequence is dominated by images of tanks and crabs. These become motifs (fig. 22-23).

The Third Lagoon
The House of Crabs
This success attracts possible investors and opportunists who see the potential to exploit the research for financial gain documented in the Third Lagoon. Here the imagery starts with an actual crab pond built for one of the opportunists (fig. 24) and visually explores the conflicting potential developments, juxtaposing grids of artificial tanks with Sri Lankan lagoons. Both are contained in the iconic drawn form of the tanks. It ends with the surface of the tanks becoming the surface of the sea (fig. 25-26).

The Fourth Lagoon
On Mapping, Mixing, and Territory
The Fourth Lagoon undertakes a thought experiment, a proposal for an industrial scale farm located at a site at the Salton Sea, California. This Lagoon is characterised by maps and aerial photographs, diagrams of proposed aquaculture systems (fig 27), and a historical timeline of the Salton Sea (fig. 28). As with the First Lagoon documentary photography, in this case of the Salton Sea area is used. The maps and technical drawings have a distancing effect, reinforcing the perspective of technoscience.

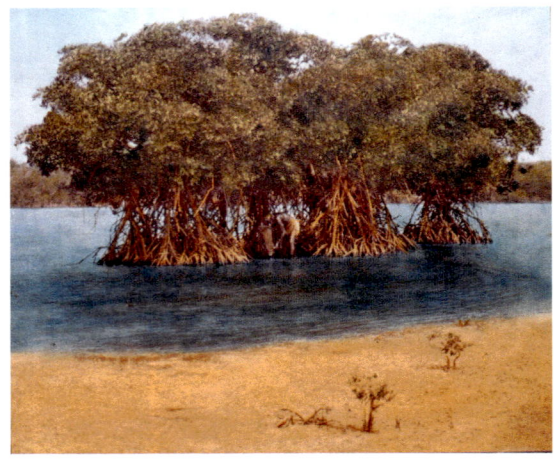

Figure 18: 'Book of the Lagoons' (1985)
First Lagoon detail (courtesy of the
Newton and Helen Harrison Family Trust)

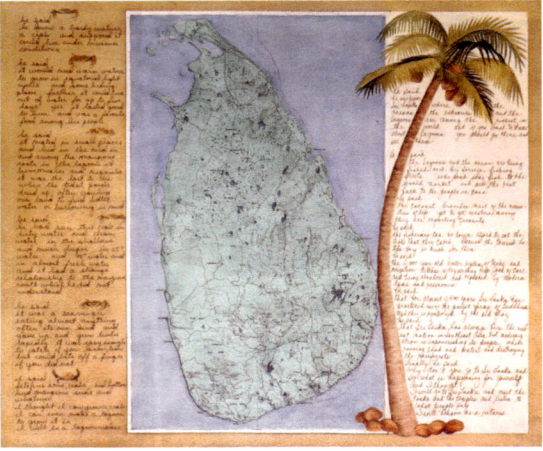

Figure 19: 'Book of the Lagoons' (1985)
First Lagoon detail (courtesy of the
Newton and Helen Harrison Family Trust)

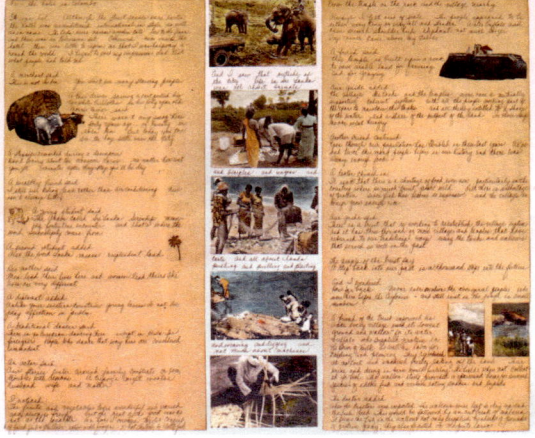

Figure 20: 'Book of the Lagoons' (1985)
First Lagoon detail (courtesy of the
Newton and Helen Harrison Family Trust)

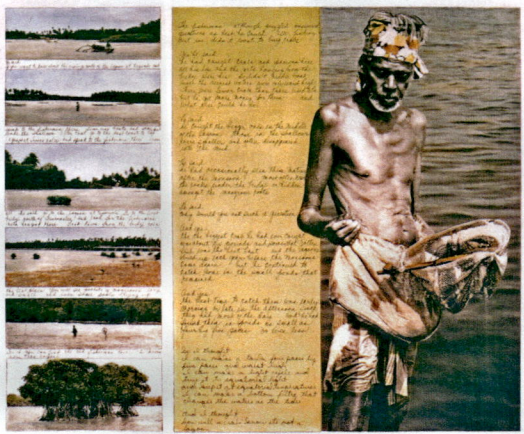

Figure 21: 'Book of the Lagoons' (1985)
First Lagoon detail (courtesy of the
Newton and Helen Harrison Family Trust)

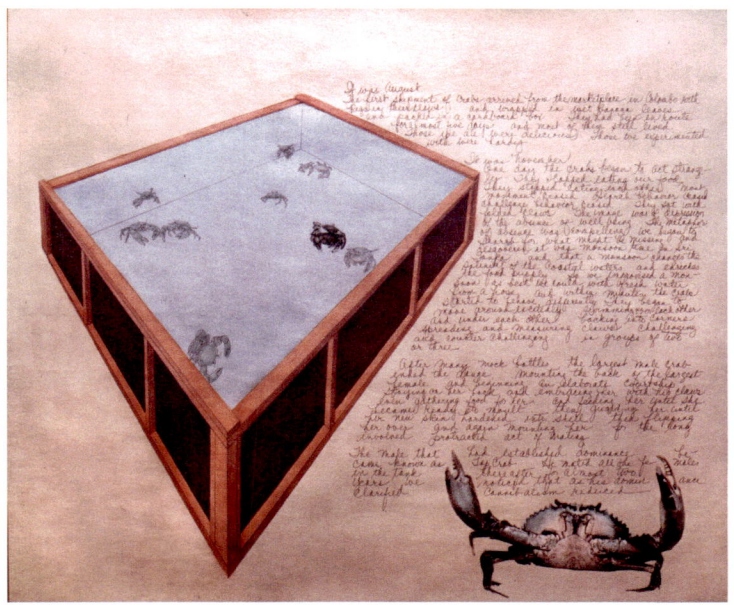

Figure 22: 'Book of the Lagoons' (1985) Second Lagoon detail (courtesy of the Newton and Helen Harrison Family Trust)

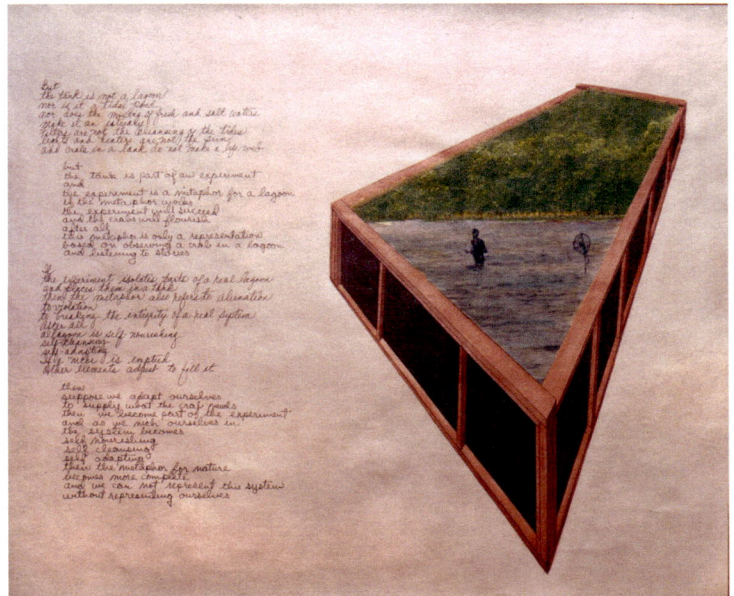

Figure 23: 'Book of the Lagoons' (1985) Second Lagoon detail (courtesy of the Newton and Helen Harrison Family Trust)

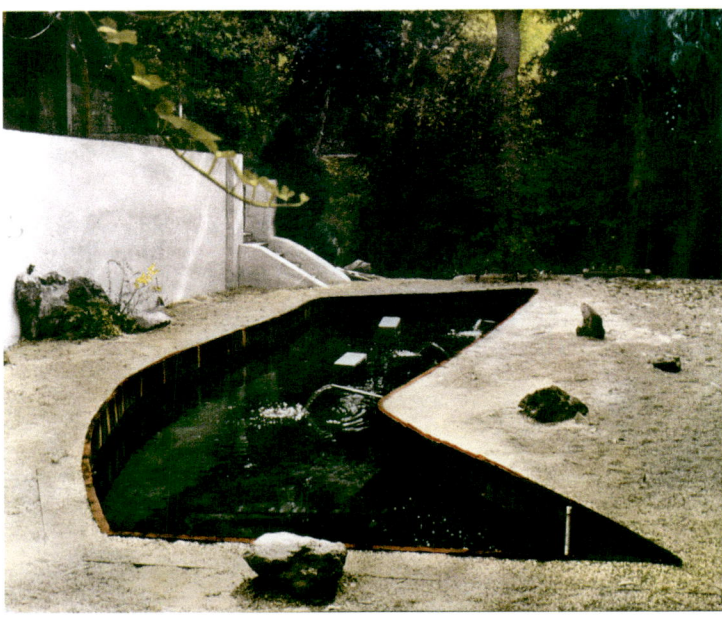

Figure 24: 'Book of the Lagoons' (1985) Third Lagoon detail (courtesy of the Newton and Helen Harrison Family Trust)

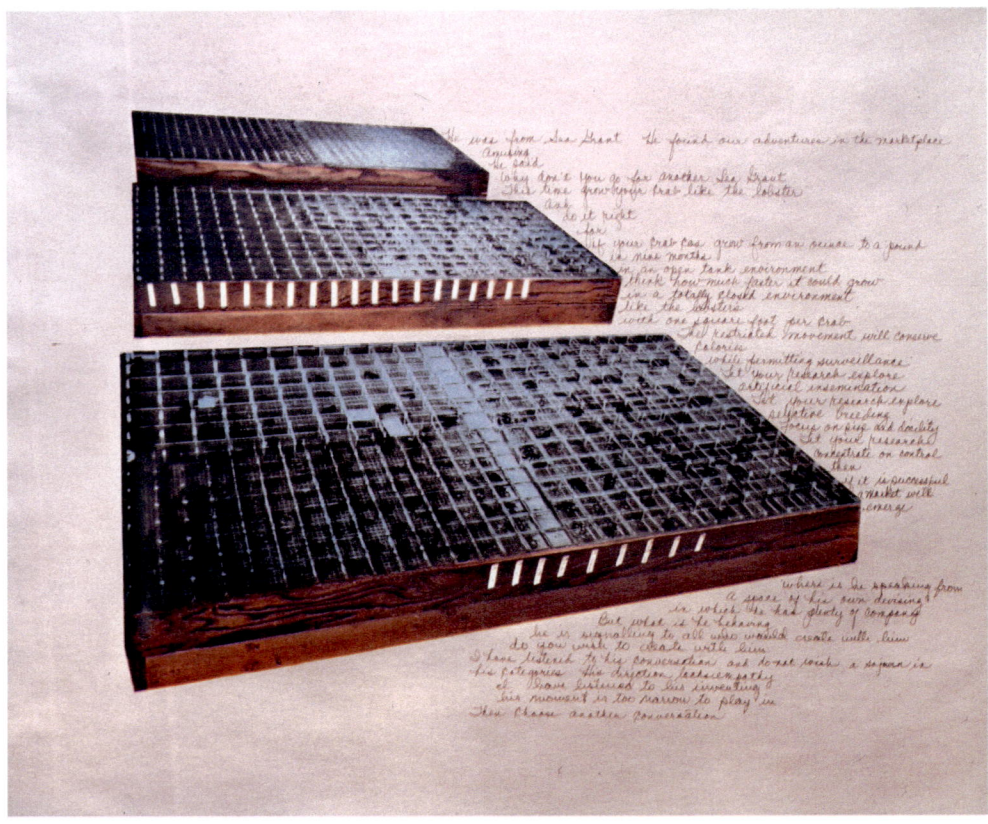

Figure 25: 'Book of the Lagoons' (1985) Third Lagoon detail (courtesy of the Newton and Helen Harrison Family Trust)

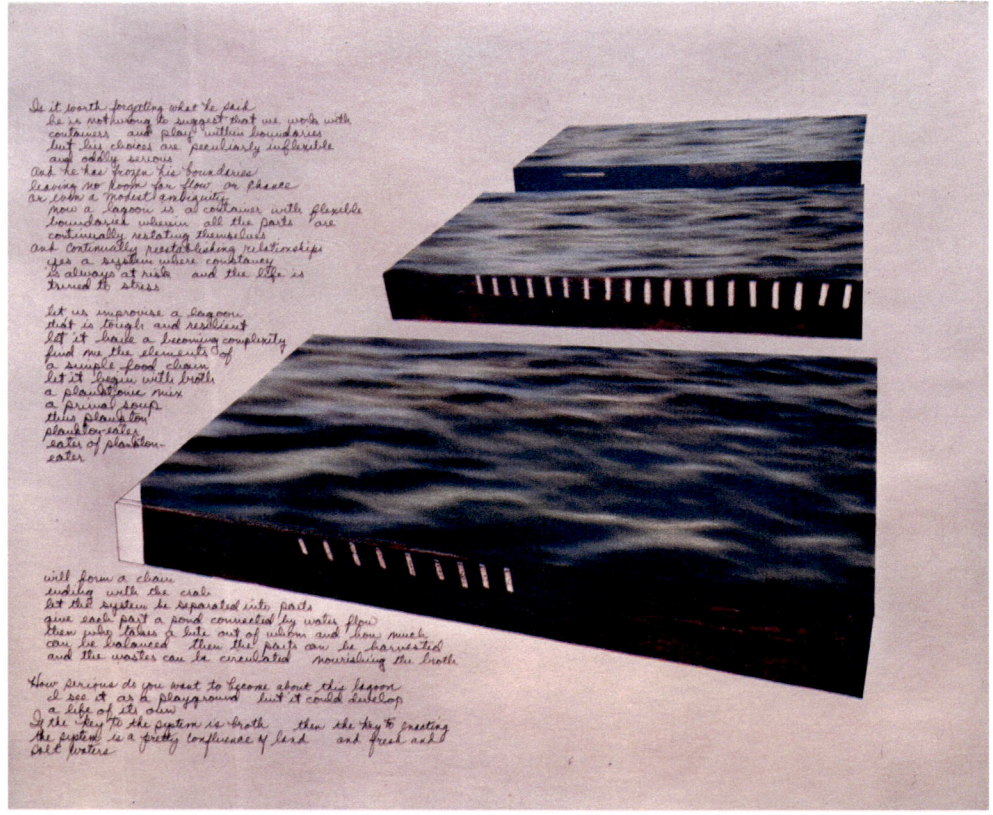

Figure 26: 'The Book of the Lagoon' (1985) Third Lagoon detail (courtesy of the Newton and Helen Harrison Family Trust)

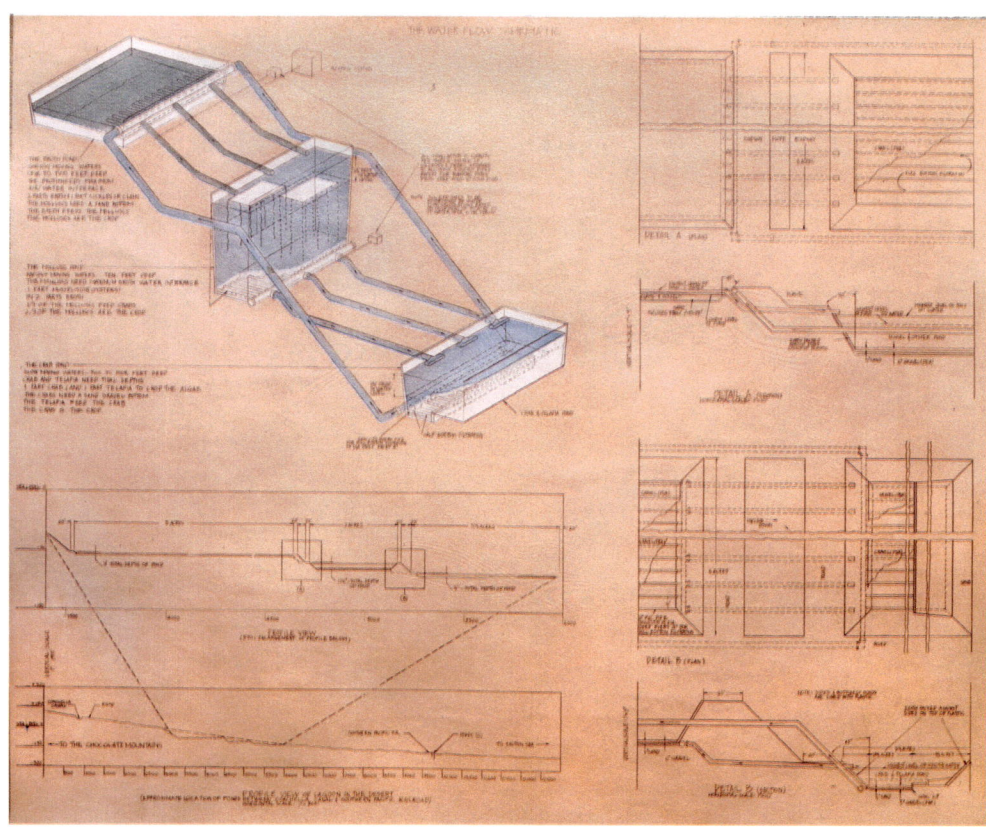

Figure 27: 'Book of the Lagoons' (1985) Fourth Lagoon detail (courtesy of the Newton and Helen Harrison Family Trust)

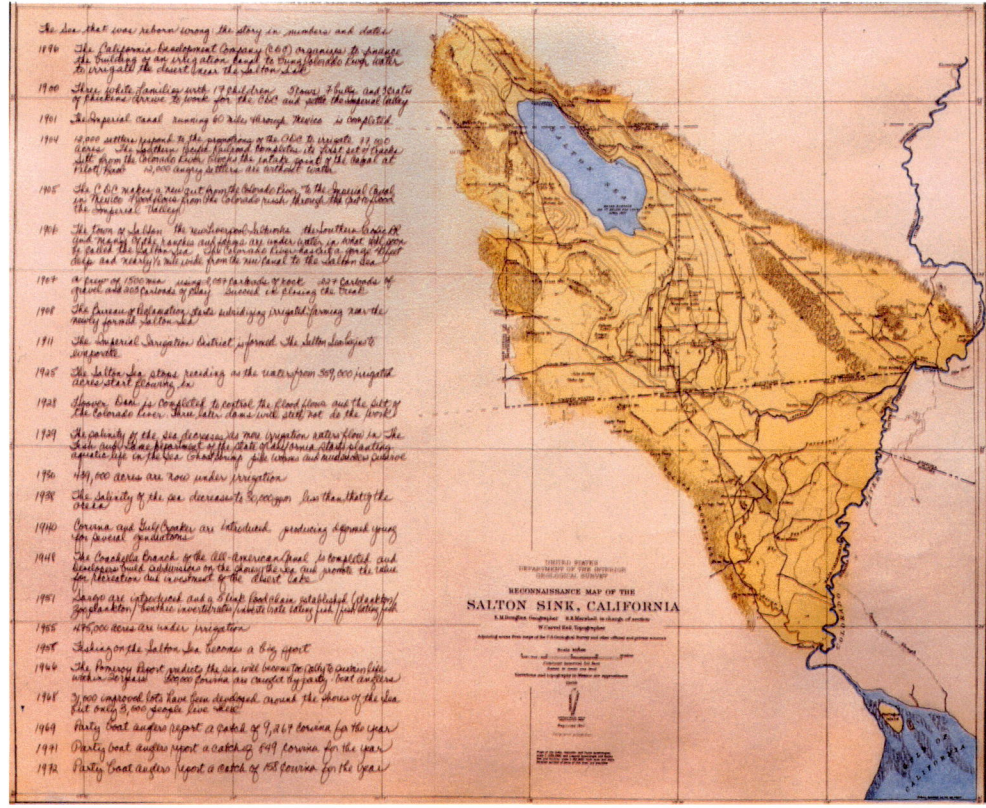

Figure 28: 'Book of the Lagoons' (1985) Fourth Lagoon detail (courtesy of the Newton and Helen Harrison Family Trust)

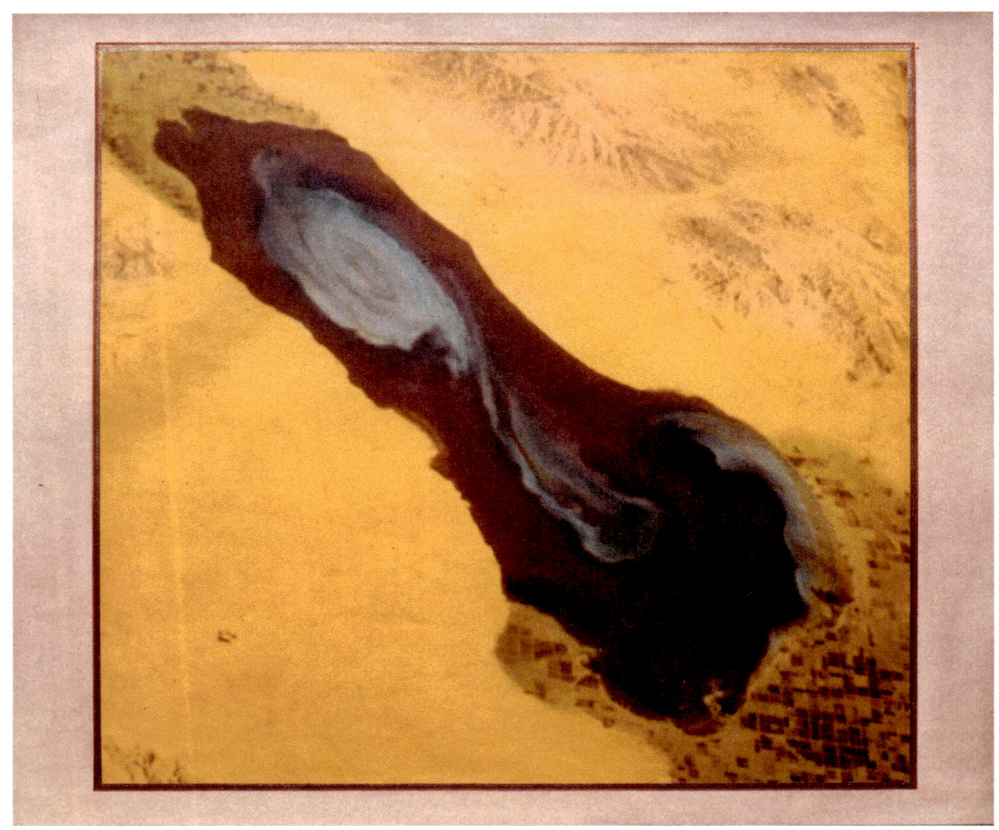

Figure 29: 'Book of the Lagoons' (1985) Fifth Lagoon detail (courtesy of the Newton and Helen Harrison Family Trust)

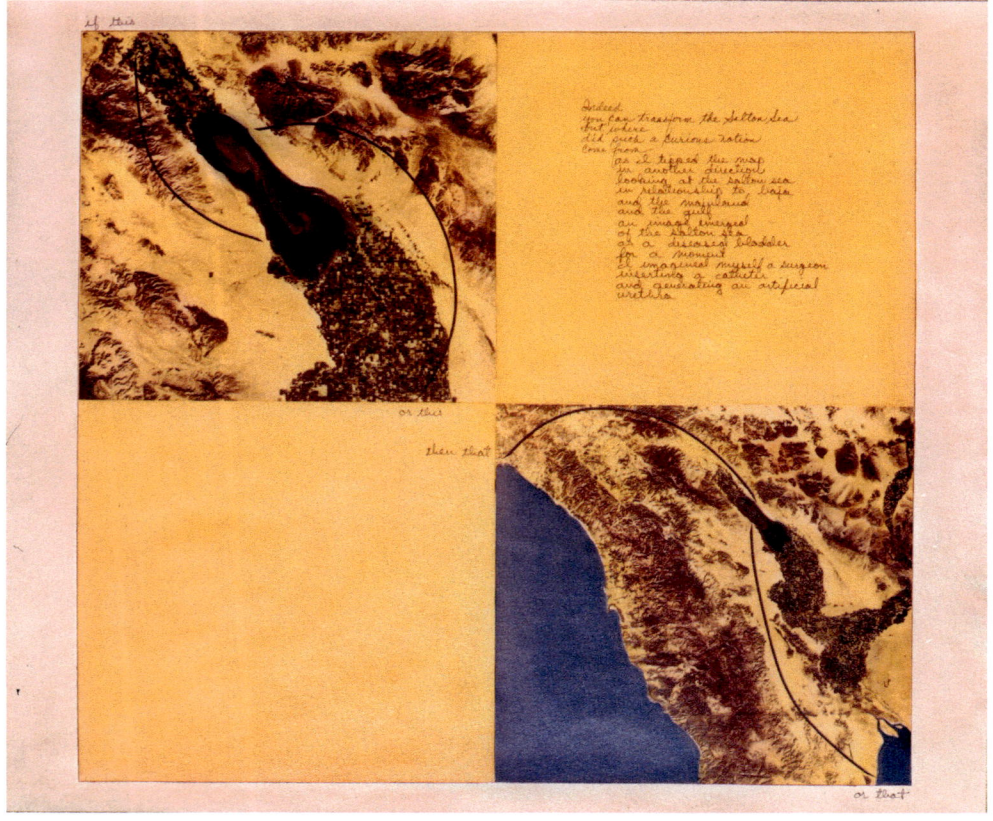

Figure 30: 'Book of the Lagoons' (1985) Fifth Lagoon detail (courtesy of the Newton and Helen Harrison Family Trust)

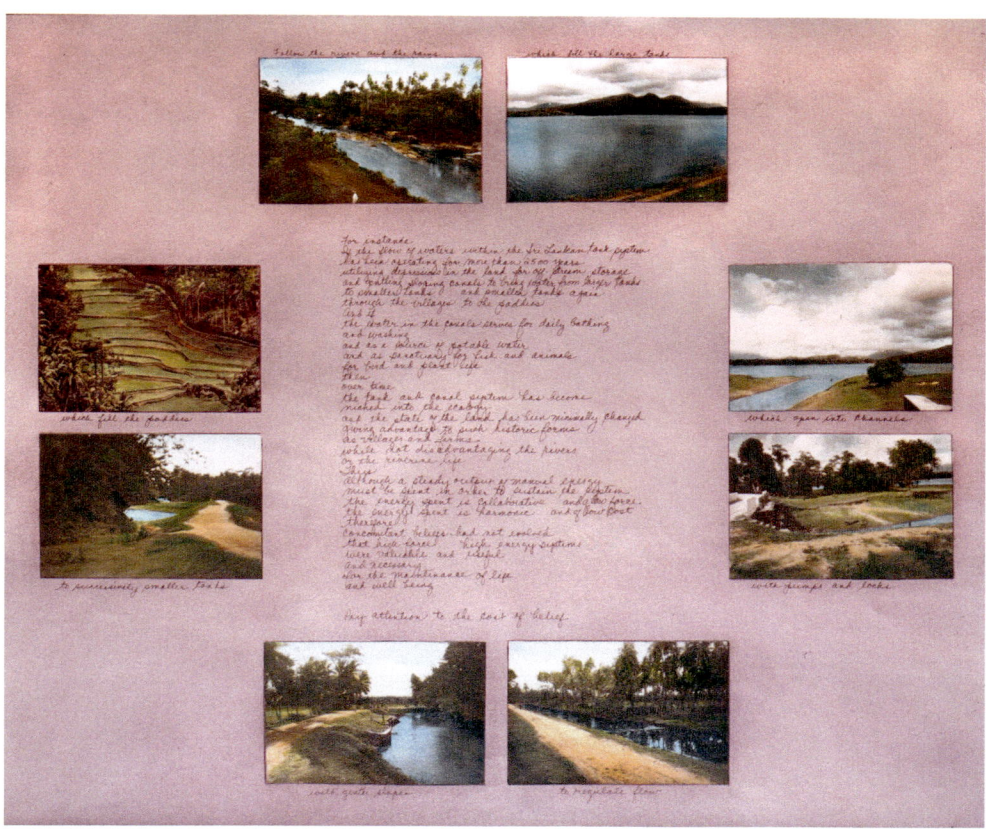

Figure 31: 'Book of the Lagoons' (1985) Sixth Lagoon detail (courtesy of the Newton and Helen Harrison Family Trust)

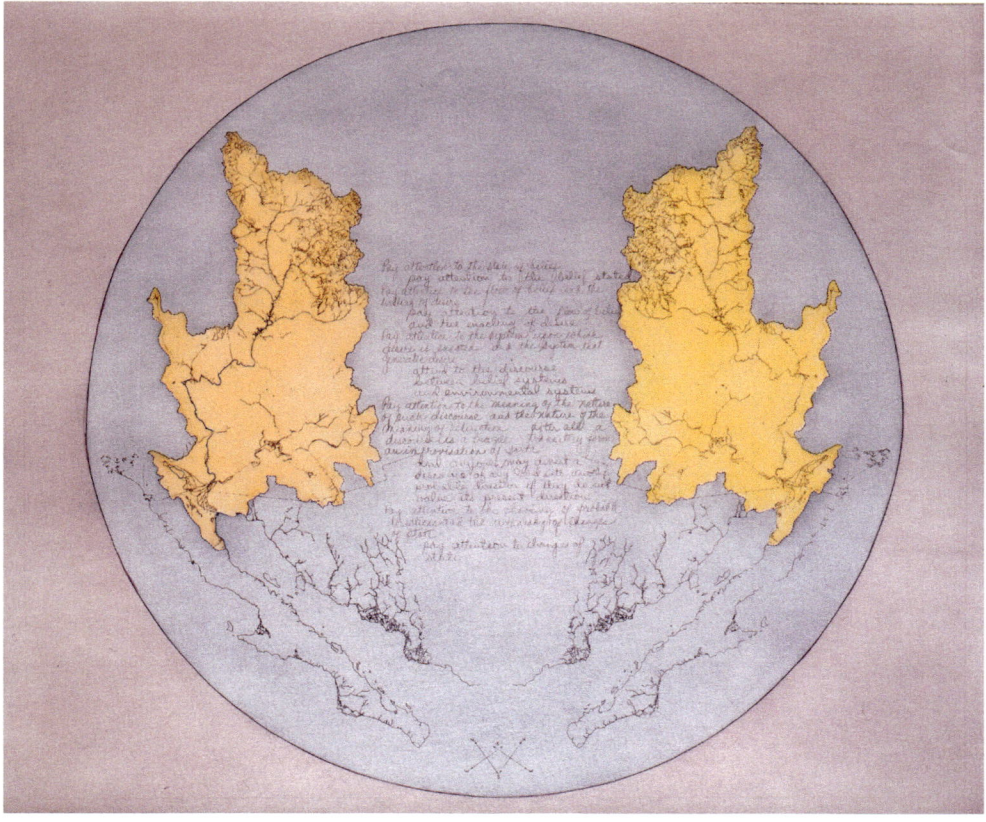

Figure 32: 'Book of the Lagoons' (1985) Sixth Lagoon detail (courtesy of the Newton and Helen Harrison Family Trust)

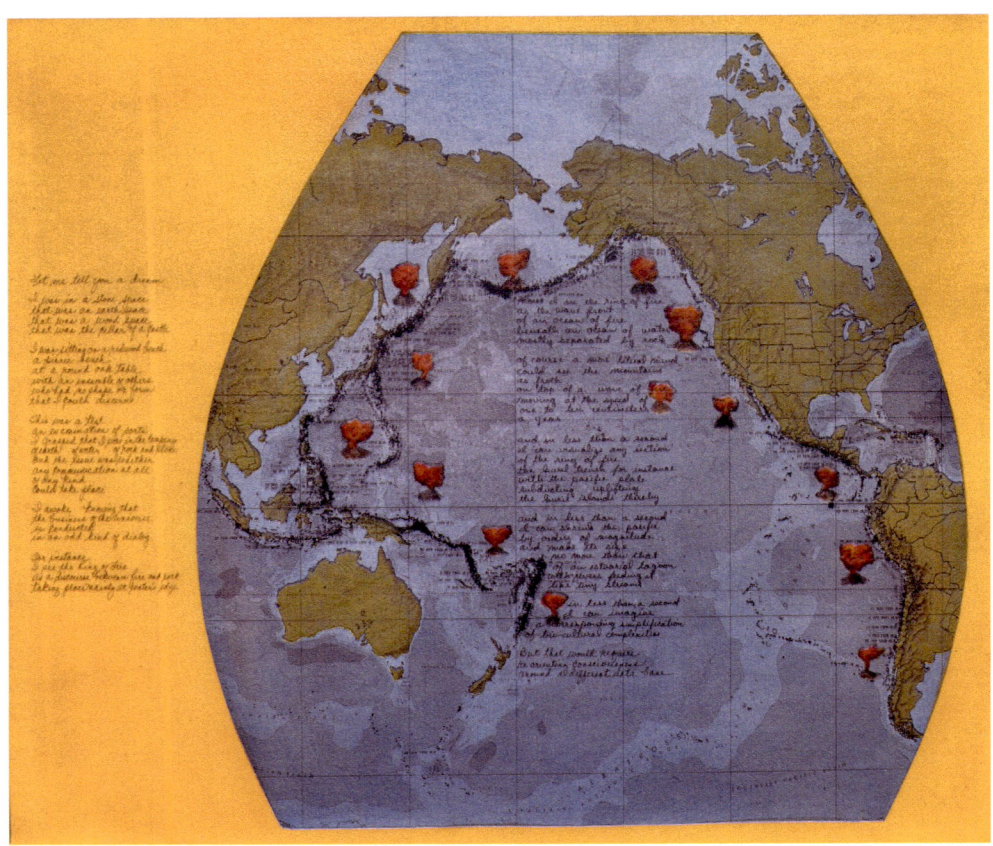

Figure 33: 'Book of the Lagoons' (1985) Seventh Lagoon detail (courtesy of the Newton and Helen Harrison Family Trust)

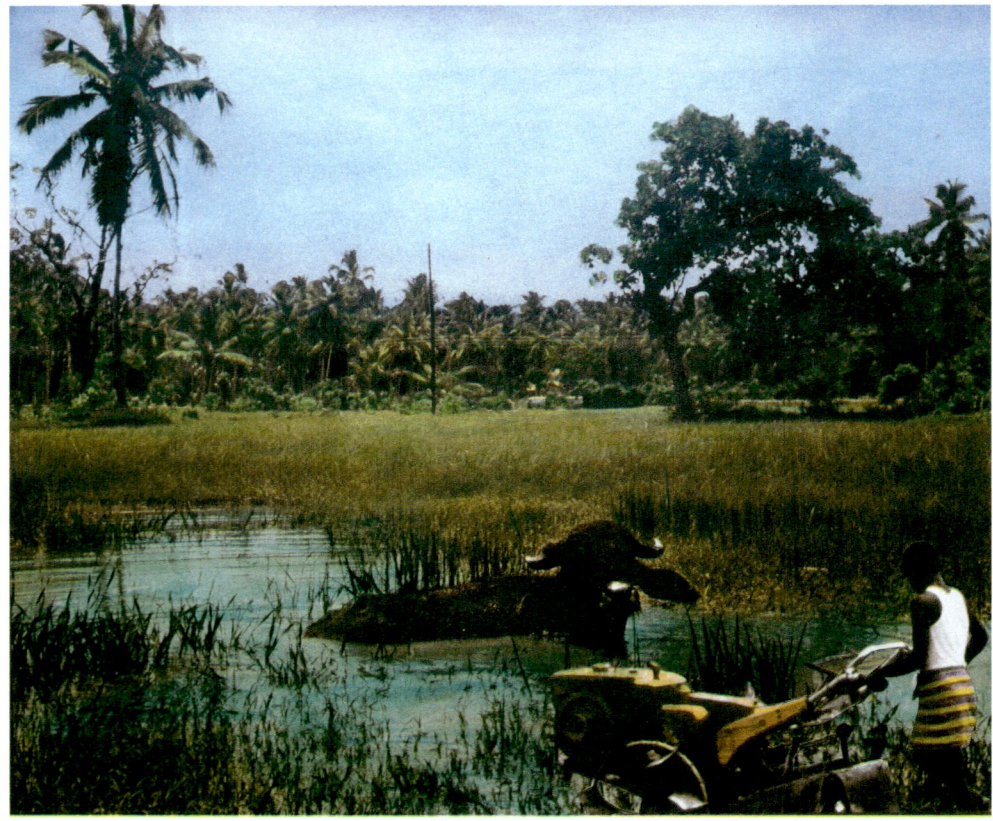

Figure 34: 'Book of the Lagoons' (1985) Seventh Lagoon detail (courtesy of the Newton and Helen Harrison Family Trust)

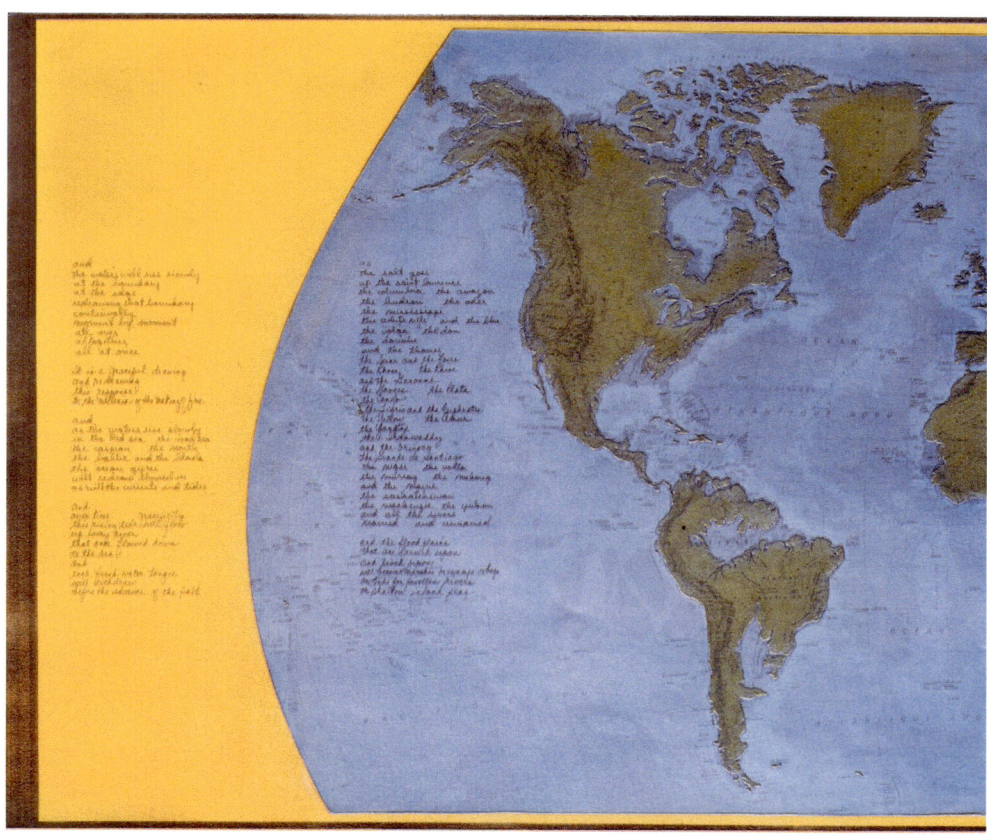

Figure 35: 'The Lagoon Cycle' (1985) Seventh Lagoon detail (courtesy of the Newton and Helen Harrison Family Trust)

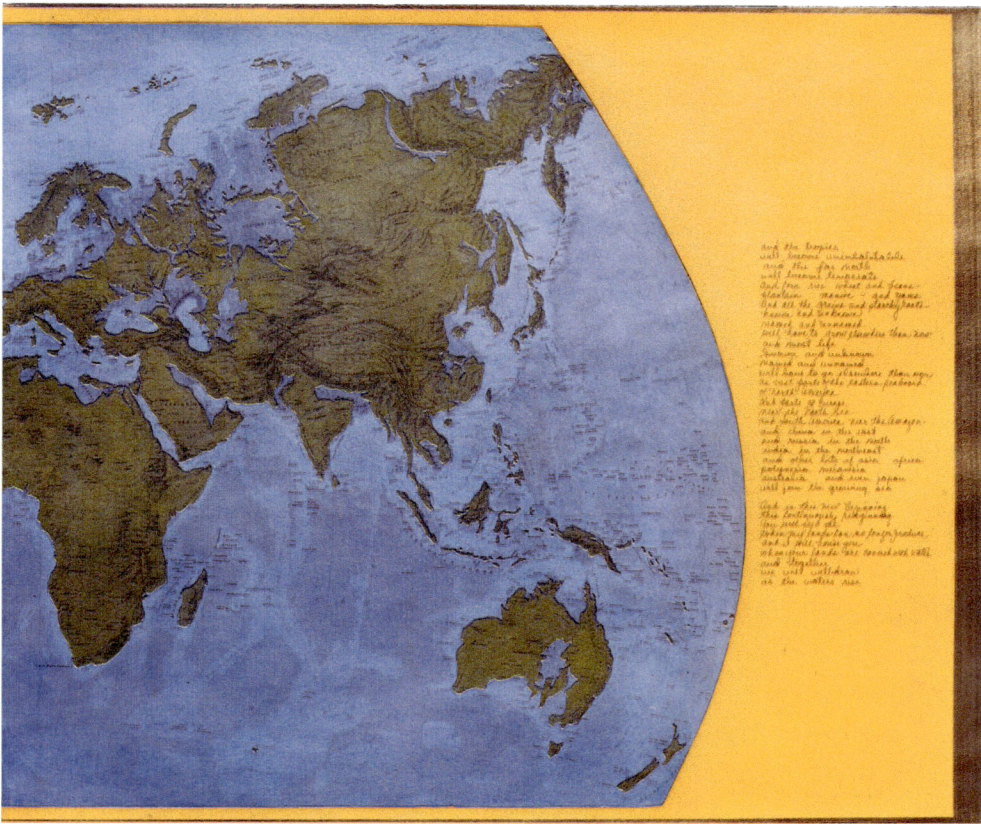

Figure 36: 'Book of the Lagoons' (1985) Seventh Lagoon detail (courtesy of the Newton and Helen Harrison Family Trust)

The Fifth Lagoon
From the Salton Sea to the Pacific
From the Salton Sea to the Gulf

The Fifth Lagoon makes explicit the potential damage of industrial scale faming in some detail through a series of 'propositions'. This device is also used in *San Diego as the Center of a World (1974)* and in *Sacramento Meditations* (1977). The imagery starts with a graphic depiction of the poisoned Salton Sea (fig. 29) and ends with a sequence of grids, picking up on the pattern of land ownership boundaries, where the negative impact of flushing the Salton Sea into the Pacific or to the Gulf of California is explored visually through maps overlayered by the text of 'If [...], Then [...]' scenarios (fig. 30). The prophetic voice calmly and thoughtfully 'walks' the reader through the horrific implications of farming at scale.

The Sixth Lagoon
On Dialogue, Discourse, and Metaphor

This triggers the invocation in the Sixth Lagoon to 'pay attention to the cost of belief' (Sixth Lagoon/84, 86) by comparing the Harrisons' artificial system to the 2,500-year-old system that constitutes the natural habitat of the crab. The first image in this section includes a multiplication of the poisoned Salton Sea image all pointing towards the text where the two characters 'face' their differences, their remembering and forgetting. This is once again juxtaposed with images of Sri Lanka's techniques of water management (fig. 31). The final circular image in this same section presents two mirroring versions of the Colorado River watershed surrounding the text 'Pay attention [...]' (fig. 32) In other works, notably *Green Heart Vision* (1994), the Harrisons use the device of mirroring maps, one backwards and one in the normal configuration to emphasise critical reflection.

The Seventh Lagoon
The Ring of Fire
The Ring of Water

The Seventh Lagoon is highly reflective of the whole journey they have undergone with the crab experiment. It begins with the Witness' dream through which both Lagoon Maker and Witness understand that the dynamics of natural systems are a form of exchange. This dialogue is set on and beside a map of the Pacific 'ring of fire' (fig. 33) and juxtaposed with an image of a water buffalo and a tractor (fig. 34). Human technological knowledge is part of this exchange but, they remark, it is a form of knowledge that lacks empathy. It struggles with anything that is not itself. The central discussion in this 'lagoon' takes place with a background of the sea. This Seventh Lagoon concludes with a series of questions about the future.

And in this new beginning
this continuous rebeginning

will you feed me when
my lands
            can no longer produce
and will I house you
when your lands are covered with water
and together
will we withdraw
as the waters rise?
(H. M. Harrison and Harrison 2006, n.p.)[5]

This passage is set on a world map modified to show sea level rise if all the ice melted (fig. 35-36). The final image in the *Book of the Lagoons* is of the sea with a solitary fisherman on a small piece of shoreline. The Second Lagoon and Third Lagoon share a visual language focusing on the material culture of experimentation, and the Fourth Lagoon and Fifth Lagoon focus on speculative mapping. Both of these sequences also end with revisiting aspects of the Sri Lankan landscapes as the visions of technological solutions break down. The intervention of images of lagoons into technological systems gives the impression of breaking the visual culture of technoscience.

Where *The Lagoon Cycle* starts with a dialogue negotiating co-operation between two individuals, it ends with this much larger question. In the initial negotiation, the individuals seem to be in control of their own fates ('In a place of my own devising' and 'A being of my own invention', (First Lagoon/26)). By the end the issue of survival has again come to reshape the story. The conclusion is focused by the waters rising and the need to offer shelter and sustenance to each other.

Bifurcation of Nature: Collisions between East and West

Whitehead's concepts are useful in exploring the distinctiveness of *The Lagoon Cycle*. His diagnosis of the bifurcation of nature is the central issue. The bifurcation, through the isolation of measurement, and the separation of observation, occurs predominantly in a particular period of Western history from the 17th century onwards that allows us to see nature as fixed, measurable, something to be used productively, exploited. Whitehead was by no means against science or indeed Western ways of thinking. He believed true science could be passed from West to East without destroying non-Western cultures (Whitehead 2022, 3). He is critical of a particular period of science from the 17th century onwards that had in its reductionism become very successful, but wantonly destructive. Stengers, drawing on Whitehead, makes the case that to escape the bifurcation we need to adopt a very different approach to reality, being prepared to think and work differently. The leap of the imagination is for her a willingness, following Whitehead, to approach the problems as an adventure and invent a field in which problems can be situated. It means being willing to understand the connections between things not limited by causality, recognising complexity and immanence. She comments that Whitehead's faith in an order of nature does not rest on imagining reality as in some sense determined and therefore measurable, but on a reality that is created, 'an aesthetic achievement' of moulding and refining our understanding of nature towards harmony (Stengers 2011, 117). The term 'harmony' as used by Whitehead does not close out contradiction or conflict. It is perhaps better understood as related to the ecological idea of 'homeostasis' – in particular, as it relates the process of constant adjusting to optimal conditions, whether as a single living entity or as an ecosystem, even up to the scale of the planet during the Holocene period.

The Lagoon Cycle might help understand that the bifurcation is a particular modern Western construction, exploring as it does the human capacity to reshape environments, to attend to or ignore externalities, and to focus on 'How?' questions, sometimes ignoring the 'Why?' questions. This construction addresses how to survive without necessarily questioning what surviving might mean. There is an important encounter early in the process of working with the crab.

> *We told him we were inventing a technologically simple*
> *aquaculture system to increase protein production*
> Second Lagoon/51

The 'him' in this passage is a scientist named John who was working with similar questions of enhancing local fisheries. This is possibly John Isaacs (1913–1980), the oceanographer from the Scripps Institution of Oceanography and Director of the University of California's state-wide Institute of Marine Resources. Issacs encouraged the artists to apply for the Sea Grant to support their enquiry, and when that was successfully completed, to apply for a second.

Collisions between Western technoscience and non-Western ways of thinking reoccur throughout the work, and in fact form a visual juxtaposition as noted above. An early example is the encounter with an elderly fisherman.

> *Above all   he said*
> *go to the Lagoon at Upouveli*
> *Go to the first bridge north of Trincomalee*
> *and look for the fisherman's nets hanging there*
> *Look down from the bridge*
> *over the flat plane*
> *You will see shallows with pockets of mangroves*
> *and even some pools drying up*
> *See if you can find the old fisherman there*
> *He knows more than anyone*

From the lagoon at Upouveli

*The fisherman   although puzzled   answered
questions as best he could   after finding out we didn't
want to buy crabs*
First Lagoon/38–41

The fisherman, trusting perhaps the apparent disinterest of his enquirers, shares his knowledge of where and when best to fish, the size of the catch in relation to seasonal changes such as monsoons and in relation to pond size (fig. 21). The artists conclude this part with the Lagoon Maker, an appealing but somewhat roguish character (and definitely not the conventional hero of an epic), confidently assuming the right to extract local knowledge, model, and re-apply it, principally for profit, in his own, quite different cultural context.

> So I thought
> I can make a tank four paces by five paces
> And waist high
> I can make a light cycle with timers
> and time it to equatorial light
> and keep it at equatorial temperature
> and make a bottom filter that changes
> the water as the tides
>
> And
> I thought
> how will a crab know it's not a lagoon.
First Lagoon/41

The contrast between a mindset based in scientific practices that isolate and study for technological and commercial benefit, and the way indigenous knowledge reflects the dependence of human survival on surrounding organisms, is palpable in the First Lagoon. Western modernisation replaces indigenous systems. Some individuals embrace the change and others fear it. As readers and spectators of the work of art, we are drawn into these conflicted emotions through the way individual characters reflect on the rise of poverty, of crime and begging that coincides with a rise in tourism. Forms of mechanisation displace traditional knowledge and custom. The tractor displaces the water buffalo. Concrete dams and reservoirs displace an ancient, highly effective irrigation system that then falls into disrepair.

*A friend said
Everybody here has such respect for "Foreign Experts"*

They're even bringing them in to plan our new water
system   No-one looks to see the long-term mess these
experts have made   of their own land   and their own
water systems
First Lagoon/36

This is one of a series of collisions between on the one hand, the West, which manifests a largely unchallenged trust in science and technology as opportunities, framed by the notion of progress and productivity, and on the other, non-Western or indigenous ways of knowing, in this case Sri Lankan, which are inherited and understand that the human is entangled together with water, crabs, and the living world.

The friend in this case might have been Ranil Senanayake, a young Sri Lankan scientist who came to the University of California, Berkeley as an undergraduate. Senanayake was the person who suggested the *Scylla Serrata* crab, and whose mother posted crabs and plant materials to California. Senanayake went on to work as a forester and scientist in Sri Lanka and across Asia. He continued to be in dialogue with the Harrisons on, among other subjects, the relevance of aesthetic judgement to landscape restoration (Senanayake 2012).

Why does the 'bifurcation of nature' matter? What does it leave hidden? It matters because it separates experience of nature from knowledge that is merely attributed to nature. Whitehead argued that nature is 'what we observe in perception through the senses' (Whitehead 2015, 2). The bifurcation separates knowledge into so called 'primary' qualities that have removed any 'bodily' aspect from 'secondary' qualities. Whitehead exemplifies the separation through a billiard ball, one of many examples. We perceive the ball as matter in its proper place and time, and its hardness, and tend to relegate qualities of colour, warmth, and sound as secondary, as psychic additions in the mind and its way of perceiving nature. '[The billiard ball's] redness and its warmth, and the sound of the click as a cannon is made off it' (Whitehead 2015, 28) are not considered part of the reality of the material object and as a consequence are separated from it. In Whitehead's notion of event, all these qualities of sound, motion, inertia, colour, and so on come together within one experience without separation or prioritisation. In the Introduction section of *The Lagoon Cycle* the dialogue addresses the same issue, recognising that the presence of the observer affects the observation through their relationship, posing the question of whether they (Helen and Newton) have possibly become each other's inventions. It reappears in the Seventh Lagoon in relation to empathy as an encounter with unfamiliar, potentially threatening experiences that take us out of the comfort zone of what is known and indeed approved, into the difficult terrain of contradiction and disagreement.

> Sometimes a forgetting takes place
> and I fall into monologue
> and repeat myself endlessly

this falling into monologue
is pleasant
it is hearing continuous approval
expecting continuing applause

Yet such falling into monologue
will self-cancel
as the energies available
are consumed

Yes   and a forgetting again takes place
as I remember that dialoguing
is very pleasant
and that it is being in dialogue
that is self-nourishing
self-cleansing
self-adjusting
Yet how can I be in dialogue
with that   with which   with whom
I have no points of similarity

Entertain empathy
and build patterns of similarity
thereby
Seventh Lagoon/93

In the *Book of the Lagoons* this sequence, along with other passages, are printed on a yellow background, a saffron yellow that is associated with Buddhism, interwoven with a view of the sea. The monologue evokes the spectre of entropy, the self-cancelling of available energy, that is endemic to a way of thinking that is so successful that it has no need to question itself. To reverse this entropy, to create a self-nourishing, self-cleansing, self-adjusting relationship, takes considerable energy, imagination, and risk (Steiner 2019, 36).

Bifurcation of Nature: Exploitation

In the Third Lagoon: The House of Crabs an entrepreneur interested in the work with the crabs as both art and science, results in a commission for a pond in his property, but in due course the differences in expectations mean that the Harrisons abandon the work.[6] A further series of interactions are reported, with an individual doing parallel research on shrimp; with a scientist working on development projects in the Middle

East; with a leading figure in the Los Angeles Asian community (who turns out to be some sort of criminal boss); as well as others. The sequence highlights with humour the various ways in which the successful breeding of the crabs evokes desires in others – in one way or another for profit.

Following on from the initial successful Sea Grant-funded research into the aquaculture system, the Harrisons are encouraged to go for a second grant.

> *Let your research explore artificial insemination*
> *Let your research explore selective breeding*
> *Focus on size and docility*
> *Let your research concentrate on control*
> Third Lagoon/59

They reject the invitation to apply for further research funding. By this point in the narrative a more reflective dialogue is taking place and the rules and conventions of this way of producing knowledge, despite its power, have lost their sway over the artists – they distance themselves.

> Where is he speaking from
> *A space of his own devising*
> *in which he has plenty of company*
> *But what is he behaving*
> He is a beacon signalling to all
> who will create with him
> Do you wish to create with him
> *I have listened to his conversation*
> *And do not wish to sojourn in his categories*
> *His direction lacks empathy*
> I have listened to his inventing
> His moment is too narrow to play in
> *Then choose another conversation*
> Third Lagoon/59

In the Fourth Lagoon another character challenges them on the problematic consequences of their technoscience thinking. This was possibly the Marxist philosopher and member of the Frankfurt School Herbert Marcuse (1898–1979) who was known to the Harrisons.[7]

> *He said*
> *there appeared to be no critical component to our ideas*
> *He asked if we really knew what we were doing*

He said
Who will own this fish farm
and who will gain from it
and who will lose

He said
if what we were doing was indeed valuable
we would immediately be co-opted
and if what we were doing was not
why were we wasting our time

He said
we were naives
and operating in ignorance of the larger whole
which was economic
and therefore we were dangerous
because we were enhancing the most destructive
economic system of all time
and where was our conscience

He said
he was interested in the power to change the system
and we might be the enemy
although he liked us personally
Fourth Lagoon/69

The challenge in the first section of the exchange with this character focuses on the basic Marxist question of 'who owns the means of production?' and the danger that the 'technologically simple aquaculture system' the Lagoon Maker is developing is embedded in capitalism, 'the most destructive/economic system of all time' (Fourth Lagoon/69). The second part of the interaction repeats some of the phrasing used in the rejection of the conversation with the scientist (above) including, 'Where is he speaking from/*A space of his own devising/in which he has plenty of company*'. But this reflection includes:

> He is not wrong to suggest
> we pay attention to advantage and disadvantage
Fourth Lagoon/69

This phrase is critical and the specific concept of 'pay attention to advantage and disadvantage', which has not occurred before, becomes very significant in the Sixth Lagoon: On Metaphor and Discourse where the first passage is a series of instructions starting

'Pay attention to the flow of waters' and ending 'Pay attention to changes of state' (Sixth Lagoon/82).

The Sixth Lagoon explores advantage and disadvantage in the specific context of the Colorado River, discussing how the land has been changed to give advantage to '*urbanisation and industrialized agriculture*'. It has been changed to the disadvantage of '*that vegetation which has adapted/to the inconstant flow of waters/and to all parts of the life web/dependent on those parts*' (referring to the river delta). The sequence ends with '*Pay attention to the cost of the giving of advantage and disadvantage*' (Sixth Lagoon/85). In contrast, the system of farming the crab in Sri Lanka that has evolved slowly over 2,500 years and in relation to local conditions can support life at all levels, 'fish and animals/and bird and plant life' and with time, human life. In the *Book of the Lagoons* these two environments (the Colorado River watershed and Sri Lanka) form a double page spread of text and image (2016, 136–37). The 'bifurcation of nature', whether framed in terms of the measurable and the observable, or in the separation of the 'How?' from the 'Why?', is addressed through the critical lens of paying attention to advantage and disadvantage and the cost of belief.

The Harrisons reveal how deeply our ways of thinking, knowing, and exchanging knowledge shape the life around us. This complexity is evoked in the idea of 'conversation', here used as a metaphor for the way language becomes the world to which it refers. They reveal how Western ways of knowing, which have been valued and practised for more than 500 years, are one possibility among many others, and a flawed one. Gradually different alternatives are woven into the poem, creating a significant shift in consciousness.

The Leap of the Imagination

To get out of the trap of bifurcated thinking Whitehead describes the 'leap of the imagination' through a metaphor.

> The true method of discovery is like the flight of an aeroplane. It starts from the ground of particular observation; it makes a flight in the thin air of imaginative generalisation; and it again lands for renewed observation rendered acute by rational interpretation. (Whitehead 1978, 5)

The leap therefore starts with a context, moves into intuition, imagination, and generalisation, and then returns to a context for more observation informed by the new perspective, rational because it is informed by this process. What it does is to give us permission to think outside of habit, to disrupt and become alert to new questions, questions that are not normally asked, or even allowed. It is then important to ask about the effects of a leap, what it does to thought, what it renders important and what it makes silent, and what it obliges one to do (Stengers 2011, 22). In *The Lagoon Cycle* the leap is not instantaneous but happens over time and in the form of discourse, an exchange between different, frequently contradictory perspectives. In the First Lagoon the leap is made through the different conversations with individuals in Sri Lanka who can help the artists to understand the life of the crab in its natural habitat. Their interlocutors include inhabitants, government officials, friends who act as guides, priests, intellectuals, diplomats, historians, mothers, artists, shopkeepers, and, eventually, an elderly fisherman. Histories of water systems, colonial oppression, and the origins of the Sri Lankan flag all contribute to a deeper understanding of place. Contradictions and conflict are integral to the shared space and welcomed as moments of learning, creating the energy to move forward with greater insight.

In the Second Lagoon, which documents the Sea Grant research, the Witness questions the Lagoon Maker's ambitious plans, including the extent to which the transposition from specific circumstances in Sri Lanka to the laboratory in California can produce the desired outcome – a functioning web of life.

> *But*
> *the tank is not a lagoon*
> *nor is it a tidal pond*
> *nor does the mixing of fresh and salt waters*
> *make it an estuary*
> *Filters are not the cleansing of the tides*
> *water from the hose is not a monsoon*
> *lights and heaters are not the sun*
> *and crabs in the tank do not make a life web*

> > But
> > the tank is part of an experiment
> > and the experiment is the metaphor for a lagoon
> > if the metaphor works
> > the experiment will succeed
> > and the crabs will flourish
> > after all
> > this metaphor is only a representation
> > based on observing a crab in a lagoon
> > and listening to stories
> Second Lagoon/44

The exchange, back and forth, generates possible courses of action. This learning is particularly evident through a key passage in which one of the critical aspects of the 'Introduction' is revisited.

If
the experiment isolates parts of a real lagoon
and places them in a tank
then the metaphor also refers to alienation
to violation
to breaking the integrity of a real system
After all a lagoon is self-nourishing
self-cleansing
self-adjusting
If a niche is emptied
other elements adapt to fill it

Then
suppose we adapt ourselves
to supply what the crab needs
then we become part of the experiment
and as we niche ourselves in
the system becomes
self-nourishing
self-cleansing
self-adjusting
then the metaphor for nature becomes
more complete
and we cannot represent this system
without representing ourselves
Second Lagoon/44

In questioning whether artificial tanks can ever function like a system in nature, the Lagoon Maker proposes to break the 'taboo' of science in which objects of enquiry, despite their physicality, are construed to be independent of any event in which they are perceived (Stengers 2011, 98).

The Witness and the Lagoon Maker's voices frequently contradict each other's strong opinions and hold contradictions in tension. This creates a vital space of exchange in which a search for rational 'truth' is replaced by a search for meaning. Their leap of imagination marks a transition from an intention to develop the aquaculture system to inhabiting a radically different imaginary. It brings two very different landscapes – the Colorado watershed (including the Salton Sea, the Pacific, and the Gulf) and Sri Lanka – into relation with each other in terms of forms of water management as well as histories. Multiple ways of knowing the landscapes as well as the crab at the heart of the story are interwoven and become generative of new possibilities.

Inventing a field

Stengers offers us the idea of 'inventing a field' as a component of breaking out of the twin traps of the bifurcation – it is not an explicit idea in Whitehead, although it is implied in the description of the 'method of discovery'. The Harrisons in a reflective essay in 2007 frame it as 'creating a field of play', conceiving of this as a compositional exercise whether imagined in a painting, an installation, or a watershed scale (2007b, n.p.). They understand the field of play is a temporary device with both spatial and temporal aspects creating a moment through which problems or questions come to be defined in ways that are meaningful. It is a way to imagine a problem unconventionally, in fact to challenge convention. The Harrisons' field of play is about raising questions to understand specific places ecologically. It is both conceptual and physical. Creating a 'field of play' in this double sense is a process at the heart of the Harrisons' practice, exemplified in every work, and discussed in their writings (2007b, n.p.). They draw attention to when the making of boundaries becomes absurd (*Meditation on the Great Lakes of North America* (1977)) (fig.51). *The Lagoon Cycle* addresses both physical and conceptual boundaries found in nature, such as a watershed, and those constructed in culture and politics, such as the boundaries of nation states. These boundaries 'increase' and 'decrease' depending on the energy that is internal and available to both nature and culture. These boundaries live and breathe, respond to force and counter force, and converse with their surroundings. This version of boundary is contrasted with the mental boundaries of the character of the scientist who encourages industrial methods of crab farming. Shifting between natural and cultural boundaries to those of disciplines, it becomes evident that different boundaries produce different fields, questions, and insights. The artists' choice of flexible boundaries and rejection of rigid boundaries creates a field that in turn becomes a 'playground', a system 'where constancy is always at risk/and life is tuned to stress', a system that could develop a life of its own (Third Lagoon/61). *The Lagoon Cycle* is in itself a field of play, a temporary device that appears to address a particular problem, but ends up, rather than resolving it, recognising that a much bigger challenge to survival is in process. It is precisely a space in which the 'problem' of survival comes to be defined meaningfully.

Adventure

The Lagoon Cycle begins as an experiment in technoscience and becomes an adventure, an important concept for Whitehead as well as for Stengers, and that, in Stengers' construction, none of the assumptions of what conventionally constitutes science, nor indeed art, remain unquestioned. For the Harrisons, conventions in scientific method give way to intuition and improvisation, a more open-ended, experiential form of enquiry that is no less rigorous but differently inflected. Intuition is a critical part of improvisation.

In the Seventh Lagoon: The Ring of Fire, The Ring of Water the Witness recounts a dream in which the elements of stone, earth, wood, fire, and water are experienced at a domestic scale, as an ensemble around a picnic bench, as a test of sorts as to whether a human could undertake any form of communication of any kind with the elements.

Let me tell you a dream
I was in a stone space
that was an earth space
that was a wood space
that was the cellar of a castle

I was sitting on a wooden picnic bench
at a round oak table
with an ensemble of others
who had no shape or form
that I could discern

It was a test
an examination of sorts
I grasped that I was in the company
of earth   of water   of rock and stone
and the issue was whether any communication
at all   of any kind
could take place

The Witness wakes to the insight

[...] knowing that the business of the universe
is conducted in an odd kind of dialogue
Seventh Lagoon/91

The dream starts a sequence of intuitions, an important aspect of Whitehead's conception of 'adventure', and an important aspect of the Harrisons' work. The Lagoon Maker responds to the Witness' intuition with a sequence of realisations about the Pacific Ocean, each one introduced with 'and in less than a second/I can [...]' The Harrisons provide a vivid description of their experience of intuition in another work, *Green Heart Vision* (1994).

Finally   we become exhausted with
reviewing so many plans
ecological   or urban   or agricultural

and so much driving the landscape
and so much studying of maps
and paying attention
to so many intense desires
often conflicting
and paying attention
to so much careful planning.
We know this exhaustion
it is the best kind
almost exhilarating
the shocking sensation
of so much overload
that the mind grows silent
and desire fades
and   in the   ensuing quiet
an image
will come
into being.
(H. M. Harrison and Harrison 1995, 3)

If intuition is the result of immersion in a context, it is through improvisation as a way of experiencing the world on its terms that ecological insights emerge. The Harrisons describe the workings of 'nature' and 'culture' in terms of an 'adventure' in passages that mirror each other, intentionally suggesting that they follow very similar patterns of behaviour. In the First Lagoon this reflection on culture follows a complex investigation into the culture of Sri Lanka, its deep history of conflict through to the present in a new wave of colonisation from the West. In the Third Lagoon 'nature' is characterised through the phenomenon of an estuarial lagoon, a particular feature of Sri Lanka and habitat for the crab. It is noticeable that the passage on 'culture' carries a sense of irony and also fragility that is absent from that of 'nature', a notion that chimes with the Harrisons' developing sense that it is nature that dictates the terms of survival to which we need to attend carefully. The emboldening in the following passages is that of the authors for the purposes of emphasis and not in the original text.

A culture is

And I thought
A culture is a cooperative adventure   *a complex system*
of shared interrelated beliefs   about the nature of reality
First Lagoon/37

And later:

> **An estuarial lagoon** is the place where fresh and salt
> waters meet and mix   It is a fragile meeting and
> mixing   not having the constancy of the oceans
> or the rivers   It **is a collaborative adventure**
> Its existence always at risk
> Third Lagoon/60

Adventure suggests an experience that is the out of the ordinary, risky, daring – abundance leading to sudden growth; the risk of scarcity decreasing a population; the risk of heavy rains expanding the estuarial lagoon, while increasing nutrients and decreasing salts; the risk of invasion by conquerors and the risk of forest fires and rains reducing a lagoon to a mud flat and then a swamp. In these adventures, everything is open to radical change.

> *But people are tough   and resilient   and improvise*
> *their existence as best they can   very creatively   with*
> *the materials to hand* **but the materials keep changing**
> **only the improvisation remains constant**
> First Lagoon/37

> Life in the lagoons is tough and very rich
> It breeds quickly   Like all of us it must improvise its
> existence   very creatively   with the materials at
> hand   **but the materials keep changing   Only the**
> **improvisation remains constant**
> Third Lagoon/60

There are subtle reversals at play in these mirroring passages. Constancy comes in the form of change and a state of always being 'at risk'. Adaptation to change takes the form of improvisation, a condition for survival itself, such as the estuarial lagoon that evolves high tolerance to sudden changes in water quality, temperature, and available food. 'Improvisation' and 'system' unexpectedly flip their conventional meanings, taking on the sense and character of the other, but never quite. Culture is a system of beliefs, values, codes of conduct, and ethics. It is a system that is also improvised. The estuarial lagoon is a place and a fragile meeting of fresh and salt water that is generative of life itself, another system created through improvisation. The relationship between system and improvisation runs through the whole work. It is enacted in the prologue:

I said
What would happen if I told the story just as
it occurred

You said
How could you
Every time we recreate the past it is different

I said
Then let us reinvent ourselves

You said
We are always doing that anyway
Introduction/26

The idea of improvisation emerges in the First Lagoon. The name given to Sri Lanka by the Arabs in one of the many invasions, was 'Serendip', supposedly the origin of the word 'serendipity', the notion of something occurring by chance but in a fortunate or beneficial way (First Lagoon/35). Chance and risk are closely aligned in improvisation, along with the fear of arbitrariness and the fear of predictability (Peters 2017, 109–12). Countries are systems. Noticing this name in Sri Lanka's history in the First Lagoon intentionally evokes improvisation as a way of imaging culture.

In moving beyond the strict scientific methods adopted for the Sea Grant research, the Harrisons, as noted above, rethink their experiment in terms of an improvisation.

> Let us improvise a lagoon that is tough
> and resilient
> Let it have a becoming complexity
Third Lagoon/61

They encounter conditions in the Salton Sea, the proposed site for industrial farming, that are already so depleted that the potential for an ecological improvisation, which would manifest high tolerance to stress and enable rapid breeding, is cancelled out. The idea of an 'improvised lagoon' proves impossible, reinstating the existing industrialised system of farming as the only option in the circumstances (Fourth Lagoon/71). This conclusion is chilling and is followed in the Fifth Lagoon by a series of scenarios, 'If [...] Then [...]' that trace the wider implications of continuing to farm industrially to the detriment of the environment. Using the Salton Sea as a repository for agricultural and municipal wastes cancels recreational functions such as swimming and fishing, and vice versa. Increasing the salinity of the water reduces the lower biota in the food chain, simplifying the biomass. On the other hand, if the salinity, herbicide, and pesticide levels are reduced, the biomass can self-complicate. The only way to restore the Salton Sea is to flush it by means of the ocean, cutting channels to the Pacific or through the Colorado River delta to the Gulf of Mexico, processes that would not only be astronomically expensive, but also highly destructive of the ecologies of both oceans.

> *For*
> *if you flush the Salton Sea and make it into an estuarial*
> *lagoon   by cutting input-output channels with locks and*
> *pumps   northward to the Pacific   or southward to the*
> *gulf*
> *then*
> *360 square miles of oversaline water   contaminated*
> *with herbicides   and pesticides   minerals   and metals*
> *will be transferred to the Pacific   or to the gulf   and as*
> *long as the irrigated agriculture continues   so will the*
> *contamination*
> *Then*
> *who will flush the ocean*
> *who will flush the gulf*
> Fifth Lagoon/79

In these passages our understanding of culture and nature – so often so problematically separated – are not conflated but are brought into a relationship where key aspects are recognised as 'mirroring' through the shared dynamic provided by improvisation. What we might normally assume as the scope of a Sea Grant funded research project is scrutinised through a much wider and deeper frame of questions. The assumption that productivity is the objective is brought into question by attending to the wider 'costs'. In one reading the venture into technoscience and innovation is exposed as fundamentally flawed and in fact dangerous to wider ecosystems in the Gulf and the Pacific. On another reading, the venture becomes an adventure.

Storytelling

Where for Stengers storytelling is an approach that is open and plural, supporting the process of experimentation through multiple viewpoints, the Harrisons say:

> We hold that the universe is a multileveled discourse, a conversation in many languages – biological, chemical, physical – most of which we cannot even perceive, much less understand. Within this discourse, every place is bespeaking the story of its own becoming. Everyone is in this conversation, as is everything. Consciousness

offers us the possibility of choosing our place and the quality of our voice in this continuous speaking, learning, responding. (Matilsky 1992, 72)

This resonates with the dream, *'[...] the business of the universe/is conducted in an odd kind of dialogue'* (Seventh Lagoon/91). The Harrisons' expansion of discourse and the role of storytelling to encompass different forms of existence (physical and chemical as well as biological) and recognise implicitly different timescales, magnifies multiple viewpoints, as well as the meaning of openness and plurality. It also highlights that the bifurcation – what we can experience and what we need of technologies to be able to understand – is not 'resolvable' but rather needs to be recognised as a dynamic we are enmeshed within that can be approached differently.

Storytelling in *The Lagoon Cycle* is multi-layered. It is a story focused by a crab that is good to eat. It is a story about colonialism and the collision of values between native inhabitants and conquerors. It is a story about economies, ecologies, and fragility experienced through the clash between indigenous knowledge that is relational, recognising interdependence between living things (First Lagoon), and Western knowledge that extracts, models, and exploits (Second, Third, Fourth, Fifth Lagoons). The Harrisons describe the work as a love story in which they uncover the power of empathy (Sixth and Seventh Lagoons) and it is through empathy that they break through to new ways of imagining and connecting to the world (Sixth and Seventh Lagoons).

What is particularly interesting is the way in which the story is told as an artwork. A sense of adventure, of daring, offers a work that cannot be easily niched into the aesthetic traditions of visual art, performance or installation, poetry or literature, but draws on all these forms. An epic poem, normally told and retold as a story, becomes a physical environment in *The Lagoon Cycle* of such a scale as to mimic the frescoes of a Renaissance cathedral, albeit breaking with those conventions of storytelling purely through images. Modernist art and the Greenbergian aesthetics of the time would have eschewed the narrative element that is core to this work as art, but arguably it is precisely this narrative element that is its most radical element, acting as a second space not just within the work itself, but also in making space for a shift in thinking and the imagination that is profoundly ecological.

We might also read the work as a feminist work in the terms described by Arlene Raven. Raven defines the work of feminist art of the time in ways that correspond to our exploration of storytelling and empathy: she lists *The Lagoon Cycle* in her chronology of feminist works (1983, xii). Feminism, as developed by Raven, extends empathy from a purely interpersonal experience into one that is concerned with building a world in common.

Feminist artists, especially, search for forms which can reach from one's own experience to embrace the varied circumstances of other people's lives. Conversely, new forms continually emerge *from* the gathering of people to share with one another and to work together. (Raven 1983, 29 italics in the original)

There are two striking qualities to the Harrisons' approach to narrative, qualities that they continue to develop throughout their lives. First, the narrative is based in their experience, but it is narrated as a myth or epic rather than as a history or biography. The real-life experience of visiting Sri Lanka, the natural habitat of the crab, came last for the Harrisons, that is, after the 'scientific' research had been completed, but in the work of art, it constitutes the First Lagoon. The Second to Sixth Lagoons predated the first in actual historical time (as they say in the Introduction, 'We didn't know it had begun until we/were already in the middle [...]' In examining myth as a philosopher and anthropologist, Levi-Strauss prioritises myth's function to make meaning. While it may be impossible to understand myths as a continuous sequence, he argues, that is, line by line, left to right, they nonetheless introduce order. Myths make meaning and it is impossible to conceive of meaning without order. Myth making across all cultures is a form of conceptual thinking, a way of introducing order into a world that is apparently chaotic: 'because the human mind is only part of the universe, the need [for myths] probably exists because there is some order in the universe and the universe is not chaos' (Lévi-Strauss 2003, 9). He makes an analogy between myths and (largely Western) music in which it is necessary to remain conscious of the totality of the whole through 'bundles of events' that appear in different moments of the story. Could this be an appropriate way to experience *The Lagoon Cycle*? What does it reveal? The Introduction can be understood as the motif introducing the key themes. In the First Lagoon the Witness and the Lagoon Maker have quite different concerns and their dialogue is sometimes at cross purposes. According to de Certeau, the whole work can be considered a fugue.

> Like a fugue, *The Lagoon Cycle* multiplies the possible modulations of dialogue in a system in which they echo each other endlessly in different tones and registers. (de Certeau in H. M. Harrison and Harrison 1985b, 21)

It is through the dialogue between the Lagoon Maker and the Witness, and with the various knowledgeable individuals, including the fisherman and the politicians and even the tourists, that they become sensitive to the differences between ways of knowing through experience and those of deduction and simplification. One might argue that recognising and exploring this difference, which we have characterised as one dimension of the bifurcation of nature, becomes an organising principle through which the meaning of the whole work is revealed to them once they have reflected upon what they have undergone. The bundles of events that Levi-Strauss refers to is here experienced through the discrete 'episodes' or 'lagoons' that effectively are the bundling together of a number of diverse and real life 'projects' and experiences. Taking form through conversation as poetry their experience takes on new meaning. The work opens and ends with questions that remain unresolved, constructing a space between the artists and the viewer/audience/spectator. It is this quality of 'in between-ness' that makes the work of *The Lagoon Cycle* a political work, one that invites the questioning and participation explored in Chapter 6.

For Stengers, storytelling is significant because it counters the idea that there is a 'right answer' and enables 'instead to put what are often difficult choices on the table, necessitating a process of hesitation, concentration and attentive scrutiny' (Stengers 2018, 3–4). This approach to knowledge places 'values' alongside 'facts', retaining the freedom to ask certain questions that conventional science normally disallows. *The Lagoon Cycle* offers a complex but compelling case for mixing 'facts' with 'values'. This is evident in the way that storytelling encompasses multiple viewpoints. The combination of text and image provides both the 'real' and a range of the 'possible'. The text shares with the reader a wide range of perspectives encountered by the Witness and the Lagoon Maker as well as their process of coming to a shared understanding, beginning with the challenge of a previous failed experiment (*Portable Fish Farm*) through to the new experiment undertaken rigorously and with the support of a research grant. The full exploration of the ramifications by means of storytelling leads them to abandon the aquaculture project. If we understand that storytelling is both the form of *The Lagoon Cycle* and also the method that is being used by the Harrisons in its development, then the process can also lead to a new understanding at a different level, an abandonment of what was taken for granted. In this case the assumption that survival is served by scientific research into the production of new sources of food is tested and its deep flaws and assumptions, in particular the absence of 'values' in the creation of 'facts', are exposed.

In what sense is *The Lagoon Cycle* an event?

Whitehead shifts our attention from substances to events. *The Lagoon Cycle* is both a sequence of activities and encounters that the artists experienced, and also an artwork that retells those in a harmonious narrative and material form. However, to read this as an event in Whitehead's terms must be to understand it as a totality in which the exhibited work is an element of the whole experience of research, learning, and artistic production.

Each Lagoon is focused by an actual experience – the First Lagoon by visiting Sri Lanka; the Second by doing the scientific research in the laboratory; the Third by how the research was responded to; the Fourth by speculating on a large-scale polycultural aquaculture system in the Colorado Desert; the Fifth by the analysis of consequences; the Sixth by connecting this analysis with the alternative of the Sri Lankan system of water tanks that are niched into their environment; and the Seventh by the intuitive leap to the larger issue of climate change, and the dream that raises the question of participating in the dialogue of the universe. The Introduction is the negotiation of a partnership and a reality between two people.

The Lagoon Cycle developed iteratively and was exhibited in sketches and versions of parts from 1974 – in that year a version of the Fourth Lagoon was exhibited at the Ronald Feldman Gallery.[8] Significant portions were included in the 'Dialogue,

Discourse, Research' exhibition at the Santa Barbara Museum of Art (Spurlock 1979) and it is clear that the work was continually being revised,[9] generating new iterations. The exhibition of the complete cycle in 1985 is a transition but not the end in Whitehead's conception. The Introduction to the complete cycle narrates the logic of telling the story in public. For Whitehead a 'perishing' is where something else becomes possible. For artists the decision that a work is finished enough to put into public is a particular form of perishing, offering new potential for experience and conversation.

The exhibition of the complete cycle in 1985, its 'perishing', allows the work to take on a new role. The creation of the exhibited version was possible thanks to the support of John Kluge and his company Metromedia, Inc. and it was subsequently purchased by the Centre Pompidou-Metz in Paris, France, and remains in the collection of that museum. The Harrisons themselves continued to perform the work through readings, for instance in the authors' direct experience during the development of *Greenhouse Britain*, and the Harrisons ascribed it a wider role informing all their subsequent works. In Whitehead's sense of event, the event of *The Lagoon Cycle* continued and perhaps continues. The Harrisons had their own understanding of this process as 'conversational drift' that includes the creation of a work, and its life once it becomes a part of the world through exhibition and performance.

Conclusions

As an artwork *The Lagoon Cycle* presents us with a whole way of seeing and feeling that cannot be reduced to 'extractable content' or 'emotional resources' (Latour 2020). The Harrisons begin with a daring question, one that is of our time and for which there is no readily available answer, that is, the question of survival, of how we feed ourselves in ways that support the web of life. Through the work we undergo an experience of researching this bold question. Their experience leads the enquiry and as audiences we become participants and interlocutors folded into their journey through the pattern of images – maps, aerial and other photographs, collages and drawings – as well as the handwritten text. We doubt with them, resist certain assumptions, question, sense, dream, and interpret experiences as they unfold. Their poetics of dialogue and discourse articulated in text and image lead us through a process of search and re-search in which what comes to be known is never separated from how something is known or why it is important/not important. The Harrisons construct a dialogue between questions of 'what' in relation to questions of 'how' and why it matters. In this way, the Harrisons establish and develop in this work a process that anyone can follow, adopt, adapt, and use in their own ways because of the clarity with which it is presented, though they demand by implication that such following must be rigorous. In this sense the work is a search for meaning rather than 'truth'.

The Lagoon Cycle as an exhibited work reconstructs a period of life, recognising the connectedness of a set of actual occasions, from working with the crabs through to dreams and intuitions. Whitehead's conception is based in faith in the order of nature. He says,

> To experience this faith is to know that in being ourselves we are more than ourselves: to know that our experience, dim and fragmentary as it is, yet sounds the utmost depths of reality: to know that detached details merely in order to be themselves demand that we should find themselves in a system of things: to know that this system includes the harmony of logical rationality, and the harmony of aesthetic achievement: to know that, while the harmony of logic lies upon the universe as an iron necessity, the aesthetic harmony stands before it as a living ideal moulding the general flux in its broken progress towards subtler, finer issues. (Whitehead 2022, 20)

Whitehead is using system in a very different sense from that of late 20th century engineering and cybernetics. As a scientist he was looking for a single idea of the universe, a focus that many philosophers might have disagreed with. This single idea needed to embrace the ongoing dynamic of organic life achieving satisfaction or harmony, as a process of emergence and as observed by humans through perception, the imagination, and aesthetics.

The Lagoon Cycle offers an aesthetic and a form of practice that profoundly shifts what we might expect from art, that is, not just to be moved, but to use both skill and intuition to question and follow through with where such questioning takes us. The voices of individual participants carry quite distinctive perspectives. The Harrisons' poetics are political. They acknowledge that life around us is changing rapidly. They construct a relation with that change through which we have the opportunity to become agents and not victims of circumstances. We engage as unique individuals within the creation of a common world.

It is in this particular work that two key foundational aesthetic ideas, improvisation and systems, become explicit and harnessed. Improvisation is a process of judging determinacy and indeterminacy. It displaces the dominant tendency in science to remove uncertainty wherever possible with an entirely different quality of encounter. Uncertainty is embraced as a state of being, a rhythm to follow, to journey across. Inconsistency and contradiction become opportunities to play, at times viewed from the distance of irony, at others harnessed as the reason to change course and open up a much bigger set of horizons. It is also here that ambiguity becomes a powerful tool to leverage thinking. Systems are understood as literal processes of movement of water, feeding of crabs, processing of waste. Systems can be constructed at different scales (the proposal for the acquaculture system in the Colorado desert, and the proposal for flushing the Salton Sea). Ecosystems such as Lagoons can appear to provide models for man-made systems, revealing the role of metaphors in these translations. Colonialism is embraced as modernisation as well as destruction. Play and adventure are at work in inventing the fields in which problems can find solutions.

In the following sections of the book, we will focus on the relation between 'system' and 'improvisation' and between 'discourse' and 'the political' as they appear in this and other early works because these are not only key qualities within their particular approach as artists; they are also potentially powerful in the development of the arts' relation to ecology.

CHAPTER 4

On Improvisation

In the last chapter focusing on *The Lagoon Cycle*, improvisation emerged as a key aspect of the Harrisons' 'leap of the imagination', bringing nature and culture into a dynamic in ways that profoundly question the basic assumptions around how the world works.[1] This chapter changes pace from a diachronic analysis of their work, to explore improvisation as a significant aspect of the Harrisons' poetics as they develop a new form of art in response to their focus on the environment. Each section of the chapter scrutinises a particular quality of improvisation as a formal approach in art making in relation to their work. Drawing on different approaches across the arts and across different cultures and histories of improvisation, the goal is to enrich our understandings of how everyday meanings of improvisation such as 'making it up as you go along' or 'using the materials to hand' become harnessed within highly skilled practices in art. These practices deepen and intensify our understanding of the Harrisons' work. These different manifestations connect improvisation with the way Whitehead develops his notion of event as emergent life. Improvisation is foundational to how the Harrisons work in the world and how the world works within them as artists. While they are not improvisers in a strictly formal sense in the arts, improvisation underpins a sensibility in their work, an approach to ideas and observations that connect them to the environments and publics in and with which they work.

The field research in Sri Lanka narrated in the First Lagoon explores culture as improvisation through the deep and complex histories of the island along with its experience of 'modernisation', a new wave of colonisation among many that the island has experienced throughout its history. These experiences are dynamic, 'an adventure' in living in relation to other human beings and 'in discourse' with land and sea, dependent upon available energies, responsive to forces of change both within and without, such as access to food and the playing out of competing interests, mostly from other humans. Improvisation in culture, they suggest, is inherent to the human condition. By the Third Lagoon, this way of imagining culture enables the Harrisons to recognise improvisation in nature as similarly dynamic – an interplay between the crab, estuarial lagoon, and local irrigation system. They generate the two passages by repeating phrases, words, and ideas in a mirroring of nature and culture through the construct of improvisation (First Lagoon/37 and Third Lagoon/60 quoted in the previous chapter).

These two passages in the First and Third Lagoons spark new possibilities in the Harrisons' imagination. The Lagoon Maker speculates on how the experiment in fish farming might be imagined as an estuarial lagoon, and an alternative to a highly controlled scientific experiment. It opens their research to the spirit of an adventure through which they might incorporate changes of state, resilience, and the accommodation of stress. Designing a system as an estuarial lagoon, however, proves to be overwhelmingly challenging. By tracing the implications of this imaginary, they recognise that their site, in the Colorado Desert near the Salton Sea, is already too damaged and further intervention puts at risk a whole ecosystem stretching from the Gulf of California to the Pacific (Fifth Lagoon). In framing their experiment as an improvisation, the Harrisons' attention focuses on 'paying attention to advantage and disadvantage' (Sixth Lagoon/88), that is, to the choices that are made where humans intervene in natural systems through technoscience and industrialisation (Sixth Lagoon). In the Sixth and Seventh Lagoons, their understanding of improvisation deepens, first in relation to the Colorado River and Gulf of California, where the natural ebb and flow of fresh and salt water is interrupted to give advantage to irrigation, urbanisation, and industrialisation, and then in relation to the lagoons of Sri Lanka, where the tanks, in contrast to the Colorado, have become part of the web of life, supporting life through an exchange of energy that is co-operative. The difference between an industrialised system and an ecological one is then poignantly evoked in the example of the tractor displacing the water buffalo (Seventh Lagoon). The tractor is first appraised as 'a bold invention/ an improvisation that will change the state of farming' (Seventh Lagoon/94) because it is 'more efficient' in terms of short timescales, modern, and cheap, bringing people into the technological domain. It does not, however, have the complexity of the water buffalo that replicates itself freely, providing milk, utilising weeds, producing fertiliser and fuel from its dung. In fact, the tractor turns the several thousand-year-old discourse and collaboration between the buffalo and its habitat into a 'technological monologue' subtracting possibilities, eventually extinguishing the fish that eat the larvae of the malaria mosquito and the snake that eats the vermin by destroying the complex interdependencies within their habitats (Seventh Lagoon/95).

In these passages improvisation becomes a way of imagining and becoming attuned to the inconsistencies and contradictions, the contingencies within living systems. The Harrisons articulate this clearly some 20 years later in discussion of their work *Peninsula Europe: The High Grounds, Bringing Forth a New State of Mind* (H. M. Harrison and Harrison 2001c).

[W]e have come to believe that inconsistency and contradiction are generated by the processes of cognition, thinking, and doing, and have the important role to play of stimulating and evoking creativity and improvisation which are inherent in the processes of the mind that have led us to do this work. (H. M. Harrison and Harrison 2007b, n.p.)

The juxtaposition of cooperation within natural systems where interventions are niched as parts of the web of life, such as the Sri Lankan lagoons (*The Lagoon Cycle*) or the high grounds of Asia (*Tibet is the High Ground* (1993)), compared with the extractive practices such as those of the Colorado catchment or channelled waters of the lower sections of European rivers respectively, expose the West's dependence upon high-energy consumption that characterises high entropy systems of industrialisation. The latter constitutes a kind of backwards skewed thinking that eventually destroys life, in contrast to living cycles of taking and returning that are generative of new life. Improvisation facilitates the 'leap of the imagination' that Whitehead suggests is key to a philosophy of the organism. It sets in motion a new adventure as an experience that makes sense of the world differently. In *Peninsula Europe*, for example, this takes form as a proposal to allow rivers to flood. The costs of flood damage, they argue, is five times less than the costs of repairs (H. M. Harrison and Harrison 2007b, n.p.).

What is improvisation?

In everyday life we tend to emphasise the meaning of improvisation in terms of spontaneity, a lack of preparation or planning, making do with the materials to hand, the amateurish or make-shift. For educational philosophers like John Dewey (1859–1952) spontaneity is essential to learning through experience. Being open and responsive to the world through the senses is a way of offering oneself to the world. We make simple actions in everyday life such as picking up a stone. The world pushes back, inviting us to feel the stone's qualities of weight, texture, and colour (Dewey 2005). Whitehead, who was a great admirer of Dewey, shares with him this way of building knowledge through experiences in the world. Learning, for both, begins in experience. Where an experimental endeavour in technoscience might set out to validate and verify anticipated epistemic constructions and concepts, the experimental act here inverts this trajectory. Being responsive to the unexpected demands an openness to what is as yet unknown and unforeseen.

Brian Massumi, philosopher and social theorist, connects experience with improvisation through play in animals, including humans. In search of a different form of politics, he turns to play to set aside deterministic narratives of environmental relations from Darwin onwards, such as ascribing mutations purely to chance, or restricting adaptation to mean adapting to an unchanging environment. Play foregoes use-value and opens a different space and quality of experience that has value for its own sake. It is in this free space, he argues, that something new can occur. It emerges out of the opportunity and desire for variation. Evoking Whitehead's construction of event, Massumi suggests that play is a place of inclusion, spontaneity, and communication. Play fights in wolf cubs mobilise the paradox between fight and play, positioning it on a knife edge. If the bite of the wolf cub is too hard, play becomes fight. Communicating through play is how the wolf cub learns to fight. There is a certain 'ludic excess' that is surplus to life as mere survival. Play is non-conforming, open to variation and novelty.

> The gap between the ludic gesture and its analogue creates a margin of manoeuvre: it opens the door to improvisation…It is actually the power of variation learned in play, the improvisational prowess it hones that gives an animal the upper hand in combat, or in flight from a predator. (Massumi 2014, 12)

Hallam and Ingold, as anthropologists, develop the idea of improvisation as a necessary and spontaneous way of coping with the world (Hallam and Ingold 2007, Douglas and Coessens 2012). They have observed improvisation across cultures and experienced how imagination, thought, and action again and again come together in situations that are both specific and unforeseen. Improvisation is dynamic, never static, never perfectly repeatable. They attribute four characteristics to improvisation. First, it is *generative*, meaning that it always creates something different, however minimally. Even in imitating, we encounter the unexpected in terms of time, the context we find ourselves in, and how we happen to be feeling. Our actions unfold differently as a result, generating variations. Second, improvisation, as indicated above, is *relational*, continuously directed towards the other, another living thing or another culture. In that sense improvisation is both socially and environmentally generative: it brings new elements into our interactions with others, humans and the more than human. It is also materially generative, an interaction between one's own body and the inner and outer world. Third, improvisation, they argue, is *time-dependent*: it is always part of a dynamic ongoing action or process, an event that is experienced in and adds to the narrative of life. It disrupts the order normally associated with chronological time: different improvisations all relate differently to different times, dependent on what came before and what comes after. Fourth and finally, echoing the Harrisons, it is 'the way we work': improvisation as an *inherent part of our human condition* becomes clear in addressing the space between living beings, the aliveness of that space, the necessity to be on one's toes in the light of ongoing change, open to the contingent while at the same time carrying over some stable element, a sense or feel for a common world.

An instrument in skilled hands

The Harrisons amply evidence the four characteristics: as a way of thinking and being in the world that is relational, generative, time-dependent, and inherent not just to the human condition, but to that of all living things. These constructs run like a leitmotif through *The Lagoon Cycle*. The play between freedom and constraint, a pairing that Whitehead also works with, is evident in the meeting of fresh and salt water in an estuarial lagoon along with the fluctuations of abundance and scarcity in cultures, always at risk and changeable.

> The human being is inseparable from its environment in each occasion of its existence. The environment which the occasion inherits is immanent in it, and conversely is immanent in the environment which it helps to transmit. (Whitehead 1985, 63)

This relation, human to environment, animal to animal and so on, is not predetermined, and like an instrument in skilled hands it can come alive with each moment of experience. That said, the flash of a new idea, spontaneity, needs to be sustained, 'co-ordinated' with its environment, to gain traction. The process of perishing of the immediate experience is a process of transition from satisfaction to becoming new potential for the next occasion of experience (Whitehead 1978, 85). Sustaining the tension between constraint and freedom is crucial to this process. For the wolf cub this is a knife edge between play and fight. In art, skill is also involved, that of handling an instrument, tool, or material where the crucial threshold may be a quality of feeling, of a work being alive or lifeless, or where radical experimentation loses an audience. Improvisation in art is a context in which skilled judgement in relation to constraint and freedom is carefully honed and given form through a diversity of approaches and at different stages of a work's development. The Harrisons' resolved works at the point of public exhibition are not obviously improvised. That said, we are invited again and again to understand their work in terms of improvisation as this, the Harrisons argue, is crucial to their ecological imagination. How might we then think about the relationship between form and content in their art? Are we experiencing dissonance between what the Harrisons talk about in the work and how they practice and give form to their work?

Terry Eagleton (b. 1943), the literary theorist, explores the significance of form to content in the work of Raymond Williams (1921–1988), a radical figure in modern literary criticism, and this is helpful here in understanding improvisation as a corporeal practice that is fundamental to the Harrisons' approach.

> He [Raymond Williams] was already preoccupied by what one might call the politics of form – of how a way of seeing or feeling, one with powerful political implications, is inherent in the structures and conventions of a work of art, not simply in its extractable content. (Eagleton 2022, 260)

Eagleton is suggesting that the integrity of form and content is important for understanding how the works of artists live within us as experiences and are formative of the ways we think and act in the world. Williams was critical of the dramatic naturalism of 19th- and 20th-century theatre, of creating an illusion of reality by representing a familiar world on stage, a world that in its realism appears to be immune to change.

> If the theatre was to reveal the anguished subjectivity of modern life, shaped as it is by the pressures of the unconscious, it would need to ditch the sofa and sideboard and draw instead on the resources of dream, fantasy and unconscious desire. (Eagleton 2022, 263)

This plea for a different form of theatre echoes Ghosh's criticism of the novel and its struggle to address climate change because of the way it apparently conserves the existing reality (Ghosh 2016). We explored this point in Chapter 1. Existing forms become unsuitable, 'inert' in Whitehead's terms, and close off perception and experience of the world we find ourselves in, rather than opening them up to change. Both perspectives, Eagleton and Ghosh, imply that art that addresses the environmental crisis demands a radically different form appropriate to these circumstances. To what extent might improvisation be critical to this?

Practices of improvisation in art vary considerably in the relation of freedom to constraint. Gary Peters, a free jazz improvisor and philosopher, points to two radically different forms. On the one hand, in traditions such as Balinese, Indian, and Flamenco, the performer draws on a host of predetermined codes, sources, rules, and practices. In these traditions, the performer in the moment of a performance in a sense 'unfixes' what is given or pre-existing, working with a vast reservoir of memory. The presence of such codes and rules often draws the criticism that works improvised in this way can sound the same. They are very conservative, risking 'mere repetition'. On the other hand, in contrast, the radical theatre of Anton Artaud (1896–1948) begins with a series of experiments (improvisations) that are eventually notated, 'fixed'. Artaud seeks to avoid the cliché of improvisation as a demonstration of capriciousness of the inspired individual. He even raises the question of whether there is a place at all for improvisation in the moment of the performance in this second modality but even he acknowledges that a sense of life, of the contingent, can never be inscribed in the text by the play or playwright. It needs the performance to come alive (Peters 2009, 94). The text-based scores of Allan Kaprow (1927–2006) like the scores created within the Fluxus movement, might be considered a third form of improvisation where a text takes the form of a riddle and invites a response in the form of performing an activity designed to destabilise everyday assumptions (Kaprow 2003; Friedman 1998).

The Lagoon Cycle is closest to improvisation in Artaud's sense of multiple improvised stages of development that reach a final resolution that is never an end. An interim public showing of the Fifth and Sixth Lagoons in 1979 at the Santa Barbara Museum of Art in an exhibition entitled 'Dialogue, Discourse, Research' reveals stages of earlier experimentation, many of which are edited out of the final work, as explored in Chapter 3 (Spurlock 1979). The configuration of text and image in the full-scale exhibition has been clearly determined by the artists rather than left open or indeterminate, unlike Kaprow scores. Even in the finalised works there are some minor variations between *The Lagoon Cycle* catalogue (1985b) and the *Book of the Lagoons*. The catalogue also clearly states that the Harrisons continually revised the text for performance.

The commonality between the Harrisons, Artaud, Balinese, Indian, and Flamenco and Fluxus-type thought experiments, is the freedom to create variation, to inhabit an in-between space and time where conformity is temporally suspended and the focus becomes the event itself, the potential for life within the exchange between the artist and their instrument or material, or between performers. Whitehead's description of event as an occasion of actual experience that draws on potential of different kinds fits with improvisation. This potential might be past experiences, cultural tropes, sounds, colours and tastes that are intrinsic to the world. Whatever the outcome, an actual occasion of experience is one in which the experience to hand is intensified and augmented, sometimes emerging as novel and, at others, as merely repetitive.

> Life lurks in the zone of indiscernibility of the criss-crossing of differences of every kind and degree. At every pulse of experience, with each occurring remix, there emerges a new variation on the continuum of life splayed across a multiplicity of co-implicating distinctions (Massumi, 2014, 34).

The Harrisons' work emerges between people, at times between each other as partners, and at other times, it draws in participants as interlocutors. Their written texts are made to be spoken aloud as frequently happened in their lifetimes in the context of lectures, interviews, and exhibitions. They suggested on many occasions that the purpose of the work was to 'explode in the mind of the interested person' (H. M. Harrison and Harrison 2001a, n.p.). Such performances were a way to start discussions at the beginning of projects, during projects, as part of the exhibition of projects, at each stage drawing participation and inviting response. By reflecting multiple voices, they keep contradictions alive and present, often with humour and a sense of irony. One example can be found in *Casting a Green Net* (1996–98) (fig. 50) in one of the sections entitled '...and stories were told'. This starts:

> He was a forester. He said wilderness areas had to come into being by themselves or not at all and he was against the manipulation of things. We asked if with that laissez-faire view, he was an optimist or a pessimist. He said that he was just a fatalist. (H. M. Harrison and Harrison 1998, n.p.)

The forester's voice is juxtaposed with that of the director of a large park, an earth scientist, a botanist, and a farmer. Prior to creating these passages shown as part of the final work, the Harrisons had undertaken intense fieldwork much like that in the First Lagoon of *The Lagoon Cycle*, becoming immersed, 'saturated' in the complexities of a specific place. Conflict and contradiction become a generative force to move forward rather than a battle to be won or lost, as they suggest 'stimulating and evoking creativity and improvisation' (H. M. Harrison and Harrison 2007b, n.p.). Once written, 'fixed' as part of the exhibition, the work becomes a resource for the Harrisons to draw from within a lecture performance, for example, telling their story to a live audience. They go further and propose that their works could become a resource for others to improvise with in new developments.

> We believe a vision, such as that embodied in 'Peninsula Europe', must have the power, the clarity, the timelessness, the openness of structure, and the ambiguity that will permit others to grasp it and work with it and test it, to create with it, to play with it, to improvise with it. (H. M. Harrison and Harrison 2007b, n.p.)

As noted earlier, Arlene Raven in her essay in the 'At Home' exhibition catalogue sees the resonances of this approach with feminism. She goes on to highlight how the Harrisons gather a support system to create works that enact the 'return...of natural resources or urban viability to these same groups'. This 'makes the people who experience their art the constituency sponsoring a project, the participants in the project, the audience, and the custodians' (Raven 1983, 33). A new and more complex relationship between artist and audience is made possible involving the audience in becoming not just 'custodians' of the original, but the next improvisers.

A fine line between communicability and adventure, between certitude and risk

For the improvising artist, constraint and freedom can be a question of judgement around what to determine and what to leave indeterminate. Such judgements preoccupied John Cage (1912–1992) over his lifetime as an avant-garde composer, musician, poet, essayist, and visual artist. He was always looking for tactics to sustain the unexpected in his work. He eschewed virtuosity in improvisation as deadening. It had become simplified out of the improviser's desire for certainty, the desire to protect formal structures from any serious disruption. Cage questioned this desire for certainty through radical experimentation, such as his 1952 composition *4'33"*. Like the Harrisons, Cage believed that uncertainty is a condition of life and therefore a core function of a work of art, but to become consciously present within the work of art, the artist needed to make choices in terms of which aspects of a composition to determine, and which to leave indeterminate. The composition *4'33"*, which involves no playing of instruments, formally frames the contingent. The score creates a specific time frame while not providing any 'content' in the Western convention of note-to-note notation. The only sounds heard are those of the audience, who effectively 'perform' the piece, inverting what is conventionally shut out, foregrounding ambient sound including the audience's coughs and sneezes. The audience co-creates the experience, ironically becoming the improviser over against the artist who provides a structure, a constraint perhaps, within which the improvisation within life itself comes into the foreground. In this way the artist's choices of control and release celebrate, intensify, and augment, uncertainty (Douglas 2018a, 18–19).

Determinacy and indeterminacy play out in the Harrisons' practice of conversational drift (mentioned in Chapters 1 and 3) in a similar way to Cage's *4'33*. The artists carefully frame or determine an opportunity for different perspectives to encounter each other in the issues of a particular project. The hope is that through this participation, a momentum is built as the conversation develops. The artists do not seek to control this momentum or its content, though they represent it in the exhibited works. In this sense conversational drift acts as a holding space, a sheltering of potential in Whitehead's thinking, in which something new might become possible. For Whitehead the direction of travel is from indeterminacy to determinacy, from incoherence to coherence. The process of 'concresence' within an event where potential moves towards satisfaction, is one in which indeterminacy 'evaporates' and potentiality passes into realisation (Whitehead 1978, 23).

There is a paradox at the heart of improvisation. We expect novelty but this is only possible in the presence of certitude, of patterns that are recognisable. Whitehead observes how history is often interpreted through constraint and freedom as a way of conferring value on what otherwise would be a meaningless succession of events (Whitehead 1985, 198). There is an equivalent in art to the meaningless succession of events in forms, styles, figures, codes, and tropes. These also need to be channelled meaningfully through the artist. It involves walking a tightrope between novelty and communicability. The Harrisons point to the dangers of novelty, so much a part of the modernist canon in art and perhaps also in science, sacrificing intelligibility.

> If it is too authoritarian, or too idealistic, or too unfamiliar in that the ideas have no precedent, or if it seems too fantastic or too far from possible, the vision will be put aside as simply one more curiosity. Moreover, a vision of the sort we propose in 'Peninsula Europe' will not work if it is wholly new information. The parts, although fragmented, disassociated from each other, must none-the-less exist in visible measure somewhere in the discourse of activities in a place. (H. M. Harrison and Harrison 2007b, n.p.)

On the one hand the work is at risk of unravelling if it leans too far into contingency, and on the other, there is a risk of becoming over-determined. What is the nature of the practice of improvisation that minimises such potential collapse? How can we imagine the tension productively?

A predicament, not something freely chosen …

A predicament emerges in a context as a problem that is difficult to solve, messy, and pivots on the artist's relationship with the past, the choice of whether to preserve or destroy what is understood as tradition. Being faced with 'the entwinement of preservation and destruction invites us to make a transition from a closed conception of the past to one that rethinks it as an open, ongoing event or occurrence whereby tradition is re-originated' (Peters 2009, 2). Peters encourages us to imagine this predicament through two metaphors. The first is the scrapyard challenge in which we are faced with the debris of the yard and invited to create something new out of the debris. The second is philosopher Walter Benjamin's (1892–1940) reimagining of Paul Klee's *Angelus Novus* (1920), in which the angel summoned to a storm in Paradise, hurtles into the future backwards. Where we might see chains of events, he fixes his gaze on a single catastrophe (history). The wreckage keeps piling up at his feet. He would like to stay and 'awaken the dead, making whole what is smashed' but the storm forces him on. The predicament of the improviser is their situatedness in the work and the agility they need in order not to be trapped in the expectations, traditions, and modalities of those around them (Peters 2009, 3). So, like Cage and the Harrisons, the exercise of choice or judgement is of paramount importance. For Massumi, predicament, in the sense of being pulled in two opposing directions, is the creative condition of organic life.

> Bodying is being in a situation, pulled in two directions at once: on the one hand anchored in what was given, and, on the other, tending to finesse a way to surpass it; the pull back of established necessity and the pulling forward to the new. (Massumi 2014, 329–30)

Given the choice between conforming to limited demands of adaptation and death, instinct in organisms finds a third way, pulling forward beyond the given, creating what Whitehead describes evocatively as 'the excess invention of a more to life' (Massumi 2014, 18).

In what sense are the Harrisons addressing 'a predicament'? The environmental crisis is a situation, into which all life on Earth is thrown and appears to be difficult to solve. As artists who have committed to rethinking what it means to be human and continue to survive in concert with other living things, they are faced with choices – what kind of artists to be, the content of the work, its positioning in relation to a public, choice of materials, form, collaborators, and so on. Their initial decision to only make work that would in some sense serve the web of life has acted as a kind of compass throughout their lives, directing them in the choices they were faced with. One might argue that this is 'fixed', a choice that determines to an extent the shape of the practice to come, including how it is experienced by a public. They made choices such as refusing to be identified as 'shock' artists, the choice not to pursue independent careers in the visual arts and education and literature, but to evolve a shared practice. This in turn has foregrounded the learning aspect of the work: they needed to teach themselves ecology and in doing so the work takes the form of a discourse in the presence of a public, one that is relevant and connected to life in its changing circumstances. The effect of their decision becomes a 'more to life', a new form of artistic practice based in partnership, not just with each other but with, for example, scientists involved in creating nature reserves (*Atempause für den Save-Fluss*, 1989), public bodies (*Green Heart Vision*, 1994), organisations (*Santa Fe Watershed*, 2005), communities (*On the Deep Wealth*, 2017) and even other artists (*Groundworks*, 2005). The shape of this phase of work, the ways in which it is deeply researched, communicated, reflected upon, critically discussed, and revisited takes the form of a series of feedback loops. Far from resulting in a static or fixed representation, the *work* of art becomes a speculative process, in movement, changeable and unstable while encountering attitudes, habits, and conventions that resist such movement and changeability.

Creating a 'more to life'

For the wolf cub excess through play equips him or her to protect a future life. For the musician, it also takes discipline and practice. Amit Chaudhuri, a musician and writer specialising in the raga tradition of Northern India, points to two concepts or forms of practice. The one 'sadhana' refers to a long-term, lifelong discipline that is focused by a goal and pursued for its own sake. 'Riyaaz' is the means or practice that makes sadhana possible. It applies as readily to other situations such as football as it does to music, and it is undertaken as an individual commitment.

> Riyaaz is the most secret part of yourself – the time you share with no one. You're listening to yourself: you're imperfect as works-in-progress are. You're self-absorbed, like a bird and like a bird, vulnerable to the danger of being discovered. Being interrupted is akin to a bird's aloneness being shattered by movement... Riyaaz comprises a continuity in the creative self... Riyaaz is an intervention in the artist's feeling of discontinuity; it's what you must do every day or every other day. (Chaudhuri 2021, 74–75)

It is from this rigour that the freedom to create, emerges. Improvisation, whether in daily life or in artistic practice, respects such constraint and thrives in it. A raga, the melodic framework for improvisation in Indian music, has prescribed ways of ascending and descending the scale, along with specific melodies that offer a palate to the musician who crafts these in performances working with the constraints of up to seven notes, a time of day and a particular emotion. In a similar way rehearsal for the free jazz improviser is a way to hear oneself 'sing' as in *re-hear-sing*, to deeply listen, discovering what is already there, given (Peters 2017, 148).

The Lagoon Cycle opens with a conversation between two people. This re-presents the daily conversation that the Harrisons hold together, through which they reflect on their work as an important part of their practice and which they describe as 'meditation' (Raven 1983, 50). The habit is formed as part of their working together from the early 1970s and repeated throughout their life together. It is contemplative, looking into the past and recognising that each time they do so, this past manifests differently in the light of new experiences, at once repetition in the form of a daily habit and novel in the sense of experiencing something differently with each repetition.

> *I said*
> *What would happen if I told the story just as*
> *it occurred*
>
> *You said*
> *How could you*
> *Every time we recreate the past it is different*
>
> *I said*
> *Then let us reinvent ourselves*
>
> *You said*
> *We are always doing that anyway*
>
> *I said*
> *Let's do it publicly*
> Introduction/26

This passage evokes the intimacy that Chaudhuri describes as being essential to the practice of improvisation. Here rather than a lone individual, this intimacy is explored as a dialogue and relationship between two people who learn to be each other, but never quite each other. Later in the *Introduction* the Harrisons engage the active part of contemplation and explore their relationship in terms of an experiment...

> To discover if we are
> each other's invention
> *But how would you know or I know*
> By listening to a conversation
> of another's devising
> *And comparing our own understandings*
> *And enacting our own believing*
> While recording each other's
> behaving

Choose any conversation
  He said he knew a hardy creature
  a crab
Introduction/26

The daily ritual appears to be more significant than the content of the conversation where it is implied there are a number of possible topics – '*Choose any conversation*'. Their conversational ritual is a kind of event that is generative, channelling the potential of undifferentiated thoughts and ideas through the exchange.

Returning to the raga as an iconic form of improvisation, it makes no distinction between 'labour, fruits of labour, preparation and performance' (Chaudhuri 2021, 73). A raga is not a 'thing', nor a composition, melody, or scale, but qualities of sounds in combination that can be 'tasted' via performance (Chaudhuri 2021, 31). The author or composer of a raga is not significant. It is the patterning of sound in the moment of an experience that matters. The work is not presented in concert halls or even in temples or courts, but in relation to time of day (Chaudhuri 2021, 41). This apparent seamlessness of an improvisation as both a known cultural institution, centuries old, and an event, an actual immediate occasion of experience, speaks to Whitehead's understanding that nature is only known to us in our experience as a complex of passing events through which we discern relations. It therefore makes no sense to separate space from time. Whitehead uses the example of Cleopatra's Needle on the Embankment in London, which can be read as 'event' depending upon the perspective of the perceiver. It can appear static to an individual passing by but to a physicist looking at its molecular structure, this is an illusion (Whitehead 2015, 106). Improvisation encourages a way of imagining ourselves in the world in time and in process rather than through spatialised objects.

Arguably in the Harrisons' work at a certain level, there *is* a clear distinction between preparation and presentation or performance or between process and object. The *Survival Pieces* and *The Lagoon Cycle*, among other works including *Making Earth*, are exhibitable as discrete works of art and replicable as performances, where authorship is celebrated in a time-honoured way according to Western custom. That said, the Harrisons have resisted becoming consumed by the institution on many occasions (Chapter 2) and have regularly sought alternative spaces in everyday life, the City Hall or Community Centre. What appears seamless in the sense that Chaudhuri is suggesting, is their 'folding in' of diverse voices, experiences, knowledges, and imaginations that continue to be sought at and after the point of exhibition, challenging this as the end point of 'producing' a work of art. They position themselves as generalists in conversation with whoever can support their learning of the issues of a place, as the earlier examples of *Casting a Green Net* demonstrate. Without these conversations there would be no work. In this way they generate the conversational drift of growing ecological awareness. This is beautifully evoked in their *Atempause für den Save-Fluss* (figs. 37-40), in which they were invited by the director of a nature reserve to help him address the

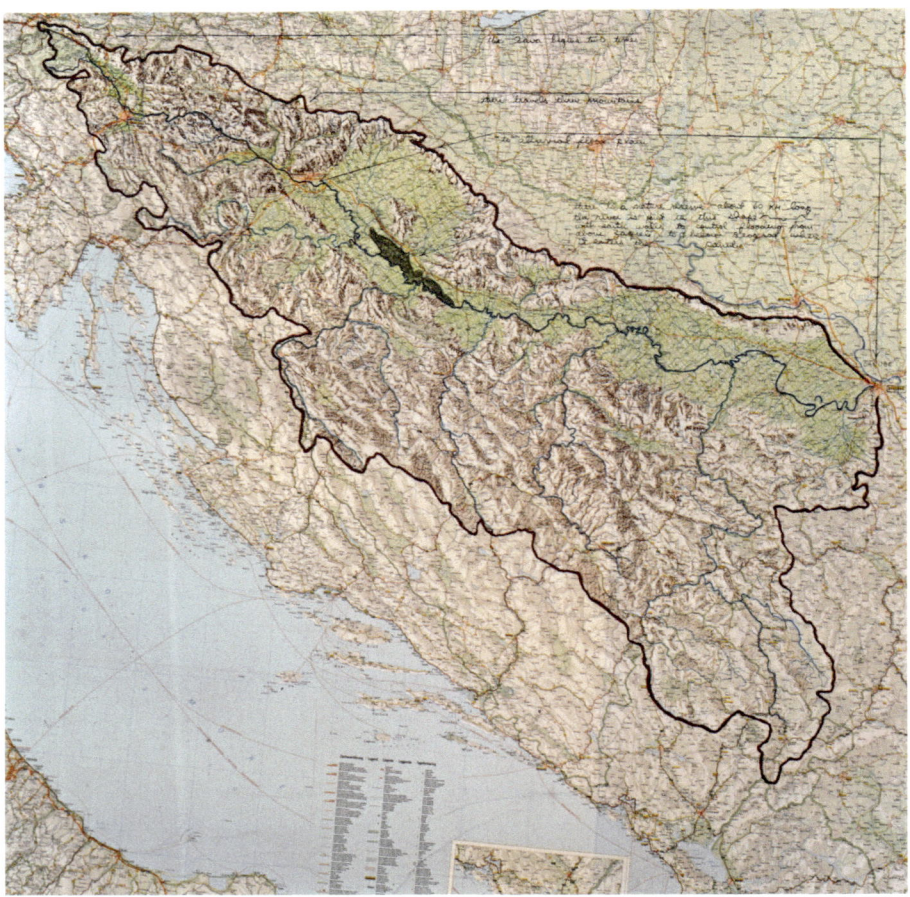

Figure 37: 'Atempause für den Save-Fluss' (1989) Watershed Map detail (courtesy of the Newton and Helen Harrison Family Trust)

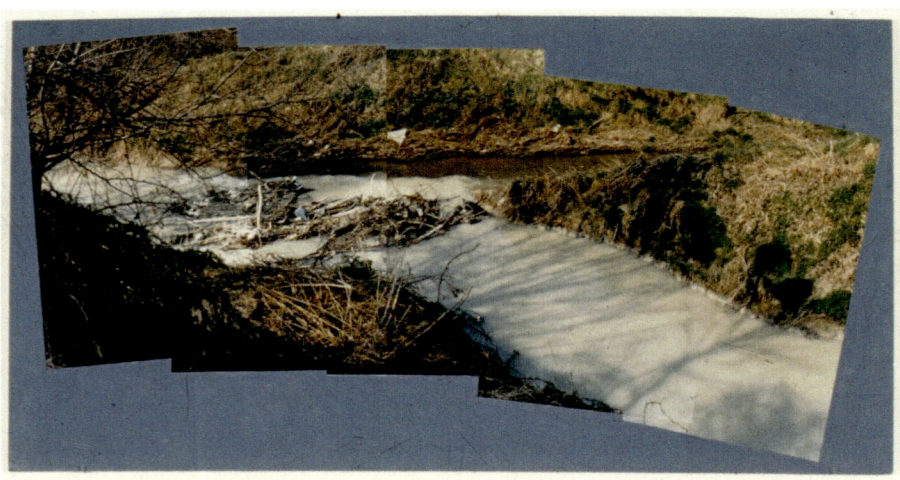

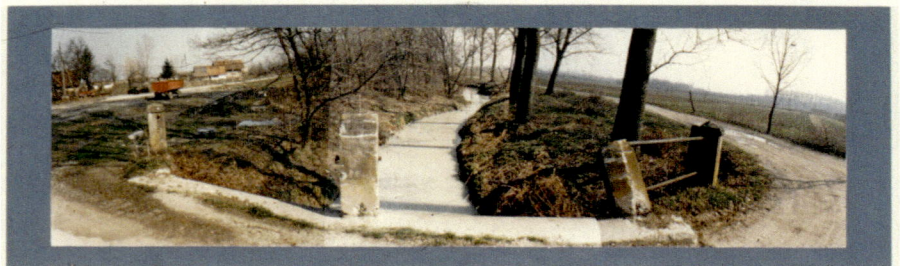

Figure 38: 'Atempause für den Save-Fluss' (1989) Polluted streams detail (courtesy of the Newton and Helen Harrison Family Trust)

threat of pollution from industrialised farming in the region of the Sava River, where the reserve was located. The conversation is about conferring value as a way to organise activity in a community, to create a change of direction based in new values.

I said
Do you value this river the Save[2]

You said
Not in its present state nor do I value
the state of the discourse around it

I said
Any state has value

You said
Then do you wish to join the conversation

I said
How do I know anybody will listen

You said
How do I know we will say anything worth listening to

I said
Even if we say anything worth listening to
will it be remembered for more than a moment

You said
Remembering and forgetting are in their totality
the sum of human understanding

I said
Then about and around this river a forgetting is taking place
and a rich history is disappearing
And a very limited present state is appearing

You said
Its present state is merely a moment in history
and is theoretically invisible

I said
Then do you value the direction of its becoming

You said
The river is like nature or for that matter a proton
its existence itself is part of a larger discourse
and
its discourse like any discourse
is the sum of its improvisations at any moment
and therefore the direction of its becoming is theoretically
invisible

I said
Forgetting the question of indeterminacy
do you value the discourse about and around this river
as best you can understand it

You said
I fear for this river's well-being

I said
Then let us find a way to join the conversation
(H. M. Harrison and Harrison 1989, n.p.)

Conversation in this work is not limited to people but to the interaction between elements in the landscape shaped by human self-interest in the form of farming and paper-
mills, channels, levees and inevitably, toxic pollution. The idea of joining the 'odd kind
of dialogue' in which 'the business of the universe/is conducted' (Seventh Lagoon/91)
here becomes the discourse of that place. By seeing and presenting the river as part of a
larger discourse, a whole watershed, that eventually leads to the Danube and Black Sea,
a 'new history for the Sava' emerges that imagines the whole region as a nature reserve
that is intent on creating a healthy ecology. If this is done the Sava restores the whole
catchment as it flows into the Danube and eventually the Black Sea.

   Ingold and Hallam suggest that improvisation is time-dependent in the sense that
what occurs is both unforeseen and never repeatable (Hallam and Ingold 2007, 1).
Conversational drift is an improvisation in the sense of taking a direction that cannot
be predetermined but is nonetheless shaped by the choices that the artists and others
make within a process that unfolds and builds momentum.

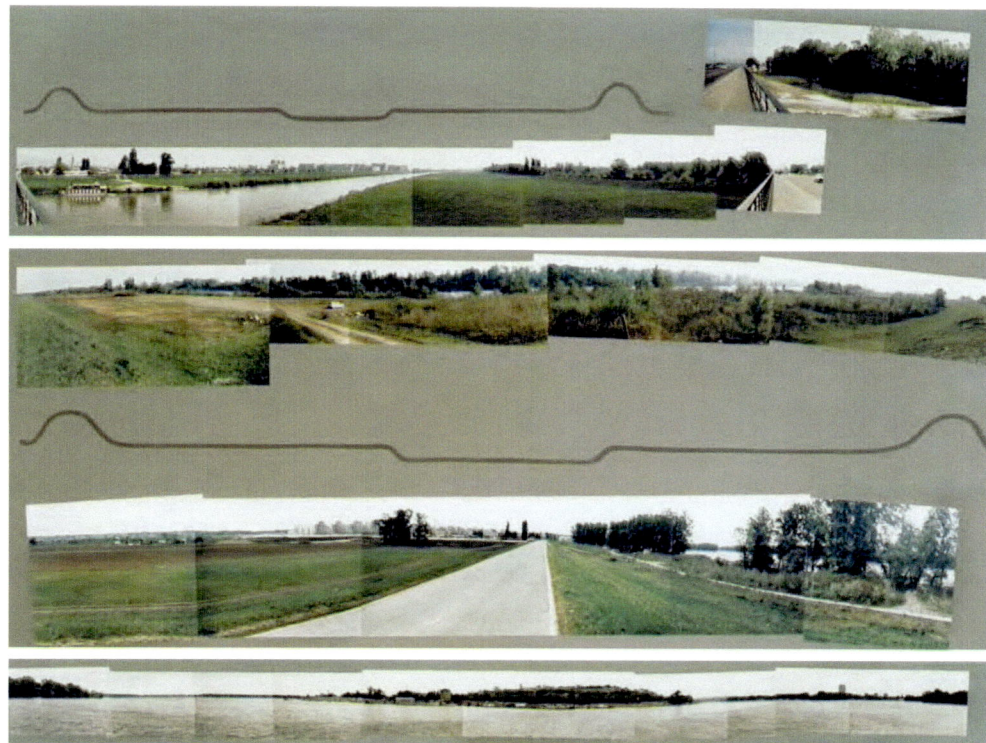

Figure 39: 'Atempause für den Save-Fluss' (1989) Re-imagining Flood Management detail (courtesy of the Newton and Helen Harrison Family Trust)

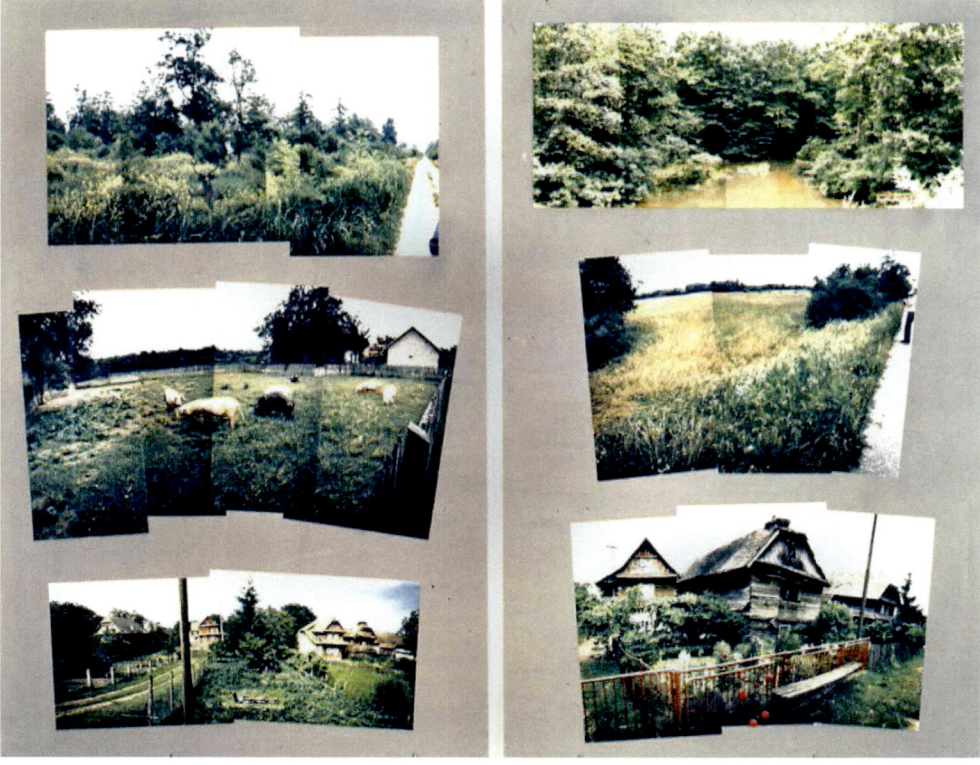

Figure 40: 'Atempause für den Save-Fluss' (1989) Detail (courtesy of the Newton and Helen Harrison Family Trust)

Generative metaphor

The sitar player desires to replicate the human voice, 'its longing to sing'. By understanding that the quality of undulation can only be produced by pulling a string and most instruments interrupt this continuity producing sequential notes, the sitar player learns to use his voice, and produce the most difficult tonal effects by 'pulling the string in his throat, bending and stretching the note significantly' (Chaudhuri 2021, 70). In imaging or seeing the sitar as voice, the sitar player develops a quality of relation in which the sitar becomes present in the singer, the singer present in the sitar. 'Seeing as' is metaphor and metaphor helps us to make sense of reality, to allow new perspectives to come into the world. For the Harrisons metaphor helps them to generate real shifts in perspective with the potential to change how things are imagined and then done. Existing metaphors of place reveal how places have developed – 'metaphor drives design' for better and for worse (H. M. Harrison and Harrison 2007b, n.p.). They are intrinsic to the stories we tell ourselves, responsible as much for the creation of predicaments as for the ways in which we might address them. Metaphor is therefore integral to improvisation.

In discussing *Atempause für den Save-Fluss*, the Harrisons reveal not only the importance of metaphor in their work, but also how they work with it.

> Any metaphor, by virtue of the beliefs embedded in it, has an implicit narrative structure. Any complex narrative has metaphors embedded in it. ...the principle is to work with the implicit metaphors that can be seen to guide human design as they affect the ecosystem. The idea is to identify among them those whose grounding (operation in the physical world) is most dysfunctional with respect to a given problem and pose alternative intentional groundings. The object here is to identify and work through the consequences of a new metaphor conceived to result in actual physical work in a cultural landscape. The metaphor in this case generates new design, and the story of its working is a narrative. (H. M. Harrison and Harrison 2007b, n.p.)

In tracing the progression from extant, and at time dysfunctional metaphors to their replacement by new more appropriate metaphors, the Harrisons approach to metaphor is reflective, critical and action orientated. This is perhaps different from the kind of metaphor found in poetry and literature. The Harrisons' metaphors are the figures of everyday speech that create our perspectives on the world, that reveal how we think about things and how we make sense of reality. Donald Schön (1930–1997) as a philosopher and urban planner is particularly interested, like the Harrisons, in how metaphors help us to address what he calls 'troublesome situations' (Schön 1993). All problems are mediated by the stories we tell ourselves in troublesome situations. The key is not to try to solve the problem, but to examine carefully how a problem is set – what underlying metaphors are at work in the way we construct the world. This is equivalent to the

Harrisons' phase of becoming aware of the metaphors at play in systems, those that are functioning and the dysfunctional.

Schön embarks on generating a 'problem setting' story and asks to what degree this new way of imagining is useful – the benefits as well as the costs. His examples are design driven and like the Harrisons, the process of responding generatively to a dilemma is at first self-critical and reflective, opening the possibility of renaming and regrouping to reach a better outcome. Metaphor in this sense is a carrying over, seeing similarities between an A and a B, understanding in what sense such similarities hold and using these insights to restructure, to reorder reality. It is neither a compromise, nor a fusion, but a shift in cognition.

In the Harrisons' work, seeing the similarities between culture and nature through improvisation enables a shift in perspective that in turn impacts on ways of acting in the world, the shift from experimentation in which the outcome is anticipated to another more open-ended form of experimentation (Douglas and Gulari 2015). What does this metaphor make matter? Metaphors are vivid ways to imagine ourselves in the world and are formative of the qualities of relations we forge through such imaginaries. The Harrisons work with metaphor with the intention of shifting the imaginary of human exceptionalism to one in which humans are in dialogue with the universe, a formative part for better or worse. In doing so they also seek to shift a deeply engrained hierarchy of values, privileging the ongoing-ness of life over human self-interest and productivity, generating a deep entanglement by which the survival of the one brings into question the survival of the other.

What does improvisation make matter?

Rethinking the arts in the environmental crisis involves questioning the conventions of art and their appropriateness for a rapidly changing world just as Whitehead's search for a different philosophy of nature involved him in questioning the foundations of science and Stengers, the questioning of the cultural values of technoscience. Whitehead's philosophy of organism is improvisatory – a process or practice from which new life emerges. In an improvisation we become hyperaware of the situatedness and contingency of the moment in which we are living, the pull of being lured towards resolution as well as the push of contradiction. In Whitehead's construction this moment draws into itself different kinds of potential to make a 'creative advance', to invent a 'more to life'. It is a refusal to be trapped into merely repeating the past, though that may be what happens from time to time. Improvisation is a counterpoint to productivity in valuing freedom channelled by carefully judged limits, between radical adventure and communicability.

Improvisation draws our attention to the degree in which 'control' and 'determinacy' haunt everyday language in post-industrial societies. We talk about 'making space for rewilding' and can mean excluding humans. Whitehead, Cage, the Harrisons, and

others celebrate the relation and immanence of humans in the world, an imaginary
for which we need new language. Improvisation transports us from a world that is
prescribed, to a world that has the potential to make and remake itself through an
understanding of dependence and interdependence as a force of cocreation.

> [W]e are in a world of colours, sounds, and other sense-objects, related in space
> and time to enduring objects such as stones, trees, and human bodies. We seem
> to be ourselves elements of this world in the same sense as are the other things we
> perceive. (Whitehead 2022, 96–97)

Having reviewed different approaches to improvisation across cultures and timescales,
it is striking that the Harrisons while drawing attention to improvisation as a shared
characteristic across culture and nature, one that breaks down this binary, their works
are not examples of improvisatory arts practice *per se*. The quality of spontaneity in improvisation does not refer to something appearing from nowhere but rather a feeling of
being drawn into and participating in something in its moment of emergence. Stengers
cites David Abrams' *The Spell of the Sensuous* (2012).

> We may think of the sensing body as a kind of open circuit that completes itself
> only in things, and in the world. The differentiation of my senses, as well as their
> spontaneous convergence in the world at large, ensures that I am a being destined
> for relationship: it is primarily through the engagement with what is *not* me that
> I effect the integration of my senses, and thereby experience my own unity and
> coherence. (Abrams quoted in Stengers 2011, 352)

Spontaneity in this sense of being in relationship with what is not me as something is
happening, is core to the feeling of a work as improvised. It inhabits the gap between
individuals, and the individual and environment. Massumi aligns it with instinct,
with the capacity to produce unexpected outcomes that do not arise out of a linear
logic, but out of the 'spontaneous propulsion/mental power to surpass the given'
(2014, 18). Whitehead call this 'appetition' (1978, 32–33). It can be felt in the play
of the wolf cubs, in the raga in which paradoxically spontaneity is made possible
through severe constraints and rigour, in the colour that a performer of a Bach prel-
ude might bring to a particular performance, in the call and response that is integral
to a Kaprow score, and in Cage's framing of ambient sound in *4.'33*. Spontaneity is
a feeling inside a process in which intuition is present, alive to the situation at hand
in ways that seek to surpass what is given. A work of art needs to make accommodation for that feeling to arise without seeking to control it, mindful that the radical
creativity of being pulled to 'the limits of chaos' (Massumi, 2014, 110) is 'potential'
and may or may not become realised in the occasion of experience. At the core of this
idea of spontaneity is freedom, the freedom from inertia and the freedom to create

the unexpected that characterises emergent life, the 'more to life' through which life is renewed.

There are moments of spontaneity in the Harrisons' process, moments where their intuitions are reported in works, but the works we experience in the gallery are prioritising a different, reflective, moment that they often referred to as the prophetic, that is, driven by the impulse to convey a message. In resolving the work of art so completely at the point it reaches a public, the Harrisons may be prioritising this message over our freedom as audiences to participate in its unfolding, not literally, but through subtle forms of inclusion such as by making present the 'gap of excess'. Their works mix retelling the words of others, sometimes humorously, with the use of the more declamatory Judeo-Christian voice, sometimes conveying portentousness. For example, in *Greenhouse Britain: Losing Ground, Gaining Wisdom* (2008a) there is the refrain, 'The news is not good, and it is getting worse'. The diversity of voices within conversational drift are 'appropriated' in the exhibited works, woven into the text in a manner that fixes them. The Harrisons' exhibited work is more 'about' improvisation than 'as' improvisation, and in the later works as the crisis deepens, this voice becomes noticeably more didactic.

> The moment is urgent   if business as usual continues
> Scotland as usual will continue to have
> a carbon footprint over three times its physical size
> to do nothing risks the death of the life web
> to do too little risks near death and a sixth extinction
> to do enough   we cannot know without the doing of it
> (H.M. Harrison and Harrison, 2017)

Looked at in terms of Whitehead's 'event' the whole process has elements of spontaneity as a lived experience along with analysis and reflection. This process includes being invited to create a work in a place, immersing themselves in that place where possible, exhibiting works, and creating ways of working that others could take up if they wished. The Harrisons' works are not examples of improvisatory art, but they do draw attention to improvisation as a characteristic of life.

Improvisation is one of two key constructs that shape how the Harrisons imagine the web of life. The other is ecosystems, the subject of the next chapter, where systems are also imagined as predicaments through a series of place-based works in which aesthetics becomes critical in working with systems.

> *Yet*
> *The business of today*
> *does not encourage continuous empathy*
> *nor spaciousness of mind*

Rather the business of today
encourages replacement
and change
It is conducted as a technological monologue
spoken so rapidly
that the consequences of an improvisation
most times
cannot be seen
(Seventh Lagoon/93)

CHAPTER 5

On the Poetics and Aesthetics of Systems

What is one to make of the use of references to 'systems' and terminology associated with systems thinking in the poetic works of the Harrisons, not least in *The Lagoon Cycle*? The Harrisons' commitment is to ecosystemic well-being and, as the previous chapter demonstrates, a key concern is with improvisation. What are they seeking to draw our attention to, to make matter? While the Harrisons' use of 'systems' terminology highlights different aspects of systems, understood as both cultural and natural, it further focuses different aesthetic concerns, fundamentally a concern with what art critic Jack Burnham called a 'systems esthetic' (hereafter 'aesthetic' unless in a quote) in a series of essays in the late 1960s. Where recent aesthetic discourse has stressed process and the relational, and systems are dynamic and relational, this discourse has focused on the human and in particular the dialogic dimension (Bourriaud 2002; Kester 2004; 2011). The Harrisons, engaging with systems through their poetics, are seeking to focus our attention on specific aesthetic aspects that are characteristic of systems in particular the contradictions between the cultural and the natural as inter- or intra-actions.

Systems are not uncontentious, often associated with bureaucracy, hierarchies, and structures of control. Some are practical resulting in food on plates, others like education shape society. Some enact genocide. Hannah Arendt said in *The Origins of Totalitarianism*:

> [W]e may say that radical evil has emerged in connection with a system in which all [people] have become equally superfluous. The manipulators of this system believe in their own superfluousness as much as in that of all others, and the totalitarian murderers are all the more dangerous because they do not care if they themselves are *alive or dead*, if they ever *lived* or never were *born*. (Arendt requoted in Kristeva 2020, 4–5 retaining Kristeva's emphasis in italics)

Arendt's attention to the forms of totalitarianism and evil focus on 20th-century manifestations in systems and the values and purposes that constitute them, including defining superfluousness and producing homogeneity. There is a design aesthetic associated with totalitarianism this is only a manifestation of an underlying aesthetic which is characterised by shaping what is superfluous and producing homogeneity. Systems have been described as 'the ontology of the control society', in particular because they can shift the focus from what to do, to a matter of 'information about how we do it' (Deleuze 1992).

However, the Harrisons are seeking a new imaginary, and they construct that new imaginary understanding the importance of systems and the potential to work with them, never believing that people are superfluous. It might be useful to think of systems in terms of 'predicament' as defined in the discussion of improvisation. Gary Peters' construction of predicament as something 'not freely chosen' but something we find ourselves 'thrown' in is most often the reality of an experience of systems. Considering systems to be predicaments in no way removes responsibility to pay attention to advantage and disadvantage.

The Harrisons use 'ecosystem' to refer to the interactions between different living things and with environments in specific places, and to 'lifeweb' or 'web of life' as the sum of all ecosystems.[1] They use the term 'systems' when discussing specific dynamics of ecosystems connected with concepts such as entropy, and for human systems including agricultural systems (*Sacramento Meditations* (1977–78)), financial and forest 'farming' systems (*The Serpentine Lattice* (H. M. Harrison and Harrison 1993)), and flood management systems (*Arroyo Seco Release/A Serpentine for Pasadena* (H. M. Harrison and Harrison 1985a)). They never use 'ecosystem' as a metaphor for a human system because in the Harrisons' analysis this becomes a form of 'naturalisation' that is dysfunctional in that is obscures the question of who is advantaged and who is disadvantaged. Each of the works above engages with key systems to offer a new way of imagining them, whether agricultural or forestry and finance, or water management.

In *The Lagoon Cycle* there are multiple references to 'systems' in the text and in the imagery, including 'the system becomes/self-nourishing/self-cleansing/self-adjusting' (Second Lagoon/44); 'the harvest preserves the system' (Fourth Lagoon/64); and 'Pay attention to the system upon which desire is enacted/and the system that generates desire' (Sixth Lagoon/88). Visually the Fourth Lagoon is characterised by drawings of a large-scale aquaculture system, but there are other indications of systems, including the British colonial order for destruction of property and living things, as well as the visual analysis of alternatives for routing the flushing of the Salton Sea. Sometimes the context is specifically ecological systems, but in others it is human, financial, or psychological. The first quote, 'the system becomes [...]', is a formulation that the Harrisons use in multiple works and texts (2007b; 2008a). It points to the characteristics of both natural and cultural systems when they are working effectively. The second quote about the harvest is also familiar across multiple works (H. M. Harrison and Harrison 1998; Firbank et al. 2009, 258) and more specifically addresses what in the Harrisons' thinking is the way humans can be within ecosystems, that is, parts that strengthen the whole. The final quote, 'Pay attention [...]', is another iteration of the provocation to pay attention to the giving of advantage and disadvantage from *The Lagoon Cycle*.

There is a range of language associated with systems thinking. 'Information' is one of the key terms in any discussion of systems (and the economisation of information in the 'knowledge economy' is one of the key aspects of technoscience that is the focus of Stengers' critique). There are specific references to information in the text, perhaps most obviously:

> *While he expected the information gained to be privileged*
> *as he expected the information gained to become profit*
> *and we expected the information gained to become public*
> *as we expected the information gained to be published*
> Third Lagoon/56

This particular sequence addresses one dimension of information, its publicness or alternatively its potential for exploitation for profit. Information has multiple dimensions even in the context of systems, as the product of cognition, and as data that shapes a system. Another example of the way the Harrisons use information is in *Atempause für den Save-Fluss* (fig. 37-40) discussed in the context of improvisation, which includes the following stanzas:

> The river is asked to process new information
> when it hits the alluvial floodplain
> and the information is mechanical.
> A new shape has been constructed for the river
> By the construction of levees and dams
> so that the river is permitted to rise and fall
> but not to spread.
> And the topology for a giant farming system created thereby.
> For the river it is the shape of catastrophe.
>
> [...]
>
> The river is asked to process new information
> when it hits the alluvial floodplain
> and the information is chemical
> and the information is toxic
> and
> where the information is most toxic
> by an unexpected congruence of circumstances
> and an unexpected confluence of waters
> there is an intersection with the nature reserve.
> (H. M. Harrison and Harrison 1989, n.p.)

Here information exists in multiple different forms and is in the interaction between the river and various human interventions. Another related term, 'data base', also appears. In the Seventh Lagoon following a moment that starts with the Witness' dream of being 'in the company/of earth of water of rock and stone' and continues with the Lagoon Maker imagining the geological processes around the rim of the Pacific Ocean, the text ends:

> *That would require reorienting consciousness*
> *around a different data base*
> Seventh Lagoon/92

In this striking use of a term (database is now commonplace) the Harrisons are linking the challenge that *The Lagoon Cycle* offers to reorient consciousness to a different imaginary: human culture organised by the well-being of the web of life. To do this the Witness suggests would need a different basis of data, one where the data is framed by an understanding of interconnectedness at multiple scales. This has both a literal aspect and an ironic one. It certainly isn't just a question of changing the data being used.

Before drawing out why and in what particular ways the Harrisons focus aesthetic attention on systems and what the resulting new imaginary might be, we will briefly focus on systems theory and key actors in its development as well as some of the other ways of working with systems developed by artists before exploring the ways *The Lagoon Cycle* can be understood as debating systems thinking, and what it might mean to understand the Harrisons' poetics as directing attention to a 'systems aesthetic'. It would be simplistic to align Whitehead's process philosophy with systems thinking, and therefore we will only turn to it at the end of this chapter as a check.

Systems: A way of thinking

What is 'systems' as a way of thinking, of designing, making matter? What is it making silent? What does it make us responsible for? Broadly speaking systems theory proposes that all phenomena can be understood as a network of relationships among elements and that all systems, whether technological, biological, or social, have common patterns, behaviours, and properties that can be explored and used to develop greater insight into complex phenomena. Ludwig von Bertalanffy (1901–1972), biologist, is widely referenced as one of the founders of the school of thought known as 'General Systems Theory' from the 1940s (though his book with that title wasn't published until 1968). Systems theory was a key focus of the 'Macy Conferences', a post-war initiative intended to create meaningful communication across scientific disciplines. The Macy Conferences on Cybernetics (1946–53) consisted of a series of 10 events that brought together an intentionally diverse group across multiple disciplines to discuss subjects critical to cybernetics but as diverse as simulated neural networks, humour, and paradox. In 1948 Norbert Wiener (1894–1964), mathematician and philosopher, defined the related term 'cybernetics' as 'control and communication in the animal and the machine'. Wiener was one of the first to theorise that all intelligent behaviour was the result of feedback mechanisms. Gregory Bateson (1904–1980), anthropologist, social scientist and linguist, was an original member of the core group organising the Macy Conferences. Bateson's books (1972, 1979) explore epistemology from a systems perspective using anthropological approaches.[2] Cybernetics in its initial formulations understood control to be exercised on systems. 'Second order cybernetics' introduced reflexivity, understanding 'cyberneticians' and other participants to be part of the systems they study and act in.[3] This latter formulation is key but fully recognising its implications remains a challenge.

By the 1960s systems had become the subject of wider cultural discourse. In 1969 Buckminster Fuller, architect, designer, writer, and futurist, published *Operating Manual for Spaceship Earth* generating a metaphor of the earth as a system. In the late 1960s Jack Burnham, critic and theorist, published a series of articles (Burnham 1968, 1969, 1971) using the concept of systems to explore the works of key artists including Gianni Colombo, Dan Flavin, Hans Haacke, Les Levine, Robert Morris, and Donald Judd as well as the Harrisons. The Harrisons use of this terminology needs to be seen in the light of this wider cultural discourse, but their engagement with systems, and their use of its concepts to draw our attention to cultural and natural dynamics and patterns, is embedded in their works over their 50-year practice.

'Systems thinking' has come to be defined by some key authors including Donella Meadows and Fritjof Capra. Donella Meadows, co-author of *The Limits to Growth* (1972), scientist and educator, quotes Robert Pirsig as the epigraph for her book *Thinking in Systems: A Primer* (2008).

> If a factory is torn down but the rationality which produced it is left standing, then that rationality will simply produce another factory. If a revolution destroys a government, but the systematic patterns of thought that produced that government are left intact, then those patterns will repeat themselves… There's so much talk about the system. And so little understanding. (Meadows 2008, 2)

Meadows uses this quote to highlight the embedded and self-replicating character of systems. Having established the importance of systems, Meadows goes on to define them as follows:

> A system is a set of things – people, cells, molecules, or whatever – interconnected in such a way that they produce their own pattern of behaviour over time. The system may be buffeted, constructed, triggered, or driven by outside forces. But the system's response to these forces is characteristic of itself […]. (Meadows 2008, 2)

This definition highlights several key aspects – that the terminology of 'systems' is a way of focusing our attention on pattern, recurring behaviour, and self-reproduction. Meadows' construction quoted above still articulates systems as sets of 'things' and Frijof Capra, the physicist and key synthesiser of ideas from chaos and complexity theory, argues for a shift in focus, from things to patterns. To understand his argument, it is worth tracing his line of thought.

> The main characteristics of systems thinking emerged simultaneously in several disciplines during the first half of the century, especially during the 1920s. Systems thinking was pioneered by biologists, who emphasised the view of living organisms as integrated wholes. It was further enriched by gestalt psychology and the new science of ecology, and it had perhaps the most dramatic effects in quantum physics. (Capra 1997, 17)

Capra identifies the key challenge of systems in terms of how they are conceived – in his argument they cannot be understood by analytic processes because the parts are not separable. He says, 'In the systems approach, the properties of the parts can be understood only from the organization of the whole'. He goes on to say, 'Accordingly, systems thinking does not concentrate on the basic building blocks but rather on basic principles of organization' (Capra 1997, 29). He elaborates this idea saying 'we realise that the objects themselves are networks of relationships, embedded in larger networks. For the systems thinker, relationships are primary' (1997, 37–38). He identifies that energy and feedback are critical to understanding systems, drawing attention to 'living systems as energetically open but organizationally closed ... [and] the recognition of feedback as the essential mechanism of homeostasis' (1997, 78). Understanding these key dynamics is critical to any attempt to understand or work with systems. Like Whitehead's conception of harmony, holism is a not uncomplicated concept. The refocusing of attention to inter- or intra-relations or even assemblages is important, but the assumption that we might then know what the totality actually is, particularly in the context of life, is a different problem.

More recently, Capra offered the following four characteristics of 'life', which further amplifies his conceptualisation (Gamble 2021). He says life organises itself in networks – its structure and behaviour are determined within the system; life is inherently regenerative (and here he references autopoiesis, a term that describes a system capable of producing and maintaining itself by creating its own parts); life is inherently creative, characterised by the phenomenon of emergence and of novelty; and, finally, life is inherently intelligent. Here again he draws on the work of Humberto Maturana and Francisco Varela, biologists who introduced the term 'autopoeisis' and developed the Santiago Theory of Cognition. The Santiago Theory builds on Wiener's conception of cybernetics: intelligent behaviour is the result of feedback mechanisms. The theory argues that cognition is the result of the continuous interaction of a system with its environment where perturbations of the system cause adaptations that enable the system to survive. Capra explains:

> The living system is autonomous, however. The environment only triggers structural changes; it does not specify or direct them. Now, the living system not only specifies these structural changes, it also specifies *which perturbations from the environment trigger them*. ... The structural changes in the system constitute acts of cognition. By specifying which perturbations from the environment trigger its changes, the system 'brings forth a world'... This definition extends cognition to everything which is in an adaptive relationship with its environment. Cognition, then, is not a representation of an independently existing world, but rather a continual *bringing forth of a world* through the process of living. (1997, 260 italics in original)

Questions remain about how autopoiesis works in ecosystems and societies (Capra 1997, 205); however, systems and ecosystems are two ways of understanding nature and culture, both characterised by interactions between elements and environments, both having coherence and being self-reproducing.[4] The one, ecosystems, is organised by particular cycles (carbon, water, and so forth) and relations (competitive, predatory, symbiotic). The other, systems, is focused by forms of organisation and control shaping flows of energies, materials, and human behaviours. Organisation and control can be centralised by a single requirement (production of crabs, timber, irrigation, flood control, and so on), or it can be decentralised, complex, adaptive, and attuned to the consequences of who and what is advantaged, and who and what is disadvantaged.

The increasing use of modelling, particularly based on computing power, has renewed the need for critique of systems-based approaches (in particular of the organising idea of isomorphism – that models are mirrors, or twins of the world rather than metaphors for them). Modelling and machine learning has amplified specific aspects of systems thinking, in particular 'that the history of ecology is enmeshed with systems theory and presupposes that species entanglements are operational or functional'. The artist and environmental engineer Tega Brain is concerned to challenge the technoscientific dominance of systems and the unquestioned assumptions ported with systems into the ecological. They go on to say 'a systematic view of the environment connotes it as bounded, knowable and made up of components operating in chains of cause and effect' (Brain 2018, 153). This analysis is completely coherent with the assumptions of cybernetics and the understanding of the human as cybernaut, steering the ship. In light of the multiple problems arising from human control, the discussion turns to the potential of machine learning to build models offering 'a more robust representation of reality, free of human judgement'. However, Brain highlights that in reality 'systems continue to reveal and confirm biases and structural inequalities rather than offering an easy pathway to their neutralization'. This is a problem of politics, not technology or data. Brain draws on theorist Françoise Vergès' argument, 'Contemporary

environmental challenges directly emerge from violent histories of colonialism, imperialism and the ongoing exploitation of marginalized communities or those living in
the global South'. In addition to the ways in which systems and machine learning-based
processes reproduce inequalities, biases, and injustices, the very focus on data, particularly large quantities of data, takes attention away from the specifics of the world.
Brain asks, 'How might we elevate engagement through the specifics of encounter
and narrative?'. Brain asks us to consider Anna Tsing, 's 'arts of noticing', arguing that
this approach offers 'tactics for thinking without either the abstraction produced by
quantification or deeply held assumptions of progress'. Another 'spin-off' of systems
thinking connected to modelling is the use of scenarios, which has become central
to climate science.[5] These important questions need to be born in mind through the
following discussion of artists engaging with systems. The focus of the next sections is
on social-cultural approaches to systems, in contrast to the dominant mathematical and
technological resulting in modelling (Brain 2018, 157–160).

Artists and systems – Haacke and Ukeles

The Harrisons are not often discussed in the context of systems and art. Critic and
writer on systems and art Ed Shanken (b. 1964) includes a contribution from the
Harrisons in his edited volume *Systems* (2015) but also highlights elsewhere four key
survey exhibitions (Shanken 2009, n.p.) none of which include works by the Harrisons.
The 1960s are elsewhere described as 'a period when visual artists began to develop new
models within which to structure and frame artistic practice by adapting methodolo-
gies from communication and literary theory, cognitive psychology, and computing'
(Sutton 2019, 13). There are aspects of systems in areas of practice as diverse as kinetic
art, social practice, and the turn to the everyday, art and technology experiments, as
well as environmentally directed work. Jack Burnham, who coined the term 'systems
aesthetics', cautioned in the Introduction to his *Great Western Salt Works: Essays on the
Meaning of Post-Formalist Art*:

> In terms of practical application, its utilitarianism and obsession with efficiency
> leave much about organic relationships misunderstood. Ultimately systems theory
> may be another attempt by science to resist the emotional pain and ambiguity that
> remain an unavoidable aspect of life. (Burnham 1974, 11)

Two artists, Hans Haacke (b. 1936) and Mierle Laderman Ukeles, can help us understand the scope of the use of 'systems' by artists. The former is consistently associated
with systems, and the latter not referenced in discussions of 'systems art', but nonetheless important from our perspective.

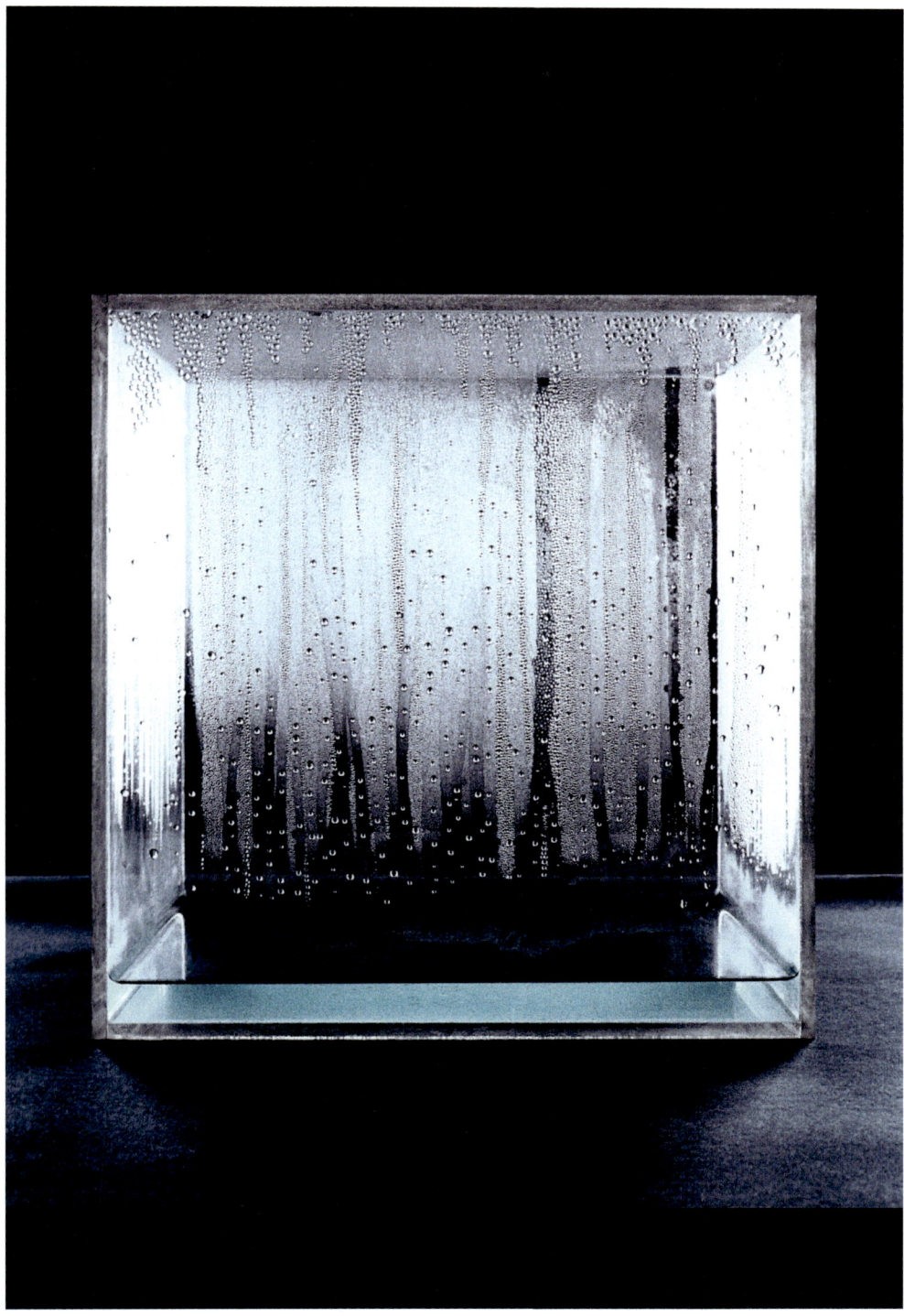

Figure 41: Hans Haacke 'Condensation Cube' (1963-67) Clear acrylic, distilled water, climate in area of display 30 x 30 x 30 in. © Hans Haacke / Artists Rights Society (ARS), New York / VG-Bild-Kunst, Bonn (courtesy of the artist and Paula Cooper Gallery, New York)

Hans Haacke created multiple works that explore different aspects of systems. In the 1960s these were concerned with growth and decay before instigating works focused by what has come to be known as 'institutional critique' from the early 1970s. His *Condensation Cube* (1963–67) (fig. 41) works with energy and entropy – the human bodies in proximity to the work, the more the water in the cube evaporates. As entropy sets in and the temperature equalises out between the inside of the cube and the surrounding atmosphere, the water condenses and becomes visible on the transparent plastic walls. Haacke's *Rhine-Water Purification Plant* (1972) is another system, in this case with a more complex goal of purifying polluted water from the Rhine. The system brought the polluted water into the Museum Haus Lange and filtered it. It was then 'held' in an acrylic tank teeming with goldfish before it was pumped into the museum's garden. These two systems are environmental and biological. Haacke also explored human systems. His notorious work *Shapolsky et al. Manhattan Real Estate Holdings, a Real-Time Social System, as of May 1, 1971* (1971) provides a completely different form of engagement with a system – in this case using excerpts from a city map, six charts, and 142 photographs and cards with data drawn from public records. The work revealed an existing exploitative system of slum landlordism and its connections with elite New York City culture. Haacke also created interactive systems including two iterations of *Gallery-Goers Birthplace and Residence Profile 1* and *2* (1969, 1970) and *MoMA Poll* (1970). These works collected data and opinions from gallery goers and re-presented those as statistics within the gallery spaces. These examples highlight the multiple ways in which systems can be represented through art, or where art can 'bring forth' a system. That being said, institutional critique has been the dominant form of artists' engagement with systems in the intervening period (Hamilton Faris 2022, 236).

Mierle Laderman Ukeles is known for her work as Artist in Residence over more than five decades with the New York City Sanitation Department. Ukeles' work is concerned with the systems of everyday life, which are largely invisible or overlooked. Her various works, including *Touch Sanitation* (1979–80) (fig. 43) during which she shook hands with all 8,500 workers in the Sanitation Department, and *The Social Mirror* (fig. 44), a mirror-plate covered Sanitation Truck (1983), are intended to focus on systems that enable everyday life. Ukeles located herself within a particular system and then developed her poetics in relation to that system and context. Her works use the materials and processes of the system, but more significantly they are reflective of the goals and purposes of the system. Ukeles conceptualised this some years before proposing the residency to the Sanitation Department in her *MANIFESTO FOR MAINTENANCE ART, 1969! Proposal for an exhibition "CARE,"* 1969 (fig. 42). In the manifesto she highlights two systems where the values are conflicted and normalised – she reverses the hierarchy of value.

    B.   Two basic systems: Development and Maintenance. The
           sourball of every revolution: after the revolution, who's

> going to pick up the garbage on Monday morning?
> Development: pure individual creation; the new; change;
> progress; advance; excitement; flight or fleeing
> Maintenance: keep the dust off the pure individual creation;
> preserve the new; sustain the change; protect progress;
> defend and prolong the advance; renew the excitement;
> repeat the flight:

(Ukeles 1997, 6)

The Manifesto goes on to differentiate the ways that feedback loops, key to homeostasis as Wiener and Capra highlights, function in these two conceptions of systems.

> Development systems are partial feedback systems with major
>   room for change.
> Maintenance systems are direct feedback systems with little
>   room for alteration.

(1997, 6)

The goal of the Sanitation Department might be understood to remove rubbish, or alternatively, as Ukeles says, 'to keep the city alive' (Conte 2015, 10). Ukeles' work addresses what the goal of the system is understood to be, and her work questions our relationship with garbage, offering a changed paradigm where garbage and the people who work with it are valued. Ukeles' focus on maintenance has been discussed in relation to the emergence of feminist art (Kester 2004), and is a key example of an 'embedded artist' (Douglas 2019). The work uses and draws attention not just to the systemic dimensions of waste management, but also importantly how understanding that it has an aesthetic dimension enables working differently. The sanitation system is typical in being understood in terms of flows of materials, and its 'aesthetic' might be considered negative, that is, that it repels our attention rather than attracts it. Ukeles' works reposition sanitation from the process of taking rubbish 'away' to being the thing that keeps the city alive. Her works use performance and choreography to make visible patterns and processes of the sanitation system through the means of the sanitation system. This is further developed in her *Seven Work Ballets* (1983–2012), which involve sanitation workers and their equipment (street cleaners (human and mechanical), garbage trucks, tugs and barges, snow ploughs) performing hour-long programmes of carefully choreographed movements. Kari Conte highlights that the choreography starts from simple questions to the workers, 'What can you do? What have you always thought about doing?' (2015, 9). Where systems such as sanitation are often invisible or only partly visible, Ukeles uses various 'techniques' familiar in the arts such as re-performing and valorising (intensifying and amplifying in Whitehead's words) everyday tasks as a poetics to draw out the aesthetic potential of the system and offer a new imaginary of it.

MANIFESTO!

MAINTENANCE ART   --   Proposal for an Exhibition

"CARE"
©1969
Mierle Laderman Ukeles

I. IDEAS:

A. The Death Instinct and the Life Instinct:

The Death Instinct: separation, individuality, Avant-Garde
par excellence; to follow one's own path to death--do your
own thing, dynamic change.

The Life Instinct: unification, the eternal return, the
perpetuation and MAINTENANCE of the species, survival
systems and operations, equilibrium.

B. Two basic systems: Development and Maintenance. The sourball
        of every revolution: after the revolution, who's going
        to pick up the garbage on Monday morning?
Development: pure individual creation; the new; change;
        progress, advance, excitement, flight or fleeing.
Maintenance: keep the dust off the pure individual
        creation; preserve the new; sustain the change;
        protect progress; defend and prolong the advance;
        renew the excitement; repeat the flight.

                show your work--show it again
                keep the contemporaryartmuseum groovy
                keep the home fires burning

Development systems are partial feedback systems with major
        room for change.
Maintenance systems are direct feedback systems with little
        room for alteration.

MAINTENANCE ART   -2-   Mierle Laderman Ukeles

C. Maintenance is a drag; it takes all the fucking time (lit.)
    The mind boggles and chafes at the boredom. The
    culture confers lousy status on maintenance jobs=
    minimum wages, housewives=no pay.

    clean your desk, wash the dishes, clean the floor,
    wash your clothes, wash your toes, change the baby's
    diaper, finish the report, correct the typos, mend
    the fence, keep the customer happy, throw out the
    stinking garbage, watch out don't put things in your
    nose, what shall I wear, I have no sox, pay your bills,
    don't litter, save string, wash your hair, change the
    sheets, go to the store, I'm out of perfume, say it
    again--he doesn't understand, seal it again--it leaks,
    go to work, this art is dusty, clear the table, call
    him again, flush the toilet, stay young.

D. Art:

    Everything I say is Art is Art. Everything I do is
    Art is Art. "We have no Art, we try to do everything
    well." (Balinese saying).

Avant-garde art, which claims utter development, is infected
    by strains of maintenance ideas, maintenance activities,
    and maintenance materials.
        --Process art especially claims pure development and
          change, yet employs almost purely maintenance
          processes.

E. The exhibition of Maintenance Art, "CARE", would zero
    in on pure maintenance, exhibit it as contemporary art,
    and yield, by utter opposition, clarity of issues.

MAINTENANCE ART   -3-   Mierle Laderman Ukeles

II. THE MAINTENANCE ART EXHIBITION: Three parts: personal, general,
     and Earth Maintenance.

     A. Personal Part:

              I am an artist. I am a woman. I am a wife. I am
                   a mother (random order).
              I do a hell of a lot of washing, cleaning, cooking,
                   renewing, supporting, preserving, etc. Also,
                   (up to now separately) I "do" Art.
              Now, I will simply do these maintenance everyday things,
              and flush them up to consciousness, exhibit them, as Art.
              I will live in the museum as I customarily do at home with
              my husband and my baby (right, or if you don't want me
              around at night I would come in every day) for the duration
              of the exhibition, and do all these things as public Art
              activities: I will sweep and wax the floors, dust everything,
              wash the walls (i.e. "floor paintings, dust works, soap-
              sculpture, wall-paintings"), cook, invite people to eat,
              clean up, put away, change light bulbs. I might save and
              make agglomerations and dispositions of all functional
              refuse. The exhibition area might look "empty" of art, but
              it will be maintained in full public view.

              My working will be the work.

              _____

     B. General Part: Everyone does a hell of a lot of noodiling
         maintenance work. The general part of the exhibition would
         consist of interviews of two kinds.

         1. Previous interviews of, say, 50 different classes and
             kinds of occupations that run a gamut from "maintenance
             man", maid, sanitation man, mailman, union man,
             construction worker, librarian, grocerystore man, nurse,
             doctor, teacher, museum director, salesman, baseball
             player, child, criminal, bank president, mayor, movie
             star, artist, etc., about what they think maintenance
             is; how they feel about spending whatever parts of
             their lives on maintenance activities; what is the
             relationship between maintenance and freedom; what is
             the relationship between maintenance and life's dreams.

             These interviews will be typed and exhibited.

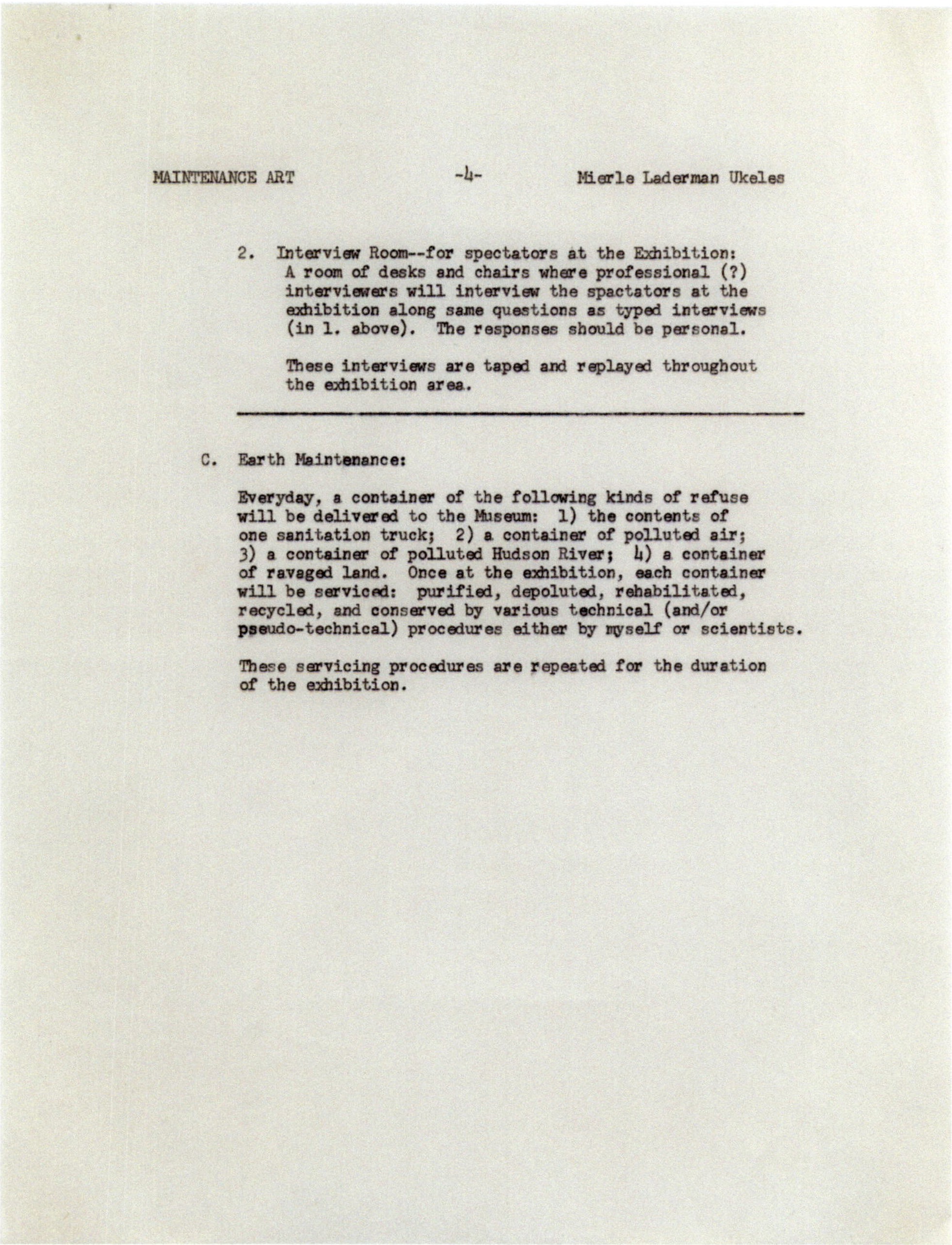

MAINTENANCE ART   -4-   Mierle Laderman Ukeles

2. Interview Room--for spectators at the Exhibition:
A room of desks and chairs where professional (?)
interviewers will interview the spectators at the
exhibition along same questions as typed interviews
(in 1. above). The responses should be personal.

These interviews are taped and replayed throughout
the exhibition area.

C. Earth Maintenance:

Everyday, a container of the following kinds of refuse
will be delivered to the Museum: 1) the contents of
one sanitation truck; 2) a container of polluted air;
3) a container of polluted Hudson River; 4) a container
of ravaged land. Once at the exhibition, each container
will be serviced: purified, depoluted, rehabilitated,
recycled, and conserved by various technical (and/or
pseudo-technical) procedures either by myself or scientists.

These servicing procedures are repeated for the duration
of the exhibition.

Figure 42: Mierle Laderman Ukeles, 'MANIFESTO FOR MAINTENANCE ART, 1969! Proposal for an exhibition "CARE"' (1969). Written in Philadephia, PA, October 1969. Four typewritten pages, each 8½ x 11 in. © Mierle Laderman Ukele (courtesy of the artist and Ronald Feldman Gallery, New York)

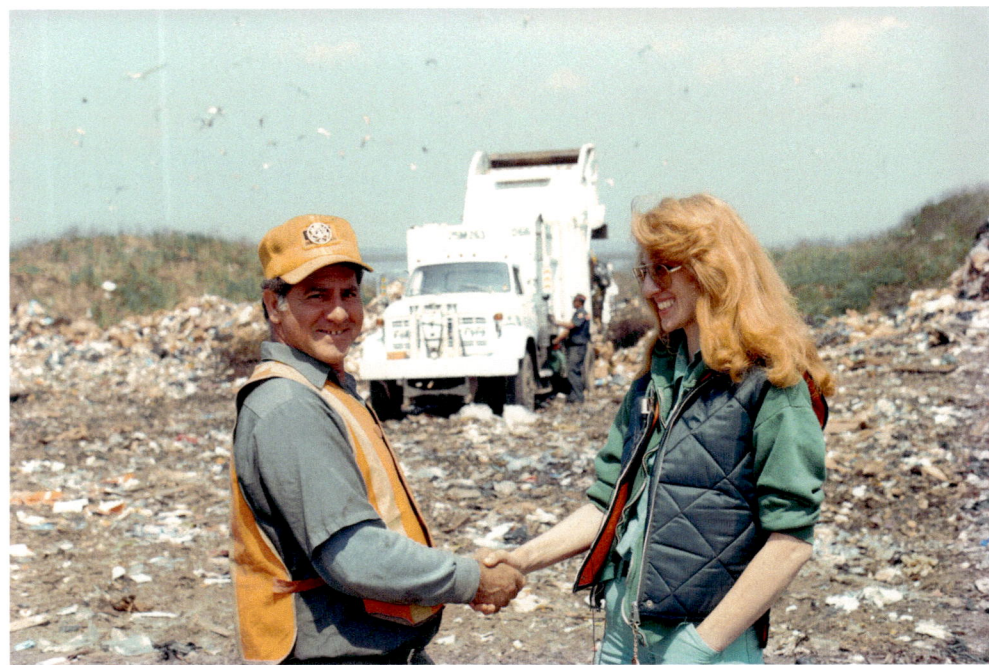

Figure 43: Mierle Laderman Ukeles 'Touch Sanitation' (1979-80) Performance documentation
(courtesy of the artist and Ronald Feldman Gallery)

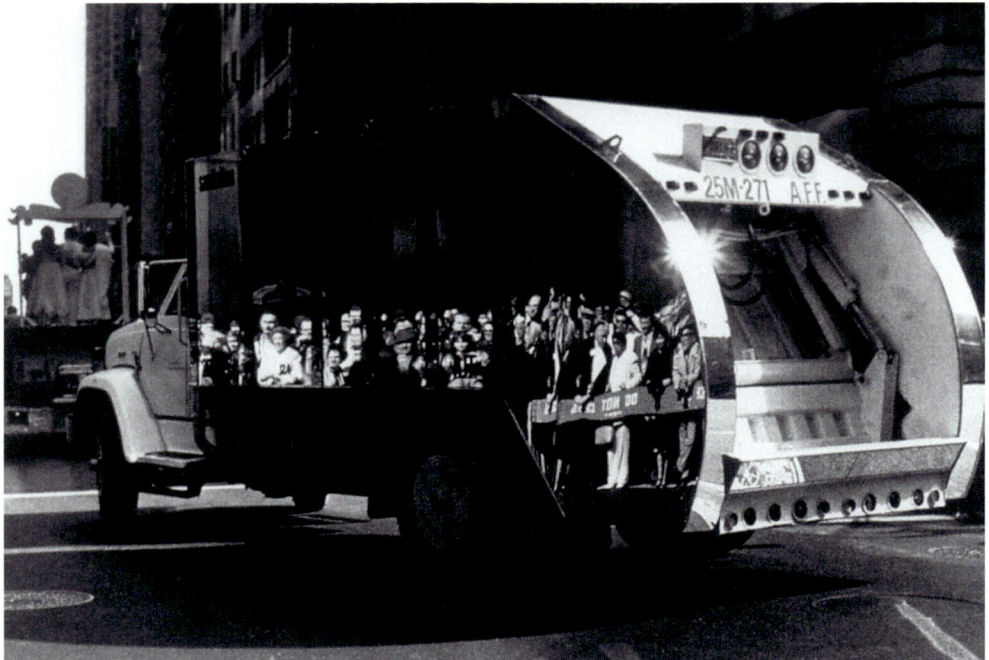

Figure 44: Mierle Laderman Ukeles 'Social Mirror' (1983) (courtesy of the artist and Ronald
Feldman Gallery)

Artists have taken up systems including focusing on key concepts such as entropy, working with information as documentation of systems, as interactive systems, and working with systems of everyday life. They all in different ways draw attention to the system as a set of things interconnected in such a way that they reproduce their own pattern over time. Those works draw attention to or work with feedback loops. Haacke's interactive works are forms of feedback loop and Ukeles' *Touch Sanitation* can be understood as inserting a new factor into a system – an element 'outside' the system (the artist) interacting with elements in the system (sanitation workers) and through repetition affecting the system. The effects that the work might have had on the sanitation system can be inferred from the support for the position of artist in residence by five succeeding Commissioners over 40 years. It has also had an effect on the art system – it remains an iconic feminist performance cited in multiple texts and exhibitions.

Burnham's Proposed 'Systems Aesthetics'

To further understand the aesthetic dimension of systems that these artists were making matter, it is worth turning back to Jack Burnham and his exploration of 'systems aesthetics'. Burnham's work is primarily concerned with art and technology and therefore we are looking to it for clues. That being said, Burnham asked whether artists' works with systems needed a new way of understanding aesthetics and this is key. Hans Haacke says in the introduction to Burnham's collected writings:

> Around 1967, Jack introduced me to the concept of systems. ... Around that time he passed on to me the biologist Ludwig von Bertalanffy's treatise *General Systems Theory*, which vastly broadened my understanding of the systems concept. I recognised then that, in effect, it applied to important aspects of my own works. I began to call them 'systems'. (Haacke in Burnham 2015, ix)

Burnham, drawing on the influential theory of paradigm shifts in science proposed by Thomas Kuhn (1922–96), proposed that 'systems aesthetic' is a similar shift of paradigm occurring in art's ontology, in how it exists in the world (Burnham 1974, 15). On one level Burnham is addressing a shift from object to process in art, which mirrors the shift from mechanistic analysis to systems thinking that Capra describes. On another level he is making a more radical proposition – that we need to pay attention to what happens with an aesthetic understanding of systems. Luke Skrebowski, a contemporary critic writing on Jack Burnham and Hans Haacke, focuses on systems aesthetics as the valuable contribution in Burnham's oeuvre. Skrebowski is specifically critical of Burnham's commitment to dissolving the distinction between art and technology – noting that Burnham is generally criticised as 'technocratic, utopian, teleological' (Skrebowski 2016, 90). Skrebowski usefully focuses on the value of Burnham's attention to aesthetics and

associated ontologies (2016, 95). He also highlights that Burnham can be seen as a pro-
genitor to relational and dialogic aesthetics as developed 30 years later by among others
Nicholas Bourriaud and Grant Kester (Skrebowski 2016, 101). The key difference, however, is that relational, and to a lesser extent dialogic, aesthetics have focused on aesthetic
as an aspect of human interactions, mostly within discourse, and the interactions of
that discourse with environments, both human-made and natural. Burnham's focus on
systems aesthetic is between human, technology, and environment. The Harrisons draw
our attention to, and work with, the aesthetic dimensions of eco-cultural contexts –
both systems and ecosystems. They focus attention within the geophysical (mountains,
rivers, seas), the vegetable (forests in particular), the animal (including the human), the
technological (for example, irrigation systems, flood control devices, machines such as
tractors), the economic and governance (competition, profit, taxes, and regulations).
They position discourse (stories and metaphors) as another dimension of systems, but
also as the way to affect how systems produce and reproduce their own pattern of behaviour over time.

Burnham's concern is whether there is significance in addressing systems as aesthetic, what the important aspects of that are, and what an artist through their poetics
can achieve. In 'Systems Esthetics' (Burnham 1968) Burnham highlights some characteristics. Primarily he argues that the 'aesthetic' lies in the 'principles' rather than the
'manifestations' – the aesthetic of systems isn't in what they look like but what organises
them – the goals and underlying organising principles. He says:

> [A] systems esthetic *is* literal in that all phases of the life cycle of the system are
> relevant. There is no end product which is primarily visual, nor does such an esthetic
> rely on a 'visual' syntax. It resists functioning as an applied esthetic but is revealed
> in the principles underlying the progressive reorganisation of the natural environ-
> ment. (Burnham 1974, 17–18. Italics in the original)

The critical aspects that Burnham is drawing attention to are the wholeness that Capra
and the other systems thinkers highlight, as well as the concern with how principles
(including metaphors) reorganise environments. Burnham led up to this claim that the
systems 'aesthetic' is in the reorganisation of the system, making two key points, saying:

> The systems approach goes beyond a concern with staged environments and hap-
> penings; it deals in a revolutionary fashion with the larger problem of boundary
> concepts. ... In evaluating systems the artist is a perspectivist considering goals,
> boundaries, structure, input, output and related activity inside and outside the sys-
> tem. (Burnham 1974, 17)

This directly correlates with Donella Meadows' essay 'Leverage Points: Places to
Intervene in a System' (1999), which, again focusing on socio-cultural dimensions,

puts 'The power to transcend paradigms' as the number one leverage point, followed by 'The mindset or paradigm out of which the system – its goals, structure, rules, delays, parameters – arises' and then third, 'The goals of the system'. Ukeles' works demonstrate the reversal of assumed values, such as production over maintenance, and the works address and intend to transcend the paradigm, not least by considering the paradigm to be aesthetic in nature.

In 'Systems Esthetics' Burnham makes two statements that are highlighted by the use of italics. These can be taken as key to his characterisation of systems aesthetics.

> *[A]rt does not reside in material entities, but in relations between people and between people and the components of their environment.* (Burnham 1974, 16 italics in the original)

Burnham is not concerned with human social interactions in themselves, but more fundamentally with all interaction. Burnham's use of the common definition of ecology invokes the holistic and self-replicating dynamic as much as the relational. The second statement is:

> *In an advanced technological culture the most important artist best succeeds by liquidating [their] position as artist vis-à-vis society.* (Burnham 1974, 16 italics in the original)

These nuance our understanding of what Burnham means when he says that all aspects of the system are relevant – none are more significant and as a consequence no parts of the system, including artists, should be fetishised. As was evidenced in the first chapter, many critics thought that the Harrisons had precisely 'liquidated' their position, becoming scientists doing experiments, or planners proposing remediation strategies. Perhaps more significantly the Harrisons frequently spoke of 'joining a conversation of place' and were known for their collaborations with many disciplines – as Burnham highlights all aspects of a system are 'literal' and are 'relevant' (1974, 17–18). Burnham goes on to say, 'As yet the implication that art contains survival value is nearly as suspect as attaching any moral significance to it' (Burnham 1974, 17). Developing this theme, Burnham quotes Morse Peckham, the literature scholar engaged with the biological sciences, who says:

> Art, as an adaptive mechanism, is reinforcement of the ability to be aware of the disparity between behavioural pattern and the demands consequent upon the interaction with the environment. Art is a rehearsal for those real situations in which it is vital for our survival to endure cognitive tension, to refuse the comforts of validation by affective congruence when such validation is inappropriate because too vital interests are at stake... (Morse Peckham cited in Burnham 1974, 17)

Imagining art as being 'adaptive' relates to the idea of systems being governed by para-digms and goals. Here adaptation means fitness for survival, and the suggestion is that art can bring into focus contradictions that are a key part of the processes of adaptation. Peckham is focusing on the role of art and its capacity to cope with contradiction or 'cognitive tension' and not to always seek coherence. It is important to understand that Capra's focus on the 'whole' and Meadows' articulation of systems' internal coherence does not mean that they aren't also characterised by contradiction. In fact, one of the Harrisons' rubrics is:

> Our work begins when we perceive an anomaly in the environment that is the result of opposing beliefs or contradictory metaphors. Moments when reality no longer appears seamless and the cost of belief has become outrageous offer the opportunity to create new spaces – first in the mind and thereafter in everyday life. (H. M. Harrison and Harrison 2006)

Peckham is effectively saying that working with contradiction is central to art and Burnham is arguing that it makes art central to survival.

The Harrisons' use of 'systems'

Turning back to *The Lagoon Cycle* and to our discussion of improvisation, the description of culture is grounded in a systems analysis,

> *A culture is a cooperative adventure   a complex system*

This one line highlights the holistic, relational, and emergent characteristics and defines culture in terms of a system. The description develops, perhaps with a degree of irony, saying:

> [...]   *Its constancy is reproduction*
> *and change   Its stability is always at risk*
> First Lagoon/37

Questions of constancy and stability, and associated risks, are central to systems thinking. The passage goes on to highlight that change is seen in the boundaries and is driven by 'the energies available'. Energy (along with information as noted above) is a key concept in systems theory. As previously noted, boundaries can be reconceptualised as constraints rather than fixed entities and in Chapter 7 the work of artist and designer Josef Albers (1888–1976) on boundaries in colour and perception will further inform our under-standing of the Harrisons' approach to this key characteristic of ecologies and systems.

This chapter opened with questioning the use of systems thinking terminology in the Harrisons' poetic works and has explored how systems thinking emerged such that by the 1960s it was an important discourse engaging artists. This led to Burnham's concept of a 'systems aesthetics', which opened an understanding of the potential to engage with systems and which forms of engagement are significant. Burnham's argument is that it is by engaging in particular with the paradigms and goals of systems that art can address them imaginatively and through the senses as part of processes of cognition. As previously noted, Burnham highlighted systems are literal, in the sense that they are the repetitions of actions and flows of materials that amongst other things are food supply chains, constitute formal education, and enact genocide. He argues that all aspects of systems are relevant, in other words that the immigrant labour we don't see is as important as the farmland that we do see, and that the humus content of the soil is as important as the price of wheat at the London Corn Exchange. It is the system or ecosystem that generates the intrusion. He also describes them as utilitarian and obsessed with efficiency. Burnham is talking about aesthetics, but his focus is on the material and the means of production and reproduction. Artists such as Haacke drawing our attention to the sources of wealth of museum board members, and Ukeles, acknowledging the work of sanitation workers, recognise the literalness of systems, and that all aspects are relevant.

The Harrisons directly engage with both the imaginative and literal aspects using the sorts of structured rationality associated with systems thinking in key passages in *The Lagoon Cycle*. They often referenced their method as 'dialectic' – based on discourse between two points of view, seeking to establish the truth through reasoned argumentation. There are three sets of 'If [...] Then [...]' sequences, two in the Fifth, and one in the Sixth Lagoon. These result from an initial debate over the use of systems thinking that starts in the Fourth Lagoon. The Lagoon Maker has used systems thinking as a form of analysis with which to conceptualise and design industrial-scale crab farming, and the Witness critiques the Lagoon Maker's approach. The Witness' pointed remark 'That's a pretty system you are proposing' (Fourth Lagoon/71) steps back to reflect and highlights the specific challenge of the use of one system – the lagoon in Sri Lanka – as a model for another – an aquaculture system in the Colorado Desert near the Salton Sea. The Witness' questioning of the 'pretty system' is a challenge to the Lagoon Maker's abductive approach, inferring that the lagoons in Sri Lanka can offer a model for a *technologically simple aquaculture system* in the vicinity of the Salton Sea.[6] As noted in Chapter 3 at the start of the Fifth Lagoon the Witness develops the critique through an 'If [...] Then [...]' sequence that explores the contradictory behaviours and goals of management of the Salton Sea – as a 'recreational area' and as a 'repository for agricultural and municipal wastes' (Fifth Lagoon/75). Both are legally 'mandated' or 'designated'. The conclusion of the sequence focuses on how the different propositions interact, and their consequences in terms of either the 'exclusion of possibilities' (resulting from continued increasing pollution) or the 'inclusion of possibilities' (resulting from decreasing levels of pollution). The Lagoon Maker responds with their own 'If [...] Then [...]' sequence immediately following (Fifth Lagoon/76). In the Sixth Lagoon (84–85) the Witness takes up the 'If [...] Then [...]' process and reframes it at another larger scale, asking questions based on observations about the whole of the Colorado River system drawing attention to what is advantaged and what is disadvantaged. The final 'If [...] Then [...]' sequence immediately follows (Sixth Lagoon/86) and turns the same observational analysis onto the system of water storage tanks and canals in Sri Lanka to drawing attention to the differences (rather than the similarities). Here the 2,500-year-old system serves multiple purposes in daily life and in farming, highlighting a very different construction of advantage and disadvantage.

> *the tank and the canal system has niched itself into the*
> *ecology*
> *and the state of the land has been minimally changed*
> *giving advantage to such historic forms as villages and*
> *farms*
> *while not disadvantaging the rivers and riverine life*
> Sixth Lagoon/86

Proposing a new system that would treat the Salton Sea as a lagoon by creating inflows and outflows, pumping systems from the ocean, needs in turn to be contextualised in the wider systems of the Colorado River to fully understand its ramifications. The proposed system in turn needs to be juxtaposed with the alternative in the water tanks and canals in Sri Lanka, both its potential similarities, but also its differences, explored. The Lagoon Maker's aquaculture system has only one purpose – crab farming – but multiple impacts, whereas the Sri Lankan system creates multiple benefits. The key point is made in the use of the word 'niched'.

Spoils Pile Reclamation

The Lagoon Cycle has so far formed the focus in discussing the Harrisons' articulation of systems. To open up a different way of approaching this issue it is useful to consider *Spoils Pile Reclamation* (1977–78), created at Artpark near Lewiston in upstate New York. *Spoils Pile Reclamation* succeeded, in some ways like *Brine Shrimp Farm* but on a larger scale, in becoming a self-generating system in which repetition is key. It involved 3,000 truckloads of material over two years, resulting in the restoration of a significant area. For a period, it achieved what in biological systems would be called homeostasis – self-regulation. But perhaps it also failed because it so dissolved itself into everyday life as to be difficult to read as an artwork in the context of other more explicitly experimental and art-like activities. There was a landscape masterplan, but that had been developed by

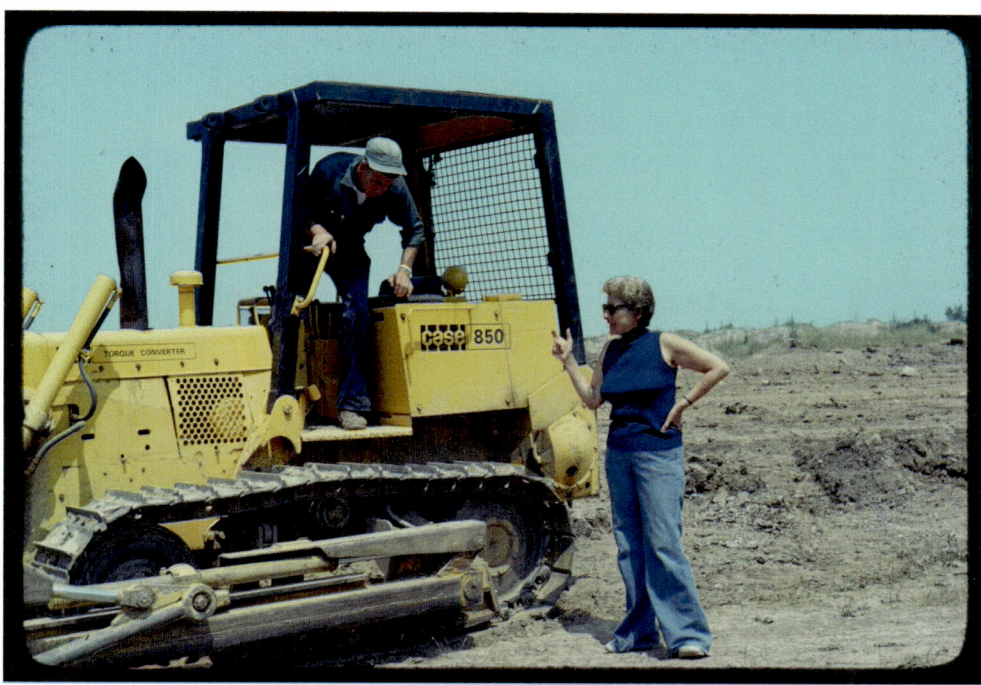

Figure 45: 'Spoils Pile Reclamation' (1977–78) Detail of work on site (courtesy of the Department of Special Collections, Stanford University Libraries)[7]

architects Hardy Holzman Pfeiffer Associates. *Spoils Pile Reclamation* had very limited fixed visual elements (fig. 46) that were wholly instructional, very reminiscent of the diagrams used in the *Survival Pieces*. It remained incomplete and does not demonstrate key characteristics of the Harrisons' mature practice in terms of metaphor or storytelling.

That being said, *Spoils Pile Reclamation* (fig. 45-46) does arise out of the formation of the Harrisons' practice even before the *Survival Pieces*. They credit their first ecological action to Newton's *Making Earth* (1969–70), a personal project recorded in photographs, and Helen's *Making Strawberry Jam*, exhibited at the Woman's Building in Los Angeles (1972). Newton developed a ritual that turned sand, clay, sewage sludge, chicken and horse manure, and leaf material into soil. He attuned himself to the process through ritual performance of the turning of the material, and by attending to the changing state, running his hands all over it, and tasting it, recognising success when it tasted good. Helen describes becoming invested in the soil Newton made and beginning to grow things in it. She made strawberry jam every day for 30 days, using less and less sugar. *Spoils Pile Reclamation* is in some ways the logical development of this personal scale work. It brings together the aspects of attunement and ritual into a 'system' over a much longer period and involving a different scale of material.

Artpark was some 172 acres, including a spoils site resulting from the construction of the reservoir for the Robert Moses Niagara Hydroelectric Power Station and a quarry that had been used for chemical industry waste. Unlike other sculpture parks,

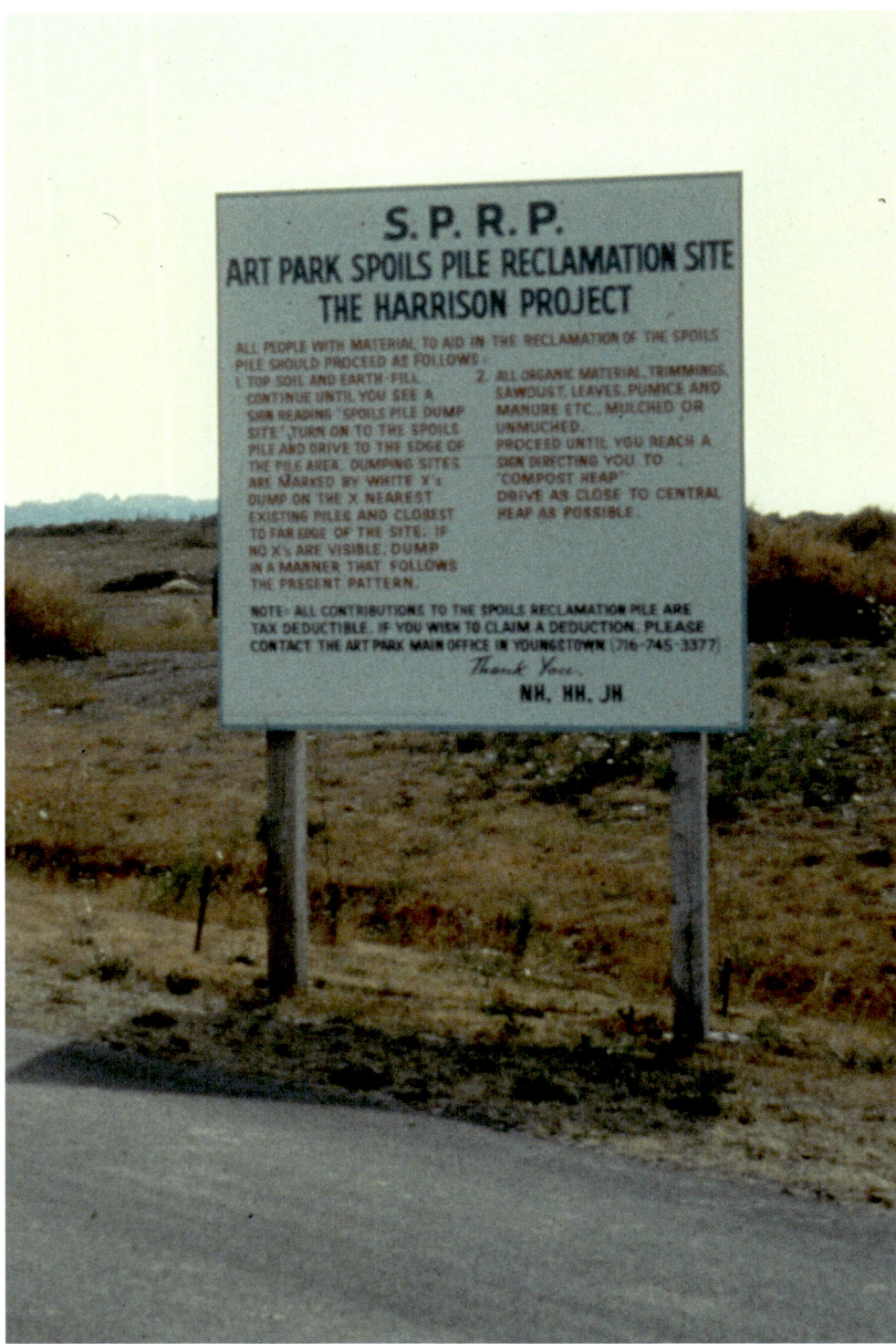

Figure 46: 'Spoils Pile Reclamation' (1977–78) Detail of signage (courtesy of the Department of Special Collections, Stanford University Libraries)[8]

the landscape hadn't been given an aesthetic. It had been designated as a new park and some areas had been remediated. Each year artists were invited to make new works for the site. It had become a radical experimental space and 'assorted projects on the Spoils Pile included minimalist boxes, assorted shelters, a series of sunken concentric rings, quixotic scarecrows destined to be set on fire like birthday candles, a working ranch (of sorts), a tree gravesite, an underground house, and films of drilling oil rigs projected onto multiple screens' (Firmin 2010, 37). The first artist to work at Artpark was Charles Simonds and others included Alice Aycock, Agnes Denes, Nancy Holt, Allan Kaprow, and Dennis Oppenheim – approximately 30 each year during the first five years.

The Spoils Pile Reclamation project begins as improvisation and becomes an emergent system: an initial improvisatory process developed its own, albeit temporary, ongoing self-replicating dynamic. Josh Harrison (b. 1956), the Harrisons' son, is credited as having found serendipitously that various utilities were doing works that resulted in significant amounts of soil, both subsoil and topsoil being available.[9] He also discovered that new regulations meant that local orchards also had to dispose of cuttings differently. Donations to the project were tax deductible. The result was a proposal, an improvisation with the materials at hand, for the remediation of 40 acres (or 16 hectares) of the site.

Given the necessity for nearby communities to pile excess fill and organic material somewhere, this work may cost less overall to do than not to do. (Edelman 1977, 41)

Josh Harrison highlighted two further characteristics of the site that informed the thinking (J. Harrison 2023). First, that the site had been a meeting point for various routes across the wider North Eastern United States from before colonisation. 'A Hopewell burial mound and portage site (both of which are listed on the National Register of Historic Places) are located there [...] because it provided a strategic trade route that bypassed Niagara Falls on the trek westward to the rest of the Great Lakes and onward to the Mississippi River' (Firmin 2010, 29). Second, the site, while attracting experimental artists, was not being widely used by inhabitants of Lewiston. *Spoils Pile Reclamation*, by involving local contractors and orchard owners as well as by transforming large parts of the site to meadow, would open up the site to greater use by local inhabitants and reinstate its role as a meeting place. *Spoils Pile Reclamation* improvised a system that started to become niched into its context by creating benefits for all involved. It used various opportunities and incentives such that the 'work may cost less overall to do than not to do' (Edelman 1977, 41). Its only signage was a board providing instructions, reminiscent of the DIY instructions associated with the *Survival Pieces* (fig. 10, 48). It was paradigmatically different from other works on the site. 'At that time we were intending to create a work of reclamation where our hand lay lightly on the earth. We had the intent of not signing the work' (H. M. Harrison and Harrison 2016, 81).

Spoils Pile Reclamation was also a compositional exercise using quantities of materials, very much like *Making Earth*.[10] This focus on quantity has an underpinning in Newton Harrison's approach to composition. Cassidy Rogers highlights Newton's concern with quantity in composition, including quoting his prospectus for a design course from 1968, saying:

> To achieve this, Newton instructed students to forego the conventional approach to composition, understood as an arrangement of parts internal to the work of art, and instead approach composition as … the study of amount. That is, how much (the amount) of any given thing [be it a work of art or otherwise] is necessary to either act of itself, or to activate any other thing [in a shared environment]. Implicit in the study of amount is the idea of interaction. It is by an evaluation of the interaction of parts that the study of amount is refined and its function defined. (Cassidy Rogers 2016, 120)

The use of quantities as compositional devices is manifest in their works from references in *The Lagoon Cycle* such as 'Each array covering sixty-two acres contains/an average of 225 acre-feet of water An acre-foot of/water contains 325,000 gallons Therefore each/array will hold an average of 73,327,500 gallons of/water' (Fourth Lagoon/65) to *The Serpentine Lattice* to 'the oxygen replenishing properties/of the quadrillions of living needles' in this case of the Douglas Fir and the Western Red Cedar (H. M. Harrison and Harrison 1993, 6). Quantities are a manifestation of what Burnham calls the 'literalness' of systems. In these various examples the one selected from *The Lagoon Cycle* is very literal. The example from *The Serpentine Lattice* (1993) has some irony to it, imagining the quantity of pine needles in a forest. The quantitative as a dimension of the systemic is foregrounded, part of the new imaginary. This offers an alternative understanding of the use of 'abstraction produced by quantification', understood by Brain as in conflict with Tsing's 'arts of noticing' (Brain 2018, 160). Here quantification and its use in composition can become a means to notice, not the detail of the individual, but the specificity of quantities in relation. Here quantity can be part of encounter and narrative as well as the literalness of a system.

It was, however, quantity that also led to *Spoils Pile Reclamation* remaining incomplete. According to the Harrisons' telling of the story:

> 3000 truckloads later, the now frantic leadership of Artpark demanded that we cease bringing truckloads of earth forthwith. We refused, saying we had covered only 8.5 of the 15.8 or 16 hectares. Therefore, the work of reclamation was unfinished, and they would be left with half a spoils pile and half a meadow. (H. M. Harrison and Harrison 2016, 79)

The project was stopped despite the Harrisons securing high-level advocates for it.[11] The comparison with *Brine Shrimp Farm* might be useful here – that had a form of visuality in the colour field but was also an artificially created and managed ecosystem which, with external inputs and periodic renewals, could successfully produce shrimp and salt

(H. M. Harrison & Harrison 2016, 25–26). However it only operated for one 'cycle', the duration of the exhibition. One might wonder if the Los Angeles County Museum of Art would have cancelled that too after two or three years of salt production and sale? The poetic texts of later works address incentives (such as the 'eco-security system' proposed in *The Serpentine Lattice* (H. M. Harrison and Harrison 1993, 7)) and argue for paradigm shifts ('Then/a new reversal of ground comes into being/where human activity becomes a figure/within an ecological field' (1993, 5)), and focus on articulating goals. Another self-sustaining installation created by the Harrisons, *Endangered Meadows of Europe*, brings together the ongoing process of meadow life in a major museum context, but was surrounded by panels containing the poetic articulation of the value and importance of meadows as 'teacher and model and prophet' (H. M. Harrison and Harrison 2001b, 17). The work was maintained for a year and then seed was used to create meadow in the Rheinaue Park in Bonn where the signage was also relocated. These sorts of regenerative, durational works actively need the dimensions of intensification and amplification through the aesthetic forms such as narrative, metaphor, and even irony in order to engage multiple dimensions of the larger systems they are nested within.

Reclamation for whose benefit?

The *Spoils Pile Reclamation* project is happening at a point where there is significant debate about the role of the arts in reclamation projects. It is synchronous with the King County Arts Commission programme in Washington State on the West Coast of the USA. That project was focused by the role of the arts in land reclamation and involved two built projects and an exhibition of proposals, the latter touring to fourteen venues across the USA. The artist Robert Morris (1931–2018) made one of the built works, *Untitled Earthwork (Johnson Pit #30)* (1979) as well as giving a keynote address at one of the two symposiums. His keynote is a seminal text in the development of critical discourse on public art. He offers a definition of the distinctiveness of place-based works, drawing attention to their temporality 'Perception of large spaces and distances is of a different order from the relatively undemanding instantaneous order for objects in closed interior spaces'. He goes on to argue that the interesting works are being done in more 'non-spectacular' and even 'densely urban' sites. Morris concludes his keynote by challenging certain key narratives – that artists are cheaper, and that art can 'wipe away technological guilt'. He asks, 'Will it be easier in the future to rip up the landscape for one last shovelful of non-renewable energy source if an artist can be found (cheap, mind you) to transform the devastation into an inspiring and modern work of art?' (Morris 1979, 13–16). He concludes saying:

> It would seem that artists participating in art as land reclamation will be forced to make moral as well as aesthetic choices. There may be more choices available than

either a cooperative or a critical stance for those who participate. But it would perhaps be a misguided assumption to suppose that artists hired to work in industrially blasted landscapes would necessarily and inevitably choose to convert such sites into idyllic and reassuring places, thereby socially redeeming those who wasted the landscape in the first place. (Morris 1979, 16)

This is a challenge to artists and the Harrisons' *Spoils Pile Reclamation* self-sustaining system, beneficial to all parties, is framed as 'cheap' – it will 'cost less overall to do than to not do'. It is also intended to create a meadow that is probably an 'idyllic and reassuring' place. The Harrisons' 'commitment' is a moral choice as well as an aesthetic one. Restoring the site might leave human responsibility unaddressed, but it is surely attending to the well-being of the web of life? In the case of remediating the landscape at ArtPark, who is advantaged and who is disadvantaged? The Harrisons do not touch on the significant human impacts of the pollution that characterised the ArtPark site, or other sites in the area such as Love Canal as documented by photographer Joel Sternfeld (Spens 2020).

Metaphor as organiser

Spoils Pile Reclamation occurs at a point where the Harrisons have been using a mixture of proposition and place-focused narrative in the various *Meditations* works (*Sacramento* and *Great Lakes* in particular) made during 1976 to 1977. They go on to articulate their 'mature' poetic voice in *The Lagoon Cycle*. However, *Spoils Pile Reclamation* has only instructions for people involved in the process. Thirty years later, in the published proposal for *Greenhouse Britain: Losing Ground, Gaining Wisdom*, the Harrisons articulate their use of texts in terms that make clear how central this has become to the practice and how it is embedded in the way they work with systems.

> We think linguistic invention is as important as visual improvisation. For the purposes of this work, we are replacing the word 'development' with the term 'settlement.' For us, the term 'settlement' as embedded in it the idea of habitat, not only for ourselves but the other living creatures (animals, birds, insects and plants) with which we share the ecosystem within which all structure is built. That is to say, human habitation would be an interactive figure in a bio-diverse sphere. (H. M. Harrison and Harrison 2007a, 8)

Metaphor has been explored in the previous chapter in the context of improvisation, in relation to Schön's conception of 'generative metaphor' and the Harrisons' argument that metaphor drives design. Metaphor is also a key part of a poetics that addresses and works with the literalness of systems. In fact one might argue that metaphor is the most significant aesthetic dimension of systems, certainly from the perspective of the

Harrisons. The Harrisons frequently highlight how changing a 'grounding metaphor' can generate new consequences (H. M. Harrison and Harrison 2007b, n.p.). We might understand that metaphors are central to what Meadows' characterises as leverage points – the 'goals and paradigms of systems' (Meadows 1999) .

At the beginning of this chapter, we suggested that it was useful to consider systems as 'predicaments'. It might also be useful to consider systems as organised by metaphors in the sense that linguists and philosophers Lakoff and Johnson discuss (1980). Complementing Schön's account, Lakoff and Johnson focus on the ways in which everyday metaphors are based in corporeal experiences including that of the body and movement. As previously noted metaphors function as 'transport' for thinking and imagination. But systems are also more than metaphors – they are also self-generating and self-maintaining. As Burnham highlights, they are 'literal' – the 'energy' moving in systems is physical, and is affected by entropy. That movement is affected by what is advantaged and what is disadvantaged. The waste in human systems mostly does not generate well-being in the wider system. The Harrisons are intent on reshaping the goals of systems in ways that enact the fundamental paradigm shift, the new imaginary, of re-niching the human within the 'bio-diverse sphere', the 'ecological field'. Metaphors are part of the Harrisons' poetics, but it is the recognition that systems can be understood *and affected* through attention to aesthetics, and in particular through a poetics that works with metaphors, that is critical.

Brain in their critique of the interpretation of ecologies through the lens of systems thinking uses exactly this device, saying:

> Stating 'I am studying a grasslands assemblage' instead of 'I am studying a grasslands system' produces a remarkable shift in expectations and assumptions. This simple substitution dismantles subtle assumptions of fixed categories of knowledge, as well as assumptions that engineering and control are always possible. (Brain 2018, 159)

The Harrisons would have approved. That being said, there are aspects of life where whether something is a 'system' or an 'assemblage' is not an either/or choice. The experience of living through cancer treatment (chemotherapy, radiotherapy, surgery) is one of assemblage – assemblage of a life each day taking small pleasures as well as adapting to necessary changes (Fremantle 2020). It is also one of a 'system', a treatment pathway with optimal points for each stage of the process. The systematic process of treatment would not ideally be conceived of through the metaphor of 'assemblage', not least because consistency is one of the key factors. However, the systematic process of cancer treatment is governed by expert judgement underpinned by an ethics.[12]

Burnham's essay 'Corporate Art' (1971), a review of the Los Angeles County Museum of Art's *Art and Technology* exhibition, is highly critical of the motivations and outcomes of the actual engagement between business interests and artists, arguing that the exhibition demonstrates that 'art and technology only coalesce on the most trivial levels' (Burnham 1971, 189). However, Burnham concludes by focusing on *Brine Shrimp Farm* (fig. 8-10) (created not with a corporate partner, but working with the Scripps Institution of Oceanography), saying:

> While this may be construed as systems art, or art which is structured to complete a natural growth pattern, many in the Art World would dismiss it as simple ecological experimentation. What is important, of course, is whether or not Harrison's work conforms to the structural principles of art. If it does, then he has made a profound commentary on the technical hopes and failures of our culture. (Burnham 1971, 192)

Burnham might define what he means by the 'structural principles of art' when he says, 'At its roots art acknowledges the existence of certain unchanging patterns to natural processes' (Burnham 1971, 191). The last section of the later essay 'Contemporary Ritual' (1973) focuses on *Survival Piece #VII: The Crab Farm*, which in due course becomes the Second Lagoon of *The Lagoon Cycle*. Rather than focusing directly on the systemic aspects of the work, he focuses on the ritual aspects, saying, 'Harrison believes that effective ritual stems from homage to our life-support systems, which in turn give sustenance and coherence to each social group that participates' (Burnham 1974, 164). He goes on to discuss Newton's process of making earth and the processes involved in *The Crab Farm*. He concludes:

> Tentative as it is, Harrison's art poses a most complex but fundamental question: namely, can we really sever ourselves from our food and material resources so that there is no longer a magical interface (ritual-art) between the two? (Burnham 1974, 166)

Jack Burnham's suggestion of a 'systems aesthetic' asks us to consider relationality beyond the discursive. It takes us into a problematic territory, for some technocratic, for others utopian or dystopian, perhaps best framed as a 'predicament'. Burnham's various indications of aspects of his systems aesthetic shine a useful 'side light' on the Harrisons' practice particularly in terms of elements we find in the work including maps and diagrams, as well as the focus on both literal quantities and logical consequences. What has become clear is that aspects of the Harrisons' poetics need to be understood in the context of systems and offer ways of engaging with systems through aesthetic understanding. Most importantly, the Harrisons' attention to patterns created by metaphors – their recurrent proposals of different metaphors to generate different patterns – needs to be understood as a poetic device directed at changing the goals and paradigms of systems. A complementary poetic device the Harrisons use, as noted elsewhere, is irony. Irony is intended to highlight the incongruity between what is intended and what is actually happening. As noted, the Harrisons describe these 'incongruities' as 'the cost of belief' – each panel or page of text in the Sixth Lagoon ends with a version of 'Pay attention to the cost of belief'.

Obvious rituals such as the feasts that characterised the *Survival Pieces* cease to appear in the Harrisons' works, though *Making Earth* forms part of exhibitions throughout their career, the last example being as part of *On the Deep Wealth of this Nation, Scotland* at the Taipei Biennial in 2018. The Harrisons' use of poetic text, combined with images and often performed, emerges as the critical element that evokes the form of a ritual for the reader, 'vision[s] that [would] explode in the mind of the interested person. [...] The work is a chant and was made to be read aloud' (H. M. Harrison and Harrison 2001a, n.p.). The ritual is part of the augmenting and amplifying.

The Harrisons' and other artists such as Ukeles' approach to systems is focused by socio-cultural dimensions, as opposed to those of for instance technoscience. This approach aligns with Meadows' conception of the leverage points. Focusing on metaphor is key in opening up what sorts of poetics are relevant to address systems through their aesthetic dimensions. Burnham crystallises the idea that it is the aesthetic dimensions that drive the progressive reorganisations of environments. It is the aesthetic dimension that drives the repetition, to connect this with Whitehead.

This needs to be understood as in juxtaposition with isomorphic approaches to systems that work on the basis that the 'system' as represented in models is a mirror of the 'world'.[13] Isomorphism assumes that the important element of the system is information. Isomorphism assumes that mirroring information is key, for instance that 'computer equals brain' or that a model is a mirror for an ecosystem, or for energy infrastructure, or for an oil rig.[14] The Harrisons demonstrate how metaphors used in landscape strategy freight certain assumptions and how, by changing metaphors, systems can change. Further they recognise that approaches that are developed in one context or system can migrate to other contexts through 'conversational drift', but that this process is 'thready' – dependent on serendipity, sometimes involving gaps, and different from context to context.

CHAPTER 6

On the Political

The Harrisons' lifelong aim to put the well-being of the life web first has political implications in that it fundamentally challenges Western notions of progress based in materialism, and economics that are built on those notions. In this chapter we explore how the Harrisons' practice takes form as an 'ecopolitical practice' and what that might mean as an art practice. In discussing their work *The Endangered Meadows of Europe* (1994), Newton Harrison points to the multi-layered character of an ecopolitical approach.

> In *Endangered Meadows* [...] you had a work with an ecological narrative, ecopolitical in nature, one hell of an aesthetic experience and a scientific product as well. This level of complexity is what we call art and science, or ecological art. It is not enough to frame, or say, 'look at this bad thing'. It is not enough to say 'look at this great phenomenon'. The real issue is to find a multi-layered narrative that bears relationship to other narratives. (Ingram 2013, 272)

We trace how they engaged in issues of public concern but distanced themselves from being easily co-opted by institutions. Taking the environment as their client, they directly engage values and belief systems. They create a provocative rather than practical space for reflection, drawing word and image normally associated with environment policy into their poetics (Kester 2011, 42, 204–7). We 'think with' Hannah Arendt (1906–1975), the political philosopher who positions the political in freedom, the freedom to think for oneself and to offer one's particular experience to the building of a common world. This is an approach to politics that is not founded in reason, moral principles, or expert knowledges. It draws on critical thought and the imagination, on the desire to participate, to encounter other perspectives unlike one's own by sharing one's perspective in public with others. We trace how Arendt constructs this position and then how her insights help us to deepen our understanding of the political in the Harrisons' work. Arendt is a political philosopher, and the Harrisons are neither political theorists nor economists, but artists. There is a surprising commonality between their approaches, a sense that public life emerges out of life itself, through exploration and experimentation more than proscribed by codes of conduct. The freedom that is necessary to this quality of public life is haunted by the spectre of totalitarianism in both of their perspectives. For Arendt this is informed by her experience of Nazism. For the Harrisons the danger implicit in adopting a principle of putting ecosystemic well-being

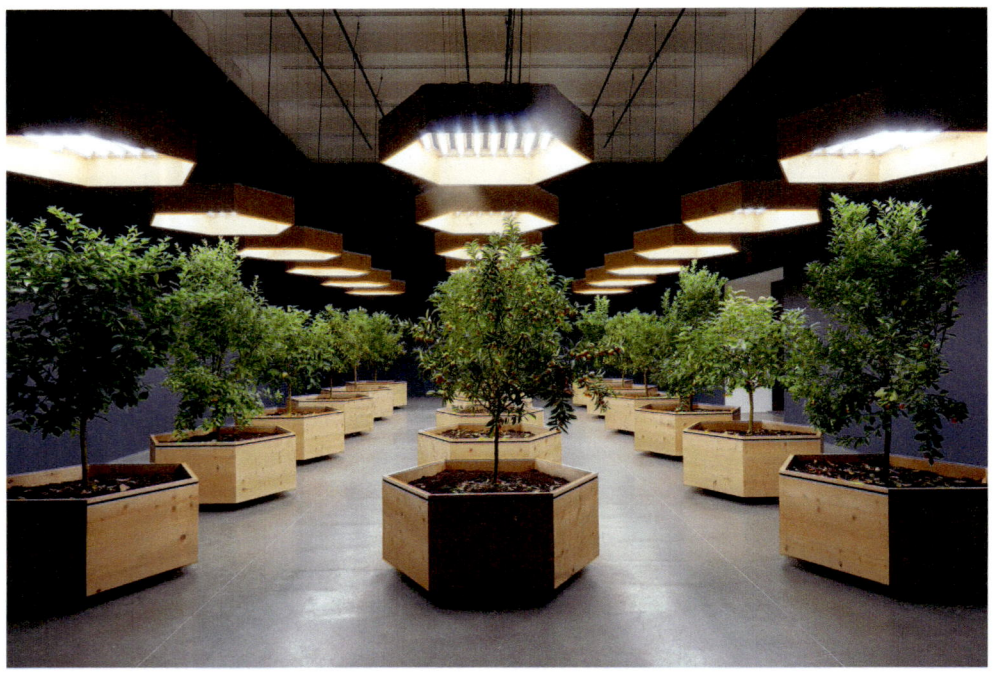

Figure 47: 'Survival Piece #V: Portable Orchard' (1972) Re-enactment for Frieze London 2017 (courtesy of the Newton and Helen Harrison Family Trust and Various Small Fires, Los Angeles / Dallas / Seoul)

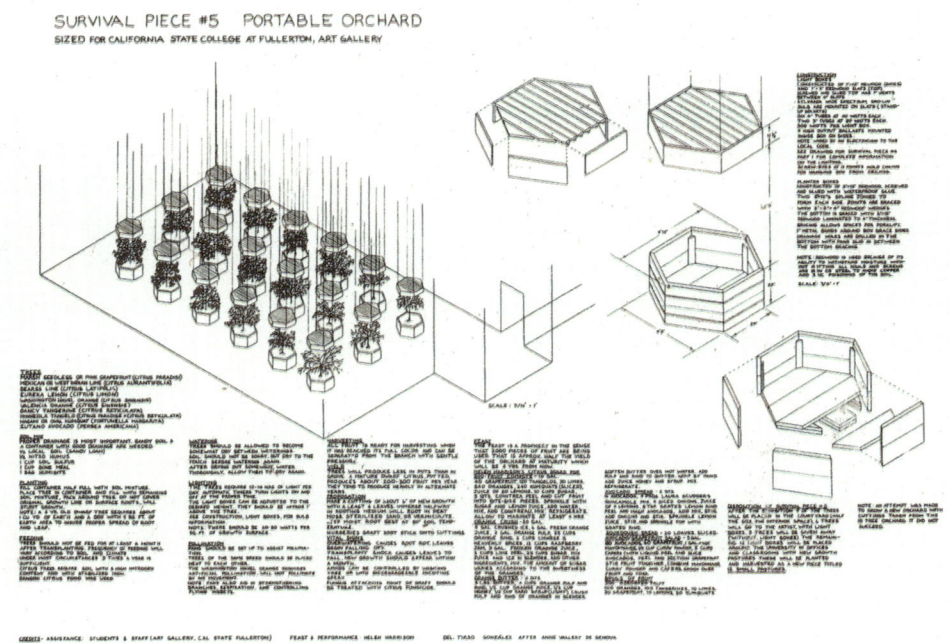

Figure 48:' Survival Piece #V: Portable Orchard' (1972-73). Graphite pencil on paper, 23 13/16 × 35 3/4 in. (60.5 × 90.8 cm). Whitney Museum of American Art, New York; purchase with funds from the Drawing Committee 2019.297.1. © Helen Mayer Harrison and Newton Harrison/ The Harrison Studio

first is that it becomes an ideology rather than a question of attention. Mandating eco-systemic well-being as a rule can in its actualisation become a form of eco-fascism, a danger they allude to with irony. In what ways do Arendt and the Harrisons incorporate aesthetics into politics? What relevance do their attempts to do so hold for today?

The Harrisons challenge governments, institutions, and organisations to undertake the implications of their commitment to the web of life. They critique the institution of art in its tendency to commodify artists and their works in ways that short circuit the meaning and power of the work to speak in public life. We touch on this in Chapter 2 where the Harrisons turn down invitations from an established gallery, refusing to set their personal interests as career artists above their commitment to the web of life. They exhibit their work in museums and galleries[1] alongside town halls (*Greenhouse Britain* (2007)), community halls (*On the Deep Wealth of this Nation, Scotland* (2017)) and public pavements (*Meditations on the Sacramento River, the Delta and the Bays of San Francisco* (1977)).They use these as 'spaces of appearance', an Arendtian term, spaces in which to reach a public through stories and debate. They re-animate the space between artist, audience, and artwork in ways that are politically charged and provocative. For example, they introduce feasts into the *Survival Pieces* in the museum and gallery spaces, for the time an unusual artistic tactic, but one that situates humans within living systems through the shared dependence on food. They also hold public conversations focused on the issues the works raise in these formal exhibition spaces that had up to then been accustomed to a different, less participative ritual form.

They produce DIY diagrams as parts of *Survival Pieces #II to #VII*, including for *Survival Piece #V: Portable Orchard* (fig. 48), so that the public could reproduce their experiments as 'backyard farming', undermining the trope of the unique work of art and positioning themselves as generalists rather than experts. They also frequently confront governments and municipalities in the ways they had imagined their territories, pointing out the contradictions between the interests of the environment and those of humans. In *Green Heart Vision* (1994-2001) (fig. 49), they respond to an invitation from the Cultural Council of South Holland by creating a work that makes clear that the planners were thinking the urban development 'backwards' (H. M. Harrison and Harrison 2016, 260). As a central element of the work they juxtapose two maps, one the wrong way round, to show an invasive set of plans and the other that respected the environment shown the right way round. They make quite practical propositions for changes in national policy, such as the redistribution of gross domestic product (GDP) in *The Serpentine Lattice*. They directly challenge Western epistemologies that result in technoscience. *The Lagoon Cycle* unfavourably compares forms of mechanised agri-culture with local practices that work in tune with the natural environment. The water buffalo in Sri Lanka outperforms the tractor in offering multiple uses and roles, not just one. Their 1977 work *Meditations on the Great Lakes of North America* (fig. 51) charges the two sovereign states of the United States and Canada with some irony in terms of whether it is possible to draw on water, commenting on the way the map had divided

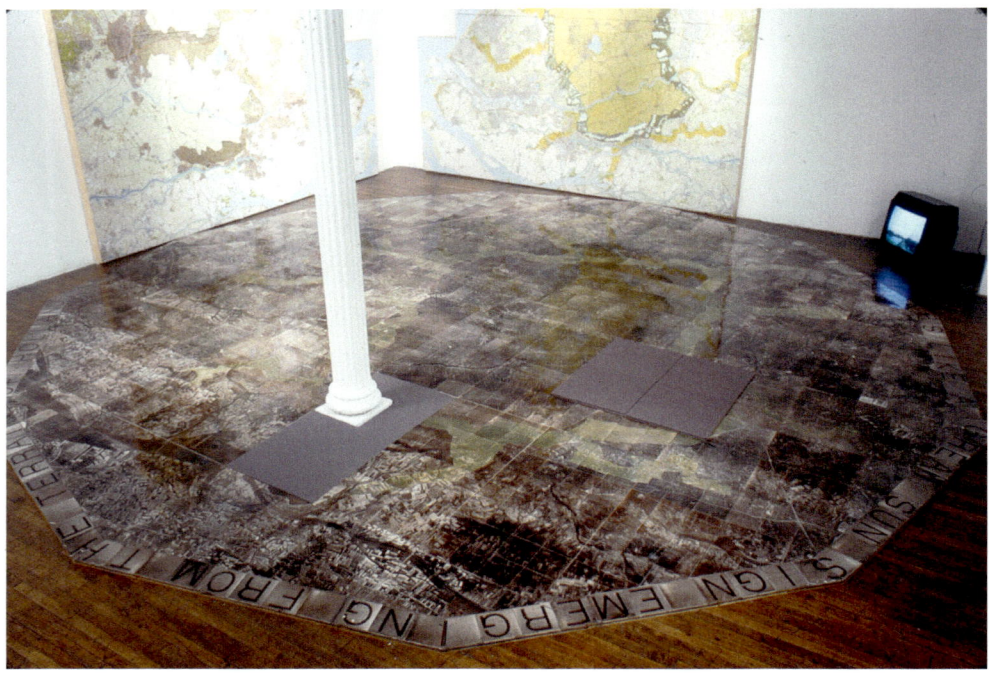

Figure 49: 'Green Heart Vision' (1994) In exhibition 'Peninsula Europe' (April 11 – May 9, 2003). Installation view at Ronald Feldman Gallery. (Private collection courtesy Ronald Feldman Gallery, New York)

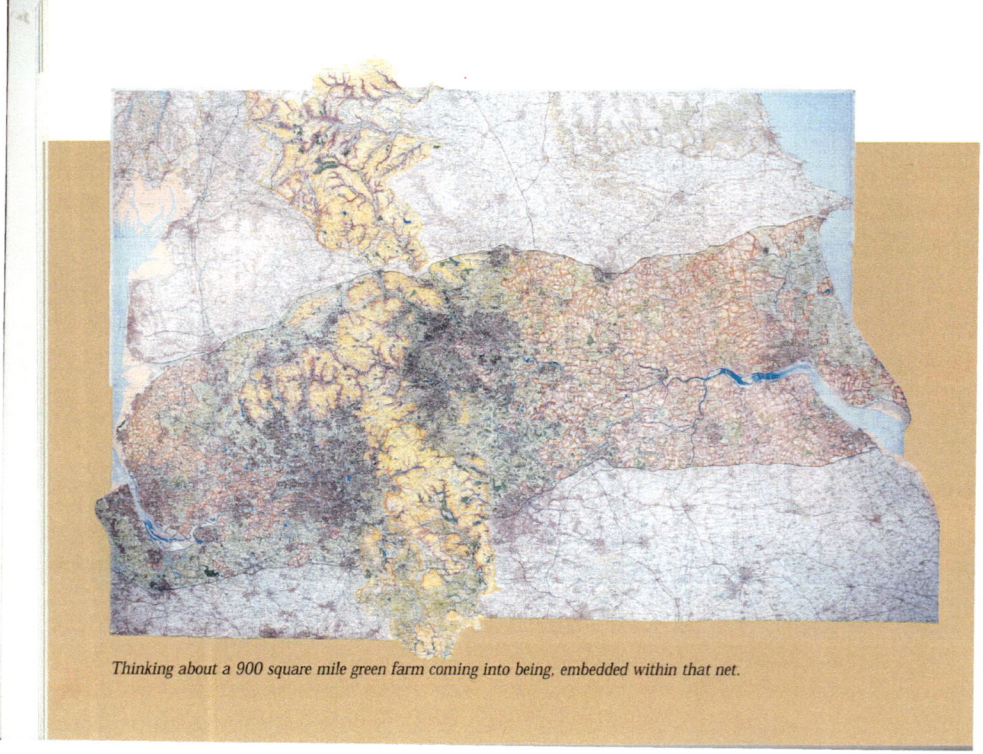

Thinking about a 900 square mile green farm coming into being, embedded within that net.

Figure 50: 'Casting a Green Net: Can it be we are seeing a Dragon?' (1998) Detail from publication (courtesy of the Newton and Helen Harrison Family Trust)

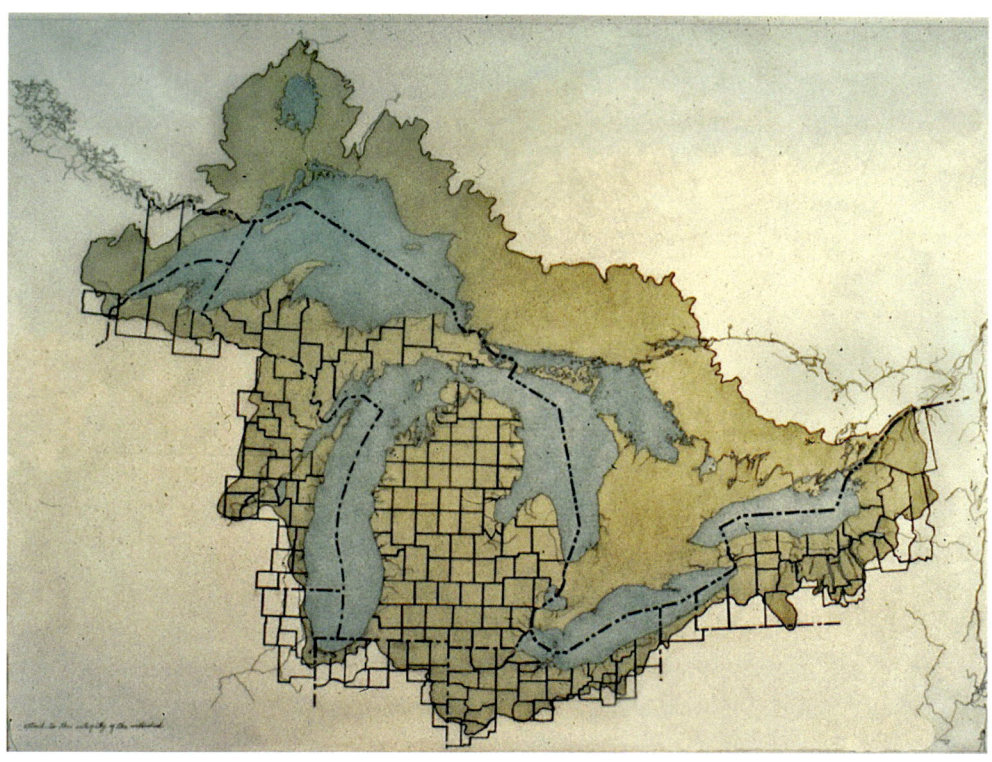

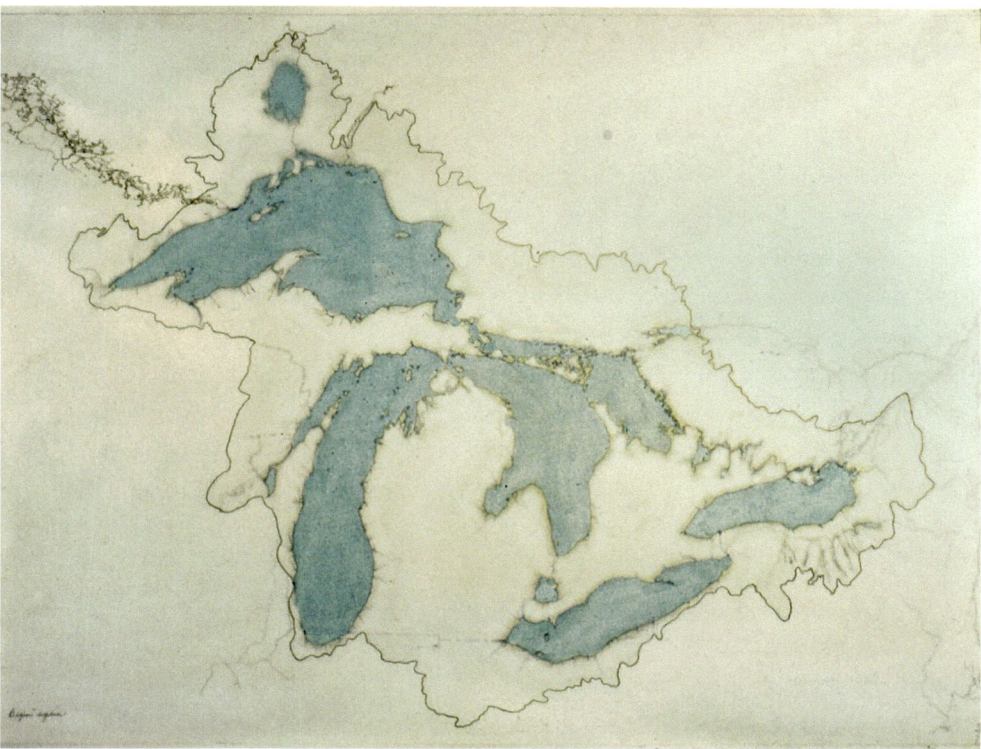

Figure 51: 'Meditation on the Great Lakes of North America' (1977) Detail (courtesy of the Newton and Helen Harrison Family Trust)

the territories across the Great Lakes with straight lines. The questions underpinning this work are highly political, evoking the spectre of cartography as a tool of imperialism. They propose to focus instead on the natural shape of the watershed in a redrawing of the map, to inhabit the niche that the natural environment has afforded. It is in this work they introduce the notion of a 'dictatorship of the ecology', consciously provoking us to reflect on the unequal power relation humans hold over the natural environment by inverting this hierarchy and presenting the natural environment as having absolute rule. Elsewhere, for example in *Epitaph* (2022) (fig. 57), they also suggest that the environment is indifferent to human survival, echoing Whitehead who suggests that active powers such as the sun are indifferent to their effects (Debaise 2017, 85–87).

These are examples of where the political is manifested through the content and process of the Harrisons' work. Both art and politics are phenomena of the public world, Arendt comments. It is through art that we engage our aesthetic sensibility and affirm life. She rarely directly deals with the natural world, let alone the ecological. She understands the political as a process of judging, of participation, and engagement in a shared sociability between humans. She draws on Kant, the Enlightenment thinker, creating an unusual reading of his various texts on the political that is based in aesthetics, taste, and judgement. Arendt argues that Kant did not explicitly develop a political philosophy. She draws on his *Critique of Judgment* as a key source for her reading of Kant's political philosophy. This reading sheds light on the Harrisons' approach to creating a world in common, with some notable differences. The Harrisons create representations that tend towards universalising. An example might be *On the Deep Wealth of this Nation, Scotland* (2017) that is constructed around the elements of air, water, atmosphere, and soil.[2] These are explored within a specific country and its ecology but the principles, and some variation of the themes, would hold true for any country on Planet Earth. Arendt's reading of Kant focuses on how to create a shared world of appearance without determining what we have in common. Her thinking on politics in the post-World War II era continues to be drawn upon in our current times. By recognising how her work and that of the Harrisons speak to each other, we may begin to get a sense, albeit a partial one, of what a political ecology that draws on the arts and aesthetics might look like in the 21st century. She constructs a politics of dialogue, persuasion, and agreement. This may be contrasted with another, more common form of politics based in interests and strategy, and the efficient management of resources (Villa 1992).

Re-finding humanity: Arendt's context for writing on the political

Before summarising Arendt's reading of Kant, it is important to draw out the context for her exploration of aesthetics and judgement as the basis for the political. It is late, unfinished work. In *The Life of the Mind* (Arendt 1981) she sets out to develop three sections – thinking, willing, and judging – explored in relation to one another. How does Arendt interconnect these three concepts to arrive at her quite distinctive formulation of the political? All three, she suggests, are activities of the mind and in their different ways preparation for acting in the world. Thinking deals with what is invisible and tends towards generalisation. Willing and judging address the particular, willing through what will be and judging through what has been. Neither willing nor judging are controlled by rules or laws, by reason. The third part on judging was never developed further than a title in her typewriter found at her death. Her *Lectures on Kant's Political Philosophy*, first published in 1982, have become the main resource for her thinking on judging and they in turn predominantly draw on Kant's late work, the *Critique of Judgment* (Kant 2007). For both writers this is unfinished work that nonetheless offers an important contribution. Both rethink the political in their respective times of significant political turmoil. For Kant this was the French Revolution (1789–1799) and for Arendt the period of Nazism (1920–1945).

Arendt's reading of Kant is original. The function of her lectures and subsequent publication is precisely to imagine and extrapolate this work. In the *Fifth Session* she states:

> If I am right that there is a political philosophy in Kant, but that, in contrast to other philosophers, he never wrote it, then it seems obvious that we shall be able to find it, if we can find it at all, in his whole work and not just in a few essays that are usually collected under that rubric. (Arendt 1992, 31)

Of Kant's three core questions that underpinned his philosophy – What can I know? What ought I do? What may I hope? – none were concerned with man as a political being. It is a 'non-written political philosophy' (Arendt 1992, 19). Nonetheless, Arendt uncovers qualities in Kant's work on judging that she recognises to be crucial to a different form of politics in a 20th century recovering from Totalitarianism.

As an extreme political form unknown before the 20th century, Totalitarianism had dangerously eroded freedom and its potential for a common world. Arendt considered that specific conditions in the 19th and 20th centuries had given rise to Nazism, beginning with antisemitism. Linked to the rise of imperialism, antisemitism is more than prejudice. For Arendt writing before our time of identity politics, she did not mean snap judgements that aim to diminish people. We need to recognise that we all have prejudices. They are both inevitable and important in a world that embraces diversity. Hatred of the Jews is a prejudice in Arendt's understanding, whereas antisemitism is altogether more extreme in seeking the alienation and eradication of a whole people, their culture and relations within other cultures in an unlimited search for power (Arendt 2017). She recoiled from the horror that such extremism had rendered human beings superfluous and therefore expendable. Its consequences for action in public life needed to be examined in a world that Arendt deemed had never found peace even in the postwar period, but that had continued war in another form, the Cold War. It is perhaps out of the experience of being a Jew and a young academic in the throes of antisemitism in Nazi Germany that she sought to re-find humanity within the ruins of such public manifestations of evil. She read in Kant's work a notion of the political founded in experience and intuition that included aesthetic experience, in the deeply human rather than in reason. It is in this sense that Arendt is important to the relationship of art to politics, a politics founded in life, the more-than-human world. The chapter therefore addresses the apparently unlikely idea that aesthetics and imagination, particularly through the arts, might bridge the widening gap between the way we imagine our world as a resource to serve human need and the inappropriateness of this construction and its increasing levels of inequality. The Harrisons share this search for an alternative. Arendt is by no means the only possible answer, but to quote one of her severest critics, it is part of the story.

> The fetishistic quality of her distinction making and her Kantian finickness in determining the political: these attest to a deeply rooted desire to preserve the possibility of meaning created by political action and redeemed by political judgement. (Villa 1992, 302)

Activist movements such as the International Degrowth Network critique our current forms of economics and neoliberal institutions structured around unconstrained exploitation of natural resources. Frequently drawing on different theories of nature, they highlight the need to question the way we have distributed wealth through access, or not, to natural resources and the concealed violence that underpins the current unequal exploitation of the world. Stengers suggests that the failure of the current scientists, politicians, and lawmakers to make the changes that the environmental crisis has necessitated is also a form of indifference. However, we must not be naïve about radical projects that address the current crisis – there is latent toxicity in counteractions. She argues that they need to be imagined as *pharmakon*, a Greek word meaning both medicine and poison. 'In its poisonous form, public action takes on fascist characteristics; in its remedial form, it leads to benevolent collaboration' (Last 2013).

The discourse of place and belonging that some areas of the ecological movement have centred upon, can quickly crystallise into nationalist claims of 'blood and soil'. Prominent figures in the early organic movement in the UK had also been closely involved with Oswald Mosley's British Union of Fascists (Raskin 2021). The targeting of over-population as a single cause of anthropogenic environmental change can quickly become a reason to block migration/immigration and reinforce notions of 'racial purity' and 'rights' based in ownership of property (Purdy 2015). The issues around which an eco-fascism might coalesce have emerged in parallel with industrial capitalism. Kirsty Campion in a review of literature on eco-fascism argues:

> Ecofascists romanticise a mystical past in which they imagine that their society was ecologically harmonious and strong. They argue that the forces of modernity, such

as industrialisation, urbanisation, materialism, and individualism have weakened their society and disrupted that ecological harmony. (Campion 2023, 927)

These writers on ecofascism go on to say that ecofascists believe that nature holds the ultimate purifying power and can restore their society to a state of harmony and strength that in turn secures it from domination from others while also achieving a positive effect on the ecosystem. The ecofascist vision of ecological harmony manifests as racial segregation based on privileged claims on territory. They draw out two constructions of this, one ecocentric and one anthropocentric. The ecocentric is constructed in terms of custodians, positioning themselves as the exclusive guardians of nature and the ecological needs of a defined place, and in the anthropocentric, the belief in protecting their 'race' and protecting the environment is essential for the race to thrive (Campion 2023, 927). The ecocentric construction might in reality be a fantasy rather than actually engaging in meaningful dialogue with other living things. The purifying power of nature can also be related to the imperial colonial project that imposes a construction of harmony that serves to justify the organisation and education of the 'savage' while also overlaying a landscape design imported by the colonisers. Ranil Senanayake, in an article on forestry that references the Harrisons, draws out the way in which landscapes are reshaped by colonisers to mirror their 'formative pleasant experiences' (Senanayake 2012, 237).

This notion of harmony may be contrasted with the way Whitehead discusses harmony within an actual occasion of experience. For Whitehead complexity and contradictions in life are crucial to augmenting and intensifying experience in the emergence of new life. This new life is what he means by harmony, reaching 'satisfaction' or resolution out of the strong pull or lure of survival (Whitehead 1978, 219–21). In ecofascism complexity and contradiction, in particular that of human relations and territories, are reduced, simplified to a sameness, that legitimises forms of exclusion.

Sam Moore and Alex Roberts in *The Rise of Ecofascism* summarise the emergence of such movements, saying:

> [W]e trace the history of these ideas and practices, from colonial nature management to the rise of scientific racism and eugenics to the 'green' aspects of Fascist Italy and Nazi Germany through to postwar overpopulation discourse, currents of environmentalist misanthropy, and lastly the securitization of the environment itself. (Moore and Roberts 2022, 3)

Thus, racism is bound into forms of nature management, and as both Moore and Roberts and Campion indicate, the inclusion and exclusion of groups, in particular through 'cultural tropes of uncleanliness, pollution and pestilence' (Moore and Roberts 2022, 1), as well as the translation of environments into resources that need to be protected, all underpin narratives. These can be read as 'adaptation projects to allow capitalist elites to stabilize their position amidst planetary crises' (Mann and Wainwright 2020, 15).

An emergent third vector of eco-fascism is focused by technoscience and the need to save the world through technology. T. J. Demos describes his own approach, saying it

> criticizes the Anthropocene thesis for its regressive and narcissistic neo-humanism, its evasion of the differential causes and effects of climate breakdown, its disavowal of petrocapitalist culpability, and its ecology of affluence. That analysis extended to diverse visual-cultural expressions of remote sensing data, the kind that offers 'whole earth' perspectives of the planet as not only devoid of social conflict but also safely in the grips of an emergent scientific mastery. (Demos 2018, 6)

This in turn relates to Geoff Mann and Joel Wainwright in their critique of the Leviathan of sovereignty, the argument for a global government, to describe how it is constituted of

> a collection of powers co-ordinated to 'save the planet' and to determine what measures are necessary and what and who must be sacrificed in the interests of life on Earth. (Mann and Wainwright 2020, 15)

The construction of ecofascism has a dimension of place, a concern with racial purity, but also a potential underpinning in the resource extractivism of technoscience required to maintain endless productivity related to colonialism. The Harrisons are not engaged in an eco-fascist project, but it is important to recognise that addressing ecological issues today brings everyone into territories where eco-fascist framings are also present. Eco-fascists have even interpreted anti-colonial arguments as justifying racial exclusion from Eurasia, conceiving immigration as a form of colonisation (Davidson 2024).

These volatile conditions have something in common with the rise of antisemitism, the sense that power can be pursued in ways that are unlimited, breaking away from the governance of nation states and increasing inequality in the process. They echo the conditions in late 19th century France and Germany where those excluded from political representation turned to extra-parliamentary action and became mobilised as a mob with the support of power-hungry intellectual elites (Arendt 2017). Arendt's analysis of the conditions that created Totalitarianism in Europe are useful to understanding emergent political ecologies. Her construction is far from being an aestheticisation of politics, as manifest, for example, in the use of aesthetics and design in Nazism – aesthetics in Arendt's construction is not used to magnify a particular ideology to show power. It is a critical practice, open to human plurality through experiences that begin with the individual and the sensory as a starting point to the sharing of experience in developing a common world.[3] As mentioned earlier in this chapter, her perspective in constructing a politics of dialogue, persuasion, and deliberation emerges out of her experience of Nazism as a Jew who emigrated to the United States in 1938 and wrote on the political in the post-war period under the shadow of Totalitarianism.

Kant's construction of the political in aesthetics

Kant foregrounds the agency and responsibility of the individual to think for oneself in concert with others. This emerges at a time when freedom continued to be heavily constrained by the Church. In his short paper entitled *What is Enlightenment?* originally published in 1784, Kant cites the multiple ways in which members of humankind have deferred to other powers to do their thinking for them, the Church, the physician, men over women. Kant stresses the path to enlightenment is founded in understanding one's own self-worth through the faculty of thinking for oneself:

> 4...For even among the entrenched guardians of the great masses a few will always think for themselves, a few who, after having themselves thrown off the yoke of immaturity, will spread the spirit of a rational appreciation for both their own worth and for each person's calling to think for himself. (Kant 1992, 1)

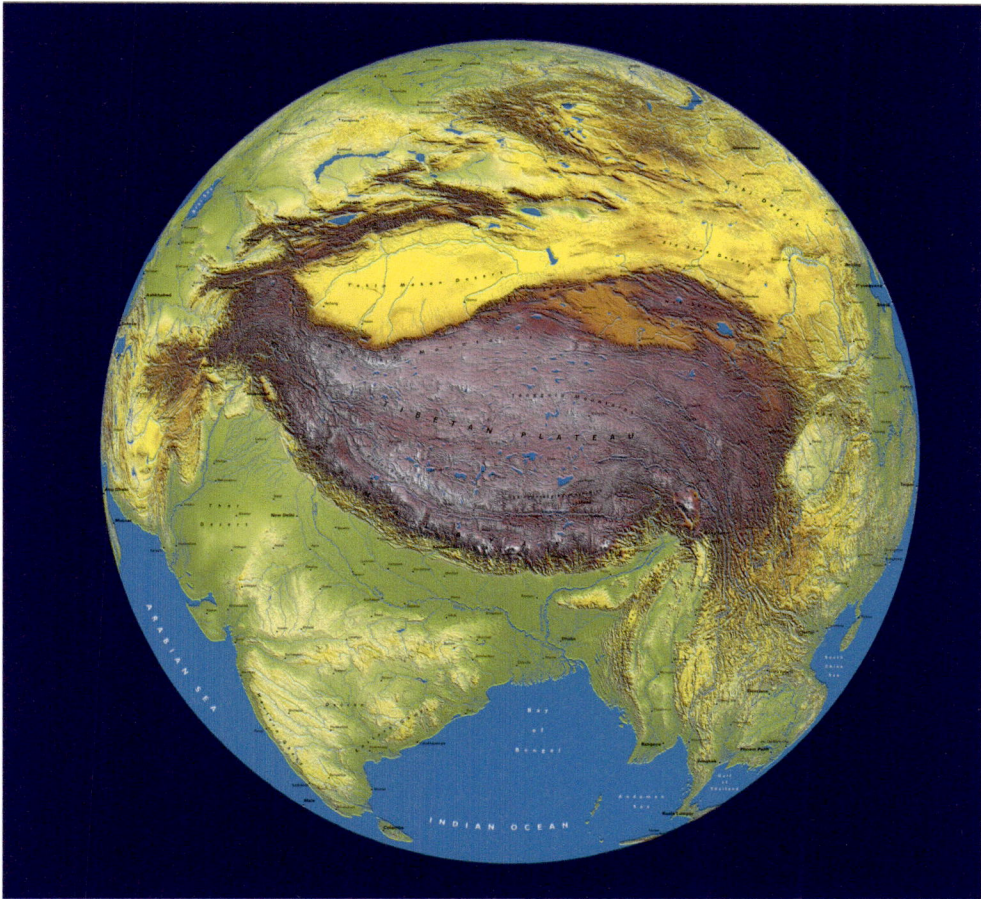

Figure 52: 'Tibet is the High Ground' (1993) (courtesy of the Newton and Helen Harrison Family Trust)

The Enlightenment in its early development meant liberation from authoritarianism.

Kant discovered judging as a 'silent sense' behind taste in aesthetics, Arendt suggests. Judging, he argued, is a practice close to the world of experience that cannot be taught, only exercised. It is not controlled by rules and laws, that is, by reason. It draws thought and understanding into its service. In his time in the 18th century aesthetics was a favoured topic that looked to the arts and the primacy of sense perception. It is through this 'hidden' faculty of judgement that we discern something to be beautiful. Kant observes that we do not arrive at appreciating the beauty of a particular rose through a process of deduction such as, 'All roses are beautiful, this flower is a rose, hence this rose is beautiful' (Arendt 1992, 13). The faculty of judgment deals in the particular without subsuming the object of our judgement into a general category, in this case 'beauty'. Through judgement we assess the beauty of an object for its own sake. This judgement occurs at a distance from our immediate sensory experience, liberated from private interest. The interval of distance offers a degree of impartiality, and, through it, we find pleasure in the world around us (Arendt 1992, 15, 42). It is an experience produced by the self interacting with the world.

Do we see such qualities in the Harrisons' work? In the early 1990s on the invitation of the Dalai Lama they were invited to make a proposal for an ecological peace park in Tibet. They chose to make their proposal in the form of a poem. Tibet was encountering significant issues with China at the time and the poetic text embodies a shift of perspective from the problems of bordering with China to the condition that both states share, the particular ecology of the region.

GREETINGS:--
We hold the ocean is a great draftsman.

In response to our millennia of manipulation of fire,
The Ocean has answered gracefully
By rising slowly,
And moment by moment
Redrawing the shorelines of the world.
And as the oceans rise gracefully
Changing all boundaries
And means of production
The ways of all living beings will change as well.

To this continuously graceful drawing and redrawing
Can we respond
By withdrawing with equal grace
To the High Ground?

It seems to us that envisioning Tibet as a World Park,
certainly high ground
Is an act of equal grace.
(H. M. Harrison and Harrison 1990, 3)

The ocean in the text evokes the human body engaged in a rhythm that is slow, 'graceful', in its back-and-forth exchange. A second metaphor of ocean as draughtsman develops this bodily connection, drawing and redrawing shorelines. Human life is personified as 'millennia of fire' that has brought about significant changes to which the ocean responds by rising, changing the conditions for all life (as it says in the Seventh Lagoon 'in an odd kind of dialogue'). The ocean's 'drawing' and 'redrawing' results in humans 'withdrawing' to a space, the proposed Buddhist peace park. The work led to a direct exchange with the Dalai Lama, clearly moved by its form of communication and quality of vision. Instead of a design for a peace park, the Harrisons offer a state of being in the interchange between ocean and land, a graceful improvisation. They propose to create a very large model of the Himalayas with the river systems exaggerated. The point of the model is to create a meeting point for all the peoples of the watershed to come together on a restoration project. *Tibet is the High Ground* (1991-2016) remained a proposal in poetry and maps (fig. 52).

What does it mean to develop politics based in judgement?

The perception of beauty in a particular thing is not confined to the person undergoing the experience. It is also in some sense free and open to all. It is communicable to others through language and form. Perception of beauty, and the sharing of aesthetic experience through language, through the arts, for instance, is fundamental to the ways in which we build a common world. It stems from the freedom to think for oneself as a pleasurable experience, and to share our perspective with others. Inevitably this engages other perspectives that differ and possibly contradict our own. Kant suggests the point of the whole exercise is to persuade, to woo another to one's own point of view (Arendt 1992, 39). For Arendt to woo is a gentle form of persuasion that is not based in a power relationship. It emerges out of a form of politics in which the individual and their experience of the world forms the foundation to engagement with others in ways that are sensory and able to be communicated.

It is like works of art that need to be communicable, to move, to offer perspectives to their audiences that are wider than their own private spheres of experience and interest. They woo us, functioning as mediators between diverse, individual sensory experiences in the world encountering one another. They create an opening, an interval for reflection in which we are invited to enlarge our imagination. We need spaces in which such exchanges can happen, spaces of appearance for activities of spectating

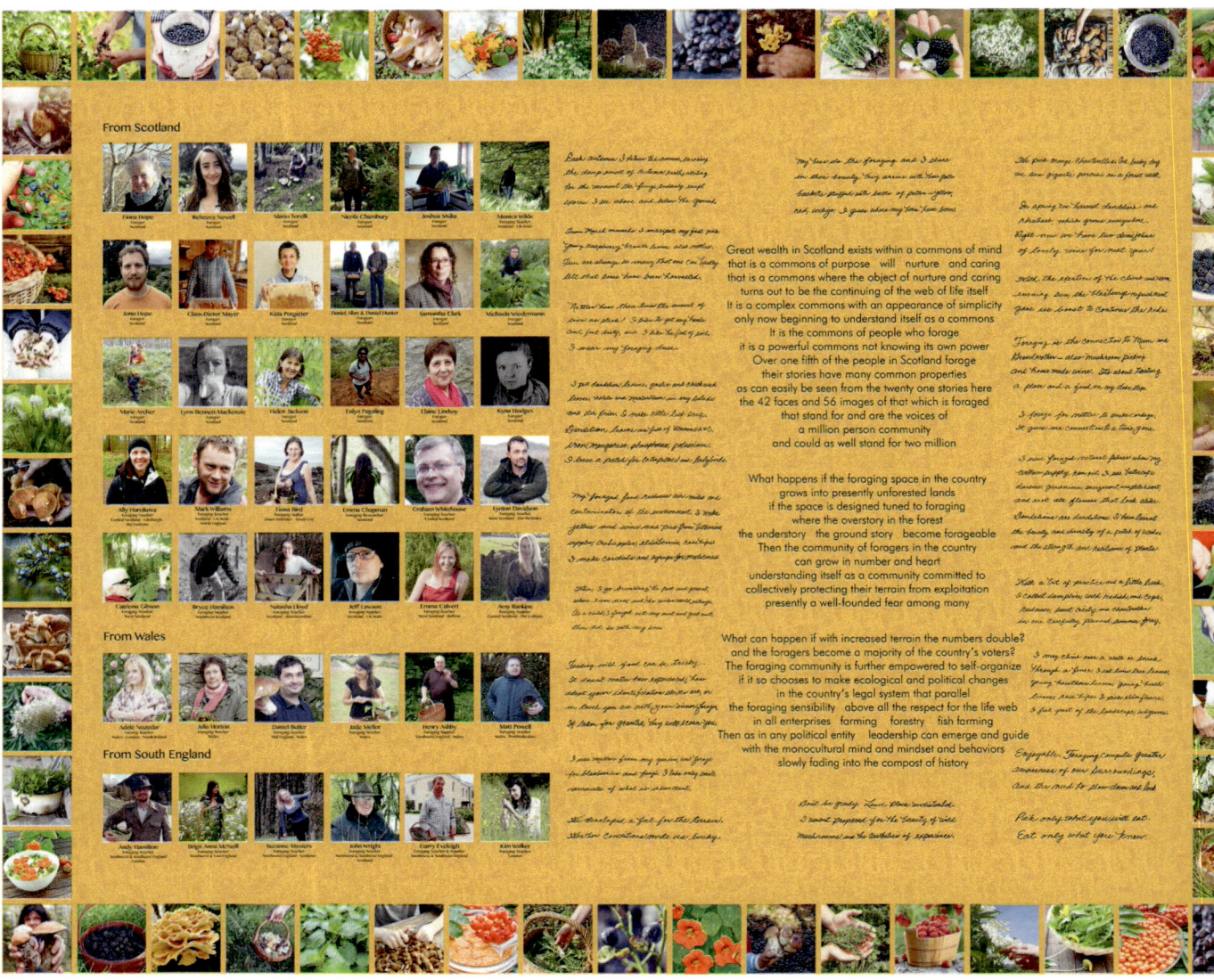

Figure 53: 'On the Deep Wealth of this Nation, Scotland' (2018) Detail of Foragers panel
(courtesy of the Newton and Helen Harrison Family Trust)

and making where we can come together to differ, to co-create meaning. Artworks offer such moments in their public presentations that are open to interpretation from different perspectives. Arendt eschewed the coercive character of truth. The notion of 'wooing' and being 'wooed' resonates with Whitehead's notion of being 'lured' towards creating harmony through the growing together of different kinds of potential, with the subtle difference perhaps that 'wooing' can emerge out of a feeling of love, where 'being lured' evokes a stronger power relation of being tempted.

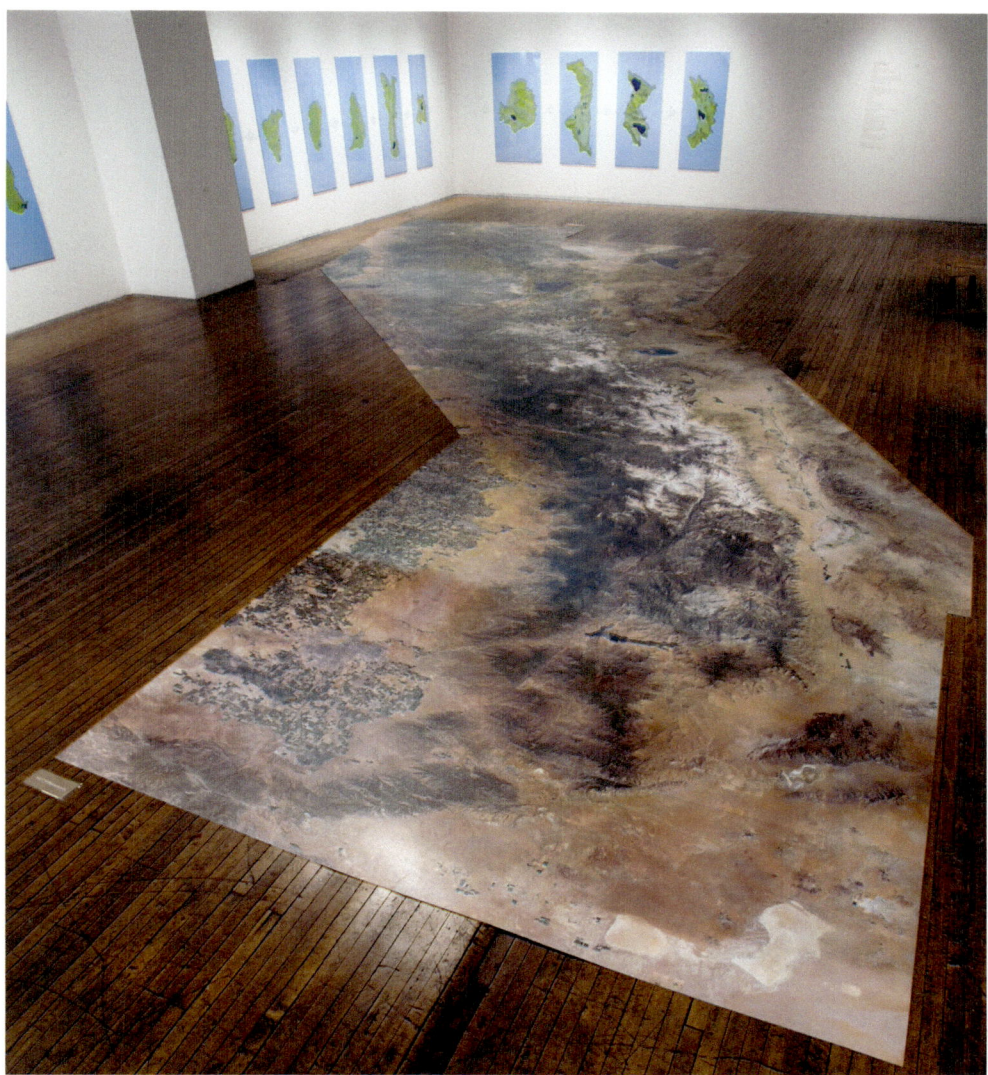

Figure 54: 'Sierra Nevada: An Adaptation' (February 9 – March 25, 2011) Installation View at Ronald Feldman Gallery, New York (Private collection courtesy Ronald Feldman Gallery, New York)

Politics in Arendt's sense can be a process of wooing or persuasion in a world of multiple, contradictory, and inconsistent viewpoints, neither a set of ideologies that are imposed through violent or non-violent means nor a set of strategies driven by goals or codes of conduct that regulate from outside. Arendt's construction of the political is a process of emergence. By participating in such spaces, we encounter other bodies in public space, other ideas to think with. If we take away the freedom to communicate publicly, we take away the freedom to think and exchange how we are experiencing the world (Arendt 1992, 40–41). It is in these spaces that the sense of a common world, *sensus communis*, emerges.

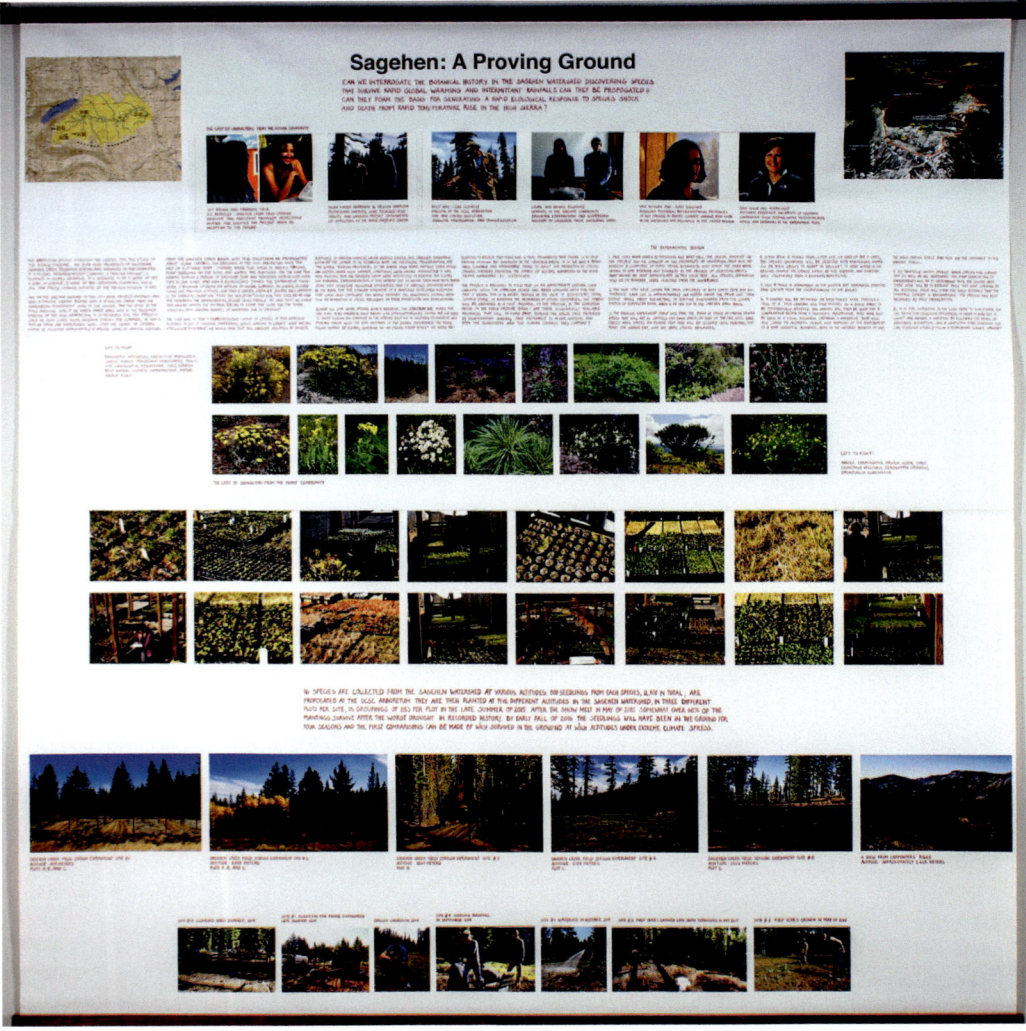

Figure 55: 'Sagehen: A Proving Ground' (2015) Inkjet print with photo collage and hand printing mounted on canvas 86 x 88 inches Collection of the Nevada Museum of Art, Gift of Helen and Newton Harrison

The Harrisons and their publics

The Harrisons' work is made to be experienced in public in this sense of an emergent discourse. They frequently performed the texts through readings. Their aesthetic tactics to woo us as audiences are multiple, including the combination of scale, colour, and materiality in the visual, and rhythm, pace, and imagery in poetic texts. Each artwork encourages us to live its issues in body and mind. They create maps you can walk on and in which you can locate where you live (*Green Heart Vision* (fig. 49), *Sierra Nevada: An Adaptation* (fig. 54)). A map can depict glacial melt as a wound or scar in the landscape (*Tibet is the High Ground*) (fig. 52). Maps can become objects of participation, such as the foragers in

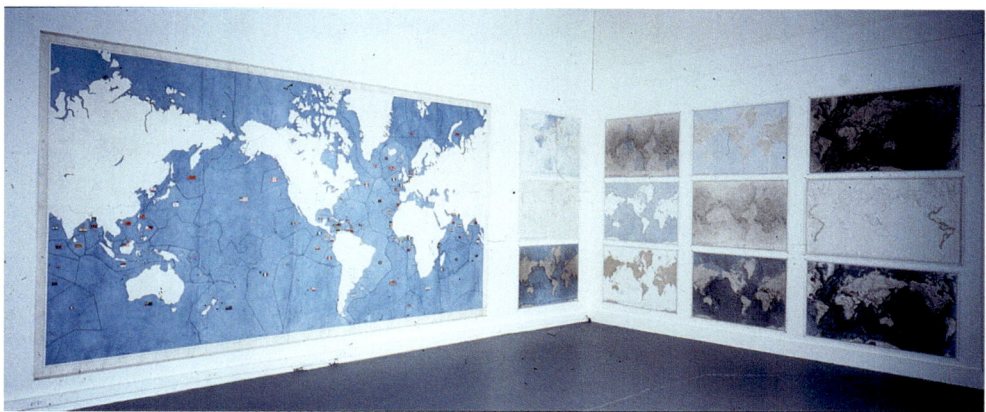

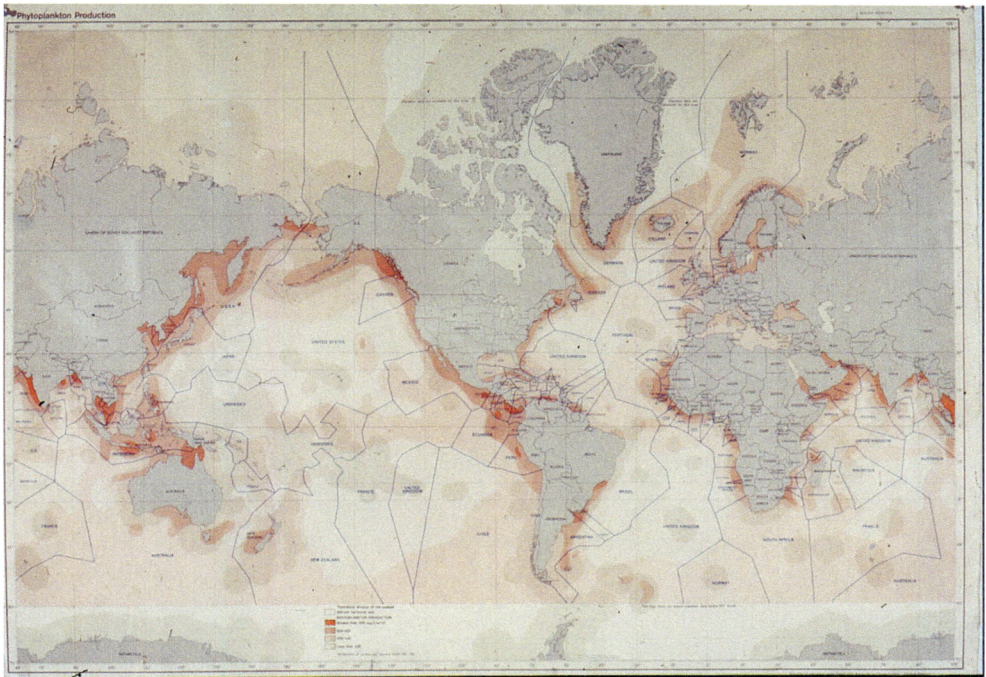

Figure 56: 'The Law of the Sea Conference: Where the Appetite is Discovered to be Endless' (1976) Installation view and Detail (courtesy of the Newton and Helen Harrison Family Trust)

On the Deep Wealth of this Nation, Scotland where private, if not secretive, individuals are 'grouped' by their identity as foragers (fig. 53). Through the resulting 'map', the Harrisons propose that foragers have the potential to become a voting block to represent their rights to the commons. In these various ways the Harrisons explore cartography to *de-territori-alise*, flipping its common use in the 19th and 20th centuries, which was to create clearly demarcated territories in the drive towards imperialism (Yao 2022).

The Harrisons' work grapples with questions that consistently problematise human relations with the web of life. Each work gives an account of place through deep research and observation, saying, 'Every place is a story of its own becoming' (H. M.

Harrison and Harrison 2001a, n.p.). In most works they garner the help of inhabitants who know their places better. Stories reveal the sometimes-skewed logics of inhabitation, in some sense putting these to the test of public opinion. The Harrisons are not seeking to be right, seeking truth, but to open the issue at hand to public scrutiny and reflective thought. This is not a narrow, atomised sense of place and inhabitation. As previously noted in each project they work with the questions: How big is here? How long is now? These become a game for the imagination where boundaries become plastic and relative, dependent on context within the web of life. The Harrisons often expose, with irony, the absurdity that drives human behaviour around narrow, short-term, self-interest. Their work *The Law of the Sea Conference* (fig. 56) exhibited at the Venice Biennale in 1976, uses a map from the United Nations Convention on the Law of the Sea presenting a hypothetical division of the sea floor and rights to minerals and fishing that demonstrated significant inequality, not just of land bound territories but also of colonised territory. Various iterations redrawing the original expose the anomalies and ironies of this kind of mapping. They subtitle the work *Where the Appetite is discovered to be Endless*. They identify a moment in global governance and expose the imperialistic narrative within it.

The Art of Narrative resides in the Ability to condense the Action into an Exemplary Moment (Kristeva 2020, 17)

Narrative or storytelling is a practice of wooing. It is not logical, but rooted in what is involved in our experience and its pleasures and displeasures, inconsistencies and contradictions. In understanding that everyone (and now we might say every living entity) has a story to tell, Arendt counters the tendency to revere individuality because each story is exposed to that of another, to scrutiny, to feelings of pleasure and displeasure not only of the self, but of others, to questions of what I must open up in myself to grapple with the experience of another, to embrace ambiguity, in other words to exercise judgement. The Harrisons expose their works to a similar form of public scrutiny not only reflecting different perspectives in the making of the work, but also inviting debate at the point of exhibition. *The Lagoon Cycle* is a story about a crab and its potential to be farmed by humans outside of its natural habitat. *The Serpentine Lattice* is a story of a great, ancient forest and its felling by humans. Dialogue within stories is as significant a device as scale and colour in their aesthetics of text and image. Some of the tropes of the Judeo-Christian voice are used because they evoke a form of impartiality. An example of this comes at the end of *The Lagoon Cycle,* which was created in a similar period to the *Great Lakes*, a voice taking on an apocalyptic resonance.

*And the flood plains that are farmed upon
and lived upon*

will become marshes   or swamps   or bogs
or beds for swollen rivers
or shallow inland seas
and the tropics will become uninhabitable
and the far north will become temperate
and corn and rice and wheat and beans
and plantain   manioc   and yams
and all the grains and starchy roots
known and unknown
named and unnamed
will have to go elsewhere than now
and most life
known and unknown
will have to go elsewhere than now
as vast parts of the Eastern seaboard of the United States
and parts of Europe near the North Sea
and much of South America near the Amazon
and China somewhere
and Russia in some parts   India
and other bits of Asia
Africa   Polynesia
Melanesia   Australia
And Japan
Will join the growing sea

And finishes with a series of questions.

And in this new beginning
This continuously rebeginning
Will you feed me when my lands can no longer produce
And will I house you
When your lands are covered with water
And together will we withdraw
As the waters rise?[4]
(H. M. Harrison and Harrison 2006, n.p.)

Implied in this last set of questions is the importance of creative exchange as the basis
for other lives, human and more than human. The quality of exchange is embodied
in the rhythm of the text. It is not just storytelling, but poetry that develops a space
between the different characters in the narrative and with us as readers. It becomes an
interval of freedom in which to ask important questions that are not asked in politics in

everyday life, questions about the difference between cultures of exchange and cultures of competition when natural resources become low. Arendt describes poetry as the most human and least worldly art. Speaking of the great poets, Whitehead suggests, 'Their survival is evidence that they express deep intuitions of mankind penetrating to what is universal in concrete fact' (Whitehead 2022, 94) . Where Arendt counters the horrors of Nazism through the importance she attributed to the narrated life (Kristeva 2020, 3), the Harrisons work with stories to come to grips with the changing environment and build understanding with others. They share stories as a means of facing reality through intuition, experience, and exchange.

Arendt's thinking stems from *amor mundi* – love for the world and the insight that it is birth itself, 'the miracle of life', that 'saves the world' (Kristeva 2020, 5). We are born first into a world that is not of our choosing, in a moment, space and culture that is not within our control. We are born again, inserting ourselves in culture and society, becoming part of life through sharing experience with other beings (Arendt 1998). Each life can be imagined as a story or narrative that can be told. All free people can enter the space of appearance and have the courage to leave one's own safe space and risk disclosure. A story grounds human life in what is specific to it, and it is through the restless, chaotic process of renewal that stories resist becoming ideologies.

Storytelling is deeply human and political in the sense that stories do not just mimic life, but also reveal their own logic in terms of who speaks, who acts, and who witnesses (Kristeva 2020, 18–19). The roles and perspectives of the Witness and the Lagoon Maker are clearly drawn at every point in the story of *The Lagoon Cycle*. They are unnamed and yet, far from being an anonymous 'Other', their identities, predispositions, and prejudices are unmistakable, even fiery. Through the exchange of sometimes polarised views, a new understanding emerges. In the Second Lagoon, the characters discuss metaphor – the hubris of the Lagoon Maker is countered forcefully by the Witness. The rhythm of force and counterforce is indicated in the italicisation of the text where the voice of the Witness is italicised, but that of the Lagoon Maker is not.

> Yet the metaphor for nature is a strong metaphor
> *an arrogant metaphor*
>   a useful metaphor
> *an improbable metaphor*
>   a playful metaphor
> *a dangerous metaphor that draws attention away*
> *from the destruction of the habitat*
>   a valuable metaphor that will lead
>   to the regeneration of habitat
> *but it's only a tank*
>   the crabs don't know it's only a tank

yet when we feed them they look up
so already they behave differently
Second Lagoon/45

The Spectator is not Involved in the Act (Arendt 1992, 63)

Stories involve actors/makers with spectators. In discussing the relationship of spectator to actor in the political realm, Arendt was very aware of the destructive virtuosic
character of public discourse in the classical *polis*, 'an organisation of the people as it
arises out of acting and speaking together' (Arendt 1998, 198). She suggests that it is
the spectator who has access to the whole event and therefore sees more than the actor
who is too preoccupied with their part in the whole. The spectator can take on more
than one perspective, weighing up different perspectives from which we are able to
judge whether 'progress' is being made. This is progress in terms of developing insight
and meaning, not material progress. Genius, a term we would now resist in describing
the specific skills of a talented artist, is required to produce an artwork, whereas the
spectator exercises judgement or 'taste' as a way of making sense, making meaning out
of the spectacle. The constraints at work here are important for an artwork to become a
meaningful work. The artist's creative freedom can be lawless if it is not constrained by
the need to be communicable to another (as discussed in Chapter 4). Arendt following
Kant calls this search for a communicable form 'spirit'.

> Spirit [...] a special faculty apart from reason, intellect, and imagination – enables
> the genius to find an expression for the ideas 'by means of which the subjective
> state of mind brought about by them...can be communicated by others'. Spirit [...]
> consists in expressing the 'ineffable element in the state of mind [Gemützszustand]'
> that certain representations arise in all of us but for which we have no words and
> therefore be unable, without the help of genius, to communicate to one another;
> it is the proper task of genius to make this state of mind 'generally communicable'.
> (Arendt 1992, 62–63)

Arendt continues that 'the very originality of the artist (or the very novelty of the actor) depends on making him/herself understood by those who are not artists (actors)'
(1992, 63). It is therefore the artist or actor that has the gift of communicability and
the spectator the means to make such works appear in public. They share the faculty of
judgement that is engaged in both processes, the making and the spectating. It is perhaps in this sense that the Harrisons believe, like the German artist Joseph Beuys, that
everyone is or has the potential to be an artist. They recognise, even desire, the refined
skill that artworks embody of vivid communication and innovation, making present
those experiences for which many of us would otherwise have no words.

The freedom to make communicable works and to engage critically with them implies careful organisation in which the freedom to speak and act becomes possible in public life through the multiplication of opportunities to appear. Appearance is fundamental to all living beings, Arendt argues, manifest in the superfluity of display in animal life that is not explainable simply as functions of the life process. Display as appearance is also generative of life. In social, cultural spaces, we have the opportunity not only to tell our stories, but also to draw out to our audiences and spectators what matters, what is meaningful, involving our and their aesthetic judgement. For Arendt, this space of appearance in which stories are told, performed, and experienced is the *polis*. It can arise anywhere, including becoming physically located and instituted by law as in the Roman City. For the Harrisons, this is the museum, art gallery, lecture theatre, meeting room, chapel, and community spaces of various kinds, and their home starting with their 'morning conversations'.

Arendt's understanding of politics, through Kant, is therefore closely aligned with the making and experiencing of a work of art. There are no right answers, but multiple perspectives that in engaging with one another, also check one another. To woo another person or group, I need to persuade them of what I am seeing and experiencing, feeling and sensing. Arendt situates the making of political life in the midst of chaos and uncertainty as a process of birth, as the invasion of the world by strangers 'whose actions and reactions cannot be foreseen by those who are already there and are going to leave in a short while'. It is a creative process of renewal (Arendt 2006, 61).

Arendt proposes as a practical solution a different form of political organisation, the council system, for those who wish to be heard in public and to have the possibility to be influential in the political direction of a country. The ballot booth is too small and singular, countries are too large for all those interested to come together, and parties are manipulative. A rational form of opinion can emerge by 10 individuals coming together, not only to express their opinions but to hear the opinions of others. In this small group it quickly becomes clear who is best to represent the group at a higher level. She acknowledges that not every citizen is interested in participating but they need to be offered the opportunity (Arendt 2013, 104–5).

Mortality, Communicability, Freedom

In *Epitaph* (fig. 57) exhibited and published in 2022 shortly before he died, Newton Harrison makes reference again to their notion of the dictatorship of the ecology. It opens with a 'Socratic type' question:

> After encountering an incurable cancer, and 3 years after Helen passed, I asked the web of life Do you have any rules beyond self-making?

The web of life responds to the question with a series of statements, including:

9. Human, Human:
    [...] it is not likely, unless you change quickly, that you will be
    able to continue. Not so for myself, after all, I have experience in these
    matters. I have regenerated, in 10 to 20 million year increments, from
    many extinctions.
    Epitaph 2022

Epitaph is intentionally dramatic, performative. Visually and in text it evokes an epic scale, bringing to mind the biblical Moses and the 10 commandments that are incised into tablets of stone for posterity. The image also consciously evokes gravestones. It is interesting to note that the web of life's responses, unlike the commandments, are not voiced as imperatives – 'Thou shalt (do or not do)'. They are more conversational, an explanation of the life-web's 'thinking' that sets out constraints within which to respond, as opposed to rules that must be followed. These are effectively presented as an invitation to think for oneself, to improvise. The life-web has gifted intelligence to all living beings through the faculty to judge what is good and bad for survival (to respond to perturbations in the terms discussed in Chapter 5). Humans are free to act intelligently and have chosen not to do so in the view of the web of life. Humans are bound by the same constraints as all other species through one single, 'all-encompassing, ultimately unforgiving rule' (N. Harrison 2022a) to exchange between one another and give back more to the web of life that it takes. Through our practices of extraction and consumption, we have refused to be guided by the constraints and the web of life is indifferent to human survival. It can recover.

16. Human, Human:
    It can be understood that I, the web of life, am indifferent to all the jus-
    tices that you talk about in social and environmental terms, especially
    distressed by your belief in endless growth. My one rule is the rule of
    exchange as practiced by each of our companion species, with your-
    selves as the very destructive exception. All others participate in the
    infinity of exchanges which bring forth my domain of livingness.
    Epitaph 2022

With bleak, absurdist irony the *Epitaph* reveals the extreme danger and precarity of the world in its current chaotic state. On the one level it rehearses a well-known, ancient narrative of Moses bringing order to human chaos at a moment of exodus from persecution to new lands, but the irony that there is no such possibility of exodus from Earth is not lost, nor are there any commandments. *Epitaph*, however, does not embody a rational form of the political based in authority, but one that grapples with the irrational

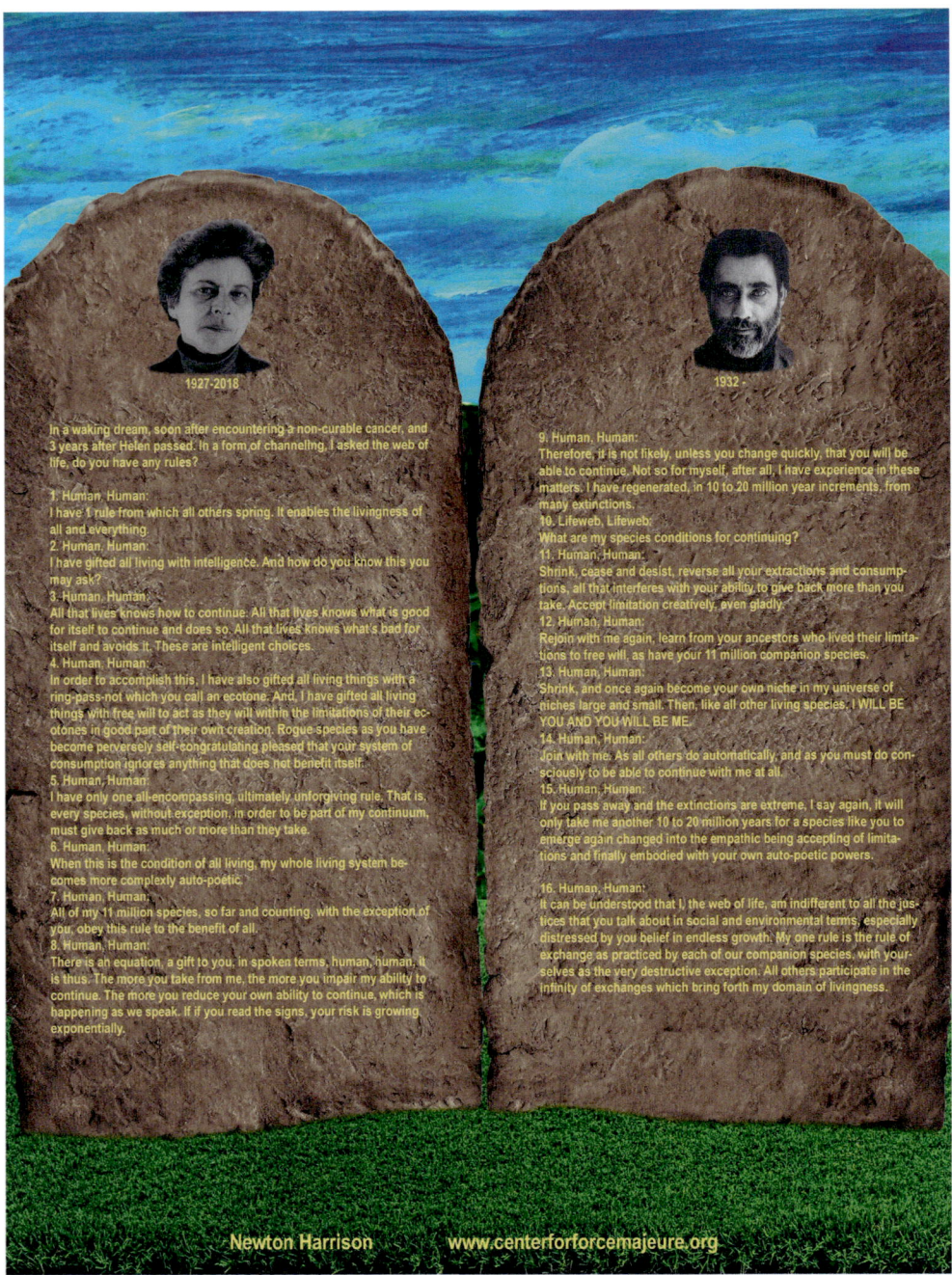

Figure 57: Newton Harrison 'Epitaph' (2022) (courtesy of the Newton and Helen Harrison Family Trust)

and even the amoral. A tension is built between rule and judgement. Humankind is expected to judge for themselves, not to obey blindly, and ultimately the web of life is not vengeful in the direction that is taken, just indifferent.

How does the political as outlined here work with codes of conduct and constitutional forms?

Arendt's formulation of politics is deliberative. Like the Harrisons she emphasises the importance of dialogue. The counterpoint to this approach is the politics of structures, strategies, and interests and the distribution of power. The latter is crucial in politics of our current times where inequality is becoming more extreme with the environmental crisis. Olúfẹ́mi O. Táíwò, a Nigerian born philosopher and academic, creates a vivid picture of what is at stake.

> [A] world where 1.6 billion people live in inadequate housing (slum conditions) and 100 million are unhoused, a full third of the human population does not have reliable drinking water, and the intersections of food, energy, and water insecurity with the climate crisis have already displaced 8.5 million people in South Asia alone, while threatening to displace tens of millions more. (Táíwò 2022, 42)

Táíwò focuses on how existing structures privilege and create elites, wittingly or unwittingly upholding a politics of inequality. Many of these elites emerge out of colonial thinking and values. They engage in identity politics, but only superficially, often using tokenism to reinforce conventional, unequal systems of values – 'the elites' tactic of performing symbolic identity politics to pacify protestors without enacting material reforms; their efforts to re-brand (not replace) existing institutions, also using elements of identity politics' (Táíwò 2022, 8).

The fable of the Emperor's new clothes runs throughout Táíwò's writing on elites as a vivid way to imagine complicity in inadequate political systems. Inequality is concrete and observable in our patterns of action and yet we do not choose to see them much as the townspeople chose not to see the Emperor's new clothes as an illusion. It is a child who calls this out in innocence. Táíwò draws attention to two forms of response: the one is a politics of deference and the other a 'constructive' politics. Politics of deference listen to the most affected, centre the most marginalised, and this in itself is important. However, it can work counter to the interests of those groups. By focusing on the marginalised, we draw attention away from the actions of bureaucracies, corporations, and algorithms, the systems of power that bring about deprivation. The discourse becomes one of weaponising the attention in the service of marginalisation, providing a cover for the abdication of responsibility. Táíwò proposes instead a constructive politics, one that characterised by imagining where we really want to be, gathering and sharing

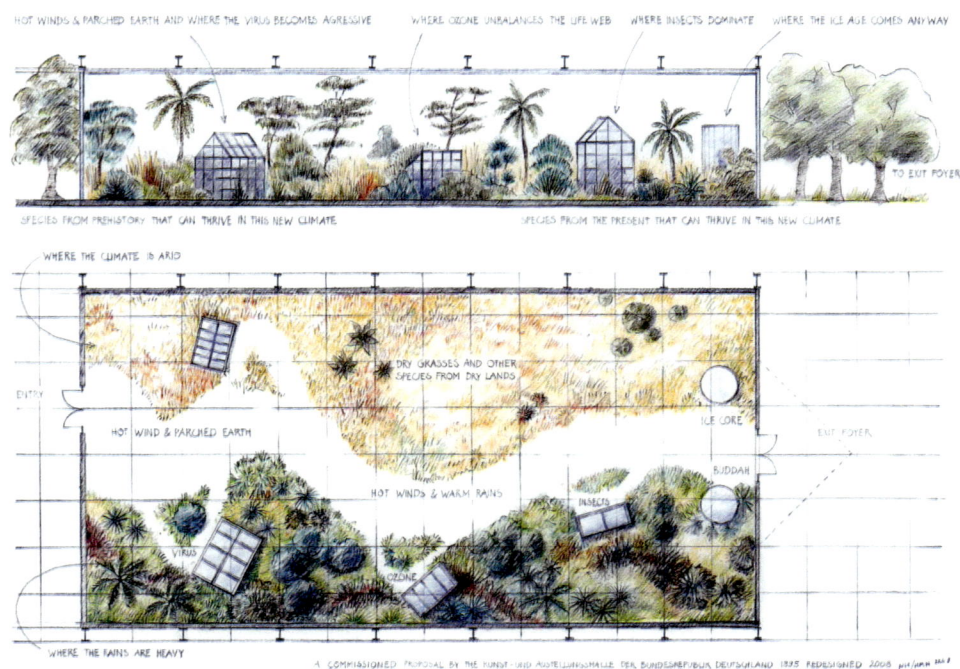

Figure 58: 'Garden of Hot Winds and Warm Rains' (1995). Drawing (courtesy of the Newton and Helen Harrison Family Trust)

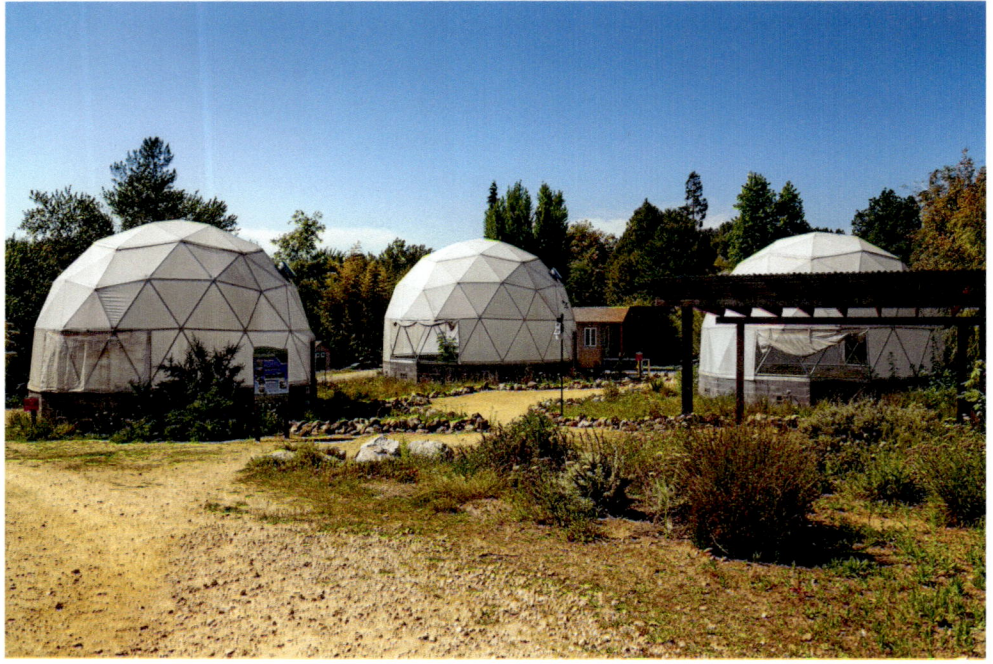

Figure 59: 'A Future Garden for the Central Coast of California' (2018) University of California, Santa Cruz Arboretum and Botanic Garden (courtesy of the Newton and Helen Harrison Family Trust)

information, and focusing on outcomes that redistribute social resources and power and for which there is accountability, building outcomes focused by specific goals rather than 'purely moral or aesthetic principles' (Táíwò 2022, 12).

Building a world in common is a shared issue, imagined from very different perspectives, the one interpersonal and the other structural. Táíwò does not reject the interpersonal.

> A constructive program does not ask us to ignore our own interpersonal, symbolic, or material needs, even though it does ask us to be disciplined in how we relate to the needs of the struggle and scores of people and generations that are immediately present. (Táíwò 2022, 67)

His analysis of elites and the interests that support them addresses a blind spot in Arendt's politics of dialogue and persuasion in emphasising the structural aspects of the political. He highlights the importance of goal setting and outcomes over process. In the 'Third Session' of 'Lectures on Kant's Political Philosophy', Arendt traces Kant's realisation that the problem of the organisation of the state cannot be reconciled with his practical reason. Moral philosophy cannot help because a good constitution needs to address the amoral. Human beings are not rational beings who require or indeed follow universal laws for their preservation. They are secretly inclined to exempt themselves, Kant's definition of evil. The ensuing collisions between private and public interests need a constitution in which individuals can check one another and, in that way, continuously engage critically with codes of conduct. The law cannot check power. It is power that checks power.

> I can want to steal, but I cannot will stealing to be a universal law; because with such a law there would be no property. (Arendt 1992, 17)

If, as Arendt and the Harrisons suggest, the political cannot be arrived through rules that are imposed, then good government becomes extremely fragile, though still possible through the shared recognition of what is in the common interest, and what stands against it. Where might we, for example, place the Harrisons' involvement of Elders of the Washoe tribe in *Sagehen: A Proving Ground* (2013) (fig. 55, 60-61). This work, one of the series called 'Future Gardens' (fig. 55, 58-61), takes the form of an experimental site where biodiversity is 'stress tested', in this case by being relocated to different elevations within the watershed. The aim is to understand what ensemble of plants can adapt to global warming in the Sagehen watershed. The experiment was undertaken on and with scientists from the University of California, Berkeley's Sagehen Creek Field Station funded by the Annenberg Foundation. Is the involvement of Washoe Elders a form of deference, a political gesture that highlights the importance of indigenous knowledge to forestry without establishing deep change, or is it the beginning of a radical shift in how forestry practice and research unfolds?

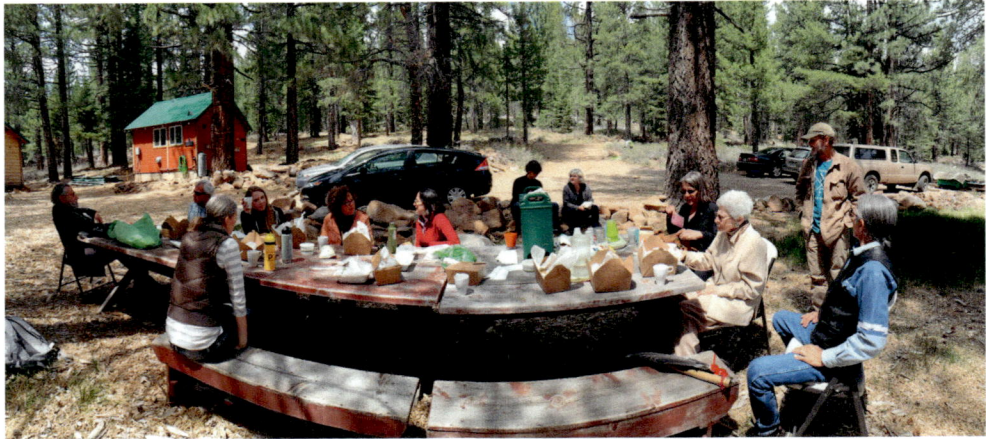

Figure 60: Test site at Sagehen (courtesy of the Newton and Helen Harrison Family Trust. Photo John Weber)

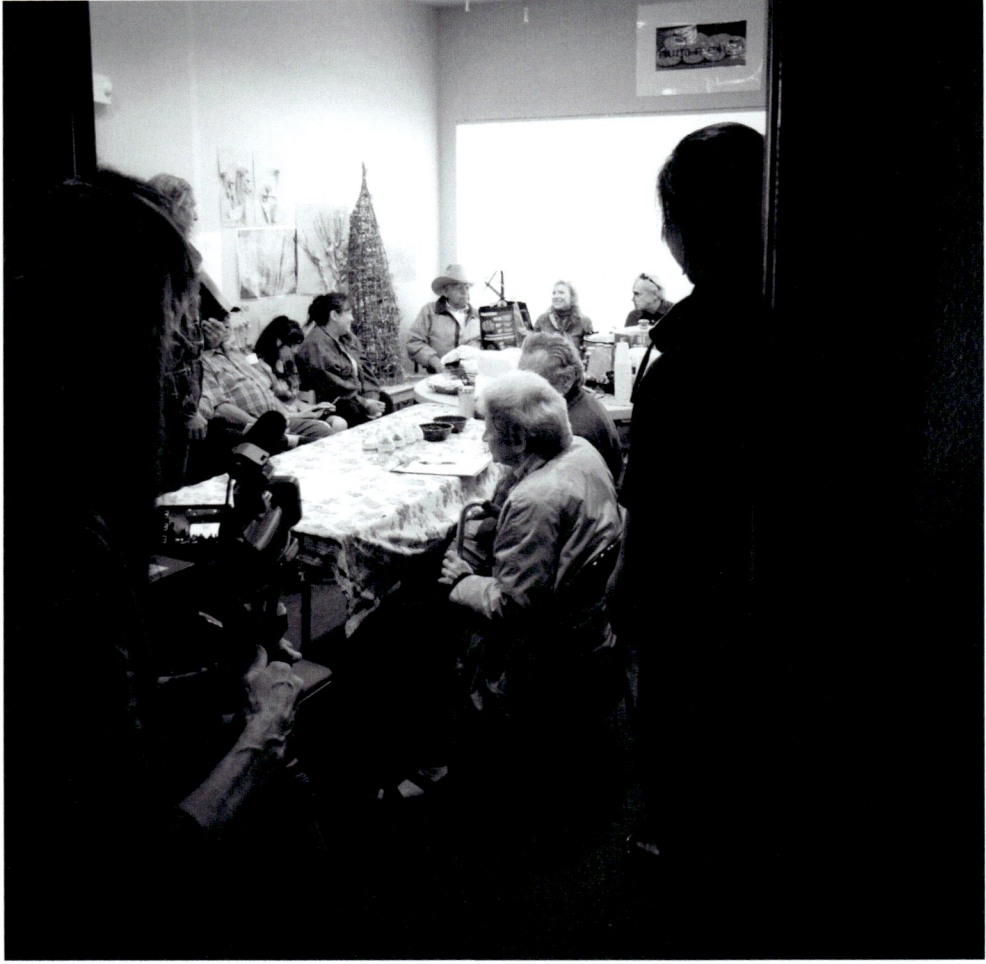

Figure 61: Workshop at Sagehen (courtesy of the Newton and Helen Harrison Family Trust)

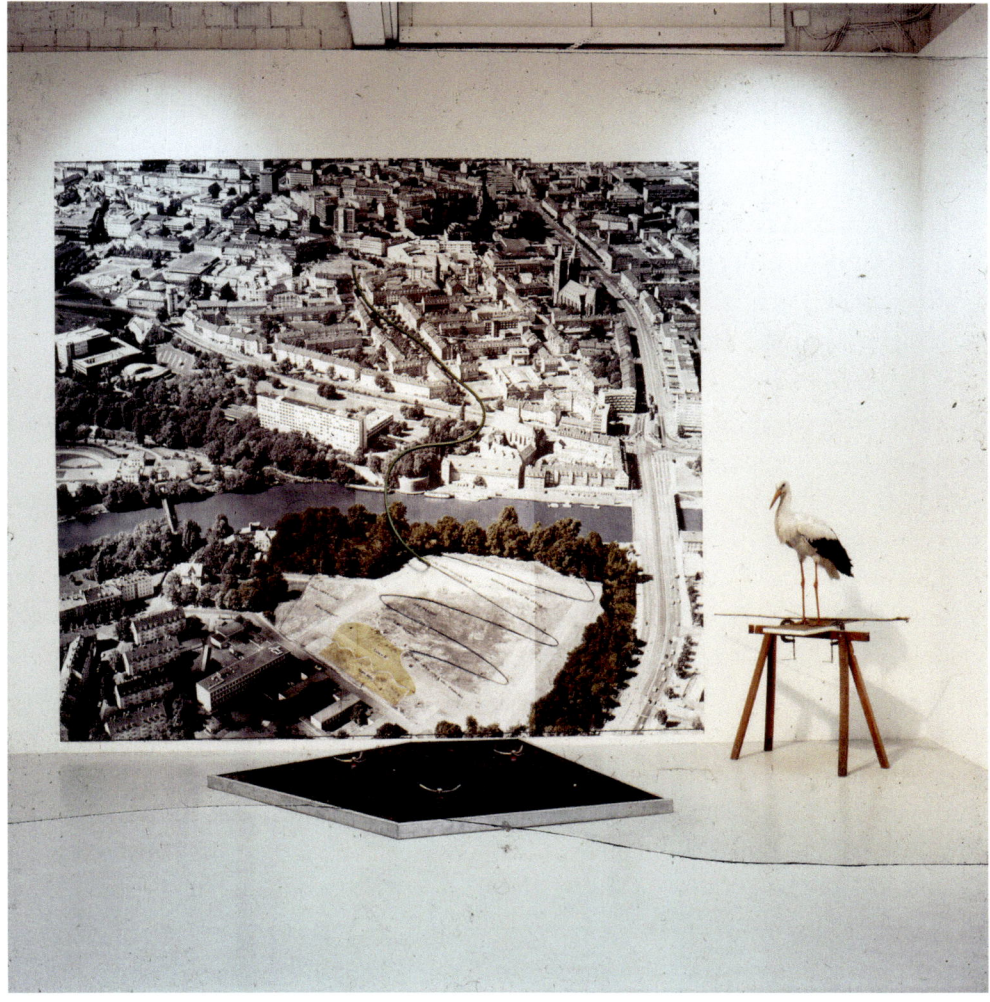

Figure 62: 'Kassel Works' (1987) Installation view, Documenta 8 (courtesy of the Newton and Helen Harrison Family Trust)

If we follow the logic of Táíwò's 'constructive' politics, then the objective of the Sagehen experiment is to understand if humans have a role in helping the ecosystem to adapt to human created global warming – a clear focus on outcome. We can argue that it imagines where we want to be – in this case in a dialogue over time with the watershed rather than simply extracting material or knowledge from it. Finally:

It would focus on building and rebuilding rooms, not regulating traffic within and between them. It would be what political scientist Adom Getachew terms a 'worldmaking' project, aimed at building and rebuilding actual structures of social connection and movement, rather than mere critique of the ones we already have. (Táíwò 2022, 12)

In the 21st century we face deep contradictions that undoubtedly are a legacy from the European Enlightenment and industrialisation. In the West we live in a political land-scape in which a hierarchy has been established between nature and the state, where our economic, social, political, and cultural practices and values reinforce one another in bending the natural environment to the will of what is called 'progress'. Unlike Arendt's following of Kant's notion of progress as a mental, imaginative freedom to think and be heard, this is a form of progress that is purely material and based in economic growth. It is also inscribed into our moral codes in a form of ideology. This is rule by experts and technocratic hubris (Yao 2022, 20–23).

The Harrisons tread this line with meticulous care, both in the quality of ecological expertise they engage with and in the way they present this to a public. They offer a clear line to where judgement can be exercised through the propositional. This can be seen in the way they frequently use an 'If [...] Then' construction, often interchanged with 'Imagine if [...] Then', a form that characterises the works from 1974 such as *San Diego as the Center of a World* that explores the then different projections of climate change, formulated as scenarios (Reeves-Evison 2021, 738). The propositional voice characterises the work of this period in a highly distinctive way, adopting the trope of urban planning to provoke ecological thinking. In 1987 they made a work for Kassel's *Documenta 8* (fig. 62) an international exhibition of contemporary art that takes place every five years and was initiated to bring contemporary art into a post Nazi Germany. The Harrisons critique the post-war design of the city in the way it turns its back on the Mulde River, once the artery and the life of the city. Their work contains this critique along with quite practical proposals to overcome it. In Newton's account the work was not well received by the curator, but its point warmly recognised by the then president of the Federal Republic of Germany, Richard von Weizsäcker.

KASSEL WORKS II:[5]
A FORGETTING HAS TAKEN PLACE

THE CLOSER THE PRESENT CENTER
COMES TO ITS PLACE OF ORIGIN
THE MORE OBVIOUS THE BARRIERS
BECOME TO THE RIVER
THAT EMPOWERED IT
AND THE TERRAIN FROM
WHICH IT SPRUNG

KASSEL WORKS III
IF
A PEDESTRIAN BRIDGE WERE BUILT
ACROSS THE STEINWEG

FROM THE CORNER
OF THE TRÄNKEPFORTE
AND
THE PATH TO THE RONDELL
ON THE RIVER
ENLARGED
REVEALING THE EXCAVATION
OF THE SECOND RONDELL
AND
THE BRÜDERKIRCHE RESTORED
THEN
COMMUNICATION
WOULD BE REESTABLISHED
BETWEEN PAST AND PRESENT
AND THE CENTER ENRICHED
THEREBY
(H. M. Harrison and Harrison 2016, 192–193)

The Harrisons make a number of works in the 1990s in post-war Germany, including *Trümmerflora on the Topography of Terror* (1988–89) that addresses the then derelict site of the Nazi Headquarters. Other works include proposals for the reclamation of industrial brown coal field sites (*Das Einzugsbeit der Mulde* (1993) and *A Brown Coal Part for South Leipzig* (1995)) as well as the ecological restoration of meadows (*Endangered Meadows of Europe* (1996)). These works address a complex political past brought about through industrialisation and World War II where the Harrisons propose designs that maximise ecological impact. They are works that throw into sharp relief the contrast between the politics of modernity around centralised control, the privileging of private interests and materialism, and a different form of the political that emerges out of aesthetic experience and produces a sense of a shared world.

Otherwise the race of devils would destroy themselves (Arendt 1992, 18)

Arendt bluntly states her sense of the predicament we have arrived at as a species in her essay *On Violence*. It emerges out of her fear of a return of Totalitarianism in the arms race between the US and the Soviet Union and the threat of nuclear war.

> To the question how shall we ever be able to extricate ourselves from the obvious insanity of this position, there is no answer. (Arendt 1970, 4)

A recent article by the political economist Geoff Mann requotes this same passage from Arendt and he continues:

> Although we don't lack for murderous leaders in charge of nuclear stockpiles, it isn't fingers on triggers that pose the greatest threat to our survival; indeed, nothing momentous need happen at all. If we simply keep doing what we are doing, then to the best of our knowledge, more and more of the planet will catch fire or be submerged under water; coastlines will wash away, glaciers collapse, and rivers dry up; soils will desiccate and blow away; and millions will be on the move or dying of disease. (Mann 2023, 17)

Mann focuses on the uncertainty that now plagues us through the inadequacy of the tools in the sciences that we have relied on in relation to climate modelling, tools that are unable to cope with the degree of uncertainty we currently face. Climate policy cannot help but become political, he argues, and current efforts are the equivalent of 'perching the gargantuan machine of contemporary capitalism as close as possible to the precipice without tipping us over the edge…a myopic and recklessly arrogant approach to the unknown fate of life on earth' (Mann 2023, 19). It is here, in this image of imminent danger, that the enormity of the challenge for a new political form becomes clear.

Bruno Latour in his 2004 book, *Politics of Nature*, proposes that a political ecology has not yet even begun to exist because we have not undertaken the work that is necessary to rethinking the two concepts of nature and politics.

> Political ecologists have supposed that they could dispense with this conceptual work, without noticing that the notions of nature and politics had been developed over centuries in such a way as to make any juxtaposition, any synthesis, any combination of the two terms *impossible*…the old distinction between humans and things, subjects of law and objects of science…had been shaped, profiled, and sculpted in such a way that they had gradually become incompatible. (Latour 2004, 2–3, emphasis in the original)

It is interesting to notice how the faculty of thinking for oneself is positioned by Latour. He references Plato's cave and the dominance of the philosopher, who as the expert, releases fragmentary knowledge to us, the lay public, as the imprisoned slaves. He suggests that the power of the philosopher has now been replaced by the scientist. We now need to escape both forms of enslavement. Like Arendt and the Harrisons, he proposes ways to reconfigure political practices that restore a balance of power through greater levels of participation, taking a significant step towards reclaiming politics for humanity. In exploring what a political ecology might mean, Latour suggests that ecological movements have sought to reposition themselves on the political chess board, without redefining the rules of the game. He shares the sense that the issue is more fundamental and complex than such movements allow, evoking Mann's precipice in a different configuration.

> Every time we seek to mix scientific facts with aesthetic, political, economic, and moral values, we find ourselves in a quandary. If we concede too much to facts, the human element in its entirety tilts into objectivity, becomes a countable, calculable thing, a bottom line in terms of energy, one species among others. If we concede too much to values, all of nature tilts into the uncertainty of myth, into poetry or romanticism. We shall never know for example whether the apocalyptic predictions with which the militant ecologists threaten us mask the power scientists hold over politicians or the domination politicians exercise over poor scientists. (Latour 2004, 4)

Latour sees that it is crucial to forgo the juxtaposition of nature with humankind, to rethink 'the requirements of freedom and the powers of necessity', to reimagine what we understand to be a common world. We can never escape our human presence and imagination in acting in the world. Rather than applying our existing politics to nature through the tendency to anthropomorphise, we need to delve more deeply into our human ways of knowing, imagining, and constituting the world, to 'describe the actual state of affairs' to understand ourselves, our humanness, better (Latour 2004, 7). Latour provocatively suggests that nature is a political construct, a division that creates the possibility of splitting life into aspects that can be objectified and therefore exploited, from aspects that are subjective and open to interpretation, if not dispute (the sensory). The problem lies in the ways we have represented nature to ourselves. We need to rethink what we have understood to be 'the collective' and take into account non-humans. This entails rethinking 'Science' as 'the sciences' exploring common worlds, rather than demarcating territories.

What to do?

A common theme emerges across all these perspectives in art and in science, in philosophy and politics, the issue of how we imagine relations between the human and natural world, and how these imaginaries, far from being fixed, are changeable and have a profound effect on how we act and who we are as human beings. The Harrisons demonstrate the powerful role of the imagination through their use of metaphor, in particular dysfunctional metaphors, metaphors that lead to bad decisions for the environment (Chapter 4–5). They ask whether assuming that we can control rivers through engineering interventions is an inappropriate way to imagine and act on rivers. In the Seventh Lagoon they ask if we can participate in a conversation at all.

Jedediah Purdy, a legal scholar and cultural commentator, gives us four different ways of imagining nature in the US that he has observed in current practice: the providential, which imagines that the purpose of the natural world is to serve human need; the romantic where nature is imbued with aesthetic or spiritual value; the utilitarian, imagining nature as a storehouse of resources expertly managed by scientists and public officials; the ecological, where nature is imagined as complex, interpenetrating systems each of which is defined by political action. He understands that everyone is now involved in thinking through and deciding the best course of action. For him it involves thinking through the interconnections between ecology, economics and politics (Purdy 2015).

What of artists? What of the Harrisons' contribution to a political ecology and their claims to be ecopolitical artists? Plato's fear of the influence of poetry in civic life would suggest that artists have no place in politics – Stengers counters this view.

> Critical thinkers have long admitted into the heart of the city the 'interstitial presence' of poets... to bring into existence that which reasons cannot board and inspect... (Stengers 2011, 505)

The politics of the post-war period to today is built on rational thinking and on a particular notion of progress based on advances in technology, industrial productivity, and consumption. Rational politics does not build a common world, but one based in competition. Arendt's politics through Kant underlines the importance of the imagination, its power to make present what is absent and to compose, construct and fabricate the world, a position that resonates with Whitehead's notion of adventure. They are ways of renewing the world. The imagination works with experience in the world, including the experience of beauty, of aesthetics. Arendt draws on works of art as exemplary in these terms. They not only affect us, but 'infect' us by provoking, delighting, entertaining (Stengers 2011, 510). For the Harrisons it is ecosystems that have this capacity if we let them, and they use their art to ask us if we are willing to participate in that dialogue. Stengers understands interstitial places as places of vulnerability, places to exchange stories and accept that these may be modified in the encounter with other stories. This is different to the 'either/or' of argumentation and rationality that leads to a kind of homogeneity where one story or world view absorbs all others and becomes dominant.

Arendt acknowledges the challenge that is presented by positioning aesthetics as key to the political.

> The most surprising aspect of this business is that common sense, the faculty of judgement and of discriminating between right and wrong, should be based on a sense of taste. (Arendt 1992, 64)

Kristeva also acknowledges the gap between the politics we actually have and Arendt's proposal.

> [T[he reader can only speculate as to what a political community based on this kind of 'aesthetic judgement' might be, a judgement that is itself based on taste, immediately communicable taste that brings reasoned understanding into its service and cannot be learned, only exercised. (Kristeva 2020, 76)

The Harrisons centre dependence or co-dependence in relation to the question of how we feed ourselves. They are not seeking solutions but provoking us to think for ourselves and from the perspective of the ecological argument. They invert a figure ground relationship, where the environment is brought to the foreground and human interests are in the background. In developing this thought through various projects and representations, they tilt towards the dangers of a totalising narrative. At the core of their imaginary is care for a common world and forms of action that support this as an aesthetic experience of mind and body. Arendt develops a form of politics that, like that of the Harrisons, is based in dialogue, persuasion, and agreement. Their approaches to the political are one-sided; the other is concerned with competing interests, strategies, and unequal power relations that are at the root of the environmental crisis. A common world can only thrive by addressing both aspects of the political, the intersubjective and the structural. Latour and Táíwò share the goal of a world in common, but by addressing the collective and structural aspects. For Latour this involves a rethinking of the sciences and the fabrication of new forms of the collective that closely observe and take into account the non-human. Táíwò's point of departures is racial politics and the imbalances of power that rehearse and challenge colonisation.

Where and how might these two perspectives on the political, the intersubjective, and the structural meet? In the conclusions to her analysis of climate change and political theory, McKinnon highlights the importance if active citizenship in the form of 'unprecedented, unflinching, and insistent pressure in political, economic, and corporate leaders to force them to make radical changes to put us in the pathway to net zero as soon as possible' (McKinnon 2022, 161). When the facts of climate change are so bleak, why should we bother to mitigate them let alone act for better policies? She offers three reasons: a 2°C rise by 2100 is not absolutely confirmed; second, even if we exceed this, any pathway to limits on warming is positive; and third, the future is anyway deeply uncertain, and we can face this future with hope. She distinguishes hope from optimism: with hope we are uncertain that some good outcome is likely, but nonetheless take action to support its possibility. In our Introduction (Chapter 1) we suggest that to be fit to undertake the challenge of a political ecology, artists need to rethink their ways of working, the aesthetics that underpin any innovation, and the ways that their works engage a public, acknowledging the hold that histories of art may have for them. Artists clearly share this challenge with others, including political philosophers in relation to different disciplines and ways of knowing the world. Artists do not, however, offer practical solutions. They draw on experience and imagination and propose different ways of perceiving what is a stake, ways that generate new experiences. The Harrisons share the importance of facing the implications of change, and of doing so with hope. They offer as ecopolitical artists a multi-layered approach in which the arts permeate the sciences, and the sciences permeate the arts, that in turn through aesthetics permeate the political. Newton Harrison comments, 'The ongoing challenge was to grasp what it might mean if the actions and interactions between, rather than entities themselves, were the realities of the universe' (Ingram 2013, 269). This is often loosely referred to as 'relationality' that implicates us in a much greater re-imagining of what relations and in-between-ness might mean as a way of life than the term has come to imply. The Harrisons in their tendency to generate totalising visions for the future inhabit the tension that human beings now experience between politics that is formulated from a global perspective and politics that addresses the local. Are these alternatives or is it possible to imagine that they are two interconnected perspectives on the same set of challenges?

For Táíwò a political perspective grows out of processes of education and learning. He draws on anti-colonial activists and politicians who have also been educationalists, such as Bissau-Guinean and Cape Verdean Amílcar Cabral (1924–1973). Cabral defined culture as more than ideological, a product of history, but as also a determinant of history, positively and negatively in man's relation with his environment (Táíwò 2022, 64). Whitehead opens *The Aims of Education* by defining culture as 'an activity of thought, and receptiveness to beauty and humane feeling' (Whitehead 1967, 1). For him, culture and education were ways of countering the effects of what he called 'inert ideas', simple repetition without thought, creativity, feeling or interest. In countering the inert, we become alive to the world and its potential. He saw education and learning as a creative process of self-development. The Harrisons frequently describe nature as their teacher in an endless process of discovery and learning.

In the next chapter we trace the way the Harrisons have learned from other artists, detail their pedagogy, and show how artists working currently have evolved their own approaches to practice that draw on the Harrisons' example.

CHAPTER 7

Artists 'Thinking with' One Another

In a recent discussion with Newton Harrison, he suggested that his interest in the work of particular artists is in their ability to ask seemingly obvious questions that, once asked, become transformative. Newton said, for instance, that Paul Cézanne (1839–1906) questioned his own seeing, asking, 'Why don't I see vanishing points in real life?' or that Rembrandt Harmenszoon van Rijn (1606–1669) was concerned with 'How little light can I use to show that a figure is spiritual?', referring to his painting of *St. Matthew* (1661) (N. Harrison 2022b). These are instances of artists making 'a leap of the imagination' in response to a bold question. It is the quality of such questions that underpin the life work of an artist and enable them and those following them to experience the world differently, drawing on the potential of the past in a new experience in the present, making work that makes sense of or interprets what they have experienced for others. Rembrandt as well as Giotto (*c.*1267–1337) among others have significantly altered the contribution that art makes to human understanding. Each question puts what went before into a new context. What is characteristic of this process is showing us what it is to be alive in the world; for instance, Rembrandt's *St. Matthew* reveals spirituality as integral to the human (rather than additional). It reveals the paradox that very little light reveals spirituality more effectively than the traditional flooding of a painting with light.

Newton went on to describe the questions he asks of another artist's work and by implication experience itself as, 'What am I seeing and what am I not seeing? How do I show what I am seeing? What are my responsibilities toward what I am seeing?' (N. Harrison 2022b). This correlates very closely with Stengers' questions. Her questions ('what [the work] does to thought, what it obliges one to do, what it renders important, and what is makes remain silent' (Stengers 2011, 22)) require us to constantly search for and make meaning, rather than presuming that meaning is given. The latter predisposes us to the inertia and repeatability of some hypothesis driven forms, in ideologies and in art. Both the Harrisons and Stengers work with these questions to be alive and alert to an actual experience and its potential for new life that alters the values of what has gone before.

Stengers' construction of 'letting [our]selves be touched by the reasons of others' (2020, 235), that is, becoming critically aware of how we work with the potential the past has to offer us, is a vivid way to trace the artists from whom the Harrisons have learned and artists who have and continue to 'think with' the Harrisons. In either direction it is not particularly relevant to trace influence in terms of style or technique.

Rather it takes the form of a deep commitment to questioning what one experiences in the world. The lure or guiding aim is to come closer to the global environment crisis in its multiple dimensions. This in turn leads to a transformation in the way some artists are approaching their work and audiences in the life around them. It is the generative power of experiencing the world combined with the responsibility to act on that experience that Stengers draws attention to.

> To make sense in common is not to convert to or submit to, or be shaped by, a common reason but to experience a transformation in our relationships with what is ours, with our reasons for acting, for perceiving things in one way rather than another. (2020, 235)

This chapter draws on conversations with the Harrisons and papers in their archive to highlight the importance of other artists that created a transformation in their thinking as their practice evolved. In addition, the chapter considers pedagogy through two examples of proposals for what a curriculum might need to be. It then turns to consider the work of current artists, and their contributions to rethinking the arts in the environmental crisis. We imagine this through Whitehead's idea of immanence: the environment that an actual occasion inherits is immanent within each occasion and each occasion is immanent within the environment that it helps to transmit (Whitehead 1985, 63). This interrupts the tendency to think of ourselves as separate subjects in a world of other objects, where the environment forms a stable background to existence. Whitehead's way of imagining enables us to see two crucial characteristics. Of critical concern to all is the formation of a 'world in common', alongside a deep care for life in which human existence is profoundly entangled with the whole of the natural world. The selected artists include Brandon Ballengée, Lauren Bon, Tim Collins and Reiko Goto-Collins, Beth Stephens and Annie Sprinkle, and Ruth Wallen. Each of these artists have been involved in ongoing dialogue with the Harrisons and engaged in a dialogue with us as authors to inform this chapter. Finally, some other artists who have re-imagined the arts in parallel are briefly considered, including Hans Haacke and Mierle Laderman Ukeles mentioned previously, and Rasheed Araeen (b.1935), Agnes Denes (b.1931), and Robert Smithson (1938–1973). These, albeit mostly US-based, artists all in various ways address the bringing together of art and ecology in response to developing understanding of the global environmental crisis.

On questions that drive practice

When Newton Harrison explored the historical artists that were key to his and Helen's development (2022b), he stressed the importance of the key question each of these artists had posed through their work. In each case the question challenges fundamental assumptions and beliefs in the way we perceive and represent the world around us

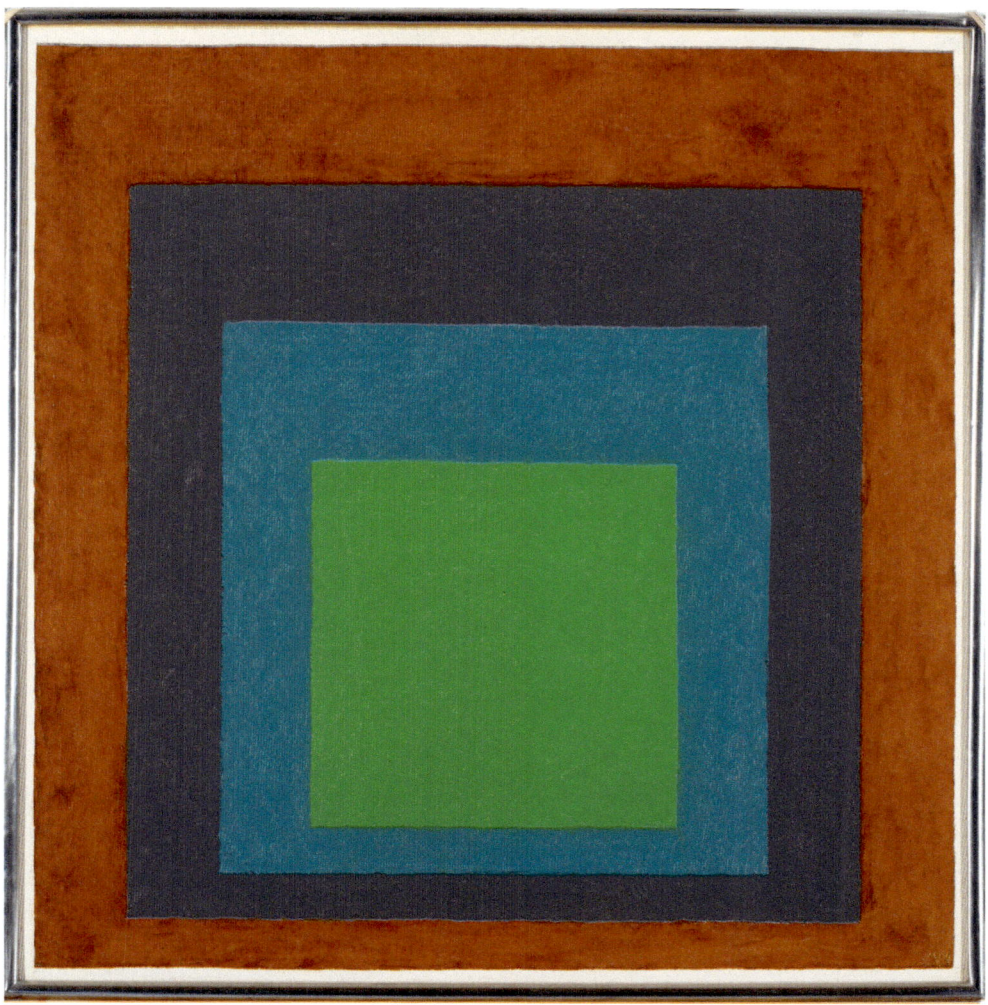

Figure 63: Joseph Albers, 'Study for Homage to the Square, Emanation' (1964) Oil on masonite, 24 x 24 in. Photo: Tim Nighswander. Photo: Albers Foundation/Art Resource, NY. © ARS, NY

through art. The Harrisons describe this way of 'thinking by questioning' as a process of identifying and working with an 'ennobling problem', that is, issues that are recognised as significant and important to address, whether or not the answer is known, and not just by specialists, but by common agreement (H. M. Harrison and Harrison 2001a, n.p.). In each case the point of the work of art is not to resolve the inconsistencies and contradictions that life presents, but to undertake a process of working them through by creating the circumstances for others to participate.

Newton Harrison discussed Cézanne and Rembrandt, and had, as noted in the discussion of *The Lagoon Cycle*, cited the form of the frescoed space as exemplified by Giotto's *St Francis*, but perhaps the most important example is Josef Albers. Albers was one of the teachers at the Bauhaus and arrived in the United States as a refugee in 1933. His *Homage to the Square* sequence, started in 1949 and comprising hundreds of works, explores colour relations through paintings of nested squares (fig. 63). Albers taught at Black Mountain College, a private liberal arts college founded in 1933 by John Andrew Rice in Black Mountain, North Carolina, after arriving in the USA, and then from 1950 at Yale. Although he had retired by the time Newton Harrison was doing his MFA at Yale, Newton was employed as a teaching assistant and taught Albers' colour theory.[1]

In *Homage to the Square* Albers creates spaces of tension and animation through the juxtaposition of colours and the boundaries between the colours. The form is almost always of nested squares – the most basic of shapes. Margit Rowell describes the dynamic as follows:

> The activity at this boundary is never the same. It allows a sharp or a fluid transition. When Albers is working with equal light intensities, the passages are barely perceptible, the angles no longer prominent, and the horizontals and verticals appear to waver. The whole configuration dissolves into indeterminate form. In other cases, however, radical contrasts of hues, or of light reflection versus absorption, draw attention to the edges as the 'hot points' of activity in light deflection, defraction, or refraction. (Rowell 1972, 27)

In the introductory discussion of Stengers' concept of 'inventing a field' (Chapter 1) we drew attention to the Harrisons articulation of 'field of play' and 'boundary'. In our discussion on systems (Chapter 5) we referenced Burnham referring to the role of the artist in 'considering goals, boundaries, structure, input, output and related activity inside and outside the system' (1974, 17) . The Harrisons themselves link the concept of 'field of play' in ecological systems to painting.

> For the painter, the field of play becomes a canvas, the physical boundaries are the edge of a canvas [...] We define a field of play in much the same way, except that the scale-shift is profound; measured in orders of magnitude. (H. M. Harrison and Harrison 2007b, n.p.)

Boundaries are thus recognised as temporary human devices, and as previously discussed in the case of the works *Meditations on the Great Lakes of North America* and *The Law of the Sea Conference: Where the Appetite is Discovered to be Endless*, they foreground the absurdity of human-instituted boundaries (Douglas 2021). Viewed from the perspective of the study of Albers, the Harrisons' approach to ecological boundaries is thoroughly informed by their understanding of the ways in which different conditions on either side of a boundary can make that waver, dissolve, or create 'hot points'. As the Harrisons put it:

> As a result, any central images that appeared seemed to exist for only a moment and thereafter to fade back into a pattern of moments grouped within moments. (H. M. Harrison and Harrison 2001a, n.p.)

Equally significant are the literary influences brought to the partnership by Helen Mayer Harrison with study of literature, in particular Chaucer (Ballengée, Harrison, and Harrison 2011, 51), and the ways that Chaucer and, for instance, Charles Dickens (1812–1870) were able to vividly engage with a larger field of human behaviour. This together with the Harrisons' involvement with key figures in the ethnopoetics movement puts their focus on the oral, spoken, and performed dimensions of texts into a wider context. There are multiple literary devices at work in the texts of the Harrisons, the most obvious of which is the distancing or pacing device of starting texts with 'And...', evoking religious texts of all faiths, or 'We hold...', evoking formality such as the Constitution of the United States. As discussed elsewhere the Harrisons play between the use of formality and everyday language (Douglas and Fremantle 2016b; Manolescu 2021, 97–102). The first five Lagoons start in very informal ways: 'For us [...]', 'He said [...]', 'But [...]', 'He said [...]', 'You can see here', 'If [...]', before changing to more directive language in the Sixth Lagoon, 'Pay attention [...]', and asking the key question, 'Do you desire [...]?' as the opening to the Seventh Lagoon.

Turning to the influence of sculpture, in an unpublished typescript, *A Short Discussion of Michelangelo, Rodin and Epstein, and Sculptural Values*, and an untitled handwritten text addressing Leon Battista Alberti (1404–1472) and Donatello (*c.*1386–1466), another dimension of analysis is evident (H. M. Harrison and Harrison, n.d.(a)). The *Discussion* focuses on the issue of line and mass in sculpture. Newton Harrison had trained in his youth in figurative sculpture and completed one public commission in the 1950s (Cassidy Rogers 2016, 95ff). The *Discussion* muses on how specific sculptures work under different ways of looking. The text starts with an instruction:

> Stand far enough away from the sculpture until it is very small but not blurred. Squint your eyes slightly in order to eliminate all from your field of vision except the work; then – and this takes a bit of training – throw the work slightly out of focus. (n.d.(a))

The text goes on to discuss what is revealed in each case: 'Michelangelo's work gets stronger and stronger and with no sense of outline roots itself in the base and grows upwards. The Epstein does not disappear but one is conscious of an outline – it reduces itself to line.' Turning to Auguste Rodin (1840–1917), 'the mass is not destroyed by line. It becomes vague and fuzzy with a kind of indecision as if he did not fully express it. He had not fully seen through weight into mass. It is for this reason that "The Thinker" appears to fall off his perch when viewed from a great distance.' The text opens up a second approach concerned with sculptural details.

> Viewed closely, an entirely different condition prevails. Here Rodin is the master and has sought a higher level of generality... The question here to be asked (after our senses have been dazzled by an exquisite facility and a virtuoso sensitivity) is do

the details truly support the statement[?] Too often in Michelangelo they tend to confuse by including too much. (n.d.(a))

If we were to undertake the same approach with the Harrisons' works, for example with *The Serpentine Lattice* (1993), momentarily setting aside the story to consider the visual form, we would certainly experience from a distance the serpentine line and the compositional mass of the elements. The exhibition at Douglas F. Cooley Memorial Art Gallery of Reed College, Portland, Oregon was contained in one room and comprised two large map-based wall images, one of the Pacific Coast from Alaska to California and the other taking that coastline as a central device and recursively exploring it to the watershed level (figs. 64-65). These two maps were complemented by two grids of photographs and a three-panel slide projection taking up most of a wall, floor to ceiling and end to end. The slide projection used material provided by Trygve Steen, a scientist and professor who had documented the landscape in its pristine, farmed, and clear-felled states. The central poetic text was positioned adjacent to the largest of the map-based images.

Working with the documentation, it becomes possible to imagine experiencing the work in the two ways described above. From a distance the strong sculptural form of the serpentine is central. Close up we become absorbed in the details that amplify the pattern with both ridgelines and watercourses forming overlayered serpentines. The other elements, projections and grids of photographs, shift among horizontals of the horizon and verticals of tree trunks in tree farms. There are changes in overall colour from heavily yellow orange (cut down trees and exposed stumps) to green and blue (looking up the trunks of redwoods and sequoias). Where the text draws attention to the scale and pattern, starting FROM SOUTHERN ALASKA/TO NORTHERN CALIFORNIA/NORTH AMERICA'S LAST GREAT TEMPERATE RAIN FOREST IS DYING, the photographs of blue tinged horizons evoke the sensuousness captured by the poetry of, for example, Gary Snyder (who is so closely associated with these landscapes) in lines such as:

Down valley a smoke haze
Three days heat, after five days rain
Pitch glows on the fir-cones
Across rocks and meadows
Swarms of new flies.

I cannot remember things I once read
A few friends, but they are in cities.
Drinking cold snow-water from a tin cup
Looking down for miles
Through high still air.
('Mid-August at Sourdough Mountain Lookout', Snyder 2010, 3)

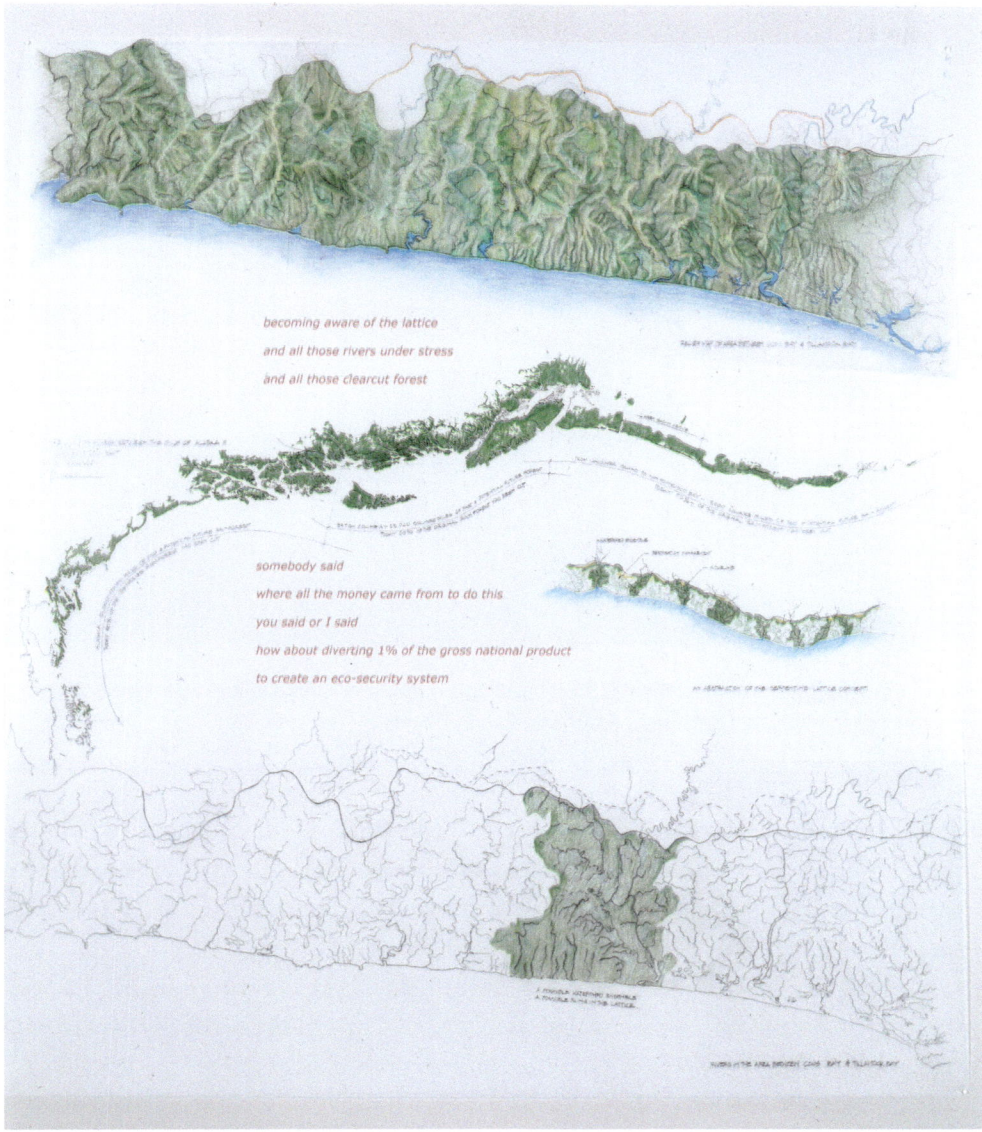

Figure 64: 'The Serpentine Lattice' (1993) Detail (courtesy of the Newton and Helen Harrison Family Trust)

The second manuscript on Alberti does not, as one might imagine at this point, address his theory of line and mass, but rather focuses on the artist and society. The manuscript shows how Alberti conceived of the artist using 'space line color dimension perfected figuration and symbolism... to "delight the eye" and "move the soul of the viewer"' (H. M. Harrison and Harrison, n.d.(a) n.p. no punctuation in MS). This is of course the humanist project, which the manuscript goes on to articulate as, 'To the creators in every field it means re-evaluation of all known forms in two lights[,] one the freedom achieved by the ancients and the second an examination of the actual world as seen and

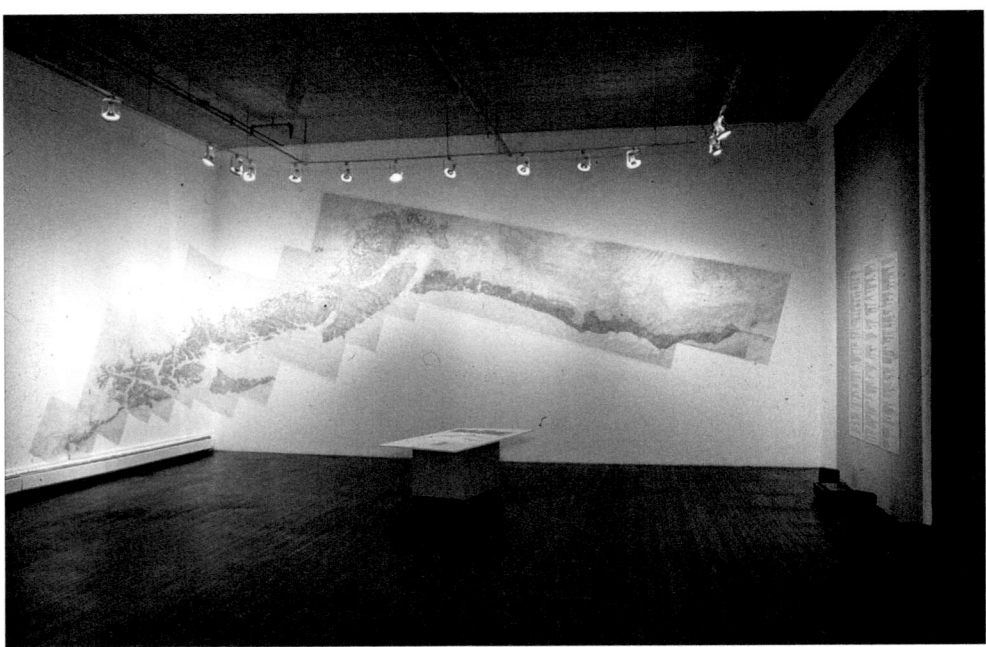

Figure 65: 'The Serpentine Lattice' (1993) Installation detail at Reed College, Portland, Oregon (courtesy of the Newton and Helen Harrison Family Trust)

felt.' It goes on to assert that where Alberti's formulation of the concept of *istoria* sets limits, Donatello's *Magdalene Pentient* (*c.*1440) breaks those limits. The *Magdalene* is 'more than the sum of the parts' because it conveys 'the ineffable' or 'the paradoxical' (n.d.(a)).

Once again, we find that underlying the ecological project the Harrisons had embarked upon, putting the well-being of the ecosystem first, there is a deep concern with matters addressed by generations of visual and text based artists.

Pedagogy: Curriculum Proposals

The Harrisons reflected on the challenge of learning and teaching that would address global environment challenges both through dialogue with other practitioners,[2] texts they authored, and even in the form of their autobiographical review of their career, *The Time of the Force Majeure* (H. M. Harrison and Harrison 2016). The Harrisons were teachers: Newton worked as a teaching assistant during his Master's at Yale; Helen's Master's degree in Philosophy of Education focused on John Dewey; Helen co-founded a Montessori school in Florence in the late 1950s; Newton worked in a Settlement School in New York City in the early 1960s (which led to *Dropouts and a 'Design for Living'* (H. M. Harrison and Harrison 1965) referenced in Chapter 2). In 1965 they were both offered teaching positions at the University of New Mexico

– Newton in sculpture, Helen in literature. Newton was appointed assistant professor of the newly formed Visual Arts Department at the University of California San Diego (UCSD) in 1967, and Helen directing the UC Extension Division's education programmes. Helen was appointed professor in the Visual Arts Department in 1980 (having resigned from the Extension Division to concentrate on their joint art practice in 1972). They both retired from UCSD in 1994 and joined UC Santa Cruz in 2010, initially through Beth Stephens' aegis, going on to form the Center for the Study of the Force Majeure.

Tim Collins et al. revisiting documentation of a dialogue from 2000 among a group of artists[3] involved in art, ecology, and teaching express the continuing problem in the following terms:

> Artists are unprepared to take a productive role in civic discourse. Students graduate without the tools and bridging experience to allow them to learn the languages and process in the areas of ecology, politics, and sociology, and are therefore unable to enter into effective creative communication. ...There isn't a single department in the country with a program area which addresses the changing meaning of nature, restoration ecology, and bio-technology. (Collins et al. 2023)

The group went on to identify the need in terms of

> 1. expand the social and aesthetic interest in public space to the entire citizen body,
> 2. re-awaken the skills and belief in qualitative analysis (versus professional-quantitative analysis), and
> 3. preach, teach, and disseminate the notion that everyone is an artist. (Collins et al. 2023)

This articulation of the challenge and what was required to address it puts a critical creative practice at the centre for the artist to be able to engage with the global environmental challenge. The ambition is for a citizen body with social and aesthetic interest in public space: a world in common. That world in common requires the notion that everyone is creative, in the sense that life is by definition creative.

In the unpublished and undated text 'Towards a New Curriculum Formation'[4] the Harrisons say,

> if we are to again think about how we might take the singular parts of our art practice and generalize them or express them, and shape them into a new form that would be generally available and usable, why, then we have to look at what prefigures the singularity in our work. (H. M. Harrison and Harrison, n.d.(b))

Here the Harrisons are asking the seemingly obvious question that once asked becomes transformative and applying this to their own practice. They frame the challenge in terms of the question 'what might students find useful to know in order to engage eco-political or eco-social issues from a profoundly ethical perspective?' They note that there are critical 'domains of literacy' but before discussing those, they position creativity and ethics as central. Resonant of Whitehead's philosophy of the organism, the pedagogy underpinning the curriculum proposal is centred on the creativity in all living things, just as improvisation is conceived as 'in common' across culture and ecosystems.

> [I]n each area there is an ongoing discourse on the nature and value and implications of creativity. All living things have, imbedded in them, the ability for continuous improvisation or creativity. (H. M. Harrison and Harrison, n.d.(b))

The Harrisons' understanding of emergence underpinning this pedagogy makes reference to Maturana and Varela's 'Santiago Theory' (Chapter 5). The construction of ethics is also drawn from the Harrisons' interest in ecological thinking.

> Each of the literacy domains that we talk about would need to be informed by what we call 'ethical creativity.' Ethical creativity, from our perspective, operates exactly in the same way as nature. That which is created, in acting toward its own wellbeing, also acts toward a larger whole. Its waste generates well-being in parts of a larger whole. (H. M. Harrison and Harrison, n.d.(b))

This formulation of ethics is quite distinct from ethical framings such as utilitarianism that would start from questions of human well-being. From Chapter 1 the focus has been on the Harrisons' ecological argument as a conceptual art move that drove the development of their practice. Here it is expressed as a question of ethics without acknowledging the significant complexities that are entailed, not least the dangers of harnessing what appear to be processes in nature as directives for human behaviours. The Harrisons focus on Margulis' conception of symbiosis (1998) rather than competition as fundamental to life but characterising this in an ethical position is not unproblematic.

The text identifies a number of 'domains of literacy' (drawing on the humanities and the sciences, processes associated with information and belief), and then turns to the real focus of the curriculum, which makes it clear that this work can only be done in groups who can choose 'an ennobling problem'. The Harrisons claim that a diverse group of people choosing to work on a common environmental challenge in a locality with the desire to prioritise the web of life will always result in ecosystemic enhancement. They argue that this generates empowerment, saying:

> We have found that this kind of investigation is revelatory in nature. In practice terms, the individual or the group can gain a sense of empowerment, as the way to engage the problem at hand emerges. (H. M. Harrison and Harrison, n.d. (b))

This claim could lose sight of the spirit of education that the Harrisons share with Dewey and Whitehead that is driven by wide-eyed curiosity, deep observation, and a sense of responsibility towards what is discovered. There can be no guarantees of 'ecosystemic enhancement'. Learning and experimentation may lead to positive and negative outcomes. The *Survival Pieces* clearly demonstrate this possibility, and they are experiences from which the Harrisons undergo the deepest moments of their own learning.

Having established the broad principles of what might now be called a transdisciplinary approach (focused on complexity and valuing of different ways of knowing), the text explores how this works through an example from the Harrisons' practice – *Santa Fe Watershed: Lessons from the Genius of Place* (2005). The starting point, as we have discussed elsewhere, are the questions 'How big is here?', 'How long is now?', and 'What is happening here, how, and what has happened here?'

They conclude by making the case that this approach has very specific benefits that directly address the wider issue of the 'bifurcation of nature' saying

> The singularity of the process is that it refuses fragmentation, it refuses the modernist framing element that sees the river as a problem or the earth as a problem, or the bark beetle as a problem. It's about seeing, creating, doing all at once. (H. M. Harrison and Harrison, n.d. (b))

This proposal for a curriculum assumes that participants have practices or disciplines, and that the task is to reorient towards addressing 'ennobling problems' through developing particular literacies, but more importantly through project-based, question-led learning.[5] That said, the Harrisons manifest a particular focus on scale as articulated in another version of the manuscript: 'If you look at this work that we do, however flawed that it may be, we seek in each case, a scale shift, that saves us from fragment-thinking and problem-solving, on the one hand, while permitting us to operate with a scale shift that lets us be in the scale of the issue we take on' (H. M. Harrison and Harrison, n.d. (b)).

The artist David Haley[6] has built on the Harrisons' works with his own approach to question-based learning that offers a different priority. In Haley's *Learning Manifesto* he argues that art should conform to Robert Pirsig's idea that the 'most moral act of all is to create the space for life to move onwards' (2022, 296). Haley draws attention to the etymology of the word 'art' in Sanskrit where *Rta* is 'the dynamic process by which the whole cosmos continues to be created, virtuously' (2022, 293). His pedagogy encompasses complex (systems) thinking and an unpacking of the idea of resilience into its different senses.

Many of the artists to whom we now turn in their ongoing conversations with the Harrisons (and perhaps more so in recent years with Newton Harrison) have debated in what ways scale plays through ecological concerns. As will be evident, they all have chosen to work durationally in specific places. In discussion Brandon Ballengée noted that the Harrisons had formed their practice in parallel with large-scale works such as Christo's *Running Fence* (1976). Art historian Suzaan Boettger explores the question of scale in this period in 'Earthworks: Art and the Landscape in the Sixties' (2002, 34 ff). Ballengée has chosen to focus on one place where the crisis is particularly sharp, offering a different response to the issue of scale.

Ballengée, Bon, Goto-Collins and Collins, Sprinkle and Stephens, Wallen

The five artist practices that are the focus of this section have been in conversation with the Harrisons over extended timescales, some from the late 1970s. Four (Brandon Ballengée, Lauren Bon, Reiko Goto-Collins and Tim Collins, and Ruth Wallen) participated in the 'Listening to the Web of Life Interdisciplinary Workshop' (Scripps Institution of Oceanography/La Jolla Historical Society, 17–18 March 2022). There are many others who we could have selected as equally relevant, including other artists who presented at the workshop in March and have also had long-term relationships with the Harrisons. Elsewhere we have discussed Cathy Fitzgerald's *The Hollywood Forest Project*, which is deeply informed by the Harrisons' work *The Serpentine Lattice* (1993). Fitzgerald takes the Harrisons' conception of storytelling, and in particular places as

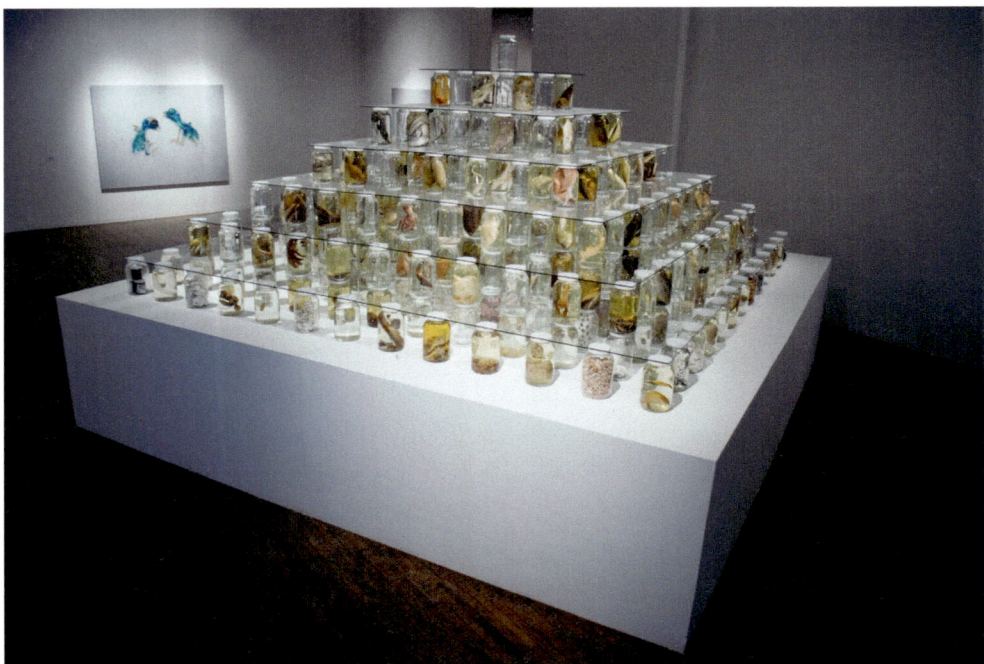

Figure 66: Brandon Ballengée 'Collapse' (2012) From 'Collapse: The Cry of Silent Forms' solo exhibition (May 5 – July 31, 2012) at Ronald Feldman Gallery mixed-media installation including 26,162 preserved specimens representing 370 species, glass, preservative solutions, 12 x 15 x 15 feet. Brandon Ballengée in scientific collaboration with Todd Gardner, Jack Rudloe, and Peter Warny. Photograph by Varvara Mikushkina (courtesy the artist, Ronald Feldman Gallery, New York, and Various Small Fires Los Angeles / Dallas / Seoul)

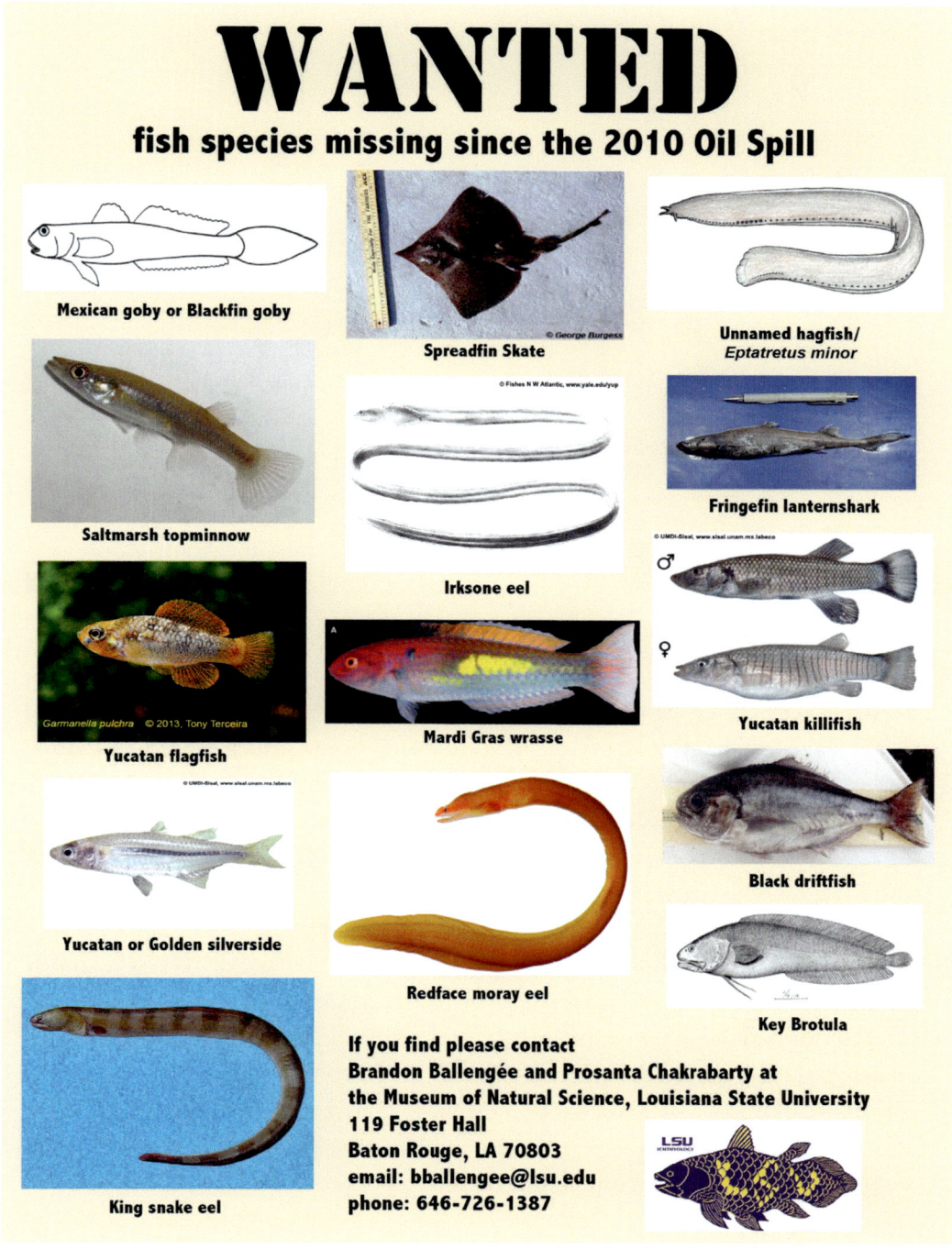

Figure 67: Brandon Ballengée 'Wanted' (2016) Gulf of Mexico endemic fishes 'missing' since 2010 Deep Horizon oil spill. This poster has been given away during outreach events and posted in marinas, schools, grocery stores, the Louisiana State Senate, and other public venues (courtesy of the artist)

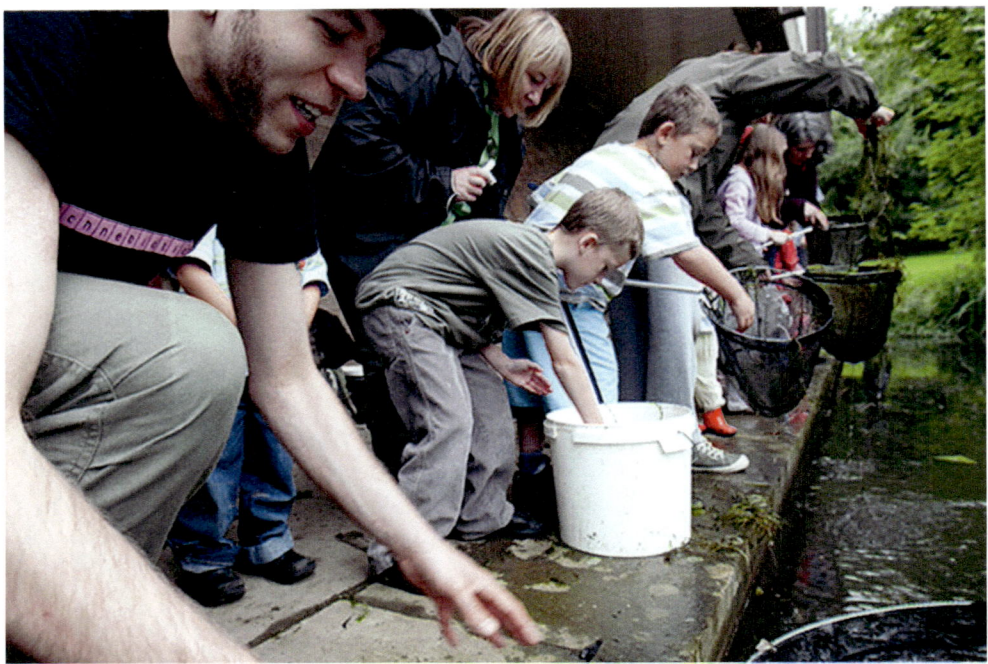

Figure 68: Brandon Ballengée 'Eco-Action, Zaragoza' (2017)

stories, into the process of transforming a small originally commercial plantation of
Sitka spruce into biodiverse woodland conforming to the principles of Continuous
Cover Forestry. Fitzgerald has used this story to persuade the Green Party in Ireland,
where she is based, to adopt Continuous Cover Forestry as policy as well as to debate
the need for legislation on ecocide. Other examples include Lillian Ball and her work
with Mangrove restoration informed by the Harrisons' work *The Endangered Meadows
of Europe* (1996).[7] Betsy Damon is a long-time friend and her work with the livingness
of water offers a parallel concern with the livingness of the world.[8] We have already
mentioned David Haley and his articulation of a pedagogy of graceful adaptation.[9]

Brandon Ballengée puts experimental and fieldwork-based science at the core of
his practice. His work in recent years, following the Deep Water Horizon mega oil spill
in the Gulf of Mexico of 2010, has become more overtly activist. This has accelerated
since moving to Louisiana in 2016. He said that the move was 'to be at the frontline for
climate impacts, work with communities here to try to become more sustainable, adapt
to the changes and retreat when we need to' (2023). This is complemented by gallery
representation in New York, for a period by the Ronald Feldman Gallery.

Ballengée's work *Collapse*, which he describes as a 'response', is a sculptural sketch of
the Gulf food chain using specimens in jars. It was created with other biologists working
on the Gulf ecosystem and is offered by Ballengée as a 'speculation' and an expression
'of concern' (Ballengée 2023) (fig.66). Other elements of this work include 'Wanted'
posters distributed across the Gulf Coast that highlight species that are missing since
the mega spill (fig. 67).[10]

Ballengée described his experience of creativity in art and science as having 'potential energy sharing' in a conversation with the Harrisons, saying:

> In certain relationships, that I have developed for a decade or more with biologists, we have this sharing energy at a level creative platform. There is no hierarchy. We talk and brainstorm collaboratively, thinking and debating ideas, also inspiring each other and there is no distinct role in this part of the process. Then we do the projects. The biggest difference, I think, is in the outcome whether or not it will be publicly revealed in a scientific journal or in an Art museum, sometimes both. (Ballengée, Harrison, and Harrison 2011, 47)

Ballengée's practice has focused on biodiversity through a series of long-term projects that use methods from the sciences, the arts, and from community development in different configurations. *Malamp*, started in 1996, is focused on causes of malformation in amphibians and has resulted in co-authored articles in science journals,[11] public exhibitions of large-scale images, and fieldwork collecting specimens of malformed amphibians with groups of volunteers in locations as diverse as the Yorkshire Sculpture Park in the UK; Parco Arte Vivente, Turin (both 2010); and North Troy, New York (2014). He calls these *Eco-Actions* (fig. 68). More recently this has involved longer term engagement with the specific context of the Gulf coast alongside work in other locations.

> My form of activism seeks to activate coastal communities through artistic and environmental inquiries into problems facing our coast, coastal habitats, and species... Here, I invite oil and gas workers, fisher folks, youth and other residents to join me in conducting ecological field sampling looking for missing species. As many of these communities are endangered, searching for missing species is a way to talk about change and loss. (2023)

Recent *Eco-Actions* include Fish Drawing workshops as well as fieldwork. Ballengée describes the involvement of inhabitants in terms of an exchange in which he learns as much as the participants do, and that is characterised by inspiration rather than didacticism.

The full realisation of this form of engagement is in the development of a nature reserve, *Atelier de la Nature*, with his partner Aurore Ballengée and their children. This was a life-time ambition according to Ballengée. The 25-acre site is being regenerated from its previous use as fields for growing soybeans. Seasonal events engage the three different local communities, Cajun, Creole, and Guatemalan, while also connecting with the Atakapa Tribe's indigenous knowledge. He shares with the Harrisons an interest in experimentation, and opening up the potential of bringing together science and art. This shared interest led to a collaboration with Newton Harrison. *A Memory in the Life of a Cajun Prairie* is a 2.5-acre site at the centre of *Atelier de la Nature* taking the form

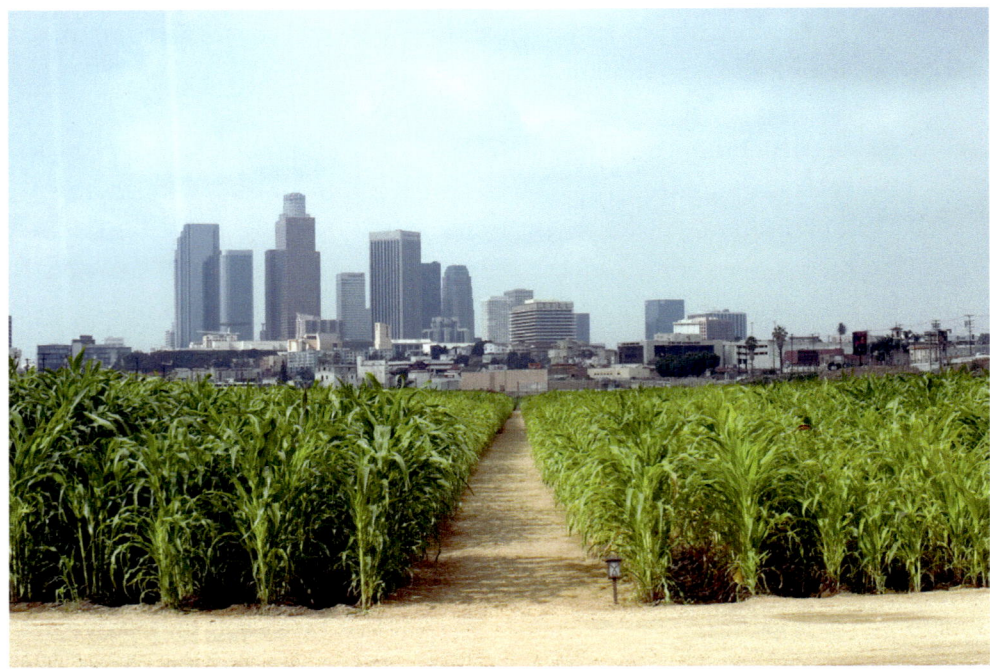

Figure 69: Lauren Bon and Metabolic Studio 'Not a Cornfield' Bioremediation and art project (courtesy of the artist)

of a 'Common Garden'[12] experiment developed in dialogue with Newton Harrison and Dr Anna Paltseva – a soil scientist at the University of Louisiana at Lafayette. This living artwork and science experiment, a version of the Harrisons' *Future Garden* works, asks whether Cajun Prairie is an effective form for sequestering carbon, how different forms of disturbance affect biodiversity (grazing sheep and fire in particular), and can this work raise awareness and inspire more widespread restoration of prairie (Ballengée 2023). As with the Harrisons' works it takes place-based and indigenous ways of knowing as a critical element in these works requiring listening to, valuing, and respecting First Nations' elders and their knowledge and understanding.

In his contribution to a collection on the legacy of the Harrisons (Fremantle and Douglas 2023) Ballengée opens by commenting on how the Harrisons 'inspired me to open my mind to the possibilities of art moving beyond objects and ideas toward concrete actions that benefit communities – ecological, biological, and social, and that connection of their special way of viewing challenges with systems thinking'. Ballengée in taking up this challenge articulates *Atelier de la Nature* as a site of landscape restoration, of experiment in the specific restoration of Cajun Prairie, focused on the well-being of the web of life. It is also as a meeting place for different cultures in the locality where three different forms of French as well as Spanish and other languages are spoken.

Where Ballengée's work reimagines the experimental as a shared activity between artists, scientists, and people living with climate change, Lauren Bon focuses her project *Bending the River* (2006–present) (fig. 70-71) on civic processes of governance

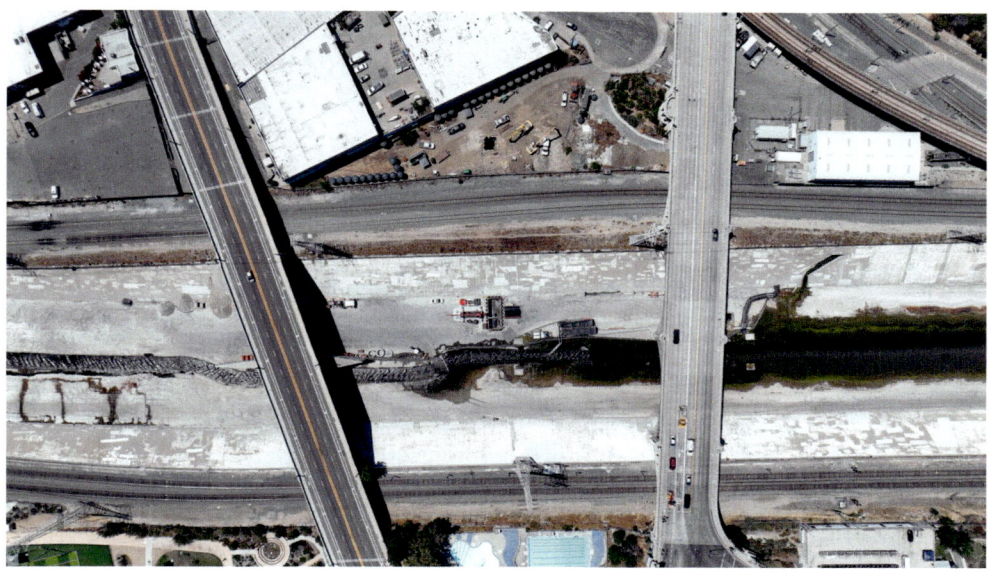

Figure 70: Lauren Bon and Metabolic Studio 'Bending the River' (2006-ongoing) Aerial view
(courtesy of Lauren Bon and Metabolic Studio)

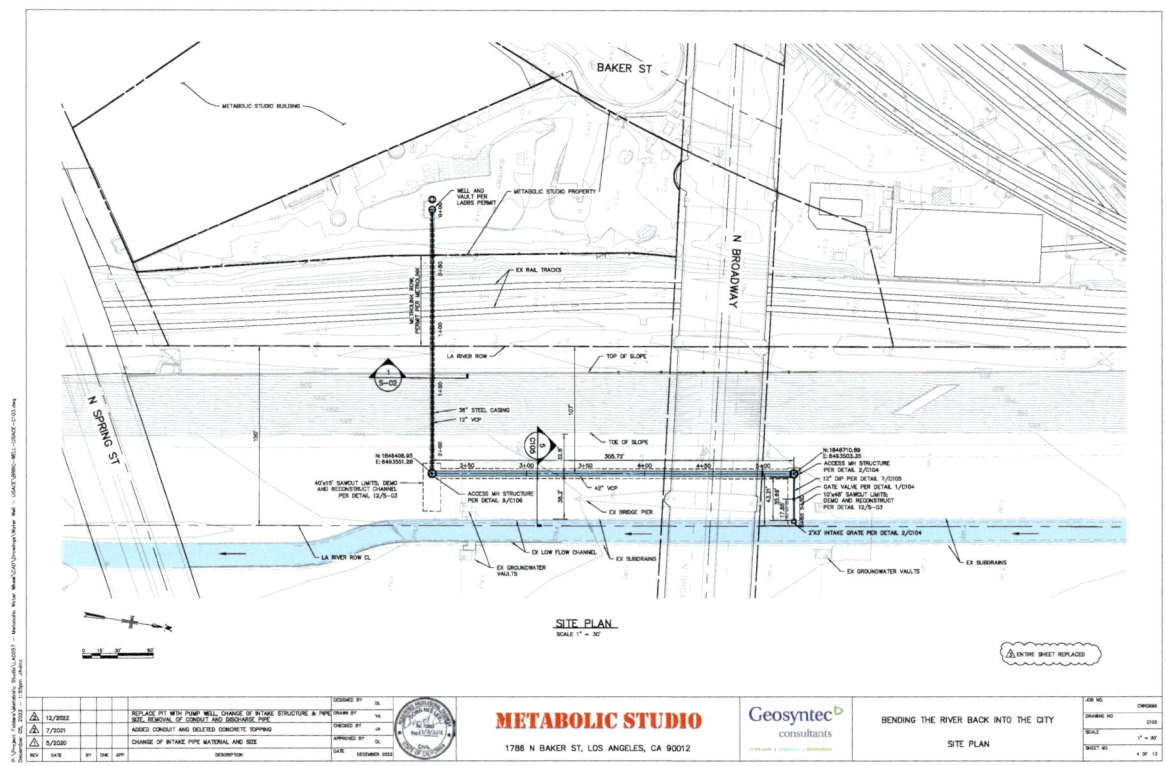

Figure 71: Lauren Bon and Metabolic Studio 'Bending the River' (2006-ongoing) Drawing
(courtesy of Lauren Bon and Metabolic Studio)

in relation to access to water as a commons, specifically focused at present by the Los Angeles River. This is a different, but equally resonant approach to attending to ecosystems. For Bon, water is not only one of the key commons; it is also a critical infrastructure, mostly overlooked, but also 'weaponised' in various ways. As with all the artists discussed, Lauren Bon's work involves collaborations with other disciplines and practices, in this case engineers and lawyers as well as land managers working for the Parks Departments.

Bon's descriptions of the Los Angeles River as we experience it today is a flood defence structure where '[p]reventing flooding prevents abundance' (Bon quoted in Stromberg 2023). This could have been said by the Harrisons and is closely related to statements of theirs such as '"flood control is the destruction of the well-being of rivers." (i.e., the well-being of the river is traded off for that of the city.)' (H. M. Harrison and Harrison 2007b, n.p.). *Bending the River* is being undertaken within the same watershed as the Harrisons' *Arroyo Seco Release: A Serpentine for Pasadena* (1985) and *Devil's Gate: A Refugia for Pasadena* (1987).[13] This shared concern with the water infrastructure of the Los Angeles' basin belies different orientations. Lauren Bon articulates her concern as 'reparation', saying 'if we are on our way out as a species, let's try and repair what we can' (Bon 2023). *Bending the River* is an experiment in water governance. It emerged out of contradictions met in *Not a Cornfield* (2005–06) (fig. 69). That project involved working with representatives of tribes who historically inhabited and farmed the watershed, planting 32 acres of corn, working with indigenous traditional seedstock on an abandoned railyard. This was the first step in the railyard's transformation into a public park. The corn acted as a bioremediator removing toxins from the soil and was the first stage in a seven-year process of remediation undertaken by Metabolic Studio. Bon described the contradiction that led to *Bending the River* as follows, 'When I did "Not a Cornfield" – I would go down to the river here with a red truck and fill it up with water and then I found out that that wasn't permitted and I couldn't understand why' (Bon and Harrison 2023). The section of the Los Angeles River and its contents are the official property of the Army Corps of Engineers ('LA River Master Plan' 2022). Technically, this even applies to rainwater coming off the roof of a private house. As highlighted in Chapter 2, contradictions revealed in one work can lead onto new works. On a bureaucratic level, *Bending the River* is made possible by securing more than 70 interconnected permits and approvals from 23 federal, state, regional, county, and city agencies. These allow a small proportion of the water in the low flow channel of the Los Angeles River to be redirected via a 300 feet clay pipe feeding a well. Solar energy is used to pump the water up out of the well through a constructed wetland before being directed to watering the park. In this basic description the elements are very reminiscent of Hans Haacke's work *Rhine-water Purification Plant* (1972). That work involved waste water being diverted from the river, pumped into a museum where it was purified, and then used to water the museum gardens (Spaid 2002, 31). This work differs in its much more complex relation with public space, not least manifest in the engagement with bureaucracy but also wider ecologies. The water used for this will be water in the canalised river derived from farmland and stormwater runoff (hence the need for the wetland to purify it), but in the process of *Bending the River*, a series of triangles have been cut through the concrete. What has been revealed is the original floodplain, in some places ground water – a river running under the river – and in others soil. As an experiment some of this soil was moved to another space where it, without any intervention, even after 70 or 80 years under concrete, seeds in the soil immediately sprouted. Bon commented that the concretisation of the river, usually demonised, had actually protected a 51 miles by ¼ mile of the watershed (Bon 2023).

Bon describes the focus of this work in the following terms:

> This work acts as a case study. My hope is to set a precedent and path forward for creative and innovative thinking about how we can better use our infrastructure and re-evaluate our commons of soil, seed, water, and community process. (Lauren Bon quoted in Stromberg 2023)

Although the sign at the entrance of Metabolic Studio, which Bon founded and leads, reads, 'Artists Need to Create On the Same Scale that Society Has the Capacity to Destroy', the approach to scale is not the same as that of the Harrisons. Where the Harrisons start with questions such as, 'How big is here?' and sought, as evident in their Curriculum Proposal, to focus on the largest relevant scale, Bon describes her process in terms of starting with an intervention that reveals the nature of the problem. The scale of *Bending the River* is relatively small on the ground (lifting 77 feet by 300 feet of concrete, installing 300 feet of clay pipe, addressing the estimated 56 acre-feet of water per year for irrigation required by the 42.5 acre park, '$8 million for the in-river portion' (Bon quoted in Stromberg 2023)), but it is large in terms of the growing engagement with bureaucracy and the potential change of governance.

Bon's focus on one small section of the Los Angeles River is a serious and ambitious effort to bring water back into public perception and value by tracing, uncovering, and honouring the underlying watershed. This work, its sheer 'daring' in Stengers' terms, along with the responsibility Bon and Metabolic Studio have taken over years to challenge civic infrastructure and the forms of governance, is making something that was 'silenced' by engineering matter again culturally and ecologically. It refocuses on water as commons rather than the apparent preserve of a government body, in this case a military engineering branch of the United States Army, the Army Corps of Engineers. Bon's construction of the commons is very much shared with Newton Harrison's recent work *On the Deep Wealth of this Nation, Scotland* (2017–18). He opened the question of how in acknowledging air, water, and soil as crucial to supporting life on Earth, we, as humans, might take care of these resources by reaching a 'commons of mind'. Encountering Bon's process that is characterised by a Deweyan 'learning by doing' in, for instance, *Not a Cornfield* (2005–06) and the subsequent process of remediation of the site inspires and informs the Harrisons initiating on the ground research with their Future Garden works, *Sagehen: A Proving Ground* (2011–ongoing).

Tim Collins and Reiko Goto-Collins have been friends with and exhibited together with the Harrisons (e.g. Kester 2005; Spaid 2002; Strelow 1999).[14] After studying their work for five years, in 1993 they travelled to the College Art Association Conference in Seattle specifically to hear the Harrisons' keynote address. On the way home to San Francisco, they visited *The Serpentine Lattice* installation at Reed College (fig. 65). Collins and Goto-Collins share a common cause in committing to making work that interconnects the human relations with the more-than-human. Learning about the Harrisons' interest in Socratic dialogue was significant to the development of their thinking about discourse. It is important to note where the Harrisons, quite uniquely, developed a singular identity, Collins and Goto-Collins are in an ongoing dialogue of shared concerns, co-create works, and are a partnership, but as with most collaborating couples, do not present as a single identity in relation to authorship of works.[15]

In Goto-Collins' doctoral research, she addressed empathy, a lifelong concern of Helen Mayer Harrison (2012). One of the key examples she drew on was her experience of *The Serpentine Lattice*. She notices in this work the Harrisons undergo a transformation from sympathy for the dying rainforest to one of empathy whereby the forest and its potential becomes a central concern. 'Diverse voices were assembled as poetic narratives using empathic projection to take the other's position through face to face dialogue, eye contact, tone of voice, and body gestures' (Goto-Collins 2012, 116). The concept of empathy is central to both Collins' and Goto-Collins' practices. They more recently expressed it in relation to forests.

> Empathy is a type of perception led by something outside of us. It is about (but it is also more than) a simple understanding and inter-relationship with human and non-human others. Empathy is beyond self-interest and most often directed at something different or foreign. It involves attention to expressions of [a] life force and engagement with the world. (Collins and Goto-Collins 2017, 8)

However, they come from a different artistic tradition than that of the Harrisons, one characterised by a 'physical conceptualism' (Collins 2013), which emerged in San Francisco where they undertook Master's degrees and practiced in the 1980s and early 1990s. This is characterised by an embrace of everyday life, a phenomenological record, and engagement with audiences directly, working in open-ended ways (Marioni 2003, 93 ff.; Tedford 2011) (fig. 72).

Collins and Goto-Collins immerse themselves in relationship to particular living things and their places over long periods of interaction. In *Plein Air* (2010–ongoing) (fig. 73), they have developed approaches that enable us to experience the respiration of living trees, seeking to evoke empathy. This is focused by the sensorium of touch, movement, and hearing, most recently drawing on traditional Japanese percussion,

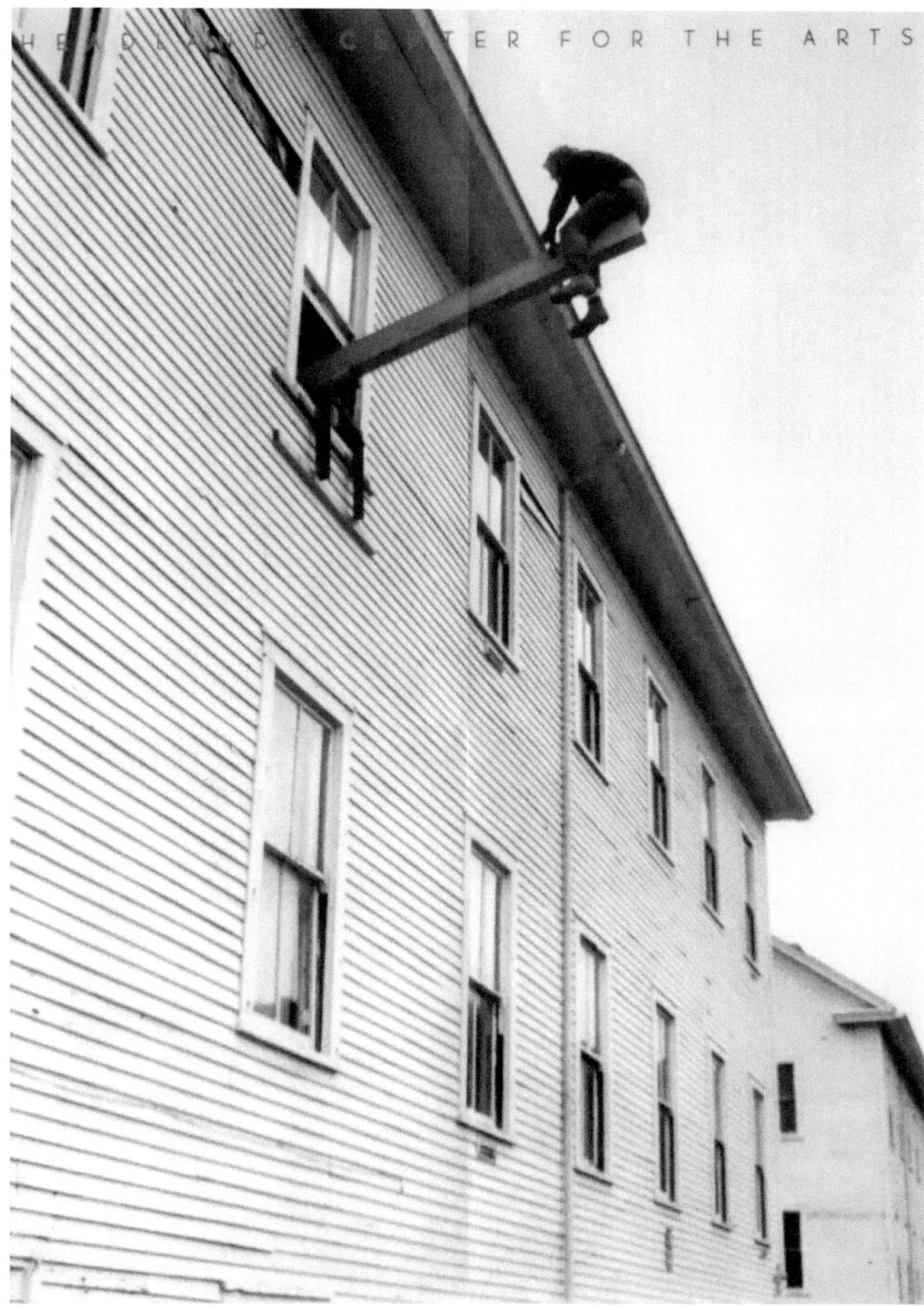

Figure 72: Timothy Collins 'Levitate' (1992) 'An artist is sitting on a sixteen-foot beam balanced eight feet out a third story window. A water trough on the other end of the beam is holding 22 gallons of water, it is leaking. The artist holds his balance against the diminishing weight of the water. Six tape recorders repeat over and over again with increasingly emotional intensity, "levitate".' (courtesy of the artist)

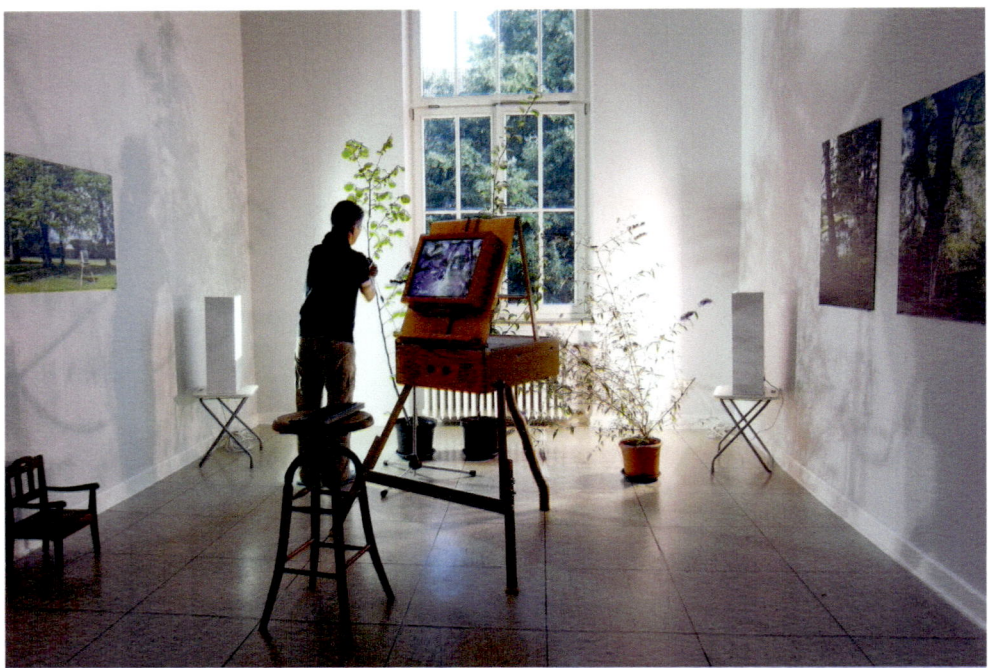

Figure 73: Timothy Collins and Reiko Goto-Collins 'Sound of A Tree' (2015) Installation,
'ON-Nuee Musik' Köln, Germany (courtesy of the artists)

woodwind, and string instruments. Sensor technologies reveal photosynthesis and tran-
spiration as data. Monitoring a single leaf for light, temperature, humidity, and carbon
dioxide data provides an understanding of the tree's reactions to dynamic local atmos-
pheric conditions. The earlier versions of this work used a Plein Air painting easel to
contain the equipment, clearly indicating the intent to position the work in relation to
the history of artists working outdoors. More recent versions have reduced the scale of
the technology to be wearable and portable, with a focus on human to leaf touch. They
have created a pair of performative, body instruments they call HAKOTO: referencing
leaf words, leaf saying, leaf things, leaf songs, in a poetic use of Goto-Collins' Japanese
language (fig 74). HAKOTO has developed as a means of performing a climate duet
that opens new empathic and aesthetic experiences with trees. The work provokes an
ensuing dialogue about nature and climate related changes to local environments.

Collins and Goto-Collins' concern with discourse is also shared with the Harrisons,
but distinct too.[16] *Plein Air* forms part of a wider programme, which includes long-term
engagement with the Black Wood of Rannoch, the most significant pinewood in the
southern Highlands of Scotland, inhabitants of the village of Rannoch, and forestry
researchers and managers caring for the Blackwood. Initiated in discussions with the
UK agency Forest Research in 2011, this has resulted in artworks, exhibitions,[17] as well
as workshops, fieldtrips, and publications. These focus on understanding and generating dialogue on the cultural dimensions of the Black Wood's significance, seeking to

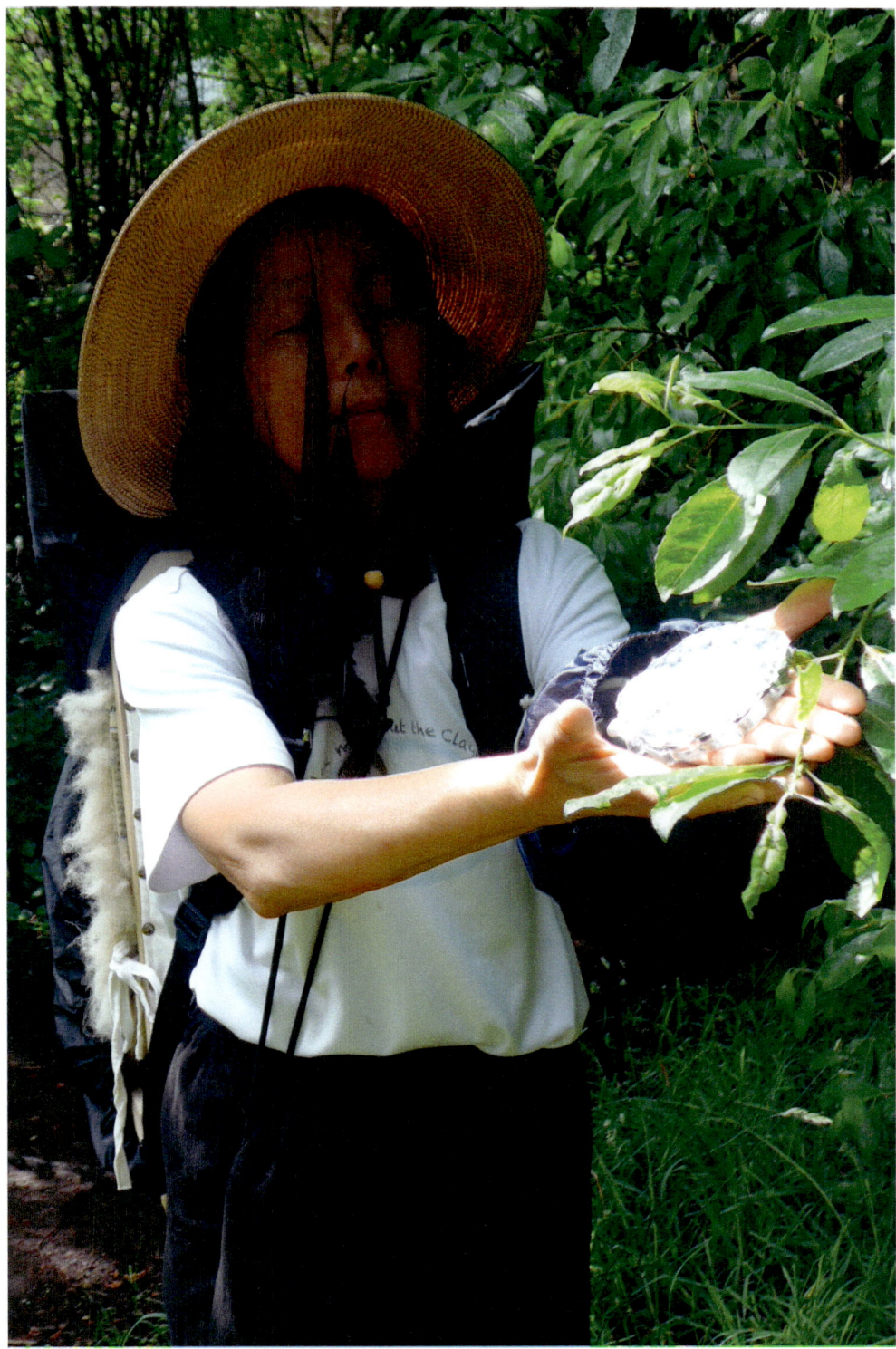

Figure 74: Timothy Collins and Reiko Goto-Collins 'HAKOTO (portable device)' (2023) (courtesy of the artists)

position this in relation to other science and conservation values, particularly in relation to ecosystem services. Evoking the Harrisons' characterisation of themselves as strangers needing to learn from inhabitants, Collins and Goto-Collins suggest:

> As urbanites and legal aliens at home in Scotland we have an interest in experiences that attract us into imaginative and critical relationship with the experience, value and meaning of ancient and semi-natural Caledonian forests. (Collins and Goto-Collins 2017, 2)

The work includes video focused on the temporal and sensory aspects of the form of this landscape (including inhabitants such as midges), the historical formation of the character of the landscape through conflicts (Collins, Goto-Collins, and Edwards 2018, 204), and the linguistic aspects – the history of the landscape as inscribed in Gaelic place names. These correlate with some of the key aspects of cultural 'ecosystem services'[18] that are intrinsic to the site: the character and how that embodies the management history and heritage as well as the wildlife. While these are intrinsic to the site, it is only through some form of articulation that cultural value can be realised (Tabbush 2010). Collins and Goto-Collins articulate the distinctive role of arts-led approaches in relation to the process of environment planning and management as focused by the creation of particular forms of discourse, distinct from either instrumental evaluation through, for example, cost–benefit analysis, or through rational deliberative processes (Edwards, Collins, and Goto-Collins 2016, 319). This approach was developed in dialogue with the Harrisons, as well as with other artists concerned with discourse and the public realm, such as the feminist activist Los Angeles-based artist Suzanne Lacy (b. 1945).

Annie Sprinkle and Beth Stephens are pioneers in conceiving of an ecosexual practice, one that understands the earth as lover (rather than mother). Their statement *25 Ways to Make Love to the Earth* (fig. 75) is a useful way to engage with the ramifications of this approach to paying attention to the web of life:

1. Tell the Earth 'I love you. I can't live without you.'
2. At first you may feel embarrassed to be lovers with the Earth. Relax. Let it go. It's OK.
3. Spend time with her.
4. Ask her what she likes, wants, and needs – then try to give it to her.
5. Massage the Earth with your feet.
6. Admire her views often.
7. Circulate erotic energy with him.
8. Smell her.
9. Taste her.
10. Touch all her all over.
11. Hug and stroke his trees.

12. Talk dirty to her plants.
13. Swim naked in their waters.
14. Lay on top of her, or let her get on top of you.
15. Do a nude dance for her.
16. Sing to her.
17. Kiss and lick her.
18. Bury parts of your body deep inside his soil.
19. Plant your seeds in her.
20. Love her unconditionally even when she's angry or cruel.
21. Keep them clean. Please recycle.
22. Work for peace. Bombs really hurt.
23. If you see her being abused, raped, or exploited, protect her as best you can.
24. Protect their mountains, waters, and sky.
25. Vow to love, honor, and cherish the Earth until death brings you closer together forever.

(Sprinkle and Stephens 2021, see fig. 75)

At once pointed, the statement is also humorous, and nuanced in its judgement of the use of genders, sometimes obvious and occasionally provocative. The last instruction fully realises the logic of the ecosexual approach.

Sprinkle and Stephens are first and foremost performance artists who also make films and write reflectively about their practice. They describe their relationship with the Harrisons in the following terms, focusing on the practical and policy-oriented aspects.

> Beginning with the premise that their client was always the Earth, the Harrisons would collaborate with a broad spectrum of experts in order to propose solutions to environmental problems. Our work, which is about being in a better relationship with the Earth and helping others to achieve this as well, is very different from that of the Harrisons, but we were inspired by their collaborative practice and lifelong commitment to addressing ecological issues. (Sprinkle and Stephens 2021, 10)

Sprinkle and Stephens' performance practice is deeply influenced by Allan Kaprow and the art movement Fluxus: Beth Stephens by Geoffrey Hendricks (1931–2018) whose work is foundational to queer art (Hendricks and Getsy 2021), and Annie Sprinkle by Dutch artist and Fluxus member Willem de Ridder (1939–2022), who was among other activities graphic designer for the alternative sex newspaper *Suck*. Both Sprinkle and Stephens also acknowledge performance artist Linda Montano (b. 1942) and her concern with art=life/life=art (Montano 2010), which manifest in a series of durational works. Sprinkle first worked with Montano in the 1980s and in 2003 Sprinkle and Stephens were affiliated with a group of artists enacting Montano's *Seven Years of Life as*

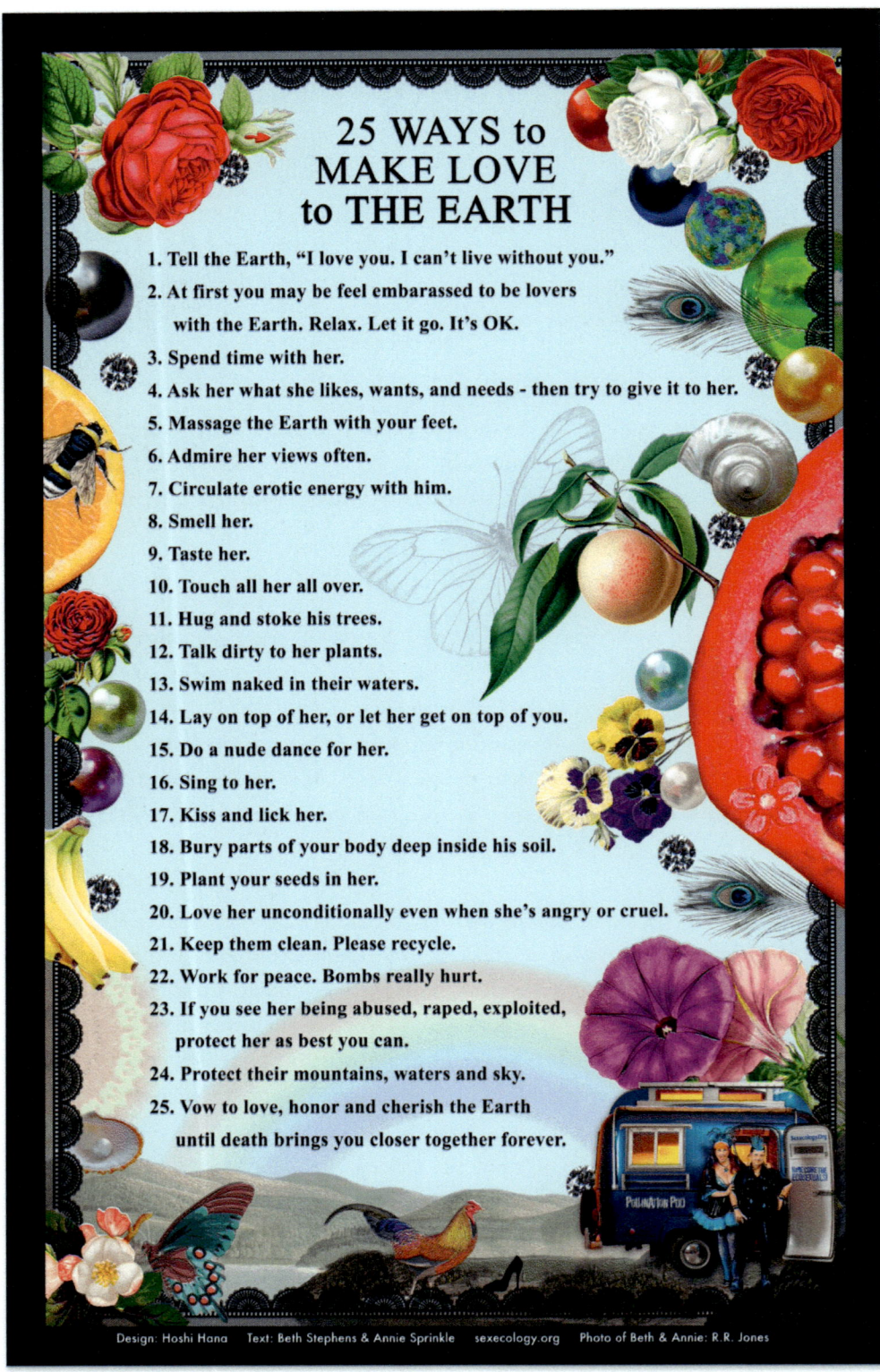

Figure 75: Annie Sprinkle and Beth Stephens '25 Ways to Make Love to the Earth' (2021) Poster (courtesy of the artists)

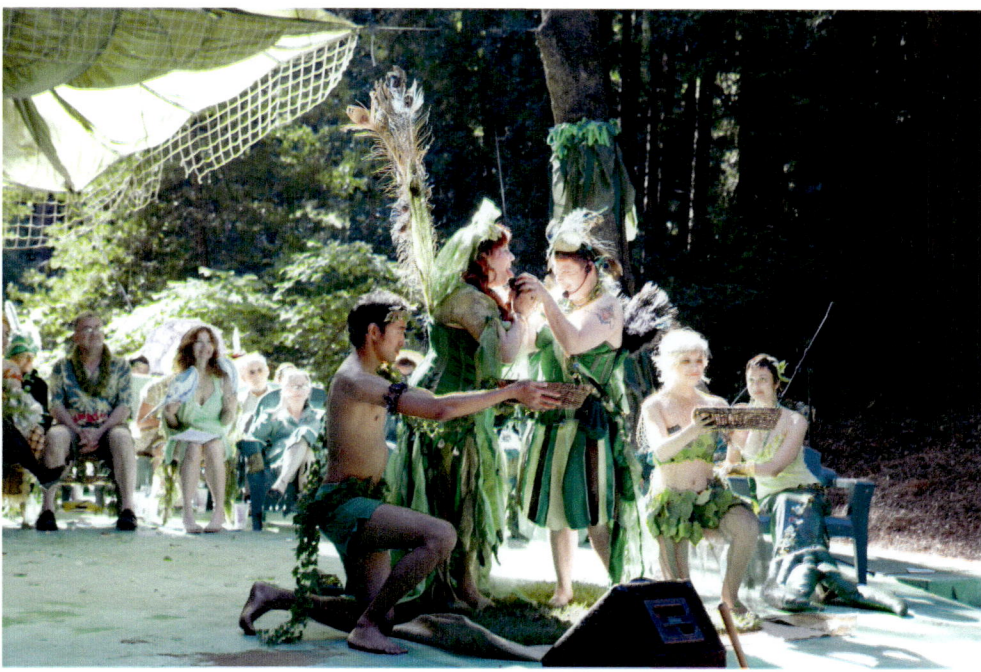

Figure 76: Annie Sprinkle and Beth Stephens 'Green Wedding' (2008) Performance with Lydia Daniller (courtesy of the artists)

Art (1984–91). Montano's *Seven Years of Life as Art* was informed by the seven-chakra structure and used the associated colours. Sprinkle and Stephens used this context to develop the Love Art Laboratory, framing it as a research project. The focus of the Love Art Laboratory was an annual wedding, each year characterised by the associated chakra colour. These were performance artworks informed by acquired immunodeficiency syndrome (AIDS) and GLBTQIE[19] activism, which transformed in the process into a key part of their ecosexual practice. They describe the transition as follows:

> We fell deeply in love with the Santa Cruz mountains and the redwood forest. In a moment of passion, we decided to marry the Earth! It was an aha moment for us. We were so caught up in the excitement of the creative possibilities that we literally got down on our knees and proposed to the Earth, who responded with what we understood was a resounding Yes! (Sprinkle and Stephens 2021, 76)

Starting in 2008 with the *Green Wedding* (fig. 76) the events become ecosexual extravaganzas – they continued to be performance works involving friends and colleagues in a range of roles, but they take on marrying different dimensions of Earth – first the Green/Heart Year the Earth literally in the form of the soil, then for the Blue/Throat Year water, the Purple/Third Eye Year the moon, and finally the White/Crown of the

Head Year, the Snow. At the *Green Wedding* the Harrisons performed the Homily, saying:

> The world of soil is bizarre. Communication is chemical and physical. Worms are its giants. Movement is slow. Fungi move through it at rates measured in centimeters per month. Bacteria move through it at rates measured in centimeters per year. The world of soil is ancient and magical, contradictory and complex. Mostly solid and opaque to light, still it acts as a sea to thousands of species that travel through it horizontally and vertically. It is the biological filter that detoxifies a large proportion of the poisons that are applied to the environment. One gram of ordinary farmyard soil can contain over one billion individual bacteria. [...]
> Consider the dynamism of healthy soil. Consider that soil covers most of the land surface of the planet. Consider that soil plays a fundamental role in stabilizing the biosphere. Consider that new soil formation has been arrested in many places. Healthy soil is a living system. Healthy soil needs to interact with the air and water. Healthy soil needs access to the products of the plants and other surface organisms. Therefore; tape this piece of paper on every bulldozer you encounter. (H. M. Harrison and Harrison 2008b)[20]

This 'Homily' draws on the Harrisons' long engagement with Earth going back to *Making Earth* in 1970.

Sprinkle and Stephens describe the *Green Wedding* as 'a queer challenge to the institution of marriage and a queer spin on environmental art' (Sprinkle and Stephens 2021, 80). They go on to say, '150 people had collaborated on the creation of the wedding. ... For the first time we conceptualized ourselves as *ecosexual*' (italics in the original). The 'queer spin' that Sprinkle and Stephens bring as they engage with the environment in their art brings the focus on 'difference' in queer theory into relation with the focus on 'difference' in ecological thinking (cf. Bateson 1979, 79–80). The synthesis of queer and ecological theory has been taken up by Timothy Morton among others (Morton 2010) and is first developed by Greta Gaard in her linking of queer theory and ecofeminism (Kagan 2020, 268). A key characteristic of both Sprinkle and Stephen's ecosexual practice and of related theory is the focus on corporeality (Kagan 2020, 271). Sprinkle and Stephens' particular approach to putting the lifeweb first and creating a world in common offers a very different but equally significant approach to reimagining art practice as making something matter. If the Harrisons' work is focused on what putting the lifeweb first might mean to, for instance, public decision-making, then Sprinkle and Stephens ask what it might mean to intimacy?

Turning to Ruth Wallen the concern with attending to the web of life, empathic relations, and creating a world in common continues and manifests in a different form of intimacy. In conversation with Collins and Goto-Collins, who are also in dialogue with Wallen, they draw attention to the interweaving of art and science, but perhaps more important is a clarity about the spiritual connection with more-than-human oth-erness that Wallen manifests in part through a Buddhist practice. This is apparent in her dialogues with trees, which seek to offer some form of understanding. Her writings focus on the cycle of life and death, of fire and regrowth, of human intervention and the longer timescales for trees. Other living things including the mycelial networks and the gobbling turkeys are all present (Wallen 2022).

Wallen is the only artist discussed who formally studied on the programme that the Harrisons taught, undertaking a Master's at UC San Diego, graduating in 1987. She has been in dialogue with them ever since and from time to time joined their morning conversations and the larger conversational drift. Prior to undertaking the MFA, Wallen had been creating ecologically focused artworks. Wallen attained an undergraduate degree in environmental sciences before undergraduate studies at the San Francisco Art Institute. From December 1978 to January 1980 Wallen was artist-in-residence at the Exploratorium in San Francisco, a museum supporting collaborations between artists and scientists. She is recognised for creating the earliest ecosystem-based artwork at the Exploratorium, in the form of wooden sculptures, positioned in San Francisco Bay in three different locations (fig. 77). The sculptures formed a substrate showing that ma-rine life was returning to the widely assumed to be lifeless San Francisco Bay as a result of the Clean Water Act of 1972. The accumulation of organisms, including species be-ing introduced as a result of global shipping, was documented using macrophotography over a period of more than a year. The work then toured as a performative lecture. The lecture performances are always followed by discussions with the audiences. Wallen is trying, by showing hundreds of images and conflating time and scale, to communicate ecological processes. Her aim is to evoke empathy in the viewers, inviting them to care about what was occurring.

Wallen's works in the 1990s and early 2000s focused on various forms of dialogue including a work entitled *Palestinian Jewish Dialogue* (2000–03) as well as works ad-dressing suburbanisation in San Diego where she lives, such as *I Love Del Mar* (1988) and *Preserving Paradise* (2007). Wallen has focused on trees in her recent work, as a result of her attention to the huge numbers of trees dying as a result of the impacts of cli-mate change, including both increased heat and drought as well as increasing numbers of insects that kill trees (Wallen 2019, n.p.). Over many years based out of San Diego this work has been informed by US Department of Agriculture Forest Service data.

> I'd been coming here for three years, drawn by a dark red spot on a Forest Service map of tree mortality in California. (Wallen 2019, n.p.)

During 2023 Wallen was invited to develop new work in the Netherlands, *Learning to think like a Forest* (fig. 79). This connected decades of work with trees, forests, and suburbanisation in San Diego and the South West of the USA to the Netherlands, focusing on the use of the terms 'native' and 'invasive'. Black Locust and Black Cherry

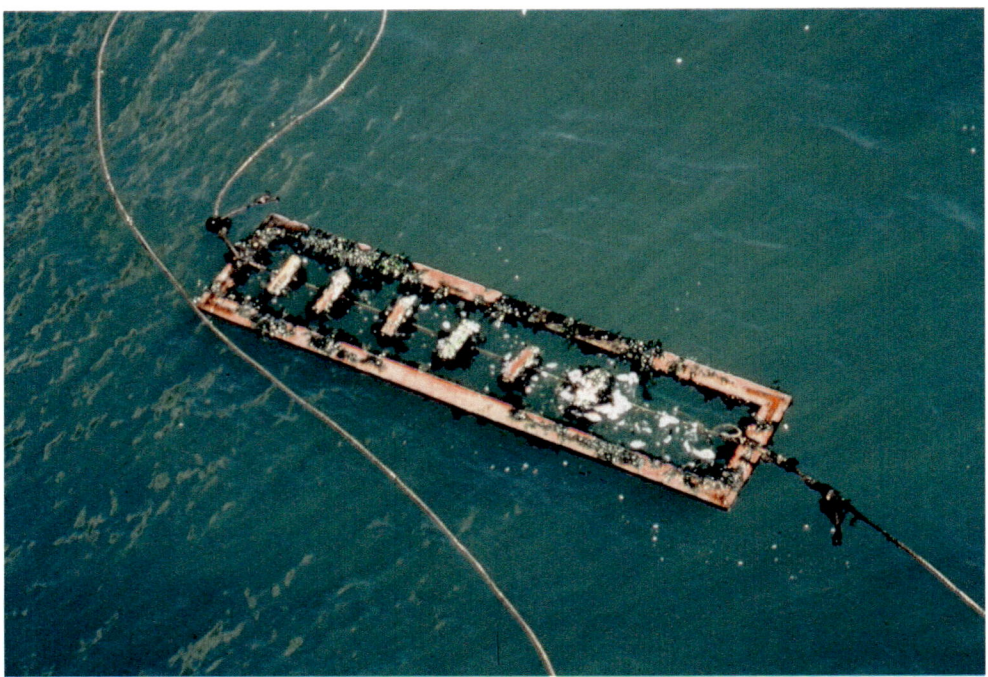

Figure 77: Ruth Wallen, 'Sea as Sculptress' (1977–1980) (courtesy of the artist)

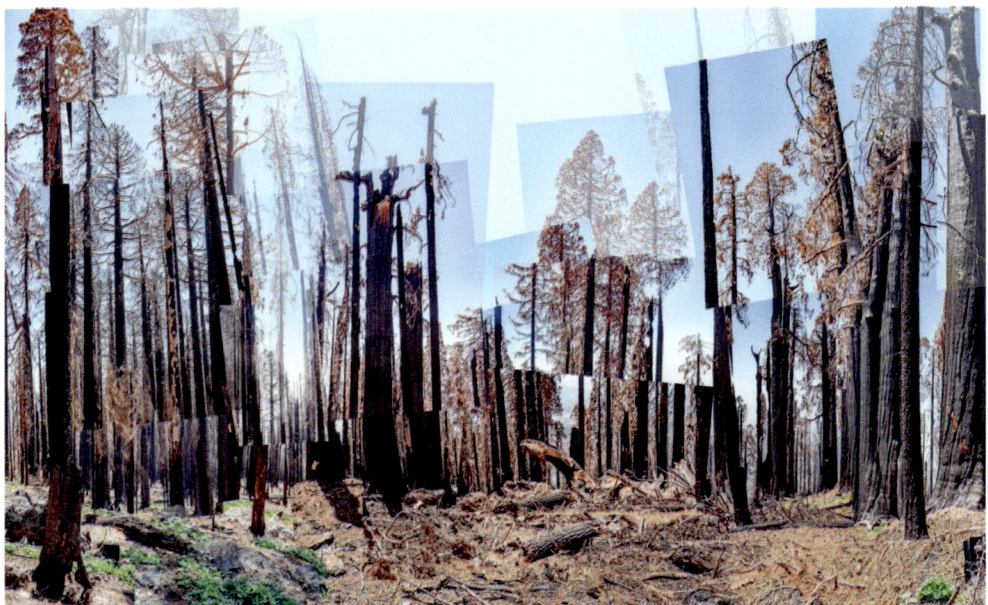

Figure 78: Ruth Wallen 'Walking with Sequoias, Sugar Bowl, Redwood Mountain Grove' (2022)
Photomontage (courtesy of the artist)

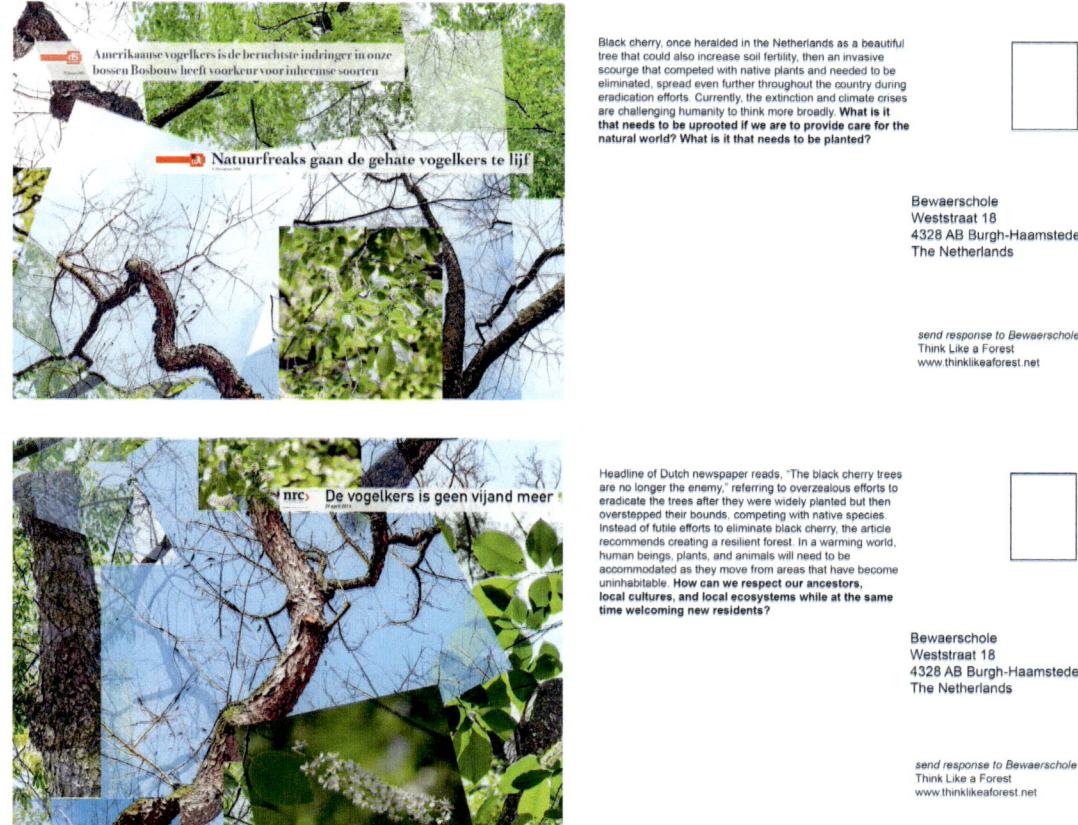

Black cherry, once heralded in the Netherlands as a beautiful tree that could also increase soil fertility, then an invasive scourge that competed with native plants and needed to be eliminated, spread even further throughout the country during eradication efforts. Currently, the extinction and climate crises are challenging humanity to think more broadly. **What is it that needs to be uprooted if we are to provide care for the natural world? What is it that needs to be planted?**

Bewaerschole
Weststraat 18
4328 AB Burgh-Haamstede
The Netherlands

send response to Bewaerschole
Think Like a Forest
www.thinklikeaforest.net

Headline of Dutch newspaper reads, "The black cherry trees are no longer the enemy," referring to overzealous efforts to eradicate the trees after they were widely planted but then overstepped their bounds, competing with native species. Instead of futile efforts to eliminate black cherry, the article recommends creating a resilient forest. In a warming world, human beings, plants, and animals will need to be accommodated as they move from areas that have become uninhabitable. **How can we respect our ancestors, local cultures, and local ecosystems while at the same time welcoming new residents?**

Bewaerschole
Weststraat 18
4328 AB Burgh-Haamstede
The Netherlands

send response to Bewaerschole
Think Like a Forest
www.thinklikeaforest.net

Figure 79: Ruth Wallen 'Learning to think like a forest' (2023) Postcards (courtesy of the artist)

were imported into the Netherlands from the Americas and became defined as 'invasive'. In the other direction Norway spruce and Scots pine (also known as Baltic pine and red pine in Europe) have been introduced into the USA and are considered invasive in places. Other examples such as the Tree of Heaven have been introduced to both locations from elsewhere.

The final example is a series of works dealing with ecological grief in the face of devastating anthropogenic forest fires. One focus is the iconic sequoia, the sequoias in several groves were killed in the past two years by 'unheard of firestorms that burnt up into their crowns' (Wallen 2023). The audience is invited to 'Listen to these seedlings'. Sequoia seeds require fire to germinate, so despite the firestorms, there is new growth. The text concerning the McIntyre Grove specifically continues, 'They are asking for a commitment to think like a sequoia, to think in tree time, to care for them for the next thousand years' (Wallen 2023) (fig. 78).

The challenge of learning to think like a forest is articulated through composite images, intended to evoke the complexity of forests rather than represent them in ways that photography conventionally does. This is a continuation of the approach developed in *Sea as Sculptress* where hundreds of images were assembled into performative lectures. Wallen describes the images as 'montages comprised of a series of glances. A meagre attempt to convey the dynamic feeling of walking in the forest – but a way for me to express respect and love for what I experienced in this living and dying place' (Wallen 2019). The montages are combined with texts, all of which contain technical information interspersed with questions such as:

> What was your favorite tree in childhood and why? Do you know where this tree comes from? How is the tree faring now?
> What is it that needs to be uprooted if we are to provide care for the natural world?
> What is it that needs to be planted?
> How can we respect our ancestors, local cultures, and local ecosystems while at the same time welcoming new residents?
> Imagine stepping into one of the tree's many cavities hollowed by ancient fire.
> Imagine stepping through this portal to imagine new ways of being and doing.
> [Black Locust] spread raises the question as to how we distinguish between the on-going processes of ecological change and disruptive transformations.
> What do the many histories of the black cherry teach us about caring for the forest?
> What is the effect of calling trees or any non-human invaders? (Wallen 2023)

In other writing the form used is of letters addressed to specific trees with whom Wallen has sat. In each case the relationship is personal, filled with grief and also hope, durational both in human terms and in recognising that tree lives are lived with a different experience of time and sensation. The artworks frequently involve multiple visits.

Wallen might invite us to learn to think like a forest, but like Bon, her concern is with addressing grief and accepting change, rather than large-scale propositions, and like Ballengée she positions herself in the place where climate change is most evident. Her 'world in common', like the others, is one that faces the ways in which our 'bifurcation of nature' has distanced ourselves from all our animate and inanimate relatives.

A Wider Reimagining of the Role of the Arts

The Harrisons' decision to focus their work on the web of life and the journey that took them on is particular and has the potential to form a powerful pedagogy. The Harrisons also were in dialogue with a wide range of artists, some of whom we have discussed. However, it is worth briefly touching on a few other artists of a similar generation who also contribute to reimagining the role and contribution of the arts in the global environmental crisis.

Chapter 5 discusses Mierle Laderman Ukeles' work in terms of drawing out what a 'systems aesthetic' might be. The focus was on how Ukeles uses the sanitation system itself, its materials and equipment, to invite us as inhabitants and audiences to 'see' it. She 'flips a metaphor', from sanitation as being 'taking things away', to sanitation workers 'keeping the city alive'. Ukeles, by choosing to locate herself within one system over a very significant duration, virtually created the idea of the 'embedded artist', but more significantly translated working with waste or discarded materials from a personal choice as an artist into a form of engagement with a social ecological system.

Both Allan Kaprow, a colleague of the Harrisons at University of California, San Diego, and John Cage, who the Harrisons exhibited with more than once, have been cited in the discussion of improvisation (Chapter 4) and both through their interest in the 'blurring' of art and life and in 'chance operations' are significant in rethinking the arts in the global environmental crisis. Another artist who has contributed to this reshaping is Robert Smithson (1938–1973). Although largely known for *Spiral Jetty* (1970) and other earthworks that are not *prima facie* ecological, Smithson's works and writings that engage with entropy continue to influence the reimagining of the role of art. Entropy has been a thread running through the discussion in this book. It starts with the Harrisons identifying 'high entropy' as a characteristic of human systems driving the global environmental crisis, and the issue recurs as a key aspect of systems thinking in Chapter 5 (as well as the form of change manifest in Hans Haacke's work *Condensation Cube* discussed in that chapter). Smithson created multiple works where entropy was the driving idea, including *Partially Buried Woodshed* (1970) at Kent State University. Invited to create a work for a festival at the university, Smithson was unable to make the proposed work *Mud Flow* because of the temperatures. He chose to have earth heaped on top of a woodshed that was part of a farm the university had recently acquired. As Robert Hobbs describes (including quoting from Smithson's own 1973 interview 'Entropy Made Visible') earth was heaped on the shed until the 'central beam cracked. The breaking of the beam was crucial to the piece: to Smithson it symbolised entropy, like the falling of Humpty Dumpty, "a closed system which eventually deteriorates and starts to break apart and there's no way that you can really piece it back together again"' (Hobbs 1981, 190). *Partially Buried Woodshed* is considered one of five extant earthworks by Smithson. Where many of Smithson's works evidence concern with entropy in relation to time and the instantaneousness of contemporary art (cf. Smithson 1966), the Harrisons' primary concern has been the characteristic of living systems to self-organise and self-replicate.

Agnes Denes is perhaps best known for *Wheatfield: A Confrontation* (1982) and *Tree Mountain – A Living Time Capsule – 11,000 Trees, 11,000 People, 400 Years* (1982–96), sponsored by the Government of Finland and the United Nations Environment Programme, but her first ecological work *Rice/Tree/Burial with Time Capsule* was made first in 1969. It was then re-enacted at ArtPark over 1977 to 1979 (at the same time as the Harrisons were developing *Spoils Pile Reclamation*). Denes says of the work:

I planted rice to represent life (initiation and growth), chained trees to indicate interference with life and natural processes (evolutionary mutation, variation, decay, death), and buried my Haiku poetry to symbolize the idea or concept (the abstract, the absolute, human intellectual powers, and creation itself). These three acts constituted the first transitional triangulation* (thesis, antithesis, synthesis) and formed the Event. (Denes 2008, 87)

Where there are synergies between the process philosophy of Alfred North Whitehead and the approach of the Harrisons, as discussed in the Introduction, Denes is explicitly concerned with Whiteheadean concepts including 'Event' and 'process' (Filippone 2017, 135). Denes says, 'My Art exists in a dynamic, evolutionary world where objects are processes and forms are dynamic patterns, where measures and concepts are relative and reality itself is forever changing' (Denes quoted in Filippone 2017, 136).

Filippone (2017) highlights the link between Whitehead's process philosophy and the idea of 'open systems' advocated by von Bertalanffy. She positions Denes' work, among a number of women artists, as key to understanding a feminist engagement with science and technology organised around a different understanding of 'utopia' – one that 'offers a political critique of patriarchal culture, subverts categories, and deconstructs power roles' (Filippone 2017, 4). In Denes' case, Filippone argues that the organising idea is 'cosmological evolution', which goes beyond Whiteheadean evolution, incorporating growth and increased complexity, and imagines humanity as involved in progressive change towards an improved future. Filippone discusses this in relation to a series of Denes' drawings of pyramids, some recognisably Egyptian, and some futuristic, organic, and fluid (Filippone 2017, 136–41). Where the feminist utopian imaginary in Denes' works offers an ecologically focused future for humanity, it is very different from the Harrisons' focus on the storytelling of ways to put the well-being of ecosystems first in specific places.

There are many artists who have contributed to the reimagining the arts and the examples cited have been selected with attention to diversity. The Harrisons' commitment is made at a time when second wave feminism is a significant social movement and is having a profound affect on the arts. This influence can be traced in Helen's participation from the Women's Strike for Peace 1961–62, her participation in exhibitions at Woman House, through to Raven's framing of the Harrisons' practice, including through inter-relatedness: 'Thus we are required to find our relatedness to people like and unlike ourselves' (Raven 1983, 50) and, as discussed in Chapter 4, in works that empower people by becoming participants (Raven 1983, 33). However, the arts and the environment and conservation movements are still characterised by a lack of cultural diversity. Pakistan-born, British-based artist Rasheed Araeen has not only contributed as an artist, he has also created *Third Text*, an academic journal and very significant platform for critical writing on art in a global context. His sculptural practice addresses the co-construction of systems using symmetry and repeating elements, starting from an intuitive response to burning bicycle tyres on the side of the road, through experiments with circular objects in London canals in the late 1960s, and developing into a recurrent concern with non-compositional and non-hierarchical cubic structures. However, it is perhaps Araeen's cosmoruralism that seeks to 'reflect on the workings of Eurocentrism and the still unrealized promises of decolonisation' where the different approach to ecological concerns is most obviously manifest. Araeen's approach focuses on the cultural intersections and seeks to provide 'a critique of modernity and its urban-industrial values and logics' (Ray 2017, 398–399), drawing on examples from locations outside of Eurocentric hegemony. These are not binary, so they create dialogues with the arts including major institutions such as the Documenta quinquennial, focusing on food and mutuality in the work *Shamiyaana* in Athens in 2017.

This chapter has explored three different strands. First, the artists whose work is in some way immanent in the Harrisons, such as Albers' focus on dynamics of boundaries and borders. Second, artists who have furthered through experimentation the potential of the Harrisons' work for the development of their own distinctive languages. Third, artists of the Harrisons' generation who have tackled similar concerns but through quite distinctive approaches. These different artists reveal the fundamental importance of learning, experimentation, and pedagogy in the relationship of art to the environment. Henry Giroux, a key proponent of critical pedagogy, focuses on the need to develop 'public imagination' and an imaginative grasp of the future. He says:

> There is no radical politics without a pedagogy capable of awakening consciousness, challenging our common sense, and creating modes of analysis in which people discover a moment of recognition that enables them to rethink the conditions that shape their lives. (Giroux 2022)

In Chapter 2 we highlighted the Harrisons' 1965 essay 'Dropouts and a "Design for Living"' as a precursor to their *Survival Pieces* and approach to the 'ecological argument'. That essay introduced a set of questions that, while directed at young people not in education, employment, or training, has resonance with Giroux's argument. The Harrisons' formulation of questions starts from asking those involved to admit their fears, but then opens out to what it means to be in the world and what a good environment is, including the aesthetic dimension. This approach seeks to open up a moment of recognition, one that is possibly most often erased, to feel a luxury or to feel 'why bother' 'nobody cares'. By caring for oneself, a dignity and power emerges that can bring a different quality to every interaction thereafter.

Conclusions

Artists Helen Mayer Harrison and Newton Harrison have made apparent that:

> Rembrandt's life work revealed spirituality through an absence of light
> Michelangelo demonstrated how little stone he needed to remove to show a human figure reaching for freedom
> Albers held tension between two or more fields of colour
> Giotto's perspective moved worshippers in the Arena Chapel into the retelling of the New Testament

If we asked the same question that the Harrisons asked of these artists, the question of how they too might have changed what is possible through art, what might the answer be? We don't know what this is, but our hunch is that they have indeed contributed to changing art's ontology in a distinctive and profound manner. Having spent the past five years and more developing this book, we know that the answer will take more time and many more imaginations to identify what this contribution is with the simplicity and accuracy with which the Harrisons discussed those artists who had played a significant role in their development.

Is it the prophetic nature of their work? Newton had wanted this to be the focus of our writing. He knew that their work had anticipated many phenomena that have since occurred. As noted in Chapter 6, Reeves-Evison describes as prophetic their use of scenario building in *San Diego as the Center of a World* (1974) five years before the first climate scenarios became public.

Is it their pioneering role in committing a life's work to bringing art to bear on the environmental crisis? When we embarked on this book, the relationship of art to ecology was a relatively minor area of concern in the art world. It has undergone exponential growth to the point that it would be challenging to find an artist of any kind who in some way or another is not drawn into the issues. It is for this reason that we avoid identifying a separate group or ideology of 'eco-art'.

If the Harrisons' contribution as pioneers is legitimate, is their work done? Art does not tend to become displaced by new knowledge and experience as happens in the sciences. While many of the proposals they made would now be considered common place, such as making space for flooding, will the Harrisons live on in the way Rembrandt, Michelangelo, Giotto, and Albers have lived on, formative of our cultural imaginary?

Does the extraordinary nature of the Harrisons' work lie in their unique process of question raising and discovery, driven by their imagination, intuition, and immense skill as artists? Their forms of enquiry manifest a coming together of poetry and the visual, the empirical with place-based knowledge and experience, the intuitive alongside rigorous research. Is it the real-world element of their work that matters? The Harrisons' question raising is radical, both in the sense of going to the limits of known ways of imagining issues as well as in the sense of getting to the root of those issues, daring to ask what many of us would leave untouched. Their commitment over 50 years to care for the environment, and having the courage to turn down significant career opportunities as artists that contradict this, are all examples. They drew in whoever could support their enquiry interleaving perspectives from science, farming, horticulture, government, and from other artists and inhabitants. This is a markedly different form of enquiry from for instance Albers' colour fields.

Do the Harrisons change what is possible in art in the way they work with the sciences? The environmental sciences had not been co-opted by the modalities of technoscience (the economisation of knowledge and the priority on commercial innovation). Increasingly the approaches that the Harrisons incorporated in works are a key part of nature-based solutions, for example, wetland restoration to manage storm surge and pollution. Perhaps the important aspect is not the fact of their doing so, but the way that they worked with science and the scope of their questioning. They put on the table difficult choices 'necessitating a process of hesitation, concentration and attentive scrutiny – and this despite the complaints of entrepreneurs, for whom time is money and who demand that everything that is not prohibited be allowed' (Stengers 2018, 3–4).

Could the Harrisons' key contribution lie in how they share their learning in such a way that those who follow grasp their experience with clarity? Unlike the world of art and its proprietorial character, the Harrisons are not afraid if other people making use of their work. This is particularly evident in the *Survival Pieces* 1970–74 that include DIY instructions for making each piece of work as a form of backyard farming (fig. 10). They highlighted and enjoyed when an assistant took the principles of the Sava River work and applied these to another river, the Drava, which is also a tributary to the Danube (*Atempause für den Save-Fluss*, 1989). The outcome of this clarity and transparency is the possibility of conversational drift that encourages participants in the conversation to play and work with the ideas in their own terms and experience.

Do the Harrisons offer new insights into nature? They construct a relationship between improvisation and systems such that improvisation is not a free for all and systems are not deterministic. Nature and culture fold over each other in ways that enable new forms to emerge, each co-creating the other.

Is it in their insistence on a new form of politics for the climate emergency, one of building a world in common from the ground of everyday life upwards, creating openings for participation and not leaving politics to experts? Others, including Immanuel Kant and Hannah Arendt, have made the same observation about the importance of a form of politics based on acting in concert and in dialogue, but this is only part of the story. It does not necessarily address processes that maintain the gains that counter the inequalities and sacrifices brought on by the changing climate. The construction of governance matters.

What about their originality of approach as artists? The Harrisons have never sought the kind of novelty that the art world seeks. Their novelty is not superficial but a form of poetics that brings together core concerns in the arts, such as metaphor, boundary, narrative, colour, scale, the lyrical and sensory in experience, to a different set of circumstances, turning these to face content that the art world had tended to marginalise.

Bruno Latour and Peter Weibel appeal to scientists in the crisis to shift their understanding of art as a practice of popularisation and ornamentation (Latour 2020, 18). It is striking that what the Harrisons sought in other artists is far from being frivolous. They point to the qualities of intensification and augmentation that Alfred North Whitehead seeks as a scientist in an occasion of experience, a moment from which life itself emerges, a moment of origination. Do the Harrisons offer this intensification and augmentation in their own work? If we can locate our whole body within the Delft tile map of the Green Heart of Holland (fig. 49) or the map of the Sierra Nevada Mountain range (fig. 54), the artwork enables us to experience what is otherwise unseen. By seeing the Pacific coastline as both serpentine and a lattice, and by entering into the landscape denuded of trees where trees should be, we can imagine the rhythms of industrial logging practices as all-consuming greed and deeply threatening to emergent life. To what extent do they enable us to imagine ourselves in 'the odd kind of dialogue that is the business of the universe'?

In what ways do the Harrisons address Ghosh's criticism of the modern novel or Williams' criticism of 19th- and 20th-century theatre as incapable of addressing the environmental crisis because both produce a world that never changes? At one level the Harrisons are born into a world in which change is palpable through the effects of industrialisation and of two major wars that in some senses have escalated production. The environment and its issues such as inequality would obviously be a matter of concern and a subject for art. They were not alone in acknowledging that this would necessitate a rethinking, a rewriting of art's place in the world and the form that practices might take, an issue shared with the artists we have mentioned among many. This rethinking was already occurring in the sciences with Whitehead, then Stengers, Latour, and others. What is not obvious is how the Harrisons went about evolving a form interconnecting dimensions of the cultural and the natural that hitherto had become increasingly divorced. They achieved this through interconnecting place-based thinking with global issues, science with art, and with other practices such as urban and rural planning, governance, and ethics.

In writing we have attempted to follow the contours and shifts in thinking that are occurring across the arts, sciences, and philosophy, in particular drawing on Whitehead to help us to challenge our own assumptions. He has indeed helped us to experience the complex, multidimensional character of the Harrisons' work, to see how it may be relevant to current challenges, sometimes showing us what an art practice that inhabits the imaginary of emergence looks and feels like, and why it is important as an ecopolitical project. *The Lagoon Cycle* shifts the imaginary from solving a problem of food production to participating in a dialogue with the universe, while coming to terms with the processes of climate change that we have set in motion.

Notes

Introduction: Seeking a Different Place for the Arts in Survival

1. Elements of the Introduction, discussion of the *Survival Pieces*, and discussion of *The Lagoon Cycle* have previously been published in a special edition (23) of *Field: A Journal of Socially Engaged Art Criticism* edited by Grant Kester.

2. A timeline of the phases of the Harrisons' practice, and the projects referenced within the text is included on pages 223–227.

3. Jane Jacobs' articulation of entropy: 'Contrast that (the loss or refraction of energy within a desert) with the energy flow through a well-developed forest ecosystem. In the forest, energy flow is anything but swift and simple, because of the diverse and roundabout ways that the system's web of teeming, interdependent organisms uses energy. Once sunlight is captured in the conduit, it is not only converted, but repeatedly reconverted, combined and recombined, cycled and recycled, as energy/matter is passed around from organism to organism. Energy flow through an intricate conduit is dilatory and digressive' (Jane Jacobs quoted in Douglas and Fremantle 2005, 4).

4. The Harrisons use plain text, italics and upper and lower case as well as punctuation within their poetic texts for aesthetic purposes.

5. We use aesthetics to describe the form of understanding and the term 'poetics' to describe specific artists' approaches to creating work.

6. Early 1970s exhibitions including 'Earth, Air, Fire, Water: Elements of Art' (Museum of Fine Arts, Boston 1971); 'Enviro-Visions' (Everson Museum, Syracuse, NY, 1972); 'A Response to the Environment' (University Gallery, Rutgers University, New Jersey, 1975); and then from the early 1990s 'Fragile Ecologies: Contemporary Artists' Interpretations and Solutions' curated by Barbara Matilsky (Queens Museum, NYC, 1992); 'Natural Reality: Artistic Positions between Nature and Culture' curated by Heike Strelow (Ludwig Forum, Aachen, 1999); 'Ecovention: Current Art to Transform Ecologies' (Cincinnati Contemporary Arts Center, 2002) and 'Ecovention Europe, Art to Transform Ecologies, 1957–2017' (Museum de Domijnen, the Netherlands, 2017) both curated by Sue Spaid; 'Ground Works: Environmental Collaboration in Contemporary Art' curated by Grant Kester (Regina Gouger Millar Gallery, Carnegie Mellon University, 2005); 'Weather Report: Art and Climate Change' curated by Lucy Lippard (Boulder Museum of Contemporary Art, 2007); 'Radical Nature: Art and Architecture for a Changing Planet 1969–2009' curated by Francesco Manacora (Barbican Arts Centre, London, 2009).

7. In 1976 they exhibited *The Law of the Sea Conference: Where the Appetite is Discovered to be Endless* at the Venice Biennale and, in 1988, they exhibited *Kassel Works* in Documenta 8.

8. Harrison solo shows at Ronald Feldman Gallery: *The Fourth Lagoon, San Diego as the Center of a World* and other works (1974); *Fifth Lagoon* and other works (1975); *Gabrielino Meditations, The Law of the Sea Conference, Great Lakes Meditations*, sketches from *The Lagoon Cycle* (1979); *Talking Water* (1980); *Barrier Islands Drama* (1982); *A Tale of 3 Cities* (1985); *Changing the Conversation* (1991); *The Serpentine Lattice* (1993); *Peninsula Europe* (2003); *Global Warming: Greenhouse Britain* (2009); *Sierra Nevada: An Adaptation* (2011); *Global Mapping* (2014). The Harrison Estate is now represented by Various Small Fires in Los Angeles, having the first exhibition with the gallery in 2017.

9. Douglas and Fremantle, 'Inconsistency and Contradiction: Lessons in Improvisation in the Work of Helen Mayer Harrison and Newton Harrison' (2016a); 'What Poetry Does Best: The Harrisons' Poetics of Being and Acting in the World' (2016b); Fremantle, 'Greenhouse Britain: Losing Ground, Gaining Wisdom (2006-09): Case Study' (2018); Fremantle, Douglas, and Pritchard, 'In the Time of Art with Policy: The Practice of Helen Mayer Harrison and Newton Harrison alongside Global Environmental Policy since the 1970s' (2020a) and 'A Timeline' (2020b); Douglas, 'Giving Absurdity Form: The Place of Contemporary Art in the Environmental Crisis' (2021); Douglas and Fremantle, 'Figure Ground Reversal: The Ecological Epistemology of Helen Mayer Harrison and Newton Harrison' (2022a); Douglas and Fremantle, 'In Conversation: A Poetics of Empathy Helen Mayer Harrison and Newton Harrison' (2022b); Douglas and Fremantle, 'Thinking with the Harrisons: What Does Now Demand?' (2023).

10. Helen Mayer Harrison died during the development of the work in March 2018.

11. The work resulted from the artist David Haley asking the Harrisons what they considered the most pressing issue to address in the UK. In due course in 2005 he became the Associate Artist on the project

12. All images are the art works of Helen Mayer Harrison and Newton Harrison unless otherwise specified.

13. 'Side light' is a term Auslag Nyrnes takes from Michel Foucault when discussing artistic research (Nyrnes 2006). For Nyrnes the 'side light' is a concern with rhetoric as a mode of understanding, distinct from the 'top light' of scientific knowledge. We are not drawing on Whitehead and Stengers as explanatory, but rather as illuminating.

14. That said like the Harrisons, Latham had a long-term relationship with a commercial gallery, in his case the Lisson Gallery in London.

'Thinking With' Whitehead, Stengers and the Harrisons

1. In the Chronology in the catalogue of *The Lagoon Cycle Survival Piece #VII* is 'Full Farm Condensed' and *The Crab Farm* is envisaged as the eight *Survival Piece*.

2. The other piece, also considered highly successful, was the result of the actual art and technology collaboration that Newton Harrison had participated in with the Jet Propulsion Labs. This was a group of plasma-based works involving glow discharge tubes. This strand of Newton Harrison's sculptural practice stopped after this point.

3. We have written about the Harrisons and 'contradiction' previously (2016a) but here we explore the issue in relation to early work revealing new aspects.

4. Newton Harrison interview by Douglas and Fremantle, 12 December 2019. They had one exhibition with Sonnabend in 1974 but also showed parts of *The Lagoon Cycle* with the Ronald Feldman Gallery in the same year (H. M. Harrison and Harrison 1985b, 101).

5. Museum of Contemporary Craft, New York, January–March 1971 and catalogue (Smith 1971).

6. Dropout came to have a different connotation as a result of Timothy Leary's call, first made in 1967, to 'Turn on, tune in, drop out. I mean drop out of high school, drop out of college, drop out of graduate school.' The term 'dropout' in the Harrisons' essay refers to young people who would now be described in terms of 'not in education, employment or training'.

7. We distinguish between Helen as an educationalist and Newton as a teacher because Helen had undertaken educational research as well as teaching.

8. It is important to acknowledge that while education was understood to be an unqualified good at the time, the formal education system has been captured by the neoliberal state and financialised so that it is now a 'debt trap' (Graeber 2014).

9. In 1974 the Harrisons developed the work *San Diego as the Center of a World*, which considered the implications of two possible futures, one of global warming and the other of global cooling, drawing on literature of the time. This is the first work to use the particular form of cartography, the Azimuthal Equidistant projection, which is a repeating figure in their works, often called by them 'big circle maps' (e.g. Fig. 2, 52). They return to world-scale maps in 1976 in a work entitled *The Law of the Sea* for the Venice Biennale and in 1980 with Seventh Lagoon. In 2013 the Harrisons are the Inaugural Recipient of the Award for Imaginative Cartography from the North American Cartographic Information Society.

The Lagoon Cycle

1. It was first exhibited as a complete work at the Herbert F. Johnson Museum at Cornell University, Ithaca, NY, and then at the Los Angeles County Museum of Art. It is part of the collection of the Centre Pompidou-Metz, Paris. A limited edition oversized book, *Book of the Lagoons*, was also created published by Laurence McGilvery (Cassidy Rogers 2016, 268). In quoting from *The Lagoon Cycle* we have followed the formatting used in the catalogue (H. M. Harrison and Harrison 1985b). The voice of the Witness is in italics and that of the Lagoon Maker is in plain text and inset further. There is no punctuation in the text, including no question marks, though there are many questions. Pauses are indicated with white space in the text. Referencing of all quotes of poetry from *The Lagoon Cycle* will take the form of the specific Lagoon and page number in the 1985 catalogue.

2. There are places where these two sources vary in the sequence, and in a few cases in the actual texts and images – for instance, in the exhibition the image of the water buffalo and the image of the man with the tractor are separate and in *Book of the Lagoons* they are composed together in a single image (Fig 34). Earlier versions of the various 'Lagoons' exhibited during the 1970s vary much more.

3. The work *Work Place*, included in the exhibition *At Home* curated by Arlene Raven in 1983, opens up other aspects of the collaboration, which was their daily practice of beginning each day with a conversation about their work, a conversation that from time to time others could join (Raven 1983; Douglas and Fremantle 2022b).

4. The 'Second Lagoon' and 'Third Lagoon' start out as *Crab Farm: Survival Piece #VII* (H. M. Harrison and Harrison 2016, 46–49) and although completed by 1974, were later exhibited as part of the 'Dialogue/Discourse/Research' exhibition at Santa Barbara Museum of Art (Spurlock 1979) and of a publication, *Book of the Crab* included in the catalogue and also printed separately, which ends 'thus ends the Book of the Crab and starts the Books of the Seven Lagoons'.

5. In the original text there is no punctuation, but whenever Helen Mayer Harrison read this text aloud she often made it end as a question. In a 2006 publication they used a question mark at the end.

6. This is documented in *The Book of the Crab*, the publication associated with the exhibition 'Dialogue, Discourse, Research' at the Santa Barbara Museum of Art in 1979. The trigger for the abandonment of this installation was a piece in the *Los Angeles Times* in December 1974 in which the entrepreneur, an actor by the name of Ted Hartley, represents the work with crabs as his own discovery supported by 'South Asian experts' (H. M. Harrison and Harrison 2016, 89).

7. Marcuse taught at the University of California San Diego from 1965 to 1970 and exchanges between the Harrisons and Marcuse are reported in *The Time of the Force Majeure* (H. M. Harrison and Harrison 2016, 48).

8. See Timeline (223–227) for details.

9. For instance, in the text of the Fifth Lagoon as reproduced in the 'Dialogue, Discourse, Research' catalogue a much more bodily metaphor is used: the Salton Sea is a womb and a bladder, the channels that would be needed are a 'urethra', the Delta as a vagina. This metaphor is abandoned.

On Improvisation

1. This chapter draws on writing by Anne Douglas, much of it concerned with connecting improvisation in music with improvisation in the visual arts. This includes 'Experiential Knowledge and Improvisation: Variations on Movement, Motion, Emotion' (Douglas and Coessens 2012); 'Improvisation and Embodied Knowledge: Three Artistic Projects between Life, Art and Research' (Douglas and Coessens 2013); 'Altering a Fixed Identity: Thinking through Improvisation' (Douglas 2013b); 'Understanding Experimentation as Improvisation in Arts Research' (Douglas and Gulari 2015); 'Improvisation as Experimentation in Everyday Life and Beyond' (Douglas and Coessens 2017); 'Venturing out on the Thread of a Tune: The Artist as Improvisor in Public Life' (Douglas 2018b).

2. In this bilingual text (English/German) the Harrisons use the German spelling "Save".

On the Poetics and Aesthetics of Systems

1. The Harrisons also talk about biological communities, particularly in relation to their 'Future Garden' works. The terminology of '(eco)system' draws attention to flows of energy and information where 'biological community' draws attention to dependencies, both of which are important in different contexts and stages to the Harrisons. For a history and discussion of these two competing conceptualisations see Shoshitaishvili (2023).
2. We have discussed the Harrisons' ecological epistemology in relation to Bateson in 'Figure Ground Reversal: The Ecological Epistemology of Helen Mayer Harrison and Newton Harrison' (Douglas and Fremantle 2022a).
3. There is another trajectory of systems thinking developed in the Soviet Union, including figures such as Bogdanov (1873–1928), and somewhat influential on British thinking (Jackson 2023). This alternative vector relates to industry and technology differently and has a more social orientation. It has recently been revisited by Dr James Fox (2023).
4. Shoshitaishvili draws attention to the work of Niklas Luhmann who develops a theory of autopoiesis in sociology "This approach allowed Luhmann to emphasize shared organizational principles in both domains, the living organism and human society, without conflating them" (Shoshitaishvili 2023, 441).
5. Theo Reeves-Evison notes that the Harrisons' work *San Diego as the Center of a World* (1974) is 'remarkable' because it uses 'scenario thinking several years before the first climate scenarios are published (Reeves-Evison 2021, 738) (see also fn.9 Chapter 2 'Thinking with' Whitehead, Stengers and the Harrisons).
6. 'If [...] Then [...]' statements can be inductive, based on observation; deductive, based on theory or premises; or abductive, inferring conclusions from observations. All of these modes occur in the work.
7. M1797, Helen and Newton Harrison Papers, box 8, folder 9.
8. M1797, Helen and Newton Harrison Papers, box 8, folder 9.
9. According to *The Time of the Force Majeure* it was new sewers but according to Josh Harrison who was the project manager for *Spoils Pile Reclamation* it was undergrounding power cables.
10. For a further discussion of the Harrisons' use of numbers in various works see *Figure Ground Reversal* (Douglas and Fremantle 2022a).
11. It is worth noting that this crisis appears to coincide with a significant change in direction for Artpark, including a complete revamp of the artist-in-residence programme (Firmin 2010, 53).
12. Brain reframes this in terms of needing both systems and assemblages in an interview (Brain 2020).
13. Dr James Fox pointed out the isomorphism–metaphor connection on the Acid Horizon podcast (A. Jones 2023)
14. The latter two examples are regularly the focus of 'digital twin' projects that construct digital models of operational systems.

On the Political

1. And as noted above with Ronald Feldman in New York and latterly Various Small Fires in Los Angeles.
2. The title references another Enlightenment thinker Adam Smith (1723–1790), whose book, *The Wealth of Nations*, first published in 1776, might also be understood to contribute to the bifurcation of nature in its conception of the division of labour, productivity, and free markets.
3. Villa (1992) appears to conflate the introduction of aesthetics into politics (aestheticism) with the aestheticization of the political. The aestheticization of politics, as defined by Arendt's colleague and friend, Walter Benjamin, is an ingredient in fascism, in which the arts are used to mythologise a totalitarian regime to affirm an existing political position. In contrast Arendt's aesthetic approach to action and the political seeks to open experience to difference.
4. As noted elsewhere there is no punctuation in *The Lagoon Cycle*. However, a publication of the final stanzas of the Seventh Lagoon includes a question mark at the end (H. M. Harrison and Harrison 2006 n.p.)
5. This is one of the examples of the Harrisons' use of the uppercase for poetic purposes.

Artists 'Thinking with' One Another

1. Newton related that Helen had helped him to 'learn' Josef Albers' colour theory so that he could secure the position. Its principles, particularly in relation to border and boundaries, became fundamental to their own practice.

2. As reported by Tim Collins et al. (Collins et al. 2023).

3. Jackie Brookner, Tim Collins, Reiko Goto, Helen Mayer Harrison, Newton Harrison, and Ruth Wallen.

4. There are two documents in the folder that contain the same proposal in two slightly different versions. They are undated. However, the latest work that they cite in detail including elements of *Santa Fe Watershed: Lessons from the Genius of Place at the Santa Fe Art Institute* 11 December, 2004-22 January, 2005 indicate that the texts were both drafted after that.

5. The Harrisons also worked with Beth Stephens, performance artist and professor at University of California Santa Cruz, on a proposal for an MFA/PhD programme (Sprinkle and Stephens 2021, 196). The next section will include a discussion of the collaborative ecosexual practice of Stephens and Annie Sprinkle. The PhD programme proposal, entitled *Art Practice: A Whole Systems Approach with a Global Reach,* was 'designed to examine complex interactions with art and the environment by studying: the history of repression; the history of radical art; an overview of the commons; ideas, practices and histories relating to the effects of economics, scientific thought, and methodology on the overall well-being of the biosphere; suggestions for an ecologically based whole systems approach to both teaching and human-induced eco-systemic stress' (H. M. Harrison and Harrison 2010).

6. David Haley was project manager for the Harrisons' work in the North of England, *Casting a Green Net: Can it be we are Seeing a Dragon?* (1996–98) and was Associate Artist with Harrisons' *Greenhouse Britain: Losing Ground, Gaining Wisdom* (2006–09).

7. Lillian Ball, *Mangrove Rescue in Bimini: Connecting Art, Restoration and Community*, Listening to the Web of Life Workshop, 17–18 March 2022 (San Diego, California, 2022), https://youtu.be/9AywEGYfuV0?t=4672 accessed 31.5.2024.

8. Betsy Damon, *Igniting Creativity, Complexity in Action*, Listening to the Web of Life Workshop, 17–18 March 2022 (San Diego, California, 2022), https://youtu.be/9AywEGYfuV0?t=2543 accessed 31.5.2024

9. David Haley, *MetaPoiesis: Art That Yields to Life*, Listening to the Web of Life Workshop, 17–18 March 2022 (San Diego, California, 2022), https://youtu.be/C52EN5SNjn8?t=4344 accessed 31.5.2024

10. Ballengée has published on this work and his MALAMP project (Cf. Ballengée 2018; Chakrabarty et al. 2016; Sessions and Ballengée 2010).

11. For example, Sessions and Ballengée (2009).

12. A 'Common Garden' experiment involves moving species from their native environments to a common environment to enable comparison.

13. In another aspect of ongoing dialogue, the Metabolic Studio and the Harrison Studio collaborated on revisiting the area of the Great Lakes, subject of the Harrisons' work *Meditations on the Great Lakes* discussed elsewhere. Where the 1977 work considered the absurdity of the fragmentation of this landscape, in 2015 the questions were focused by the question of refuge. Judging that the East and West Coasts of the continental United States would become increasingly uninhabitable because of extreme weather and sea level rise, attention turned to the land between the Rocky Mountains and the Great Lakes as a refuge for the those who must withdraw. The research was a deep look at the ecological landscape through the lens of the 'force majeure'. The report draws attention to all those aspects of infrastructure that bear on the ecological health of the region.

14. Tim Collins' presentation lists the works of the Harrisons they saw in person: *Ideas and Provocations in Environmental Artsworking*, Listening to the Web of Life Workshop, 17–18 March 2022 (San Diego, California, 2022), https://youtu.be/J9MGSARetCE?t=2242 accessed 31.5.2024.

15. As noted elsewhere the Harrisons in practice conceived of themselves as a 'Mom and Pop act' and in performances frequently had disagreements. However, all the work until Helen's death was from 1974 attributed to the two of them equally and indivisibly.

16. Collins and Goto developed two major initiatives, 'Nine Mile Run' and '3 Rivers 2nd Nature', in Pittsburgh from 1996 to 2005, which opened up discourse around the post-industrial landscape and the Allegheny, Monongahela, and Ohio rivers. These projects focused on reimagining nature and countering the idea that a post-industrial landscape was a wasteland (Collins 2001, Kester 2005).

17. *The Forest is Moving: Tha a' Choille a' Gluasad*, Perth Museum and Art Gallery (2013), *Sylva Caledonia*, Summerhall Arts Centre in Edinburgh (2015), and *A Caledonian Decoy*, Intermedia Gallery, Centre for Contemporary Art, Glasgow, (2017).

18. Ecosystem Services is a widely adopted framework used by scientists and policy makers to articulate the goods and services provided by ecosystems to humans. The framework is criticised as being anthropocentric.

19. Sprinkle and Stephens add 'E' for ecosexual.

20. This text originally appears associated with the work *Making Earth Again* exhibited in 'Revered Earth' (Mazeaud et al. 1990, 44–45). In the associated publication the text is laid out in poetic format.

Timeline

Periods	Date	Work	Exhibition/Venue/Publication
Survival Pieces	1970	*Making Earth*	
		Making Strawberry Jam	Woman's Building, Los Angeles
	1971	*Part One of an Ecological Nerve Center*	'Fur & Feathers', Museum of Contemporary Crafts, New York City
		Survival Piece #I: Air, Earth, Water, Interface: Annual Hog Pasture Mix	'Earth, Air, Fire, Water: Elements of Art', Museum of Fine Arts, Boston
		Survival Piece #II Notation on the Ecosystem of the Western Saltworks with the inclusion of Brine Shrimp (figs. 8-10)	'Art and Technology', Los Angeles County Museum of Art
		Survival Piece #III Portable Fish Farm (figs. 11-14)	'11 Los Angeles Artists', Hayward Gallery, London and touring
		Survival Piece #IV La Jolla Promenade	La Jolla Historical Society
	1972	*Portable Orchard: Survival Piece #V* (figs. 47-48)	California State University, Fullerton
	1972	*Full Farm: Survival Piece #VI*	Contemporary Arts Museum Houston, Texas
	1972		*Full Farm Condensed: Survival Piece #VII*[1] in 'Enviro-Visions', Everson Museum of Art, Syracuse, NY

---

1   *Full Farm Condensed* is recorded as *Survival Piece #VII* in the biography of 'The Lagoon Cycle' catalogue (1985). However, *The Crab Farm* is given that designation in 'In the Time of the Force Majeure' (2016).

Periods	Date	Work	Exhibition/Venue/Publication
The Lagoon Cycle	1974	*Survival Piece #VII: The Crab* Farm,[1] which became the *Second Lagoon*	
	1974	*San Diego as the Center of a World*	Ronald Feldman Gallery, New York City (exhibition also includes first version of *Fourth Lagoon: On Mixing, Mapping and Territory*)
	1975	*Fifth Lagoon: From the Salton Sea to the Pacific, From the Salton Sea to the Gulf*	First version included in 'A Response to the Environment', University Gallery, Rutgers University, New Jersey
	1976		The *Fourth* and *Fifth Lagoon*s are published by the Ronald Feldman Gallery
	1976	*The Law of the Sea Conference: Where the Appetite is Discovered to be Endless* (fig. 56)	Venice Biennale
	1976	*Meditation on the Gabrielino, Whose Name for Themselves is No Longer Remembered, Although We Know That They Farmed With Fire and Fought Wars By Singing*	Long Beach Museum of Art, CA
	1977	*Meditation on the Great Lakes of North America* (fig. 51)	University of Wisconsin–Milwaukee and touring
	1977–78	*Spoils Pile Reclamation* (figs. 45-46)	Artpark, Lewiston, NY
	1977–78	*Meditations on the Sacramento River, the Delta and the Bays of San Francisco*	San Francisco Art Institute, CA. Catalogue includes *The Fourth Lagoon: On Mixing, Mapping, and Territory; The Fifth Lagoon: From the Salton Sea to the Pacific, From the Salton Sea to the Gulf; Study in Metaphor: Scale and Pressure for the Sixth Lagoon; Ring of Fire: Sketch in Metaphor for the Seventh Lagoon; Meditations on the Condition of the River Seine and the Excavation at Les Halles; Meditation on the Gabrielino, Whose Name for Themselves is No Longer Remembered, Although We Know That They Farmed With Fire and Fought Wars By Singing; More on the Endless Appetite* (part of *The Law of the Sea Conference*); *San Diego is the Center of the World and Notions for Others*

Periods	Date	Work	Exhibition/Venue/Publication
	1979	*Fourth* and *Fifth Lagoon* (the proposals for large-scale crab farming and exploring the implications). Text differs significantly from final form.	In 'Dialogue/Discourse/Research: David Antin, Eleanor Antin, Helen Mayer Harrison/Newton Harrison, Fred Lonidier, Barbara Strasen', Santa Barbara Museum of Art. Catalogue includes *Book of the Crab*, which narrates the research into crab farming, recreated in *The Lagoon Cycle* as the *Second* and *Third Lagoon*
	1982	*Barrier Islands Drama: The Mangrove and the Pine*	'Five Artists in the Florida Landscape', The John and Mable Ringling Museum of Art, Sarasota, FL
	1983	*Work Place*	'At Home', Long Beach Museum of Art
	1984		Parts of 'Barrier Islands Drama' in 'Artistic Collaboration in the 20th Century', Hirshhorn Museum and Sculpture Garden
	1985	*Arroyo Seco Release/A Serpentine for Pasadena*	Baxter Art Gallery, California Institute of Technology, CA
	1985	*The Lagoon Cycle* & *Book of the Lagoons* (figs. 8, 15-36)	Herbert F. Johnson Museum of Art, Cornell University, Ithaca, NY and Los Angeles County Museum of Art
Watersheds	1987	*Devil's Gate: A Refugia for Pasadena*	Downtown Gallery, Los Angeles ArtCenter College of Design
	1988	*Kassel Works* (fig. 62)	Documenta 8
	1988	*Trümmerflora on the Topography of Terror*	Martin-Gropius-Bau, Berlin, Germany
	1989	*Atempause für den Save-Fluss (A Breathing Space for the Sava River)* (figs. 37-40)	Moderna Galerija, Ljubljana, Slovenia and touring
	1990	*Das Einzugsgebiet der Mulde (The catchment area of the Mulde (river))*	
	1990	*Making Earth Again*	'Revered Earth' Center for Contemporary Arts, Santa Fe, New Mexico
			Parts of *The Lagoon Cycle* and *Breathing Space for the Sava River* in 'Fragile Ecologies: Contemporary Artists' Interpretations and Solutions' Queens Museum, NYC

Periods	Date	Work	Exhibition/Venue/Publication
	1993	*The Serpentine Lattice* (figs.64-65)	Douglas F. Cooley Memorial Art Gallery of Reed College, Portland, Oregon and the Ronald Feldman Gallery NYC
Becomes part of the *Force Majeure*	1993	*Tibet is the High Ground* (fig. 52)	Ronald Feldman Gallery, NYC
	1994	*Green Heart Vision* (fig. 49)	Jeruzalemkapel Gouda, the Netherlands
	1995	*A Brown Coal Part for South Leipzig*	Sächsische Landesvertretung beim Bund, Bonn, Germany
	1996	*Endangered Meadows of Europe*	Rooftop of Kunst- und Ausstellungshalle der Bundesrepublik Deutschland, Bonn, Germany and then permanent installation, Rheinaue, Bonn
Becomes part of the *Force Majeure*	1996	*The Garden of Hot Winds and Warm Rains* (first 'Future Garden' proposal) (fig. 58)	First exhibited in 2003 at Ronald Feldman Gallery, NY
	1998	*Casting a Green Net: Can it be we are seeing a Dragon?* (fig. 50)	'ArtTranspennine', The Bluecoat Gallery, Liverpool, UK
	1999		*Casting a Green Net* in 'Natural Reality: Artistic Positions Between Nature and Culture', Ludwig Forum, Aachen
Becomes part of the *Force Majeure*	2002	*Peninsula Europe: The High Ground, Bringing Forth a New State of Mind*, including *The Mountain in the Greenhouse*	Ludwig Forum für Internationale Kunst, Aachen, Germany, and touring
			Various works from 1970-1997 'Ecovention: Current Art to Transform Ecologies', Cincinnati Contemporary Arts Center, 2002
	2005	*Santa Fe Watershed: Lessons from the Genius of Place*	Santa Fe Art Institute
	2005		*Fecal Matters* in 'Groundworks', Miller ICA, Carnegie Mellon University, Pittsburgh, PA

Periods	Date	Work	Exhibition/Venue/Publication
Force Majeure	2007	*Greenhouse Britain: Losing Ground, Gaining Wisdom* (figs. 3-6)	Centre for Contemporary Art and the Natural World, Exeter, UK and touring
			The Mountain in the Greenhouse in 'Weather Report: Art and Climate Change', Boulder Museum of Contemporary Art, Colorado, 2007
	2009		*Full Farm: Survival Piece #VI* included in 'Radical Nature Art and Architecture for a Changing Planet 1969–2009', Barbican Art Gallery, London
	2011	*Manifesto for 21st Century*	
	2011	*Sierra Nevada: An Adaptation* (fig. 54)	Ronald Feldman Gallery, NYC and Nevada Museum of Art
	2011	*Sagehen: A Proving Ground* ('Future Garden' work) (figs. 55, 58-61)	Work made for Nevada Museum of Art – Center for Art + Environment (2015)
	2017		Parts of *Green Heart Vision* and *Endangered Meadows of Europe* in 'Ecovention Europe, Art to Transform Ecologies, 1957–2017', Museum de Domijnen, the Netherlands
	2018	*On The Deep Wealth of this Nation, Scotland* (figs. 1-2, 53)	Taipei Biennial, Taiwan and various venues in Scotland
	2022	*Epitaph* (fig. 57)	Serpentine Galleries, London

References

Antin, David. 1970. 'Art + Ecology'. *ArtNews*, November 1970.

Arendt, Hannah. 1970. *On Violence*. New York: Harcourt, Brace & World.

———. 1981. *The Life of the Mind: One/Thinking, Two/Willing*. (One Volume Edition). San Diego: Hartcourt Brace Jovanovich.

———. 1992. *Lectures on Kant's Political Philosophy*. Edited by Ronald Beiner. Chicago: Univ. of Chicago Press.

———. 1998. *The Human Condition*. 2nd ed. Chicago: University of Chicago Press.

———. 2006. *Between Past and Future: Eight Exercises in Political Thought*. Penguin Classics. New York: Penguin Books.

———. 2013. *Hannah Arendt: The Last Interview and Other Conversations*. Brooklyn, NY: Melville House.

———. 2017. *The Origins of Totalitarianism*. London: Penguin Classics.

Auping, Michael. 1982. *Common Ground: Five Artists in the Florida Landscape*. Sarasota, Fla: John and Mable Ringling Museum of Art.

Ballengée, Brandon. 2018. 'Crude Life'. *Issues in Science and Technology*, no. 2: 66–71.

———. 2023. 'Searching for Ghosts of the Gulf'. *Field: A Journal of Socially Engaged Art Criticism* 23. https://field-journal.com/issue-23/6940 (accessed 9.6.2024).

Ballengée, Brandon, Helen Mayer Harrison, and Newton Harrison. 2011. 'Helen and Newton Harrison in Conversation with Brandon Ballengée'. In *Mediated Environments*, edited by Andrea Gleiniger, A. Hilbeck, and Jill Scott, 45–58. Transdiscourse 1. Wien and New York: Springer.

Bateson, Gregory. 1972. *Steps To an Ecology of Mind: Collected Essays in Anthropology, Psychiatry, Evolution, and Epistemology*. 2000th ed. Chicago and London: University of Chicago Press.

———. 1979. *Mind and Nature: A Necessary Unity*. 2002nd ed. New York: Hampton Press.

Benthall, Jonathan. 1971. 'Newton Harrison: Big Fish in a Small Pool'. *Studio International*, December 1971.

Boettger, Suzaan. 2002. *Earthworks: Art and the Landscape of the Sixties*. Berkeley: University of California Press.

Bon, Lauren. 2023. Thinking with Newton Harrison Interview by Anne Douglas and Chris Fremantle. Zoom recording.

Bon, Lauren, and Newton Harrison. 2023. 'Transcription: Lauren Bon Presentation with Newton Harrison'. *Field: A Journal of Socially Engaged Art Criticism* 23. https://field-journal.com/editorial/lauren-bon-presentation-with-newton-harrison (accessed 9.6.2024).

Bourriaud, Nicholas. 2002. *Relational Aesthetics*. Paris: Les Presses Du Reel.

Brain, Tega. 2018. 'The Environment Is Not A System'. *A Peer-Reviewed Journal About* 7 (1): 152–65. https://doi.org/10.7146/aprja.v7i1.116062.

———. 2020. Misbehaving Systems: In Conversation with Tega Brain Interview by Rhian Morris. https://fiber.medium.com/misbehaving-systems-in-conversation-with-tega-brain-5b39c5d03531 (accessed 9.6.2024).

Burnham, Jack. 1968. 'Systems Esthetics'. *ArtForum*, September 1968.

———. 1969. 'Real Time Systems'. *ArtForum*, September 1969.

———. 1971. 'Corporate Art'. In *Dissolve into Comprehension: Writings and Interviews, 1964–2004*, edited by Melissa Ragain, 184–92. Writing Art Series. Cambridge, Massachusetts: The MIT Press.

———. 1973. 'Contemporary Ritual: A Search for Meaning in Post-Historical Terms'. *Arts*, March 1973.

———. 1974. *Great Western Salt Works: Essays on the Meaning of Post-Formalist Art*. New York: George Braziller.

———. 2015. *Dissolve into Comprehension: Writings and Interviews, 1964-2004*. Edited by Melissa Ragain. Writing Art Series. Cambridge, Massachusetts: The MIT Press.

Campion, Kristy. 2023. 'Defining Ecofascism: Historical Foundations and Contemporary Interpretations in the Extreme Right'. *Terrorism and Political Violence* 35 (4): 926–44. https://doi.org/10.1080/0954655 3.2021.1987895.

Capra, Fritjof. 1997. *The Web of Life: A New Synthesis of Mind and Matter*. London: Flamingo.

Carson, Rachel. 1962. *Silent Spring*. Boston, MA: Houghton Mifflin.

Cassidy Rogers, Laura. 2016. 'The Social and Environmental Turn in Late 20th Century Art: A Case Study of Helen and Newton Harrison after Modernism'. PhD Thesis, California: Stanford University.

Chakrabarty, Prosanta, Glynn O'Neill, Brannon Hardy, and Brandon Ballengee. 2016. 'Five Years Later: An Update on the Status of Collections of Endemic Gulf of Mexico Fishes Put at Risk by the 2010 Oil Spill'. *Biodiversity Data Journal* 4 (August): e8728. https://doi.org/10.3897/BDJ.4.e8728.

Chaudhuri, Amit. 2021. *Finding the Raga: An Improvisation on Indian Music*. New York: New York Review Books.

Chisholm, D. 2011. 'The Art of Ecological Thinking: Literary Ecology'. *Interdisciplinary Studies in Literature and Environment* 18 (3): 569–93. https://doi.org/10.1093/isle/isr077.

Collins, Timothy M. 2001. 'Conversations in the Rust Belt'. Edited by Bernd Herzogenrath. *Critical Studies, From Virgin Land to Disney World: Nature and Its Discontents in the USA of Yesterday and Today* 26: 251–76.

———. 2013. 'Re: The Museum of Conceptual Art: A Prolegomena to Hip', e-mail message to author 3 December 2013.

Collins, Timothy M., Jackie Brookner, Reiko Goto-Collins, Helen Mayer Harrison, Newton Harrison, Ruth Wallen, and Josh Harrison. 2023. 'Art and Change: The Emerging Social and Ecological Impetus'. In *Paying Attention to Make Art: Twenty-Nine Voices on the Legacy of Newton and Helen Mayer Harrison*, edited by Chris Fremantle and Anne Douglas. The Nature of Cities. https://www.thenatureofcities. com/2023/03/18/paying-attention-to-make-art-twenty-nine-voices-on-the-legacy-of-newton-and-helen-mayer-harrison/ (accessed 9.6.2024)

Collins, Timothy M., and Reiko Goto-Collins. 2017. *The Caledonian Decoy*. Glasgow: Collins and Goto Studio.

Collins, Timothy M., Reiko Goto-Collins, and David Edwards. 2018. 'A Critical Forest Art Practice: The Black Wood of Rannoch'. *Landscape Research* 43 (2): 199–210. https://doi.org/10.1080/01426397.20 17.1318119.

Conte, Kari. 2015. 'The Ballet Book: Choreography and Labor'. In *Seven Work Ballets*, edited by Kari Conte, 9–16. Amsterdam: Kunstverein Publishing.

Conzen-Meairs, Ina. 1991. 'Art after Physics'. In *John Latham – Art after Physics: The Museum of Modern Art, Oxford, 13 October 1991 – 5 January 1992*, edited by Museum of Modern Art, 9–36. Stuttgart: Mayer.

Davidson, Miri. 2024. 'Sea and Earth'. *NLR/Sidecar*, 4 April 2024. https://newleftreview.org/sidecar/posts/ sea-and-earth?pc=1592 (accessed 9.6.2024).

Debaise, Didier. 2017. *Speculative Empiricism: Revisiting Whitehead*. Translated by Tomas Weber. Speculative Realism. Edinburgh: Edinburgh University press.

Deleuze, Gilles. 1992. 'Postscript on the Societies of Control'. *October* 59 (Winter 1992): 3–7.

Demos, T.J. 2018. 'To Save a World: Geoengineering, Conflictual Futurisms, and the Unthinkable'. *E-Flux*, 2018. https://www.e-flux.com/journal/94/221148/to-save-a-world-geoengineering-conflictual-futurisms-and-the-unthinkable/ (accessed 9.6.2024).

Denes, Agnes. 2008. *The Human Argument: The Writings of Agnes Denes*. Thompson, Connecticut: Spring Publications.

Dewey, John. 2005. *Art as Experience*. Perigee trade pbk. ed. A Perigee Book. New York, New York: Berkeley Publ. Group.

———. 2011. *Democracy and Education*. LaVergne, TN: Simon & Brown.

Douglas, Anne. 2013a. 'Drawing and the Score'. In *Sound & Score: Essays on Sound, Score and Notation*, edited by Paulo de Assis, William Brooks, Kathleen Coessens, Virginia Anderson, and Orpheus Instituut. Orpheus Institute Series. Leuven: Leuven University Press.

———. 2013b. 'Altering a Fixed Identity: Thinking through Improvisation'. *Critical Studies in Improvisation / Études Critiques En Improvisation* 8 (2). https://doi.org/10.21083/csieci.v8i2.2122.

———. 2018a. *Redistributing Power? A Poetics of Participation in Contemporary Arts*. Bristol: University of Bristol/AHRC Connected Communities Programme.

———. 2018b. 'Venturing out on the Thread of a Tune: The Artist as Improvisor in Public Life'. Edited by James Oliver. *Associations: Creative Practice and Research*. Melbourne: University of Melbourne Press.

———. 2019. '"...The Eye of the Stranger": A Practice Led Research Perspective on the Embedded Artist'. In *Embedded Artists: Artists Outside the Art World – The World in Quest of Artists*, edited by Frédéric Martel and Hartmut Wickert, 48–74. Zurich: Zurich University of the Arts.

———. 2021. 'Giving Absurdity Form: The Place of Contemporary Art in the Environmental Crisis'. *Arts* 10 (4): 81. https://doi.org/10.3390/arts10040081.

Douglas, Anne, and Kathleen Coessens. 2012. 'Experiential Knowledge and Improvisation: Variations on Movement, Motion, Emotion'. *Art, Design & Communication in Higher Education* 10 (2): 179–98. https://doi.org/10.1386/adch.10.2.179_1.

———. 2013. 'Improvisation and Embodied Knowledge:three artistic projects between life, art and research.' In *(Re)thinking Improvisation: artistic explorations and conceptual writing*, edited by Henrick Frisk and Stefan Östersjö. Malmö Academy of Music: 29–41.

———. 2017. 'Improvisation as Experimentation in Everyday Life and Beyond'. In *Experimental Encounters in Music and Beyond*, edited by Kathleen Coessens. Leuven, Belgium: Leuven University Press.

Douglas, Anne, and Chris Fremantle. 2005. 'Leaving the (Social) Ground of (Artistic) Intervention More Fertile: An Ecology of Practice in the Everyday'. In *SK2 Aesthetic Practice and Aesthetic Insight*. Bergen, Norway: University of Bergen. https://web.archive.org/web/20100828112655/http://sensuousknowledge.org/category/sk2/ (accessed 9.6.2024).

———. 2016a. 'Inconsistency and Contradiction: Lessons in Improvisation in the Work of Helen Mayer Harrison and Newton Harrison'. In *Elemental: An Arts and Ecology Reader*, edited by James Brady, 153–81. Manchester: Gaia Projects.

———. 2016b. 'What Poetry Does Best: The Harrisons' Poetics of Being and Acting in the World.' In *The Time of the Force Majeure: After 45 Years Counterforce Is on the Horizon*, edited by Helen Mayer Harrison and Newton Harrison, 455–60. New York: Prestel.

———. 2022a. 'Figure Ground Reversal: The Ecological Epistemology of Helen Mayer Harrison and Newton Harrison'. In *Imaginative Ecologies: Inspiring Change through the Humanities*, edited by Diana Villanueva-Romero, Lorraine Kerslake, and Carmen Flys-Junquera, 81–106. Nature, Culture and Literature, vol. 17. Leiden ; Boston: Brill.

———. 2022b. 'In Conversation: A Poetics of Empathy Helen Mayer Harrison and Newton Harrison'. *Women's Eco Artists Dialog Magazine*, 2022. https://directory.weadartists.org/in-conversation-a-poetics-of-empathy 9.6.2024).

———. 2023. 'Thinking with the Harrisons: What Does Now Demand?' *Field: A Journal of Socially Engaged Art Criticism* 23. https://field-journal.com/issue-23/thinking-with-the-harrisons-what-does-now-demand (accessed 9.6.2024).

Douglas, Anne, and Melehat Nil Gulari. 2015. 'Understanding Experimentation as Improvisation in Arts Research'. Edited by Professor Kate Pahl And Professor Tarquam Mckenna. *Qualitative Research Journal* 15 (4): 392–403. https://doi.org/10.1108/QRJ-06-2015-0035.

Eagleton, Terry. 2022. *Critical Revolutionaries: Five Critics Who Changed the Way We Read*. New Haven: Yale University Press.

Edelman, Sharon. 1977. *Artpark 1977 The Program in Visual Arts*. Lewiston, New York: Artpark.

Edwards, David M., Timothy M. Collins, and Reiko Goto-Collins. 2016. 'An Arts-led Dialogue to Elicit Shared, Plural and Cultural Values of Ecosystems'. *Ecosystem Services* 21: 319–28.

Filippone, Christine. 2017. *Science, Technology, and Utopias: Women Artists and Cold War America*. Science and the Arts since 1750. London and New York: Routledge, Taylor & Francis Group.

Firbank, Les, Helen Mayer Harrison, Newton Harrison, David Haley, and Bruce Griffith. 2009. 'A Story of Becoming: Landscape Creation through an Art/Science Dynamic'. In *What Is Land For? The Food, Fuel and Climate Change Debate*, edited by Matt Lobley and Michael Winter, 251–63. London: Routledge.

Firmin, Sandra, ed. 2010. *Artpark: 1974-1984*. New Jersey: Princeton Architectural Press.

Fox, James David. 2023. 'Dis/Agreement in Participatory Organisations: Low Theory and Democratic Governance in Cybernetics'. PhD Thesis, Colchester, Essex: University of Essex.

Fremantle, Chris. 2018. 'Greenhouse Britain: Losing Ground, Gaining Wisdom (2006–09): Case Study'. In Valuing Nature Programme. Cardiff, UK. https://rgu-repository.worktribe.com/output/249255 (accessed 9.6.2024).

———. 2020. 'The Art of a Life Adapting: Drawing and Healing'. *Leonardo* 53 (1): 83–84. https://doi.org/10.1162/leon_a_01833.

Fremantle, Chris, and Anne Douglas, eds. 2023. *Paying Attention to Make Art: Twenty-Nine Voices on the Legacy of Newton and Helen Mayer Harrison*. The Nature of Cities. https://www.thenatureofcities.com/2023/03/18/paying-attention-to-make-art-twenty-nine-voices-on-the-legacy-of-newton-and-helen-mayer-harrison/ (access 9.6.2024).

Fremantle, Chris, Anne Douglas, and Dave Pritchard. 2020a. 'In the Time of Art with Policy: The Practice of Helen Mayer Harrison and Newton Harrison alongside Global Environmental Policy since the 1970s.' In *The Routledge Companion to Art in the Public Realm*, edited by Cameron Cartiere and Leon Tan, 300–314. Abingdon, Oxon and New York: Taylor & Francis (Routledge).

———. 2020b. 'The Harrisons' Practice in the Context of Global Environmental Policy and Politics from the 1960s to 2019: A Timeline.' In *The Routledge Companion to Art in the Public Realm*, edited by Cameron Cartiere and Leon Tan, 315–32. Abingdon, Oxon and New York: Taylor & Francis (Routledge).

Friedman, Ken, ed. 1998. *The Fluxus Reader*. Chicester, West Sussex and New York: Academy Editions.

Galafassi, Diego, Sacha Kagan, Manjana Milkoreit, Maria Heras, Chantal Bilodeau, Sadhbh Juarez Bourke, Andrew Merrie, Leonie Guerrero, Guðrún Pétursdóttir, and Joan David Tàbara. 2018. 'Raising the Temperature': The Arts in a Warming Planet'. *Current Opinion in Environmental Sustainability* 31: 71–79.

Gamble, Morag, dir. 2021. *What Is Life? Fritjof Capra Explains the 4 Characteristics of Life*. https://www.youtube.com/watch?v=Moe_4iC6kBg (accessed 9.64).

Ghosh, Amitav. 2016. *The Great Derangement: Climate Change and the Unthinkable*. Chicago and London: University of Chicago Press.

Giroux, Henry. 2022. 'Critical Pedagogy in a Time of Fascist Tyranny'. Human Restoration Project. https://www.youtube.com/watch?v=4WM1G5Ovy54 (accessed 9.6.2024).

Goto-Collins, Reiko. 2012. 'Ecology and Environmental Art in Public Place: Talking Tree: Won't You Take a Minute and Listen to the Plight of Nature?' PhD thesis., Robert Gordon University.

Graeber, David. 2014. *The Democracy Project: A History, a Crisis, a Movement*. London: Penguin Books.

Haley, David. 2022. 'The Art of Inquiry: A Learning Manifesto'. In *Ecoart in Action: Activities, Case Studies and Provocations for Classrooms and Communities*, edited by Amara Geffen, Ann Rosenthal, Aviva Rahmani, and Chris Fremantle, 292–96. New York: New Village Press.

Hallam, Elizabeth, and Tim Ingold, eds. 2007. *Creativity and Cultural Improvisation*. 1st ed. Routledge. https://doi.org/10.4324/9781003135531.

Hamilton Faris, Jaimey. 2022. 'Towards Infrastructure Art: Containerization, Black Box Logistics, and New Distribution Complexes'. In *Nervous Systems: Art, Systems, and Politics since the 1960s*, edited by Johanna Gosse, Tim Stott, and Judith F. Rodenbeck, 235–60. Durham: Duke University Press.

Haraway, Donna. 2011. *SF: Speculative Fabulation and String Figures: = SF: Spekulative Fabulation Und String–Figuren*. 100 Notes – 100 Thoughts 33. Ostfildern: Hatje Cantz.

Harrison, Helen Mayer, and Newton Harrison. 1965. 'Dropouts and a "Design for Living"'. In *New Perspectives on Poverty*, edited by Arthur B. Shostak and William Gomberg, 174–78. Englewood Cliffs, New Jersey: Prentice-Hall.

———. 1985a. *Arroyo Seco Release / A Serpentine for Pasadena, Baxter Art Gallery, 30 January – 3 March 1985*. Pasadena, California: California Institute of Technology.

———. 1985b. *The Lagoon Cycle*. Ithaca, NY: Herbert F Johnson Museum of Art, Cornell University.

———. 1989. *Atempause für den Save-Fluss: Die Summe Seiner Geschichte, Beginn Einer Neuen Geschichte*. Berlin: Nueuer Berliner Kunstverein.

———. 1990. *Tibet Is the High Ground*. Del Mar, California: The Harrison Studio.

———. 1993. *The Serpentine Lattice*. Portland, Oregon: Douglas F. Cooley Memorial Art Gallery, Reed College.

———. 1995. *Green Heart Vision*. Den Haag, Holland and Del Mar California: The Harrison Studio and the Cultural Council and Province of South Holland.

———. 1998. *Casting a Green Net: Can It Be We Are Seeing a Dragon?* San Diego, CA: Harrison Studio & Associates, unpaginated

———. 2001a. *From There to Here*. San Diego, California: The Harrison Studio, unpaginated

———. 2001b. 'Knotted Ropes, Rings, Lattices and Lace: Retrofitting Biodiversity into the Cultural Landscape'. In *Biodiversity: A Challenge for Development, Research and Policy*, edited by Wilhelm Barthlott, 13–31. Berlin: Springer-Verlag.

———. 2001c. *Peninsula Europe: The High Grounds*. San Diego, California: The Harrison Studio, unpaginated.

———. 2006. 'Seventh Lagoon: The Ring of Water'. *Structure and Dynamics: eJournal of Anthropological and Related Sciences*. https://escholarship.org/uc/item/45z287n2#main (accessed 9.6.2024).

———. 2007a. 'Greenhouse Britain: Losing Ground, Gaining Wisdom'. Harrison Studio & Associates (Britain). http://greenhousebritain.greenmuseum.org/blog/wp-content/uploads/greenhouse-britain-final-july-07.pdf (accessed 9.6.2024).

———. 2007b. 'Public Culture and Sustainable Practices: Peninsula Europe from an Ecodiversity Perspective, Posing Questions to Complexity Scientists'. *Structure and Dynamics: eJournal of Anthropological and Related Sciences*. https://escholarship.org/uc/item/9hj3s753 (accessed 9.6.2024).

———. 2008a. *Greenhouse Britain: Losing Ground, Gaining Wisdom*. Installation.

———. 2008b. 'Green Wedding Homily'. Love Art Laboratory. 17 May 2008. https://loveartlab.ucsc.edu/2016/06/13/green-wedding-homily/ (accessed 9.6.2024).

———. 2010. The Harrisons Interview by Annie Sprinkle and Beth Stephens. https://sprinklestephens.ucsc.edu/research-writing/the-harrisons/ (accessed 9.6.2024).

———. 2016. *The Time of the Force Majeure: After 45 Years Counterforce Is on the Horizon?* Munich, London, New York: Prestel.

———. 2017. *On the Deep Wealth of this Nation, Scotland* 2017. Santa Cruz, Center for the Study of the Force Majeure. https://www.centerforforcemajeure.org/deep-wealth-of-this-nation-scotland (accessed 9.6.2024).

———. n.d.(a) 'A Short Discussion of Michelangelo, Rodin and Epstein, and Sculptural Values'. Special Collections, Stanford University. Box 184, Folder 7. Helen and Newton Harrison Papers M1797.

———. n.d.(b) 'Towards a New Curriculum Formation'. Special Collections, Stanford University. Box 184, Folder 12. Helen and Newton Harrison Papers M1797.

Harrison, Josh. 2023. 'Re: Spoil Heap Reclamation', email to the author 9 January 2023.

Harrison, Newton. 1996. 'Stories from an Unorthodox Classroom'. https://theharrisonstudio.net/wp-content/uploads/2011/03/classroomstories.pdf (accessed 9.6.2024).

———. 2021a. 'Helen's Town: The Impulse to Begin Again'. *Ecopoiesis: Eco-Human Theory and Practice* 2 (2). https://en.ecopoiesis.ru/aktualnoe/news_post/harrison-newton-helens-town-the-impulse-is-to-begin-again (accessed 9.6.2024).

———. 2021b. *Newton Harrison Interview*. Los Angeles, Calif: Various Small Fires.

———. 2022a. 'Epitaph: Channeling the Lifeweb'. *Ecopoiesis: Eco-Human Theory and Practice* 3 (2): 53–56.

———. 2022b. On learning from other artists Interview by Anne Douglas and Chris Fremantle. Zoom recording.

Hendricks, Geoffrey, and David J. Getsy. 2021. 'Outing Queer Fluxus'. *PAJ: A Journal of Performance and Art* 43 (1): 95–106. https://doi.org/10.1162/pajj_a_00551.

Hobbs, Robert Carleton. 1981. *Robert Smithson: Sculpture*. Ithaca: Cornell Univ. Press.

Ingold, Tim. 2013. *Making: Anthropology, Archaeology, Art and Architecture*. London and New York: Routledge.

———. 2015. *The Life of Lines*. London and New York: Routledge

———. 2021. *Correspondences*. Cambridge, UK Medford, MA: Polity.

Ingram Allen, Jane. 2008. 'A Marriage Made on Earth: Helen Mayer Harrison and Newton Harrison'. *Public Art Review*, Spring/Summer 2008: 28–30.

Ingram, Mrill. 2013. 'Ecopolitics and Aesthetics: The Art of Helen Mayer and Newton Harrison'. *The Geographical Review* 103 (2): 260–74.

Jackson, Michael C. 2023. 'Rebooting the Systems Approach by Applying the Thinking of Bogdanov and the Pragmatists'. *Systems Research and Behavioral Science* 40 (2): 349–65. https://doi.org/10.1002/sres.2908.

Jones, Adam, dir. 2023. 'Cybernetics and the Left: Communist Synergy or Capitalist Machines?' *Acid Horizon*. Acid Horizon. https://pod.link/1512615438/episode/371b5594c39be49c60a401f3154f4ed2 (accessed 9.6.2024).

Jones, Caroline A. 2018. 'Helen Mayer Harrison (1927–2018)'. *Artforum*, 7 April 2018. https://www.artforum.com/passages/caroline-a-jones-on-helen-mayer-harrison-1927-2018-74887 (accessed 9.6.2024).

Kagan, Sacha. 2020. 'Introduction: Queer Convivialist Perspectives for Sustainable Futures'. *World Futures* 76 (5–7): 267–86. https://doi.org/10.1080/02604027.2020.1777834.

Kant, Immanuel. 1992. *An Answer to the Question: What Is Enlightenment?* Translated by Ted Humphrey. Hackett Publishing. https://www.nypl.org/sites/default/files/kant_whatisenlightenment.pdf (accessed 9.6.2024).

———. 2007. *Critique of Judgment*. Translated by John H Bernard. New York: Cosmo Classics.

Kaprow, Allan. 2003. *Essays on the Blurring of Art and Life*. Edited by Jeff Kelly. Berkeley: University of California Press.

Kester, Grant. 2004. *Conversation Pieces: Community and Communication in Modern Art*. Berkeley: University of California Press.

———. 2005. *Ground Works: Environmental Collaboration in Contemporary Art*. Pittsburgh, PA: Carnegie Mellon University.

———. 2011. *The One and the Many: Contemporary Collaborative Art in a Global Context*. Durham and London: Duke University Press.

Kristeva, Julia. 2020. *Hannah Arendt Life Is a Narrative Alexander Lectures*. Translated by Frank Collins. Toronto: University of Toronto Press.

'LA River Master Plan'. 2022. Los Angeles County and Los Angeles County Public Works. https://larivermasterplan.org/about/master-plan-2022/jurisdictions-ownership-and-rights/ (accessed 9.6.2024).

Lakoff, George, and Mark Johnson. 1980. *Metaphors We Live By*. Chicago and London: University of Chicago Press.

Last, Angela. 2013. '400Ppm: Passing A New World Threshold'. *Society and Space*, 2013. https://www.societyandspace.org/articles/400ppm-passing-a-new-world-threshold (accessed 9.6.2024).

Latour, Bruno. 2004. *Politics of Nature: How to Bring the Sciences into Democracy*. Cambridge, Mass: Harvard University Press.

———. 2020. 'Seven Objections Against Landing On Earth'. In *Critical Zones: The Science and Politics of Landing on Earth*, edited by Bruno Latour and Peter Weibel, 13–19. Cambridge, MA: MIT Press.

Latour, Bruno, and Peter Weibel, eds. 2020. *Critical Zones: The Science and Politics of Landing on Earth*. Cambridge, MA: MIT Press.

Lévi-Strauss, Claude. 2003. *Myth and Meaning*. Repr. Routledge Classics. London: Routledge.

Mann, Geoff. 2023. 'Treading This Air'. *London Review of Books*, 7 September 2023.

Mann, Geoff, and Joel Wainwright. 2020. *Climate Leviathan: A Political Theory of Our Planetary Future*. London: Verso.

Manolescu, Monica. 2021. 'Imagining the Lagoon in Helen Mayer Harrison and Newton Harrison's "The Lagoon Cycle"'. *Ranam: Recherches Anglaises et Nord-Américaines* Landscapes and Aesthetic Spatialities in the Anthropocene (54): 89–109.

Margulis, Lynn. 1998. *The Symbiotic Planet: A New Look at Evolution*. 1st ed. Science Masters. New York: Basic Books.

Marioni, Tom. 2003. *Beer, Art, and Philosophy: A Memoir*. San Francisco: Crown Point Press.

Massumi, Brian. 2014. *What Animals Teach Us about Politics*. Durham (N.C.): Duke university press.

Matilsky, Barbara. 1992. *Fragile Ecologies: Contemporary Artists' Interpretations and Solutions*. New York: Rizzoli.

Mazeaud, Dominique, Robert B Gaylor, Suzi Gablik, Melinda Wortz, and Diane Armitage. 1990. *Revered Earth*. Santa Fe, NM: Center for Contemporary Arts of Santa Fe.

McKinnon, Catriona. 2022. *Climate Change and Political Theory*. And Political Theory Series. Cambridge, UK Hoboken, NJ, USA: Polity.

Meadows, Donella. 1999. 'Leverage Points: Places to Intervene in a System'. *Sustainability Institute*, 1999.

———. 2008. *Thinking in Systems: A Primer*. Vermont: Chelsea Green Publishing.

Meadows, Donella H., and Club of Rome, eds. 1972. *The Limits to Growth: A Report for the Club of Rome's Project on the Predicament of Mankind*. New York: Universe Books.

Montano, Linda. 2010. Linda Montano Interview by Annie Sprinkle and Beth Stephens. https://sprinklestephens.ucsc.edu/research-writing/linda-montano/ (accessed 9.6.2024).

Moore, Sam, and Alex Roberts. 2022. *The Rise of Ecofascism: Climate Change and the Far Right*. Cambridge, UK and Medford, MA: Polity.

Morris, Robert. 1979. 'Robert Morris Keynote Address'. In *Earthworks, Land Reclamation as Sculpture: [Exhibition Catalog]: A Project of the King County Arts Commission*, edited by King County Arts Commission, 11–16. Seattle, Washington, USA: Seattle Art Museum.

Morton, Timothy. 2010. 'Guest Column: Queer Ecology'. *Proceedings of the Modern Languages Association of America* 125 (2): 273–82.

Nyrnes, Auslag. 2006. 'Lighting from the Side: Rhetoric and Artistic Research'. *Sensuous Knowledge Journal "Focus on Artistic Research and Development"*, no. 3: 1–17.

Peters, Gary. 2009. *Philosophy of Improvisation*. Chicago and London: University of Chicago Press.

———. 2017. *Improvising Improvisation: From out of Philosophy, Music, Dance, and Literature*. Chicago and London: The University of Chicago Press.

Purdy, Jedediah. 2015. *After Nature: A Politics for the Anthropocene*. Cambridge, Massachusetts: Harvard University Press, [2015] London.

Raskin, Ben. 2021. 'There Is an Interesting Discussion to Be Had about Permanence, and Sense of Place, and Long-Term Relationships with Soil'. *Mother Earth*, 2021. https://issuu.com/soilassociationcharity/docs/mother_earth_summer21-issuu-corrected (accessed 9.6.2024).

Raven, Arlene. 1983. *At Home*. Long Beach, California: Long Beach Museum of Art.

Ray, Gene. 2017. 'Imagining Mutuality: A Reading of Raseed Araeen's Art Beyond Art'. In *Rasheed Araeen*, edited by Nick Aikens, 393–400. Zürich: JRP Ringier.

Reeves-Evison, Theo. 2021. 'The Art of Disciplined Imagination: Prediction, Scenarios, and Other Speculative Infrastructures'. *Critical Inquiry* 47 (4): 719–48. https://doi.org/10.1086/714536.

Rowell, Margit. 1972. 'On Albers' Color'. *ArtForum*, January 1972.

Schön, Donald. 1993. 'Generative Metaphor and Social Policy'. In *Metaphor and Thought*, edited by Andrew Ortony, 138–63. Cambridge: Cambridge University Press.

Senanayake, Ranil. 2012. 'Analog Forestry as an Art Form'. *Journal of the Royal Asiatic Society of Sri Lanka* 57 (2): 229–46.

Sessions, Stanley K., and Brandon Ballengée. 2010. 'Explanations for Deformed Frogs: Plenty of Research Left to Do (a Response to Skelly and Benard)'. *Journal of Experimental Zoology Part B: Molecular and Developmental Evolution* 314B (5): 341–46. https://doi.org/10.1002/jez.b.21351.

Shanken, Edward A. 2009. 'Reprogramming Systems Aesthetics: A Strategic Historiography'. In *Proceedings of the Digital Arts and Culture Conference*. University of California, Irvine. https://escholarship.org/uc/item/6bv363d4 (accessed 9.6.2024).

———, ed. 2015. *Systems*. Whitechapel: Documents of Contemporary Art. Cambridge, Mass: MIT Press/Whitechapel Art Gallery.

Shoshitaishvili, Boris. 2023. 'Is Our Planet Doubly Alive? Gaia, Globalization, and the Anthropocene's Planetary Superorganisms'. *The Anthropocene Review* 10 (2): 434–54. https://doi.org/10.1177/20530196221087789.

Skrebowski, Luke. 2016. 'Jack Burnham Redux: The Obsolete in Reverse?' *Grey Room* 65 (October): 88–113. https://doi.org/10.1162/GREY_a_00205.

Smith, Paul J. 1971. *Furs and Feathers*. New York City: Museum of Contemporary Crafts of The American Crafts Council.

Smithson, Robert. 1966. 'Entropy and the New Monuments'. *ArtForum*, Summer 1966.

Snyder, Gary. 2010. *Riprap and Cold Mountain Poems*. Anniversary ed. Washington, D.C., London: Counterpoint.

Spaid, Sue. 2002. *Ecovention: Current Art to Transform Ecologies*. Cincinnati: Contemporary Arts Center.

Spens, Christiana. 2020. 'Domestic Bliss'. *Studio International*, May 2020. https://www.studiointernational. com/index.php/domestic-bliss-review-gallery-of-modern-art-glasgow (accessed 9.6.2024).

Sprinkle, Annie, and Beth Stephens. 2021. *Assuming the Ecosexual Position: The Earth as Lover*. Minneapolis: University of Minnesota Press.

Spurlock, William. 1979. *Dialogue/Discourse/Research*. Santa Barbara, CA: Santa Barbara Museum of Art.

Steiner, Frederick. 2019. 'Toward an Ecological Aesthetic'. *Socio-Ecological Practice Research* 1 (1): 33–37. https://doi.org/10.1007/s42532-018-00004-0.

Stengers, Isabelle. 2011. *Thinking with Whitehead: A Free and Wild Creation of Concepts*. Cambridge, Mass: Harvard University Press.

———. 2018. *Another Science Is Possible: A Manifesto for Slow Science*. Translated by Stephen Muecke. English edition. Cambridge ; Medford, MA: Polity.

———. 2020. 'The Earth Won't Let Itself Be Watched'. In *Critical Zones: Observatories for Earthly Politics*, edited by Bruno Latour and Peter Weibel, 228–35. Cambridge, Mass.: The MIT Press.

———. 2023. *Making Sense in Common: A Reading of Whitehead in Times of Collapse*. Translated by Thomas LaMarre. Posthumanities 66. Minneapolis and London: University of Minnesota Press.

Strelow, Heike. 1999. *Natural Reality: Artistic Positions Between Nature and Culture*. Stuttgart: Daco Verlag.

Stromberg, Matt. 2023. 'The Artist Working to Reclaim the LA River's Water'. *Hyperallergic*, 12 September 2023. http://hyperallergic.com/844126/the-artist-working-to-reclaim-the-la-rivers-water/ (accessed 9.6.2024).

Sutton, Gloria. 2019. 'Has Haacke: Works of Art, 1963–72'. In *Hans Haacke: All Connected*, edited by Gary Carrion-Murayari and Massimiliano Gioni. London and New York, NY: Phaidon Press Limited.

Tabbush, Paul. 2010. 'Cultural Values of Trees, Woods and Forests'. Farnham, Surrey: Forest Research.

Táíwò, Olúfémi. 2022. *Elite Capture: How the Powerful Took over Identity Politics (and Everything Else)*. London: Pluto Press.

Tedford, Matthew Harrison. 2011. 'The Museum of Conceptual Art: A Prolegomena to Hip'. *Art Practical*, 12 April 2011. https://web.archive.org/web/20150203023107/http://www.artpractical.com/feature/the_museum_of_conceptual_art_a_prolegomena_to_hip/ (accessed 9.6.2024).

Tsing, Anna L. 2016. *The Mushroom at the End of the World: On the Possibility of Life in Capitalist Ruins*. New Jersey: Princeton University Press.

Ukeles, Mierle Laderman. 1997. 'Maintenance Art Activity (1973) Artist Project: Mierle Laderman Ukeles'. Edited by Miwon Kwon and Helen Molesworth. *Documents* 10: 5–22.

Villa, Dana R. 1992. 'Beyond Good and Evil: Arendt, Nietzsche, and the Aestheticization of Political Action'. *Political Theory* 20 (2): 274–308.

Walker, John Albert. 1999. *Art and Outrage: Provocation, Controversy, and the Visual Arts*. London: Pluto Press.

Wallen, Ruth. 2019. 'Walking with Trees'. *Dark Matter: Women Witnessing* 9. http://www. darkmatterwomenwitnessing.com/issues/Oct2019/articles/Ruth-Wallen_Walking-with-Trees.html (accessed 9.6.2024).

———. 2022. 'The Stickiness of Touch'. *Women's Eco Artists Dialog Magazine*, 2022. https://directory. weadartists.org/the-stickiness-of-touch-caring-for-boulders-front-range-forests (accessed 9.6.2024).

———. 2023. *Learning to Think like a Forest*. https://www.ruthwallen.net/think-like-a-forest (accessed 9.6.2024).

Whitehead, Alfred North. 1948. *Essays in Science and Philosophy*. London: Rider and Company.

———. 1967. *The Aims of Education: And Others Essays*. New York Toronto Oxford: Free press.

———. 1978. *Process and Reality: An Essay in Cosmology Gifford Lectures Delivered in the University of Edinburgh during the Session 1927–28*. Edited by David Ray Griffin and Donald Wynne Sherburne. Corr. ed. New York London: the Free press.

———. 1985. *Adventures of Ideas*. 19. [print]. New York: The free Press.

———. 2015. *The Concept of Nature*. Cambridge philosophy classics edition. Cambridge Philosophy Classics. Cambridge: Cambridge University Press.

———. 2022. *Science and the Modern World*. Lowell Lectures 1925. Milton Keynes, UK: Z&L Barnes Publishing.

Yao, Joanne. 2022. *The Ideal River: How Control of Nature Shaped the International Order*. Manchester: Manchester University Press.

Index